STUDIES IN SPANISH RENAISSANCE THOUGHT

ARCHIVES INTERNATIONALES D'HISTOIRE DES IDEES

INTERNATIONAL ARCHIVES OF THE HISTORY OF IDEAS

82

CARLOS G. NOREÑA

STUDIES IN SPANISH RENAISSANCE THOUGHT

STUDIES IN SPANISH RENAISSANCE THOUGHT

by

CARLOS G. NOREÑA

MARTINUS NIJHOFF / THE HAGUE / 1975

To Victoria, my favorite daughter

ISBN 90 247 1727 2

PRINTED IN THE NETHERLANDS

CONTENTS

INTRODUCTION

In spite of its carefully planned – and fully justified – modesty, the title of this book might very well surprise more than one potential reader. It is not normal to see such controversial concepts as "Renaissance," "Renaissance Thought," "Spanish Renaissance," or even "Spanish Thought" freely linked together in the crowded intimacy of one single printed line. The author of these essays is painfully aware of the complexity of the ground he has dared to cover. He is also aware that all the assumptions and connotations associated with the title of this book have been the subject of great controversy among scholars of high repute who claimed (and probably had) revealing insight into human affairs and ideas. That these pages have been written at all therefore needs some justification.

I am convinced that certain of the disputes among historians of ideas do not touch upon matters of substance, but rather reveal the taste and intellectual idiosyncracies of their authors. Much of the disagreement is, I think, a matter of aesthetics. Those who find special gratification in well-defined labels, clear-cut schemes, and comprehensive generalizations, can hardly bear the company of those who insist upon detail, complexity, and organic growth. The nightmarish dilemma, still unresolved, between Unity and Diversity, between the Universal and the Individual, haunts the History of Ideas. To have the best of both worlds (a typical Spanish attitude), I have resolved to use traditional labels, but to use them casually and with great flexibility. By "Renaissance," therefore, I mean a noticeable quickening in the pace of cultural change toward the end of the fifteenth century, reaching to what one might be more inclined to call 'Baroque,' probably toward the early decades of the seventeenth century. Whether this 'Renaissance' signaled a 'radical break' with the so-called Middle Ages or not, is a matter of scarce interest to me. It all depends on what is meant by the expression 'radical break;' the answers are likely to be different for each individual, for each nation, and for each decade.

What is of far greater interest to me is the old controversy about the significance of Philosophy during the Renaissance period. Philosophical prejudice prevents me from dogmatically believing that philosophical expression always follows the religious or artistic unfolding of the human mind. I am willing to concede, for instance, that Renaissance Philosophy was unequal to seventeenth or nineteenth century Philosophy in the novelty of its paradigms, in the comprehensiveness of its systematization, or in the accuracy of its technical idiom. But I cannot believe that man's artistic taste, political thought, economic structure, system of values, religious beliefs, and educational institutions can change as quickly as they did during the Renaissance without a matching upheaval in the world of ideas. Whether the new ideas caused those changes or were caused by them, is for dogmatic philosophers to decide on the basis of their grand premises and principles. The historian of ideas is busy enough exploring the winding path of human intellectual achievements. The inconclusive, latent, propeadeutic, transient, precursory, and protean character of Renaissance thought – fascinating as it is – makes this task much more difficult and the findings much more modest.

The central claim of my title is by far the most controversial, and probably the one most important to me. Of those who have no scruples in talking about 'the Renaissance' and who place special value upon intellectual history, only a small minority is willing to include Spain in their research. If the Renaissance is described as a movement of ideas which either secularized human existence or prepared it for the Reformation, Spain, obviously, does not easily qualify for further consideration. The four ensuing chapters attempt only to convey the impression that Spain had her full share in the vitality of Renaissance intellectual life; that, particularly during the reign of Charles V, and to a lesser extent under Philip II, she was still a lively partner in the community of European nations; that some of her achievements formed a relevant and influential aspect of European philosophical traditions; and, finally, that the intellectual ostracism of the centuries to follow was not the inevitable result of intellectual pauperism, but the regrettable consequence of religious and political censorship.

These chapters do not pretend to focus upon the greatest representatives of Spanish Renaissance thought. In fact they were chosen for practical and personal reasons of which the author is well aware and the reader can comfortably ignore. Each one of them, however, in its own right, aims to draw attention to a different aspect of Spanish intellectual life in the sixteenth century. The first chapter does not actually deal with Renaissance thinkers, but rather with thinkers at whom Renaissance criticism was aimed. The second chapter discusses the origins of International Law and the thought of Francisco de Vitoria. In the third chapter we move on to the reign of Philip II, and present Fray Luis de León's philosophy of language. The last chapter deals with the naturalistic philosophy of man which inspired Juan Huarte's *Examen de Ingenios*. Throughout the book I have attempted to relate these past expressions of philosophical reflection to contemporary themes and concerns. As is the case with any book, this one was made possible by the help and generosity of many individuals and institutions. My wife presented me with a wondeful son between the completion of Chapters Two and Three. My daughter urged me to finish a book she knew I would dedicate to her. Professors Joseph Silverman and Richard Popkin helped me in many more ways than they themselves knew. Mrs. Joan Hodgson, of the Interlibrary Loan at Santa Cruz (University of California), kindly procured all the books and articles mentioned in the Bibliography. Mr. David Burkes, Mrs. Eveline Kanes, Mrs. Helen Smith, Ms. Kerstin Thule and Ms. Beth Beurkens edited the text with incredible patience. The University of California Administration made available the badly-needed research aid and leave of absence. But, mostly, it was a Senior Fellowship of the National Endowment for the Humanities which, toward the end, provided me with the time and the means to make the final effort.

Finally, I want to thank all the publishers who generously allowed me to quote part of their books: the *Biblioteca de Autores Españoles* for the Spanish text of Juan Huarte's *Examen de Ingenios*; the Clarendon Press for the English translation of Francisco de Vitoria's *Relectiones;* the Gregg press for the text of Vives' *In Pseudo-Dialécticos;* the *Biblioteca de Teólogos Españoles* for the Latin text of Vitoria; the *Biblioteca de Autores Cristianos* for the Spanish original of Fray Luis de León; Herder Book Company for the English Translations of *De Los Nombres de Cristo.*

CHAPTER I

SPANISH LOGICIANS OF MONTAIGU COLLEGE

We begin our study of Spanish Renaissance thought with a chapter dedicated to a remarkable but practically forgotten group of Spanish logicians teaching at the University of Paris in the first decade of the sixteenth century. The purpose of this introduction is twofold: to present the reader a strong "chiaroscuro" contrasting the languid medievalism of terminist logic with the exciting novelty of humanistic ideals, and to show the Parisian background of early Spanish Renaissance thought.

In spite of these remarks the very title of this chapter might be intriguing to the reader. Renaissance studies traditionally start with an account of the ideas and attitudes made fashionable by the Italian humanists of the quattrocento and spread throughout Europe by Italian masters or their disciples. Although Italian influence was of considerable importance in Spain, as several of our studies will show, the special character of the Spanish Renaissance demands some clarification regarding the intimate connection between sixteenth century Spanish thought and the most conservative and medieval of all the institutions of that time, the University of Paris.

A. THE UNIVERSITY OF PARIS AND TERMINIST LOGIC

At the beginning of the century Spanish intellectual life was still clearly oriented toward Paris. To the most talented and ambitious intellectuals of that age Paris remained the glamorous institution of times past. An academic degree from Paris was a reliable guarantee of success. Both the Spanish Universities and the Spanish Episcopate of the sixteenth century drew a large mumber of their members from among Parisian graduates. When Cardinal Cisneros founded the University of Alcalá at the beginning of the century he turned toward the Parisian University to recruit a brilliant faculty. From Paris he borrowed such masters as Sancho Carranza de Miranda, professor of dialectic and physics, the master of Juan Ginés de Sepúlveda; Miguel Pardo, the brother of the famous logician Jerónimo Pardo (*See below* pp. 13-14); Pedro de Lerma, a disciple of Raulin and a constant apologist of Erasmus; Gonzalo Gil, the first theology professor of Alcalá; Dionisio Vázquez, another apologist of Erasmus and well-known biblical scholar; Fray Alfonso de Córdoba, one of the founders of Alcalá and later a professor of Nominalism at Salamanca; Pedro Sanchez Ciruelo, professor of mathematics at Paris and the first lecturer of Thomistic theology at Alcalá. The Universities of Salamanca and Valladolid were equally proud of their former Parisian faculty members. In 1517 the University of Salamanca sought two masters of Aristotelian philosophy *ad modum Parisiense* and contracted the services of two Parisian masters, Juan Martínez Siliceo and Fray Domingo de San Juan. Antonio de Alcaraz, Rector of the University of Valladolid, had previously been the Rector of the University of Paris (1520) and the *procurator* of the French Nation (1517).

The University of Paris was also the intellectual cradle of an impressive number of illustrious thinkers whose names will constantly appear in these pages: Franciso Astudillo, Pedro de Maluenda, Domingo de Soto, Fernán Pérez de Oliva, Luis de Carvajal, Juan Martínez Población, Juan Gélida, and the famous Jesuits Miguel Torres, Juan Polanco, and Jerónimo Nadal. More importantly the Parisian University was a decisive influence in shaping the intellectual style of the two greatest representatives of the Spanish Renaissance during the reign of Charles V, Juan Luis Vives (to whom we have dedicated a book), and Francisco de Vitoria (*See below*, Chapter Two), whose contrasting life and thought illustrate with utmost clarity the different departures and choices offered by that historical situation.

The extraordinary influence of Paris upon Spanish thinkers of the sixteenth century is probably one of the distinguishing features of the Spanish Renaissance, and reveals its resilient attachment to medieval patterns of thought and its solid commitment to continuity and tradition. At the beginning of the century the University of Paris was clearly a medieval institution, in spite of the zeal of such reformers as Standonck and Maillard, and notwithstanding the appearance of some brilliant Italian masters like Balbi and Andrelini and the first impulses of French humanism inspired by Budé, Lefèvre d'Etaples, Fichet, Gaguin, and Clichtove. The University as an institution was a medieval castle assailed only from outside by formidable winds. The only changes introduced since the glorious days of Philip Augustus were symptoms of old age rather than promises of new life. The autonomy of the University was threatened by the Crown and by the Church. The increasingly powerful French kings resented the jurisdictional independence, the legal autonomy, and the truly international character of the influential academic community on the left bank of the Seine. In 1446 Charles VII severely restricted the legal privileges of the University; in 1473 Louis XI went so far as to forbid the teaching of nominalism at Paris, a form of intellectual censorship which was defiantly ignored by the faculty and revoked eight years later. The Popes, on the other hand, incensed by the popularity of conciliatory doctrines among the Parisian theologians, attempted frequently to control and direct through Cardinal legates the *curriculum* and the discipline of the school. In 1462 Pius II denied the University one of its most cherished privileges, the *cessatio*, or the right to strike. The Papal prohibition against teaching Civil Law, and the ecclesiastical scruples against the study of medicine by the clergy decisively weakened those two important departments, which, instead became strong at Bologna andMontpellier, respectively. The number of students attending Paris was constantly decreasing, from around ten thousand in the fourteenth century to only five thousand at the beginning of the sixteenth, the size of other Universities such as Louvain and Salamanca. The days of Paris as the last court of appeal of Catholic orthodoxy were quickly approaching an end. The nationalization of the University by Francis I and the renewal of Oxford, Salamanca, Heidelberg, Padua, and Louvain (among others) would eventually strip Paris of the central position it had enjoyed in medieval Christianity.

The administrative and academic structures of the University at the beginning of the sixteenth century were basically the same as in the Middle Ages. The University was divided into four departments or 'Faculties' (Law, Medicine, Arts, Theology); both students and teaching staff were divided into four different 'Nations' and several Colleges or pensionates. The convents of the monastic orders (*studium generale*) were equivalent to collegial residences with an increasingly independent academic life of their own. The character was primarily ecclesiastical: the 'Faculty' of Theology enjoyed special privileges, but the Rector of the University was chosen from among the 'artists' or philosophers, by far the largest and most heterogeneous group made up of unmarried laymen and secular priests. The *curriculum* and the teaching methods had remained practically unchanged for centuries. The regulations introduced by the Cardinal Legate D'Estouteville in 1452 were still observed in the sixteenth century, and even those were practically a repetition of rules imposed on the University by Urban VI in 1366, with the exception of one significant change which allowed married laymen in the school of Medicine, a decisive step toward the secularization of that particular department. Students were admitted into the Arts Faculty at the age of fifteen after having demonstrated sufficient familiarity with the Latin grammars of such old fashioned authors as Alexander de Villedieu and Eberhard de Béthune. The first two years were almost exclusively dedicated to the study of the Aristotelian *Organon;* at the beginning of the sixteenth century, however, the *Summulae Logicales* of Peter of Spain was practically the only textbook in use. During the third and final year of Philosophy the student would take Physics, Metaphysics, Ethics, and Mathematics. This incredible disproportion between the time allocated to Logic (two full years) and to philosophy proper was first attacked by Humanists who deplored the absence of Grammar and especially Rhetoric from the University *curriculum*. Later on it was the target of Renaissance thinkers who criticised the absence of speculation in the Faculty of Arts. In speaking of 'Scholastic philosophy', therefore, a sharp distinction is to be understood between the Arts course taught by secular priests and laymen mostly interested in dialectic and to some degree in physics and ethics, and the metaphysical questions discussed by members of the monastic orders in their Theology courses, questions such as the proof of God's existence, immortality of the soul, and their like. The tendency to identify 'scholasticism' almost exclusively with the latter brand would render meaningless much of the Humanistic opposition to traditional education in the sixteenth century.

After three years in the Faculty of Arts the student received his master degree or *licentia docendi*. In Paris most of the students would then proceed to the Faculty of Law (mostly ecclesiastical law) rich in promises of Church stipends and benefices, or to the Faculty of Theology where they spent eighteen long years with the books of the Scripture and the *Liber Sententiarum* of Peter Lombard. Theological studies at Paris did not fare much better than philosophy itself. Textual criticism of the New Testament was narrowed down to corrected editions (*correctorium*) of the Vulgate. In spite of the recommendations of the Council of Vienna in 1311 the study of Greek and Hebrew was practically ignored. Patristic theology was superficially introduced to the students in anthologies, dictionaries, and manuals four hundred years old. The catalogue of books printed in Paris between 1469 and 1500 reveals the proportions of the crisis: two thirds of the titles belong to terminist logic and the great Ockamist masters of the fourteenth century, Buridan, Marsilius of Inghem, Albert of Saxony, and Nicholas Oresme. The editions of Aristotle's *Ethics* and the *Organon*, plus a few, unrepresentative works of Albert the Great, Saint Thomas, Saint Bonaventure complete the list.[1]

Neo-scholastic historians of philosophy have traditionally characterized the philosophical *curriculum* at Paris during the fifteenth and sixteenth centuries as a regrettable diversion form the high path of metaphysical speculation inaugurated by the genius of Saint Thomas in the thirteenth century. Other scholars, however, have pointed to the extraordinary achievements of fourteenth century thought: terminist logic and nominalist physics. These scholars have discovered in terminist logic unsuspected similarities with contemporary mathematical logic, and in nominalist physics a significant and remarkable step toward the scientific method of Galileo's generation. Leaving aside for now the study of nominalist physics we intend to deal here in some detail with terminist logic because of its extraordinary relevance to the understanding of the Renaissance in general, and, especially the large role played by Spanish thinkers in such a school of thought.

It is well known that the early Humanists directed their abrasive attacks and criticisms against traditional philosophy as it was taught in Paris around the turn of the century. The Italians were particularly incensed against the Parisian nominalists, whether logicians or physicists. The Italian Averroist Nifo and the leader of the Alexandrists, Pomponazzi, accumulated more insults than arguments against those Parisian *juniors* who had the audacity to ignore Aristotle's authority in explaining the motion of projectiles or the laws of syllogistic inference. Albert of Saxony was referred to as *Albertulius*, and Richard Suiseth, the author of *Liber Calculationum*, was nicknamed *Captiumculator;* finally the entire Parisian group was labeled *recentiores*, *moderni*, *juniores*, *terministae*, and *sophistae*. The Italian Humanists were appalled by the useless subtlety, by the repulsive parlance, and by the total lack of concern with aesthetic values of the Parisian philosophers. If only by way of contrast

[1] The University of Paris in the first half of the sixteenth century is the special subject of two interesting books. Augustin Renaudet, *Préréforme et Humanisme à Paris pendant les premières guerres d'Italie* (*1494–1517*), 2nd ed., (Paris, 1953); and Ricardo G. Villoslada, *La Universidad de Paris durante los estudios de Francisco de Vitoria O.P.* (*1507–1522*), Analecta Gregoriana, (Rome, 1938).

the study of Parisian thought in the quattrocento is of capital importance to pass judgment upon the criticism of Humanist and early Renaissance thinkers.

Contemporary testimonies abundantly show that in the eyes of many the intellectual confrontation of the day was between Italian Humanists and Renaissance thinkers (later reinforced in some devious ways by central and northern European Reformers) on one hand, and on the other by a stubborn group of Scottish and Spanish logicians at Paris. Ramus described the humanistic movement in the French capital as a reaction against *Scotos et Hispanos*. Vives was painfully aware of the important role played by his countrymen in the teaching of terminist logic when he wrote:

> Most intelligent people blame the Spaniards for these disorders, and they are right. The Spaniards, men of indomitable character, apply all their energies to the defense of this fortress of foolish ignorance; intelligent as they are they have become the best in teaching all the aberrations which have given Paris such a disreputable name the world over. In other Universities you will find a mixture of insane and true knowledge; Paris alone is exclusively dedicated to finicky trifles.[2]

At the beginning, then, of our study of Spanish Renaissance thought we find ourselves facing the extraordinary fact that the most illustrious exponents of the 'barbaric dialectics' which provoked at least partially the bitter Humanistic reaction were Spanish professors at the University of Paris. The intriguing feature of this historical event is that precisely what the otherwise enlightened Humanist and Renaissance thinkers criticised with utmost contempt is viewed today as one of the few redeeming achievements of late medieval thought. The rise and the fall of terminist logic – a quick dramatic process completed in hardly two centuries – is another mysterious chapter in the puzzling history of logic. No other manifestation of the human mind displays the erratic and apparently discontinuous growth which is characteristic of logical theory. According to Kant and his disciples Logic was born perfect in the Aristotelian *Organon*, or rather in the syllogystic of the *Prior Analytics*. The history of Logic for them was only a history of partial aberra-

[2] The Latin text of *In Pseudo-Dialecticos* is found in the third volume of *Juan Luis Vives Opera Omnia* (Valencia, 1790), edited by Gregorio Majans. (Hereafter called *Vives Opera Omnia*, volume and page).
"Pars maxima doctorum hominum totam hujusce rei culpam in Hispanos, qui istic sunt rejicit, qui ut sunt homines invicti, ita fortiter tuentur arcem ignorantiae, et optima ingenia, ubi intenduntur, valent, tradunt se se his deliramentis, fiunt in illis summi, ... reliquis omnibus in studiis, etsi sunt vana et futilia nonulla, esse tamen solida multa, in unis Parisiis vix esse nisi nugacissimas nugas, ..." (*Vives Opera Omnia*, p. 38.)

tions – Prantl calls them 'Byzantine aberrations' – from the perfection of the past. Others, like Bertrand Russell, were convinced that Aristotelian logic was either false or useless, and had no interest whatsoever in any logician who had lived before Leibniz. The serious studies of Peirce, Lukasiewickz, Boehner, Bochenski, Benson Mates, Moody, and others, have definitely established that the two greatest logical advances beyond the narrow boundaries of Aristotelian syllogistic, namely the propositional calculus of the Stoics and terminist logic of the fourteenth century, were abortive movements without any significant following.[3] Stoic logic was practically ignored during the Middle Ages and terminist logic never recovered from the attacks of the Humanists, and for all practical purposes it collapsed into sudden silence by the middle of the sixteenth century. Bochenski's history of formal logic jumps from Paul of Venice – a fifteenth century compilator of terminist logic – to Frege's *Grundgesetze der Arithmetik* (1893) with only a short reference to Arnault's *Logic of Port Royal.* The swift demise of terminist logic, however, was accompanied and followed by the intense but short-lived popularity of both the topical dialectic of Agricola and Ramus' methodology. These two movements are obviously of little interest to the historian of formal logic, but are highly relevant to the intellectual history of modern Europe and intimately related to some overriding concerns of Spanish Renaissance thought. Their significance, however, will first appear after a careful evaluation of the movement they helped to neutralize, terminist logic.

Until the twelfth century medieval logic centered around Aristotle's *Categories* and *De interpretatione* plus the commentaries on these books by Boethius and Porphyry. This impoverished version of Aristotelian logic – later described as *logica vetus* – was enriched in the twelfth century with the discovery of the remaining books of the *Organon*, *logica nova.* Saint Albert the Great's tracts on logic are an encyclopedic compilation of this traditional logic, the boundaries of which go beyond the narrow treatises of neoscholastic logic, but do not yet compare with the wealth of logical theory developed in the thirteenth century by the two founders of terminist logic (*logica moderna*), William of Sherwood (died 1249), and Peter of Spain (died 1277). Sherwood's most characteristic contribution to the development of medieval logic was his thorough

[3] L. M. Bochenski, *A History of Formal Logic,* trans. Ivo Thomas, (Indiana, 1961); Phil Boehner, *Medieval Logic. An Outline of its Development from 1250 to 1400,* 3rd ed., (Manchester, 1966); Ernest E. Moody, *Truth and Consequence in Medieval Logic,* (Amsterdam, 1953). See also the classical book of Karl v. Prantl, *Geschichte der Logik im Abendlande,* 2nd. ed., 3 vols. (Graz, 1955).

study of syncategorematic terms or logical constants, a clear testimony to the growing consciousness of the purely formal character of logical theory. Closely related to the study of syncategorematic terms was Peter of Spain's semantical theory of supposition, the medieval counterpart to the modern theory of quantification and the functional calculus of the first order. The work of Sherwood and Peter of Spain was further developed and elaborated by the great logicians of the fourteenth century William of Ockham (died 1358), William Burleigh (died 1343), John Buridan (died 1358). and his disciple Albert of Saxony (died 1390). Less known but perhaps equally important were the Oxford logicians of the Mertonian school of mathematical physicists, William of Heytesbury, Robert Swineshead, John Dumbleton, and Ralph Strode.

As a logician Ockham was not a radical innovator, but rather a painstaking analyst and an intelligent systematizer. The neo-classical division of logical treatises into a logic of terms, a logic of propositions, and a logic of inferences – an unfortunate distribution – stems from Ockham's logical treatises. In the history of philosophy, however, Ockham deserves great honors for having dispelled the existing confusion between logic and metaphysics. Ockham fought the notion of a metaphysical logic or a logical metaphysics with the conception of logic as a science of speech, *scientia sermocinalis*, a linguistic discipline of second intentions totally neutral to any explanatory theory of Mind or Reality.[4]

Burleigh was the first medieval logician to place the tract on consequences at the beginning of his logical treatise, revealingly entitled *De puritate artis logicae*. More striking still is the fact that the book does not contain any special chapter on syllogistics, a matter which is treated under the more comprehensive and basic heading of inferential theory. Burleigh's clear insight into the purely formal character of inferential theory seems to have powerfully influenced the work of Albert of Saxony, whose treatise *Perutilis Logica* was an ingenious combination of Ockham and Burleigh. Buridan was mostly responsible for the fusion of

[4] The abundant bibliography on Ockham has recently been enriched by important studies. See, for instance, "Der Stand der Ockham-Forschung," *Franziskanische Studien*, XXXIV (1952), pp. 12–31. Reprinted in Boehner, Philotheus. *Collected Articles on Ockham*, Ed. by Eligius M. Buytaert. ("Franciscan Institute Publications, Philosophy Series" No. 12). (New York, 1958); González, Anselmo, "Guillermo de Ockham, *De praedestinatione*: Introducción de Anselmo González," *Ideas y Valores*, VI (1963–64), pp. 303–360; Moody, Ernest A. "William of Ockham," *The Encyclopedia of Philosophy*, ed. Edwards, P., Vol. VIII, pp. 306–317. (New York: The Macmillan Co. and The Free Press, 1967); Shapiro, Herman. *Motion, Time and Place According to William Ockham*. "Franciscan Institute Publications, Philosophy Series" No. 13. (St. Bonaventure, N.Y.: The Franciscan Institute, 1957).

nominalist epistemology and terminist logic, an association which has led to some confusion among historians of ideas. The impressive body of logical theory contained in the works of these fourteenth century masters was enlarged and summarized by a large group of second rank logicians whose names were still highly popular in Paris at the beginning of the sixteenth century, Pierre of Ailly (died 1426), Paul of Venice (died 1428), Bricot (died 1516), Bruxellensis, Pierre Tartaret (died 1495, rector of the University of Paris in 1490 and a well-known Scottish philosopher), John Wessel (died 1498), Gabriel Biel (died 1495), John Dorp (died in the first half of the sixteenth century), and others.

This short historical summary brings us now to the group of Spanish logicians teaching in Paris at the beginning of the sixteenth century to whom this chapter is dedicated. But before we deal directly with their work it might be worthwhile to pause for a short time to ponder the significance, the advances, and the limitations of this form of medieval logic which they cultivated with such "intolerable detail and thoroughness' (Prantl: "unertraegliche Ausfuehrlichkeit"). Only then shall we be able to pass judgment on the criticism of the Humanists and on the role played by this group of Spanish logicians in the intellectual history of Europe.

As a *scientia sermocinalis* terminist logic intended to make explicit the formal structure implied in the usage of language for the purpose of discriminating formally valid from formally invalid inference schemes. This process of explication – reducing *praxis* to *ars*, as medieval philosophers would have put it – consisted in prescribing a set of rules governing the syntactical relationships of a given concrete language, Latin, in a metalanguage which described the syntactical form of linguistic expressions. Such a science of language – a science of *intentiones secundae* in terminist jargon – was understood to be completely independent from any metaphysical speculation and debate, and to be an independent, neutral and uncommitted school of thought, *schola non affectata*. The fact that the late medieval Faculty of Arts dedicated most of its time and energies to the study of an art which by definition was indifferent to the speculative debates of the Theologians is indeed a clear proof of the positivistic and sceptical trend brought into medieval thought by the critical spirit of Duns Scotus and William of Ockham. The revival of bold metaphysical speculation by Renaissance Platonists and Aristotelians was an antithetical reaction to the mundane endeavors of terminist logicians. Terminist logic, furthermore, was not only uninterested in epistemological or metaphysical explanations, it also professed a total contempt for the dia-logical aspect of language, for language as an *ars communicandi* between human beings in social intercourse. The aesthetic, the pragmatic, and the social aspects of the human idiom were of no interest to the terminist logicians. It was up to the Humanists to emphasize the intimate connection between beautiful form and clear content, to recognize the power of the word in teaching and in persuading, to discover the impact of language on the social consciousness of the individual. Humanist criticism, however, failed entirely to give credit to the enormous achievements of terminist logicians and unfairly aggravated some of their obvious deficiencies. An objective statement of both at this point should help us to evaluate Humanism itself and its opposition to logic.

The positive side of terminist logic – not to be confused with the narrow version of medieval logic to be found in neo-scholastic manuals – can best be appreciated by pointing to its novelty with respect to Aristotelian syllogistics and to its similarities with contemporary mathematical logic. There are three important advances of late medieval logic beyond peripatetic logic. The first is included in the treatises on the properties of terms (Books VI, VIII, IX, X, XI of Peter of Spain's *Summulae Logicales*), somehow improperly called *Parva Logicalia*. These tracts contain a theory of truth-condition as a set of formal definitions of the one-place logical predicate 'time'. Two new notions, *significatio* and *suppositio*, introduced into medieval logic an analysis of quantification which offers striking similarities with the first order predicate calculus of contemporary logic and permits expression of the rules of supposition in the theorems of modern calculus. By means of the *suppositio* terminist logic was able to deal extensively – not intensively – with the range of a predicate in reference to individuals. Temporal determinations of the copula were included in the chapter *De copulatione*, while the universal, existential qualifiers, and adjectival determinations were dealt with in the sections *De ampliatione*, *De restrictione*, *De Apellatione*, and *De Distributione*. It is worthwhile to emphasize that the theory of supposition was built not upon the semantical but rather upon the syntactical aspect of language, not upon the relation of designation but upon the logical relation of predication.

The second original contribution of terminist logic was the study of the logical operations or constants called syncategorematic terms. Both the atomistic syncategoremata (essential to the quantitative analysis of the supposition), and the molecular syncategoremata ('it', 'unless', 'if not', 'or', 'and' ...) permitted the truth functional treatment of sentential connections and opened the doors to a thorough study of the propositional calculus. To this section belong the innumerable and long tracts called *De exponibilibus*, which deal with the logical operations of exclusive, exceptive, and reduplicative propositions. The medieval distinction between categorematic and syncategorematic terms was a significant step toward a distinction between the variables and the constants of logical discourse which make up the symbolism of contemporary logistics.

The third and by far the most important improvement of terminist logic beyond the Aristotelian tradition was the theory of consequences or inferential theory. Terminist logicians were inclined to subsume all forms of valid inference, including the syllogism, under the type of inference of conditional propositions. Guided by this principle, terminist logicians were able to develop a propositional logic much more comprehensive than the traditional assertoric, term logic of Aristotelian extraction. The historical sources of this trend are far from clear. The enthymemata of Aristotle in the *Topics*, Aristotle's study of modal consequences in *De interpretatione*, Boethius' work on hypothetical syllogisms, and the Stoic Megaric tradition of propositional logic, are the obvious historical ancestors, but contemporary scholars do not yet agree upon the continuity or discontinuity of such a tradition. In any case, no one disagrees with Lukasiewicz when he says that "propositional logic was founded by the Stoics, developed by the scholastics, and axiomatically constructed by Frege".[5] To these basic contributions of late medieval logic we should add the endless treatises on semantical antinomies (*De insolubili* and *De impossibilibus*), fallacies (*Sophismata*), and the progress made in modal logic.

In spite of these respectable achievements terminist logic was doomed from its very start to the elephantiasis of which it suddenly died in the first half of the sixteenth century. The very innovations which fed the body of logical theory inevitably produced the abuses and excesses which proved fatal to its growth. The source of this chronic disease was precisely the attempt, firstly, to abstract from a concrete language (Latin) the formal rules dictated by the semantic and syntactic functions of the sign in that particular language; and, secondly, to formulate such rules in a descriptive metalanguage consisting of terms of second intention and syncategorematic terms common both to the object language and to the syntax language. In direct contrast with medieval terminist logic, contemporary mathematical logicians proceed

[5] "Zur Geschichte der Aussagenlogik," *Erkenntnis* V (1935), p. 127.

not to abstract but to construct purely formal systems the laws of which are formulated in an artificial language using symbols not only for the variables of the object language but also for the constants of logical operations. The scholastic attempt to 'abstract' a formal system of logic from the usage of a concrete, living language, not only imposed certain limitations on the results, but also led to excessive complication, repetition, and logical gaps. Furthermore, the language of second intentions in which formulae are not exhibited but described became in time an unintelligible jargon, a true monster generously fed by the amazing subtlety, endurance, and acumen of terminist logicians. Paradoxically, the logical analysis of a living language was formulated in a sub-language which was at the same time the object described and the tool of description. At the end of the fifteenth century terminist logic had reached a dead end. The great masters of the fourteenth century and the commentators and systematizers of the fifteenth had already exhausted most of its possibilities. A new growth could only mean a fresh distortion or another abuse. Unfortunately, the Scottish-Spanish group we are about to review represents this last stage in the history of terminist logic.

B. MONTAIGU COLLEGE AND THE SPANISH LOGICIANS

Most of the logicians we will introduce were students, teachers, or at least disciples of scholars related to the Montaigu College. The history and the character of this institution powerfully influenced the intellectual climate of Paris in the first half of the sixteenth century, and is, therefore, a very important chapter in the history of the Northern Renaissance.[6]

Founded in 1344 by the Archbishop of Rouen for the sake of poor students, Montaigu's first hundred years of existence were languid and obscure. Toward the end of the fifteenth century, however, the College was entirely reformed by John Standonck, a disciple of the Brethren of the Common Life, and the most austere and remarkable apostle of the *Devotio Moderna* at Paris. Under his leadership the students of Montaigu led an intensive religious life in harmony with a thorough dedication to intellectual pursuits. At the beginning of the sixteenth century Montaigu was not only the best disciplined and the most religious of all the Parisian colleges but also the very center of the

[6] See Renaudet, *Préréforme et Humanisme*, pp. 175–177, 267–269, 309–312, 463–467, and 655–658. Also, Marcel Godet, *La congrégation de Montaigu*, (Paris, 1912).

University's intellectual life. In 1500 the poor students of Montaigu were organized by Standonck as a religious congregation, which was, in the opinion of some scholars, the model of Loyola's Jesuit Order fifty years later. The prestige of Montaigu can be measured by the names of the *alumni*, Erasmus, Juan Luis Vives, Rabelais, Calvin, Domingo Soto, Juan Celaya, and Saint Ignatius of Loyola.

After Standonck's death, the college was governed by two of his closest associates, Noel Beda and John Mair. At that time Montaigu had a teaching staff of thirty masters and about four hundred students. It was under Beda and Mair that Montaigu became a powerful center of reactionary orthodoxy and terminist logic. The conservative trend was attributable to Beda, whom Erasmus used to call *cacactilis bestia*, an unflattering title which resists literal translation. In the second book of *Pantagruel* Rabelais was even harder on the college and its austere director. Beda's constant attacks on Erasmus, Lefèvre d'Etaples, Luther, and even Marguerite of Navarre and Francis I, were finally too much for the French Parliament. In 1536 Beda was sent into exile to the Abbey of Mount Saint-Michel where he died the following year.

The reactionary climate fostered by Beda was unfortunately, but not without cause, coupled with the revival of terminist logic championed by the Scot John Mair and the Spaniard Jerónimo Pardo. Chronologically Pardo preceded Mair by a few years, and according to some historians (Prantl, for instance) was Mair's teacher at Montaigu. Although we know very little about Pardo's life and character, his name deserves a very special mention, first because he was the co-founder of the movement; and secondly, because his textbook of terminist logic, *Medulla dialectices*, first printed in 1500 and later reprinted by Mair in 1505, remained for half a century a classical summary of the subject. In spite of its pretentious title – probably an atrocity of the editor – Pardo's book was a rare example of moderation and good sense. As was traditional in the superabundant tracts of terminist logic Pardo's treatise was cumulatively built upon the findings and particular achievements of practically all past logicians from Ockham and Buridan to the most recent masters like Bricot, Dorp, and Pierre Crockaert. Pardo follows Albert of Saxony in the study of consequences and fallacies, but sticks to Ockham in the chapter on modal logic and to Paul of Venice in the discussion of the hypothetical syllogism. The treatise is divided in ten parts: 1) The truth and falsity of propositions; 2) General theory of consequences (inferential theory); 3) Contradictory propositions; 4) Conversion; 5) Hypothetical syllogism; 6) *Ampliatio;* 7) *Appellatio;* 8)

Modal propositions; 9) Syllogistic; 10) *De descensu* (inferences based upon the quantification of the supposition). Comprehensive as the book was it obviously lacked formal order and perspicuity.

Pardo's disciple, John Mair (also known as John Maior, Maioris, or Lemaire) was by far the most influential master of Montaigu College. A discipline of Standonck, Raulin, Bricot, and Tartaret, he became in time the respected patriarch of an entire generation of Parisian masters such as Almain (Vitoria's master in theology), Jean Dullaert (Vives' teacher in Beauvais College), Cambraith, Pierre Crockaert (*See below* pp. 19-20), Gaspar Lax, the Coronel brothers, and many others. Mair's strong influence helped to shape the distinctive features of Montaigu's philosophical attitudes. Personally, Mair was an austere man who kept untarnished his admiration for the reforming zeal of Standonck. Intellectually he managed to blend in equal proportions the critical tendencies of nominalist epistemology and a loyal submission to Catholic dogma, in spite of his share of gallicanism and conciliarism. Although Mair's name is also associated with theology, the main source of his reputation was undoubtedly his contribution to the growth of terminist logic. More than anyone else, Mair was responsible for the excessive attention and time given to dialectic at Montaigu College, and by so doing he clearly drew the line of confrontation between medieval learning – of which he was called 'the depository' – and the fresh, new approaches of Renaissance Humanism. The decisive experiences of men like Erasmus, Ramus, Vives, Rabelais and Vitoria, during their studies at Paris cannot be fully appreciated without the sharp contrast between their restless projection into the future and Mair's medievalism. As the founder of Montaigu's school of terminist logicians Mair was a prolific writer and editor. His first original book was a commentary to Peter of Spain's *Summulae logicales* (1505), a book which Mair considered "the door to Logic" (*totius logicae ianua*). Mair's own books displayed all the nefarious abuses common to this last stage of terminist logic: prolix and digressive, burdened by an endless disarray of examples and counter examples, excessively subtle and obscure in their staccato of distinctions and sub-distinctions, obdurate in their analysis of logical minutiae. The syntaxis and the vocabulary of the Latin jargon used by Mair and his followers were related to classical Latin only by a far-fetched kinship, although the introductions and dedications of the same books often proved beyond any doubt that their authors were also capable of Ciceronian cadences and even Horatian meters. The ungainly homeliness and total lack of concern for beauty which these books betray was not an accidental shortcoming, but rather the conscious result of a frame of mind perfectly formulated by Mair himself in his famous slogan: "Science does not stand in need of comely words."

Mair's achievements in logic were furthermore associated with a moderate version of nominalist epistemology. Montaigu's nominalism, like that of Mair himself, was an interesting trend, being more a philosophical attitude than a well-defined epistemological theory. In fact most of the Montaigu teachers took a very eclectic position concerning the ontological status of the universals, the classical issue which had divided medieval philosophers into the two irreconcilable groups of 'Realists' and 'Nominalists.' According to Mair and his disciples the difference between the two schools of thought was only a matter of words, an attitude which we shall find in other Spanish 'Parisians' such as Vives, Soto, and Vitoria .Montaigu's eclecticism was not the result of fuzzy thinking. It was rather an act of positive independence from the narrow Thomism of the Dominicans and the Scotism of the Franciscans. Mair's description of Montaigu as an independent school was faithfully respected by his disciples. When Pierre Crockaert left Montaigu to become a Dominican in the Convent of Saint-Jacques none of his colleagues accused him of betraying his philosophical allegiances. In fact, even as the champion of the Thomistic revival in Paris during the first half of the sixteenth century Crockaert, remained always a loyal disciple of John Mair. A striking example of Montaigu's special brand of nominalism were the subtitles of Celaya's books (*See below*, pp. 45-46); "*Secundum triplicem viam beati Thomae, Realium et Nominalium.*" Since eclecticism is such an important ingredient of Spanish Renaissance thought, especially among the Augustinians and Jesuits, this outstanding character of Montaigu College is of particular relevance to our study.

Two other features of Montaigu can be attributed to Mair's leadership. The first was a progressive attitude toward Aristotelian physics, the second an overriding concern with ethical problems. Mair's achievements in physics are closely related to the outstanding work of Domingo de Soto whose ideas deserve much more attention than they have so far attracted.[7] More importantly, Mair's critical attitude toward Aristotelian physics was instrumental in making possible the scientific revolution of the following century. As for ethics it is clear that Montaigu's efforts found a receptive audience among humanists,

[7] See, however, William Wallace's article "The Enigma of Domingo de Soto," *Isis*, 59 (1968), pp. 84–401.

reformers, pedagogues, and jurists involved in shaping new forms and categories of life in those decades of quickening change.

Most of the disciples of John Mair were Scottish and Spanish. The Scottish group – David Cranston, Robert Cambraith, William Mendeston, Robert Walterson, George Lockert – continued in Paris the remarkable British tradition of Ockham, Swineshead, Burleigh, and Strode, a tradition which Italian humanists like Petrarch and Salutati had repeatedly scorned. There were also some disciples from the Low Countries – Jean Dullaert and Pierre Crockaert – and a few Frenchmen like Jacques Almain, Jerome of Hangest, and Robert Cènau. Here, however, we shall limit ourselves to the Spanish disciples of Mair, not only because of the character of this book, but also because, as Vives would remind us, they were the most loyal, the most representative, and the most criticized. The Spanish logicians of Montaigu can be divided into three groups: The first is made up of the immediate disciples of Mair, Antonio Coronel and Gaspar Lax of Sariñena. Juan Dolz and Fernando Enzinas make up the second group. Finally Juan Celaya represents the closing of the school around the middle of the century.

Antonio Nuñez Coronel was the favorite disciple of Mair. Following the example of his master, Antonio Coronel (as history knows him) became one of the most prolific writers of Montaigu. His books did not add much substance to the already luxuriant growth of terminist logic, but magnified rather the aberrations in which it was fatally entangled. The titles of the books give a fair idea of their contents: *A treatise on 'exponibile' and fallacies* (1509), *Logical questions according to Realists and Nominalists* (1509), *Commentary on the Posterior Analytics of Aristotle* (1510), *The Rosary of Logic* (sic!) (1512), *Commentaries on the Aristotelian Categories according to Realists and Nominalists* (1513), *A treatise on Syllogistics* (1512), *A treatise on Terms* (1518). Antonio Coronel and his brother Luis were typical representatives of Spanish intelligentsia at the turn of the century. Born in Segovia between 1470 and 1480 they began their intellectual training at Salamanca; soon they felt the admiration for Paris where they arrived around 1500. Luis became in time an influential theologian in the Sorbonne College, while Antonio joined Montaigu and its logicians. Probably around 1517, like so many other Spanish students and teachers at Paris, the Coronel brothers left France for the Low Countries where they soon reached influential positions as counselors and preachers at the Imperial Court. In their crusade against Lutheranism in the Low Countries they first took a very critical and severe attitude toward Erasmus, but their friendship with

Juan Luis Vives helped to mollify their attitude. Antonio Coronel died soon thereafter, but his brother Luis played an important part in the history of the Erasmian movement in Spain as secretary to Alfonso Manrique, Archbishop of Sevilla and Grand Inquisitor until his death in 1531. In his case, as in so many others, the personal contact with Vives in Bruges proved a decisive factor in his intellectual and religious orientation.

The second direct disciple of John Mair was Gaspar Lax of Sariñena, known in Paris as the 'Prince of the Sophists,' a most flattering title for the times. Gaspar Lax had been born in Zaragoza in 1487. After obtaining his doctoral degree he went to Paris and taught for several years at Montaigu. One of his best known disciples, Juan Luis Vives, praised the extraordinary memory of Gaspar and informs us that later in his life Gaspar Lax, together with his master Jean Dullaert, deeply regretted having dedicated the best years of his life to the pursuit of such a wasteful discipline. Lax's conversion probably took place after he was compelled to leave Paris in 1524 by the Royal Edict of Francis I against foreign teachers and students. Back in Spain, Gaspar Lax became a theology professor and the Rector of the University of Zaragoza where he had Saint Francis a Borgia – the second General of the Jesuits – and the future Pope Calixt II among his disciples. Lax owes his fame to the important role he played in the Parisian University. Without fear of exaggeration we can characterize Lax as the most degenerate representative of terminist logic in the first half of the century. The organic ailments of such discipline reached in his works fatal proportions. The jargon of his multitudinous books – he wrote no less than seventeen treatises of logic – became totally unintellegible. To the reader who knows Latin the following definition of a necessary proposition might give a fair idea of Lax's tortuous style:

> Propositio necessaria sic potest diffiniri. Est propositio secundum aliquam significationem non destruens suam necessitatem idem quam est significans taliter qualiter necessario est, vel significat taliter qualiter impossibiliter est, quidquid non consequatur impossibilitas aut contingentia.[8]

The casuistic treatment of logical questions made necessary by the lack of axiomatization and proper symbolism teased Lax's undeniable intelligence into an endless sequence of ever increasing concreteness. The definition of *obligatio* in one of his tracts is followed by no less than twenty five objections and counter-objections. To make things worse,

[8] Quoted by Marcial Solana, *Historia de la Filosofía Española. Epoca del Renacimiento*, 3 vols., (Madrid 1941), III, p. 26.

Gaspar Lax and his contemporaries were utterly convinced that in comparison with the logical efforts of past times their own outlandish monstrosities were, as he himself wrote to a friend, "clear and perspicuous, useful, sweet, and bright." Some of the titles of his books give an impression of the style and the content: *Exponibilia Magistri Gasparis Lax Aragonensis de Sarinyena correcta et revisa per ipsum cum nonnullis additionibus eiusdem* (1512); *Insolubilia Magistri Gasparis Lax ... noviter impressa et per ipsum correcta* (1511); *Tractatus de oppositionibus propositionum categoricarum et de earum aequipollentiis* (1512); *Tractatus syllogismorum* (1510). To these books we should add two mathematical treatises which were also very popular in Paris: *Arithmetica speculativa* (1515) and *Proportiones* (1515). The reputation of Gaspar Lax was such that one of his disciples reported to the Spanish Ambassador in the French Court:

> Master Gaspar Lax has such a total mastery of the dialectic art and of philosophy in general that nobody would ever believe that one single person has so much intelligence, if it were not because of the testimony of his contemporaries who respect him as the unquestionable leader.[9]

Gaspar Lax was in many ways the leader of the second and last generation of Montaigu logicians among whom we find three more Spanish names: Juan Dolz from Aragón, Fernando Enzinas from Valldolid, and the Valentian Juan Celaya. Our information concerning the first two is very meager. Dolz arrived in Paris around 1505 and was probably a disciple of Lax in Montaigu. From his master, Dolz soon acquired the publishing obsession. Long before he obtained his doctoral degree as a teaching assistant in the College of Lisieux, Dolz published three books in three years: *Termini* (1510), *Syllogismi* (1511) and *Disputationes super primum tractatum summularum* (1512). Their unfathomable jargon and their lack of originality (being a repetition of Mair and Cambraith's logical tracts with some added complications) were ominous signs of Montaigu's impending collapse.

Enzinas and Celaya, on the other hand, were already figures of transition. Enzinas was a professor of Arts in Beauvais College. Between 1518 and 1528, the year of his premature death, the young Spaniard published seven logical treatises in the best (or worst!) tradition of Mair's school. We have enough data, however, to think that in the later years of his short and promising life Enzinas was progressively detaching himself from his early entanglements and becoming increas-

[9] "Quem penes potestas omnis est dialecticae artis atque philosophiae vix crediderit quispiam tantam ingenii lucem in homine nisi omnes sui contemporanei logici qui eum pro duce in suis argutiis colunt atque observant clare viderent." Quoted by Solana, *Historia de la Filosofía Española*, III, p. 33.

ingly interested in the new perspectives of Renaissance Humanism. In the introduction to one of his later books, which he reluctantly agreed to publish under considerable pressure from his admirers, Enzinas confessed that he himself did not think too much of his own *ineptiae*. Vives, who knew him well and admired him immensely, was convinced that Enzinas was clearly approaching the moment of final 'conversion.'

Juan Celaya is the last and probably the most interesting Spanish figure in the short-lived but intense school of Montaigu logicians, in spite of the fact that his name has been entirely left out of the classical histories of logic or medieval philosophy. Born in Valencia around 1490 Celaya sojourned to Paris before completing his studies of Grammar, probably in 1505, four years before the same journey of a better known Valentian, Juan Luis Vives. In Paris Celaya studied Arts under Gaspar Lax, Jean Dullaert, David Cranston, Robert Cènau, and the Coronel brothers. The first sign of Celaya's independent spirit was his reluctance to engage in the publishing race his colleagues were tirelessly running. In fact he criticized with severity the books of his countryman Juan Dolz, signifying a breach of loyalty toward the school which was showing signs of increasing disintegration. Celaya's teaching began at Coqueret College where he had among his colleagues one of the most famous logicians of those times, Robert Cambraith, and among his disciples one of the most influential men of Spain in the first half of the sixteenth century, Juan Martínez Siliceo, the future Archbishop of Toledo. From 1515 to 1522 Celaya taught in Santa Barbara, but in 1524 he returned to his native Valencia where he became the permanent Rector of the University until his death in 1558. As in the case of Gaspar Lax and many others, Celaya's intellectual activity in Spain meant a total break with terminist logic; in Valencia Celaya taught theology with enormous success and universal applause. His frame of mind, however, remained conservative and scholastic. He feared the paganizing trend of humanistic education and sincerely distrusted Erasmian irenics.

As a writer Celaya displayed some qualities carefully avoided by his Parisian colleagues. His logical books – most of them commentaries on Porphyry and Aristotle – were orderly conceived and clearly executed. His rare pursuit of lucidity led him in fact toward the frequent use of geometrical symbolism to express logical rules, a device previously introduced by John Mair and Pierre Tartaret. Geometrical figures were introduced by Celaya only as mnemonic devices to facilitate the learning of logical intricacies, not as substitutes for the tortuous metalanguage of second intentions. Moreover, the labyrinthic convolutions of Celaya's diagrams proved beyond any doubt the limitations of geometrical symbols toward the formalization of logic. On the other hand, Celaya's frequent use of the spatial model as a key to solving the riddles of the mental world was highly symptomatic of the increasing trend toward the visualization of intellectual constructs nurtured by the new techniques of letter printing and progressively revealed in Ramus' dichotomies and schemes. The fact that some of Celaya's disciples later became intimate friends and admirers of Ramus suggests the existence of some deep bonds between the two schools of thought.

Celaya's eclecticism and intellectual cosmopolitanism were also revealed in the wide range of his philosophical interests. Refusing to become exclusively absorbed in the study of logical *minutiae* Celaya focused his attention on two other philosophical disciplines more closely associated with life itself – *disciplinae quae ad vitam attinent*–ethics and physics. His commentaries on Aristotle's *Physics*, *De Coelo*, *De generatione et corruptione*, and *Ethics* have lately attracted the attention of scholars (Durhem). Celaya's interest in ethical problems was indirectly fostered by the very humanists he so deeply distrusted, and was also the result of the speculative scepticism rampant in late medieval thought.

With Juan de Celaya and his contemporaries the school of Montaigu was closed for all practical purposes. Some stubborn but uninteresting efforts lingered on in some quarters of Europe – Spain especially – throughout the sixteenth century. But the failures of the school itself, and more importantly, the devastating criticisms of the Humanists, were enough to neutralize its impact in the world of ideas. Interestingly enough one of the most fierce and intelligent critiques directed against Montaigu was written by one of its *alumni*, a friend of Celaya, the Spanish Humanist Juan Luis Vives, to whom we shall now direct our attention.

C. VIVES' CRITICISM OF TERMINIST LOGIC

In the fall of 1509 a young man from Valencia was admitted as a student of Arts in Montaigu College. In doing so Juan Luis Vives joined a large and distinguished cluster of Valentian teachers and students in Paris, among whom we should mention Celaya, Juan Martínez Población, Juan Gélida, and Pedro Juan Oliva. Vives was not an ordinary man. By race, character, early education, and the events of his life, he was destined to become an intense, lonely, cosmopolitan man, passionately eager to understand the quick change of his historical occasion, to find the prudent middle way between a blind loyalty to tradition and radical novelty. While others were at the mercy of the erratic waves on the surface, Vives was in search of the basic stream of history. Although he was not one of those rare geniuses in whom human consciousness reaches higher levels of understanding, his entire work revealed the direction of the ascent with scattered flashes of prophetic insights into the future mixed with routine tributes to past habits of thought. For this reason his work was full of baffling contrasts. Known as a Humanist he despised poetry and fiction, and considered Plato and Aristotle the representatives of man's childhood. He was both pessimist and optimist about the possibilities of man's nature. He believed in God but refused to become dangerously involved in the religious disputes of his contemporaries. He wrote a summary of Aristotelian speculation, but was convinced that knowledge is primarily a tool of action and a set of strong beliefs.[10]

The presence in Paris of a large number of students from Valencia was no mere accident. Toward the end of the fifteenth century Valencia was the most prosperous city in the Kingdom of Aragón, a loose confederation of three different regions, Catalonia, Valencia, and Aragón proper. Together with Barcelona, Valencia was, by its very geographical position, a cosmopolitan center of trade, wide open to the clear horizons of Mediterranean culture, and closely associated with southern Italy since the conquest of Naples by the Aragonese. As a result of these circumstances the city soon became an important center of Spanish Renaissance culture, one of the few Spanish towns to bear a certain resemblance to the intellectual blossoming of the Italian urban elites. In 1473 Valencia had the privilege to establish the first Spanish printing press, and in 1501 a Valencian Pope, Alexander VI, founded in the city the first of twenty new institutions of high learning opened in Spain during the sixteenth century. Unlike other Spanish Universities, however, Valencia was more a municipal than an ecclesiastical center. In 1508 Vives entered the Gymnasium already split by the conflict between the conservatively minded grammarians and the admirers of the patriarch of Spanish Humanism, Antonio de Nebrija. One of Vives' most conservative teachers – *insipiter barbarus*, as Vives' biographer calls him – did not hesitate to use Vives' rhetorical talents to attack the op-

[10] For further information on Vives and complete bibliography I will refer the reader to my book *Juan Luis Vives*, (The Hague, 1970).

posite faction, and gave Vives the assignment of writing a speech against Nebrija. We do not know whether Vives actually complied with this order, but we do know that years later Nebrija was the only Spanish scholar ever admired and recommended by Vives. In any case we are certain that Vives' local background and early education prepared him admirably for the immense critical task which became his vocation.

Another important ingredient of Vives' independence and even rebelliousness was his Jewish ancestry. Until very recently Spanish scholars have either ignored or denied this important fact. Neither Menéndez y Pelayo nor Bonilla even bothered to mention such a possibility. Today, after the conclusive findings of Américo Castro, Abdón Salazar, Angel Losada, and especially, Miguel de la Pinta and José María de Palacio, we can establish beyond any reasonable doubt the following facts.[11] The parents of Vives were both Jewish converts, and both of them were brought to Court by the Inquisition on suspicion of heresy. Vives' father was "delivered to the secular arm," a sinister expression which was equivalent to death by fire. Vives' brother and sisters were forever deprived of any right to the paternal or maternal property. These are the shocking facts; any attempt to understand Juan Luis Vives without taking these events into sober consideration would be irrational and/or wicked. Although Vives' baptism remains shrouded in mystery we have no reason to doubt that he was in fact baptized as an infant, a practice he would later criticize. Probably he received also from the beginning an intense Christian education since his parents knew well that after the decree of 1492 local circumstances made such a training a matter of survival for the child. Although Vives thus became and remained for his entire life a sincere Christian, the Jewish heritage which was his is obviously one of the most important features of his personality. As a Spanish Jew Vives belonged to a well defined ethnic group which for centuries had managed to impose upon the Christian rulers a policy of tolerance and even privilege against the base religious fanaticism of the lower classes. Vives' parents belonged to an enlightened and respected elite; from them Vives inherited a practical bent of mind, a pervasive feeling of communal responsibility, a sense of urgency in attempting to fulfill the promises of a better future,

[11] Américo Castro, *The Structure of Spanish History*, (Princeton, 1954); "Un aspecto del pensar Hispano-Judío," *Hispania*, 35 (1952), pp. 161–172; Angel Losada, "Luis Vives en la actualidad internacional," *Revista de Filosofía*, VII (1952), pp. 151–155; Miguel de la Pinta y Llorente and José M. de Palacio, *Procesos Inquisitoriales contra la familia judía de Juan Luis Vives*, Consejo Superior de Investigaciones Científicas, (Madrid, 1964).

but also a great detachment from the established order, institutional education, and Spanish narrow-mindedness.

Vives disliked Paris from the very first moment of his arrival. One of his later books, *Lingua Latinae Exercitatio* (1538), describes with colorful detail the conceit of the richer students, the folly of academic honors and degrees, the endless and futile disputes, the lack of humanity and refinement among the faculty members, the archaism of the textbooks, the pointless dullness of terminist logic. "The University," he wrote, "looked like an eighty-year-old woman, sick, decrepit, and in imminent danger of death." Six years after his departure from Paris Vives wrote a passionate and bitter denunciation of the University. This short pamphlet, *In Pseudo-Dialecticos* (1519) took the form of a letter to Vives' former fellow student at Paris, Daniel Fort, also from Valencia. *In Pseudo-Dialecticos* was neither the first nor the most mature of Vives' writings. It was preceded by ten short essays published by Vives in Louvain between 1514 and 1518. Some of those writings were prayers and meditations in the tradition of the *Devotio Moderna*; some were humanistic essays, and one an extremely original summary of the history of philosophy. All of these writings clearly prove that Vives' negative reaction to terminist logic was, if not the result, at least the natural consequence of his conversion in Paris to humanistic ideals and new religious attitudes.

In Paris the young and restless Spaniard met for the first time the intellectual avant-garde of Transalpine Europe. The moderate scepticism of Northern pietism and the concealed pagan flavor of Italian humanism were properly represented in Paris by a phalanx of reformers and scholars ready to scale the walls of the citadel of a world-view they considered obsolete and retrograde. The sharp contrasts between Vives' formal education at Paris and the daring novelty of his extracurricular learning brought to him an intense and clear-sighted awareness of the radical cultural change his generation was going through.

In Montaigu College, besides the tortures of terminist logic, Vives was exposed to the spirit and piety of the congregation of Windesheim, a group organized after the death of Gerard Groote in 1384 as a mystical reaction against the impoverishment of a theologically centered devotion by the criticism of Ockham's philosophy. Both the Brethren of the Common Life and the canons of Windesheim turned to the Scripture, to the Fathers, and to the German mystics (especially Ruysbroeck, Groote's personal friend) in search of spiritual nourishment. Their special brand of piety – which they proudly called *Devotio Mo-*

derna as a challenge to the similar claim of the 'modern' logicians – was definitively formulated by Thomas à Kempis in his book *Imitatio Christi*, which together with Loyola's *Spiritual Exercises* would give to Catholic piety its typical Counter-Reformation profile. The spiritual temper of Juan Luis Vives was therefore forged in a movement which was intimately related to the Reformation, the Erasmian movement, the Spanish mystics, the spirituality of the Jesuits, and the special religious character of much Transalpine Humanism. The final result was a typically northern European version of devout education and life-oriented Humanism to which Vives, at least in the early stage of his life, gave his most enthusiastic allegiance. Vives' passionate indictment of medieval logic in *In Pseudo-Dialecticos* has to be understood in this context.

The opposition of the *Devotio Moderna* to the mundane, wasteful, and disproportionate emphasis on logic of late medieval philosophy found a warm echo among some of the most cherished ideals of the Humanists. Italian Humanism had reached Paris with remarkable delay, but the presence of French armies in Italy during the reign of Charles VIII of Orléans (1483–1498) expedited its final victory and increased the range of its influence. In the third quarter of the fifteenth century, a personal friend of Bessarion, Guillaume Fichet, had introduced Paris to the *Elegantiae Latinae* of Valla; and Robert Gaguin, the General of the Trinitarian Order, had given a perfect example of how to combine a refined humanistic taste with an intense religious life. The presence in France of Italian masters such as Girolamo Balbi and Fausto Andrelini, and the revival of classical Greek studies through Tissard and Aleander prepared the day for the emergence of three illustrious men intimately associated with Juan Luis Vives: Guillaume Budé, Lefèvre d'Etaples, and Erasmus of Rotterdam. In 1509 Budé was absorbed in his study of Justinian's *Digest*, Erasmus was in England, and Lefèvre had withdrawn into the monastery of Saint Germain-des-Prés to prepare his edition of the Psalms in five different languages. Vives' early correspondence reveals an unbounded admiration for all three of these giants of Northern Humanism. Furthermore, the first written productions of Vives, those which preceded *In Pseudo-Dialecticos*, betray an amazing familiarity with classical culture and authors totally alien to the established dialectical studies he pursued at Montaigu. *In Pseudo-Dialecticos*, therefore, is not only an extraordinary document of sixteenth century criticism, but also an autobiographical page of Juan Luis Vives' diary. The essay (or letter) begins with some personal remarks:

In conversations with some of my closest and most educated friends we often talk about the renaissance of letters in this our century we are so proud of. My friends, however, deplore the fact that precisely in Paris, where all enlightenment should originate, some men have tenaciously embraced the most vain, silly, and ugly of all barbarisms.

Most intelligent people blame the Spaniards for these disorders, and they are right. The Spaniards, men of indomitable character, apply all of their energies to the defense of this fortress of foolish ignorance; and capable as they are, have become the champions of all the aberrations which have given Paris such a disreputable name the world over. In other Universities you might find a mixture of insane and sane knowledge; Paris alone is entirely dedicated to finicky trifles.[12]

As a Spanish student from Paris Vives felt obviously hurt by the reputation of his *alma mater* and the role played there by his own countrymen. His letter to Fort, still in Paris, was an urgent appeal to all the Spanish masters there to abandon as soon as possible the mistaken path of terminist logic, and to apply "their extraordinary personal talents to the study of beautiful disciplines, so that, superior as we (the Spaniards) are to other nations in individual gifts, we might excell also in learning and true scholarship." To make his request more persuasive Vives reminded his readers of his own bitter experience:

I felt that those who criticized Paris also criticized me in some way since I was one of the group, nor have I yet completely forgotten all the asinine people I met there nor all those dreadful words such as *tantum*, *alter*, *alius*, *uterque*, *incipit*, *desinit*, *immediate*, and the rest. In fact this is one of the main reasons why I dare to talk about the subject. If I did not know all the details of this discipline they seem to be so proud of, I would certainly refrain from discussing it. I know well that these insolent people would right away claim that I condemn what they are doing because I do not understand it. Now, you, my dear Fort, and all my fellow students at Paris, you are my witnesses that I did not only taste this insanity, but I also penetrated its most recondite secrets...[13]

12 "Homines doctissimi, et amantissimi mei, quibus cum familiariter dum commentor, incidimusque in mentionem renascentium litterarum; id enim fere agimus, ut gratulemur nostro seculo maxime queri illi solent Parisiis, unde lux totius eruditionis manare deberet, mordicus homines quosdam foedam amplecti barbariem, et cum ea monstra quaedam disciplinarum, velut sophismata, ut ipsi vocant, quibus nihil neque vanius est, neque stultius ...
Pars maxima doctorum hominum totam hujusce rei culpam in Hispanos, qui istic sunt rejicit, qui ut sunt homines invicti, ita fortiter tuentur arcem ignorantiae, et optima ingenia ubi intenduntur, valent, tradunt se se his deliramentis, fiunt in illis summi, ... reliquis omnibus in studiis, etsi sunt vana et futilia nonnulla, esse tamen solida multa, in unis Parisiis vix esse nisi nugacissimas nugas, ..." (*Vives' Opera Omnia*, III, pp. 37 and 38.)

13 "Tum etiam quod ad me quoque partem illius vituperationis attinere existimarem, qui aliquando ex isto numero fui, nec sunt mihi adhuc asini omnes, et portentosa illa vocabula, tantum, alter, alius, uterque, incipit, desinit, immediate, obliterata, quae una est atque ea praecipua causa, quare de hac ista re loqui audeo; nam si haec quibus homines inepti

After these introductory remarks Vives proceeds to criticize terminist logic. His objections center on a double theme: A) logic is not a prescriptive, but an inductive set of rules about language; B) logic is not a theoretical science but a practical instrument of all other disciplines. The presentation of these fundamental ideas was both repetitious and disorderly; the style, while though noble at times, was too frequently gross and ill-mannered. The document betrays an assorted array of mixed influences and trends of thought: a humanistic emphasis on form and practicality; a pietistic contempt for the mundane character of logical speculation; Agricola's attention to topics and probable argument; and a deep-seated contempt for (and ignorance of) medieval logicians and scholars before Peter of Spain.

Vives repeats again and again that linguistic usage and convention dictate the rules of dialectic, and not vice versa. In this respect dialectics follows exactly the same procedures as the other two linguistic arts (*artes sermocinantes*), grammar and rhetoric.

These three arts are about a language received from people, not about a language they themselves impose upon people. Greek and Latin were spoken first; only later were some grammatical, rhetorical, and dialectical rules formulated. Language was not directed by them, but they followed language and adapted themselves to it. We do not speak Latin in this or another way because Latin grammar so prescribes it; on the contrary, grammar dictates those rules because that was the way Latin people spoke. Exactly the same applies to rhetoric and dialectic, which deal with the same language as grammar. Dialectic finds the true, the false, and the probable in the language ordinary folk speak. Rhetoric finds the ornament, the beauty and the elegance. To ignore all this is to profess a supreme ignorance.

The grammarian does not dictate whether an expression is to be considered correct Latin, he only finds it and teaches it. The same applies to dialectical l rules, which are not executory. The rules existed long before dialectic was invented. The dialectician only teaches what the usage of language prescribes.[14]

gloriantur, nota mihi non essent, ne hiscere quidem in his auderem, novi enim quid confestim solita sua insolentia jactant: Damnat quia non intelligit.

Verum Tu es ipse testis, sunt et alii condiscipuli mei, me non degustasse solum has insanias, sed etiam intima paene illarum penetrasse, ..." (*Vives Opera Omnia*, III, pp. 38, 39.)

14 "Sunt enim hae tres artes de sermone, quem a populo accipiunt, non ipsae tradunt; nam prius fuit sermo latinus, prius graecus, deinde in his formulae grammaticae, formulae rhetoricae, formulae dialectices observatae sunt, nec ad illas detortus est sermo, sed illae potius sermonem sunt secutae, et ad eum se se accommodarunt, neque enim loquimur ad hunc modum latine, quia grammatica latina ita jubet loqui, quin potius e contrario, ita jubet grammatica loqui, quoniam sic Latini loquuntur; res eodem modo se habet in rhetorice et dialectice, quarum utraque in eodem sermone versatur, quo grammatica: unde est illud verum et falsum praesupponere congruum: dialectica itaque in hoc vulgari, et qui est omnium in ore sermo, verum, falsum, probabilitatem invenit, rhetorice vero ornatum, splendorem, gratiam, quae qui ignorat, is profecto imperitissimus est, ...

Ideo grammaticus non jubet eam esse latinam, sed docet, ..." (*Ibidem*, III, pp. 41 and 42.)

The emphasis on usage – *ex instituto moreque Latinorum* – as the source of all linguistic disciplines (grammar, rhetoric, and dialectic) was inspired by the typical humanist position that dialectic was a theory not so much of thought as of statement, *scientia de sermone, ars de verbis,* as Vives himself described it. This position, derived from Quintilian, had been formally adopted by Agricola. It was Vives' contention that Aristotle himself had conceived logic as a set of inductive laws derived from usage and expressed in ordinary and idiomatic Greek for a very practical purpose.

Does anyone think that Aristotle patterned dialectic to a language of his own creation and not to the Greek of the ordinary folk? It is not the task of the dialectican to give language a new force, but rather to teach the rules sanctioned by old usage. Thus the Logic of Aristotle is contained entirely in short precepts. The book on *Categories* teaches the nature of terms. *On Interpretation* explains the sense of propositions. *Posterior Analytics* deals with demonstration; *Topics* with probable argument and invention; *On Sophistical Refutations* with fallacies and cavillation.[15]

Precisely because logic is a theory of verbal communication more concerned with linguistic phenomena than with mental operations of reasoning Vives rejected with the same acrimony the artificial jargon of terminist logicians and the attempts of some of his Montaigu professors to find an adequate algebraic or geometrical symbolism to express the syntactic rules of language.

Could you, please, tell me which language are you dealing with in this dialectic of yours? Is it French or Spanish, Gothic or Vandal? Latin it is certainly not! The dialectician ought to use words and expressions which are understandable to everyone who speaks that language, Latin if the dialectician wants to write in Latin, Greek if he so chooses. These people, however, are not understood by those who know Latin perfectly well, not even by their own colleagues.

A wonderful thing this dialectic which they claim to write in Latin and not even Cicero would understand if he came back to life!

Add to that all the admixtures never concocted before by any pharmacist, all their e, f, g, h, k. Some of these writers, in their wild dreams about

[15] "Atqui Aristoteles ne minimam quidem regulam diffinivit in tota sua dialectica, quae non congrueret cum ipso sermonis graeci sensu, quo docti homines, quo pueri, mulierculae, plebs denique universa utebatur.

Neque enim dialecticus novam facit traditque vim linguae, sed ex vetere et usitatissima regulas observatas docet, quemadmodum antea disserui; cujus porro philosophi logica brevibus praeceptis tota constat, dictionum videlicet natura quae docetur in libris Categoriarum, Enuntiationum viribus quae in Perihermenias, tum formulis collectionum quae in prioribus Analyticis, adjectis, et quae demonstrant in posterioribus, et quae probabili suadent ratione, quaeque ad inventionem faciunt, in topicis, et quae astute cavillantur, in elenchis ..." (*Ibidem*, III, p. 53).

all kinds of different *suppositiones* and their like, had to have recourse to the tenth letter of the second alphabet. The truth is that they were jealous of the exclusive use of those symbols by mathematicians, and therefore also claimed for themselves the use of the entire alphabet, so that their readers were given the impression that they too were men of great learning.[16]

Vives' criticism of the intolerable jargon and abortive symbolism points indeed to a central defect of terminist logic, but in a curious and oblique manner which at the same time betrays his own humanistic limitations regarding the conception of logic. *In Pseudo-Dialecticos* reflects a somewhat superficial acquaintance with Agricola's dialectical work. Himself a disciple of the Brethren of the Common Life, Agricola had written during the incunabular period, but his manuscripts were profusely printed in the first quarter of the sixteenth century by Bartholomew Latomus (a personal friend of Vives) and were popularly received throughout the Low Countries and the Rhineland. To Agricola the rules of invention – corresponding roughly to the *Topics* of Aristotle – were the most important part of the dialectical art yielding, as they were supposed to, a methodical guide to the discovery of arguments on any subject. As one of the three linguistic disciplines dialectic was an important tool to convert a man into an influential teacher, a powerful political speaker, a persuasive negotiator, or a prudent judge in the court of Law. Terminist logicians agreed with Agricola in considering dialectic a linguistic discipline. But while Agricola insisted upon considering language as a vehicle of social communication, the logicians sought to discover the formal framework and deep structure of language as an expression of human thought. Terminist jargon and symbolism, both inadequate for the reasons expressed above, were to Vives a betrayal of the pragmatic character of dialectic. To the professors of Montaigu they were an expression of the formal rigor of logic-

[16] "Jam de quo quaeso sermone est ista vestra dialectica: De Gallico'ne an de Hispano? an de Gothico? an de Vandalico? Nam de Latino certe non est; dialecticus enim iis uti debet verbis, iis enuntiationibus, quas nemo non intelligat qui sciat linguam illam, qua is loquitur, velut Latinam, si latine se dialecticus profitetur disserere, Graecam, si graece; at isti non dico non intelliguntur a doctissimis latine, cum se latine dicant loqui, sed interdum ne ab hominibus quidem ejusdem farinae, seu ejusdem potius furfuris.

An putat quispiam Aristotelem suam dialecticam ad sermonem, quem ipse sibi confinxerat, et non potius ad vulgarem illum Graecum, quem totus populus loquebatur, accommodasse?

Mira profecto istorum dialectica, cujus sermonem, quem ipsi latinum esse volunt, Cicero, si nunc resurgeret, non intelligeret; ...

Adde etiam commistiones majores, quam ullus unquam pharmacopola facit, e. f. g. h. i. k. ita ut nonnulli ad decimam usque litteram secundi alphabeti jam recurrerint, mira suppositionum genera somniantes et confundentes; inviderunt scilicet isti homines mathematicis, quod illi soli litteris uti viderentur, ideo et ipsi quoque totum alphabetum suos in usus transtulerunt, ut nemo sit cum haec videat, qui possit negare ejusmodi homines esse litteratissimos." (*Ibidem*, III, pp. 40, 41, 44.)

al laws which ordinary language often violates. Vives' discussion of the notion of *rigor* is perhaps the highest point of this document, the clearest indication of the irreconcilable gap between two diametrically opposed conceptions of philosophy itself. Vives described his own understanding of what *rigor* was supposed to mean in the following terms:

I shall proceed now to explain what is the meaning of this rigor they are constantly speaking about, hoping they will finally understand what they have so far ignored; and hoping too that in the future they will use it more correctly than in the past.

Each language has its own characteristic, or as the Greeks put it, its own idiom. Each word of the language has a unique power to mean something. Uneducated people frequently use words loosely, in an abusive manner. Learned men sometimes yield to the popular usage, although among themselves they speak and feel differently. There are not too many cases of this, and most of them are related to abstruse philosophical issues which simple people do not understand as precisely as philosophers claim to do. A simple example, taken from Cicero's *De Fato*, illustrates this point: 'We abuse language in our ordinary conversation when we say that somebody desired or rejected something for no reason whatsoever, when we frequently mean without any prior or apparent reason. Or when we say that a glass is empty we obviously do not speak as the physicians who do not accept the possibility of vacuum, but only in the sense that the glass does not contain any water, wine, or oil.'

Rigor is therefore the propriety, the innate and authentic power and exact meaning of Latin sentences.[17]

According to Vives, then, learned language differs from ordinary language only in idiomatic propriety, in precision, and in a few technicalities. The language of philosophy and theology need not be an esoteric, pseudo-scientific jargon, but rather a grammatically correct, easily understandable, idiomatic, and elegant language. The masters

[17] "Sed ut intelligant quod ipsi omnes ignorant, prudentiusque posthac et aptius uti possint ipso rigore, docebo eos quid sibi velit rigor hic, quem toties in ore habent.

Est in unaquaque lingua sua loquendi proprietas, quod a graecis ἰδιώμα dicitur; sunt et vocibus sua significata, suae vires, quibus nonnunquam indoctior ipsa multitudo abutitur doctores indulgent utcunque plebi in sermonis usu, ipsi inter se se et aliter sentiunt, et loquuntur quamvis haec non usque adeo multa, et fere in philosophicis abditisque sint rebus, quas ipse populus non ita exacte callet ut a philosophis intelliguntur: dabo unum ex Cicerone exemplum quo ipsa tota res intelligatur, qui in libro de Fato ad hunc loquitur modum: 'Communi igitur consuetudine sermonis abutimur, quum ita dicimus velle aliquid quempiam, aut nolle sine causa, ut dicamus sine externa et antecedente causa, non sine aliqua; ut cum vas inane dicitur, non ita loquimur ut physici, quibus inane esse nihil placet, sed ita ut, verbi causa, sine aqua, sine vino, sine oleo vas esse dicamus . . . est ergo, ut apertius eloquar, ipsa proprietas, ipsa expressa, nativa, ac germana vis, ipse rectus, verusque sensus orationum latinarum . . ." (*Ibidem*, p. 48).

of such language – in the case of Latin – were not the medieval logicians – least of all Peter of Spain, "totally ignorant of Latin" (*Latine inscientissimus*) – but rather Cicero, Quintilian, and Boethius. In theology Saint Augustin (not Saint Thomas) demonstrated the correct path to follow:

One of these logicians heard one day that Saint Augustine was a great dialectician. Without delay he grabbed one of the Saint's books and passionately read it to see if he could find a proof of that fame. You can imagine his consternation when he was not able to find a single word about *de asinis* and *alter alterius*, not a word about *instantiae*, *reduplicationes*, *exclusivae*, not a single reference to any of those problems which they discuss in the *parva logicalia*. He simply could not understand that such a sharp and able debater could talk about the Trinity without ever mentioning incomplete and complete distributions, immediate and mediate suppositions, complete and incomplete individuations, and all that jargon which makes the syllogism sound divine and without which terminist logicians are convinced our Holy Faith in the Trinity would have been destroyed by heretics.[18]

Vives was never able to understand that logic in its attempt to formulate the methods and principles used to distinguish correct from incorrect reasoning was perfectly entitled to transcend the vagueness, the equivocation, the ambiguousness, the metaphorical and emotive coloring of ordinary language by means of an artificial symbolic language free from all those defects. This incapacity to grasp the legitimacy of such a task was caused, first, by his humanistic over-emphasis upon the practicality of the discipline and the dia-logical character of discourse; secondly, by the resounding failure of terminist logicians to construct such an artificial language. To Vives even the limited achievements of the Montaigu school were ridiculous riddles, cryptic puzzles, and childish charades:

Once you understand what they say, you realize it is nonsense. What happens is that when these people debate in public they declare themselves winners without any consideration for the opinions of others, not because they have really won, but because their opponents were flabbergasted by their linguistic tricks and unusual way of speaking about suppositions, am-

[18] "Fuit ipsorum quidam, qui cum fama et sermone hominum accepisset Divum Augustinum magnum fuisse dialecticum, incidissetque in manus ejus libellus quidam illius, avidus legit ut aliquem inde casum, aliquam instantiam arriperet; miratum ferunt ipsum, in homine tam logico ne verbum quidem esse de asinis, et alter alius, non de instantiis, non de casibus, non de reduplicativis, de exclusivis, nec de aliqua ex iis rebus, quae traduntur in parum seu parvis logicalibus; quin quod homo subtilissimus acerque disputator, quum de Trinitate dissereret, nullam fecerit mentionem de distributione completa et incompleta, de particularizatione, de singularizatione completa et incompleta, de suppositis mediatis, et immediatis, quibus syllogismi illi divini fiunt, quis sine jam olim haeretici totam nostram de Trinitate sanctissimam fidem fuissent demoliti ..." (*Ibidem*, pp. 54–55.)

plifications, restrictions, and appellations... Who will not be amazed to hear that the King of France, surrounded by a large number of servants, has no servants because he does not have the servants who belong to the Spanish King? What if somebody boldly says that although Varro is a man, he is not man because Cicero is not Varro? or that no man has a head although there is no man without a head? or that there are more non-Romans than Romans in a room where there are one thousand Romans and two Spaniards? or that all the people in the world are blind because some are blind?... What about those silly jokes like: 'The Antichrist and the Chimaera are brothers', 'nothingness and nobody bite each other inside a sack', 'the donkey of the Antichrist is the son of the Chimaera'...[19]

Vives' objections to terminist logic, misdirected as they frequently were, proceeded from a serious pedagogical concern. To him logic was a propaedeutic discipline pragmatically oriented to the study of those other disciplines which "shape the spirit and the life of man" (*quaeque et animum et vitam instituunt*) such as Ethics, History, Rhetoric, Political Science, and Economics. *In Pseudo-Dialecticos* contains the bitterest denunciation of the Parisian curriculum which assigned two years to the study of dialectics and one to the rest of Philosophy.

More than once I heard Dullaert and Gaspar Lax, my teachers (whose names I sincerely respect), painfully complaining about having wasted so many years of their lives in such a useless and wasteful exercise... As for you, my dear Fort, I am sure you now understand that it is much more intelligent to dedicate our short lives to the study of true and authentic arts; you realize that those who do not will soon become the object of ridicule and shame.

Even those who study the right kind of dialectic should not give too much time to it. The study of dialectic is not for its own sake, but for the sake of other disciplines. Who could tolerate a painter exclusively dedicated to taking care of his pencils and colors, or a shoemaker wasting all his time in waxing the thread or sharpening his knives and needles? Such abuse would be intolerable even in the case of the useful and good kind of dialectic; can

[19] "Ita turbato eo, quicum certant, mira et inusitata vocabulorum forma atque ratione, miris suppositionibus, miris ampliationibus, restrictionibus, appellationibus, ipsi tunc sibi ipsis nullo publico consilio atque sententia decernunt triumphum de hoste novis verborum praestigiis turbato, non victo: ... Si cum videat regen Galliae maxima famulorum manu stipatum, alter ajat, Regem hunc famulos non habere, quia non ejus sint illi, qui Regi Hispaniae famulantur? Tum etiam si asserat, Varronem cum sit homo, hominem tamen non esse, quia Cicero non ipse sit Varro; caput nullum hominem habere, cum tamen nullus homo capite careat; plures esse non Romani quam Romani in hac aula, in qua sunt Romani mille, Hispani duo; omnesque homines, qui sunt in orbe esse non videntes, quia sunt caeci nonnulli ...

Transeo illa, quae magis ad risum faciunt ex sua tanta fatuitate; Antichristus et Chimaera sun fratres; nihil et nemo mordent se in sacco; Asinus Antichristi est filius Chimaerae ..." (*Ibidem*, pp. 42 and 43.)

you imagine the terrible waste of time involved in this silly verbosity which corrupts all the other disciplines?[20]

Vives' criticism of terminist logic ends with a response to a possible objection: "Many of these dialecticians do not deny that what they teach is irrelevant, but they claim that it sharpens the intelligence of youngsters" (*quod puerorum acuant ingenia*). Vives' response was bitter and direct. The study of terminist logic, he claimed, was not only wasteful but destructive. Those who taught it were men deprived of common sense, practical prudence, social manners, civic responsibility, and witty conversation:

> When these people leave the nest of their schools to mix with normal and prudent folk, they act so stupidly that one gets the impression that they grew up in the backwoods. You should see the expressions on their faces when they are confronted with reality. They just behave as if they were coming from a different world, to such an extent that they ignore real life and common sense. You could swear they were not human beings. Their words, habits, and behavior are so different from that of the rest of us that it is hard to see what they have in common with mankind. Consequently they are totally inept to conduct serious business, to be legates or ambassadors, to be arbitrators in public or in private, or to deal with social problems.[21]

Those were serious accusations from the mouth of a humanist. Those who taught matters irrelevant to the betterment of individual and social life should be "expelled from the classroom by public decree as public enemies of morality and learning" (*edicto publico expelli tamquam corruptores et morum et eruditionis*). And those monks who taught such mundane art should be ashamed to recognize how much damage they

[20] "Dullardum ego et Gasparem Laxem praeceptores olim meos, quos honoris gratia nomino, querentes saepe summo cum dolore audivi, se tam multos annos rei tam futili, atque inani impendisse; ... Te vero, mi carissime Fortis, ... vides aetatem brevem multo satius esse veris artibus tradere, vides brevi illa qui habuerint, fore omnibus despectui atque ludibrior; ...

Quid quod tametsi in ipsa bona veraque dialectica versarentur, non tamen deberent tanto in ea tempore desidere; ars enim est dialectica, quae non sua causa addiscitur, sed ut reliquis artibus adminiculum praestet, ... Quis ferat pictorem in componendo penicillo, in terendis coloribus, sutorem in acubus, in subulis, smiliis, ceterisque cultris acuendis, in torquendo incerandoque filo, in setis illi addendis, totam aetatem consumere? Quod si haec etiam in bona dialectica ferenda non sunt quae est quidem ars neutiquam aspernanda, quantum erunt in illa omnium artium corruptrice garrulitate ferenda?" (*Ibidem*, pp. 63, 64, 58, 59.)

[21] "Illi quidem, cum ad conventum prudentiorum hominum ex scholastico tecto educuntur, ita stupent, ac si essent in silvis educati; mira ibi et insueta illis facies omnium rerum, in alium quendam orbem perductos eos esse credas; ita usum vitae et communem sensum ignorant; ita impeditos, ita implicitos eos videas, sive quid agant, sive loquantur, ut illos non esse homines jures; adeo sicut sermo, ita et mores et actus omnes ab homine abhorrent, ut nihil illis cum ceteris hominibus commune praeter formam judices; hinc quoque fit, ut negotiis gerendis, legationibus obeundis, administrandis rebus, aut publicis aut privatis, tractandis populorum animis ineptissimi sint ..." (*Ibidem*, p. 60.)

inflict upon individual souls and the welfare of the entire Church (*quanta cum jactura et animae et totius religionis haec a monachis et discuntur docenturque*).

Vives' censure of Parisian education ends with a note of unexpected optimism. The corruption of learning has obviously reached bottom and the future can never be as bad as the past:

> Everywhere, in every nation, I see men of great intelligence, daring, free, independent, tired of being slaves, ready to shake off the yoke of this mad and violent tyranny. These men will rescue our freedom as individuals and bring back to the republic of letters the sweetest liberties.
>
> I learned from my parents and teachers what experience has confirmed in many different ways, namely, that bad habits cannot be easily cured unless they have reached an intolerable degree of depravation... 'The better order' – says the proverb – 'is born from the corrupted one, and the worst is always followed by the better'. I do not believe that a change is far away anymore; darkness cannot grow any thicker now; men have endured long enough all this foolish nonsense; our spirit, naturally inclined toward better things, has obviously reached the end of its tolerance.[22]

Together with Erasmus' *Praise of Folly*, Ulrich von Hutten's *Litterae virorum eruditorum*, and Rabelais' *Gargantua and Pantagruel*, Vives' *In Pseudo-Dialecticos* must be counted as one of the most devastating (although less humorous) attacks against medieval education written in the sixteenth century. The book was published in Paris, Louvain, and Basel; soon it was read all over Europe. Thomas More read the book and wrote to Erasmus in the following manner:

> Everything that Vives writes is delightful, but I experienced a special pleasure in reading his book *In Pseudo Dialecticos;* not only because he makes such fun of their useless tricks, fights them with valid arguments, and destroys their foundations with irresistible force; but especially because he uses exactly the same approach I had in mind to use against them before I read the book.[23]

[22] "Erigunt enim se se apud nationes omnes clara, excellentia, liberaque ingenia impatientia servitutis, et jugum hoc stultissimae ac violentissimae tyrannidis ex cervicibus suis animose depellunt, civesque suos ad libertatem vocant, vindicabuntque totam prorsus literariam civitatem in libertatem longe suavissimam ... Ego sane sic a parentibus, sic a prudentissimis viris accepi, sic rerum usu ac experientiis didici compluribus, pravas consuetudines non facile in melius viribus cujusquam commutari, nisi cum ipsae in tantam pravitatem pervenerint, ut omnibus fiant intolerabiles: ... unde est illud vulgare hominum sermone proverbium: Nasci optimum ordinem ex perversissimo, bonasque leges ex malis moribus procreari ..." (*Ibidem*, p. 62.)

[23] "Itaque vt nihil est illius quod non mirum in modum delectet omnes, ita me profecto quae scripsit in Pseudodialecticos peculiari quadam voluptate perfundunt: non ideo tantum (quanquam ideo quoque) quod illas ineptas argutias lepidis cauillis eludit, validis argumentis oppugnat, ineuitabili ratione a fundamentis eruit atque subuertit, sed et praeterea quod ibi video quaedam iisdem fere tractata rationibus, quas et ipse mecum olim, quum nihil adhuc

Erasmus answered:

> I am glad to see that your opinion of Vives coincides with mine. He is one of those who eventually will overshadow Erasmus' name . . . He has an extraordinary philosophical talent . . . Nobody else is better prepared to demolish the armies of the sophists; especially because he was once a prominent sophist himself.[24]

One year after the publication of *In Pseudo-Dialecticos* Vives travelled from Louvain to Paris for a short visit as a tutor of Cardinal Croy. Unexpectedly the Parisian academic community welcomed him in the most friendly manner:

> I thought (Vives wrote to Erasmus) that a visit to Paris at that time would be rather unpleasant having just published the *In Pseudo-Dialecticos*, explicitly against the Parisian sophists . . . but what happened was entirely different. As soon as I notified them of my arrival they came to see me and greeted me with welcoming and polite words.
>
> Many times during and after the meals we talked about you (Erasmus). O my Erasmus, I wish that you would permit me to praise you as they did . . . According to them you have brought Saint Jerome back to life, your notes on the New Testament have done more for the Christian religion than a thousand years of scholastic discussions. They even enjoy your *Praise of Folly*. Finally whether you like to hear it or not, these people think that you are supreme, admirable, and perfect. There is certainly nothing they would not do for you; they want you to know that their homes and everything therein, their families and friends are entirely at your disposal.[25]

Viuis legissem, collegeram." [Erasmus' correspondence is quoted from *Opus Epistolarum Des. Erasmi Roterodami*, eds. P. S. Allen and H. M. Allen, 12 vols. (Oxford, 1906–1965) (here *EE.*)] (*EE.* IV, 1106, 64–70.)

[24] "De Lodouici Viuis ingenio gaudeo meum calculum cum tuo consentire. Is vnus est de numero eorum qui nomen Erasmi sint obscuraturi . . . Est animo mire philosophico. . . . Non alius magis idoneum qui profliget sophistarum phalanges; in quorum castris diu meruerit." (*EE.* IV, 1107, 5–11.)

[25] "Et nouos mihi asciscerem amicos, quibuscum praesens verbis coniuntioneque vitae et absens suauissime literis oblectarer. Illud perincommode rebar accidisse, quod eo tempore aduersum Pseudodialecticos scripsissem, eosque nominatim Parrhisienses; vnde non dubitabam quin multos illius notae homines quos modo sophistas appellant, animo parum in me propitio sensurus essem. Verum re ipsa longe aliud sum expertus quam ipse mihi nimis profecto meticulosa et suspicaci cogitatione confinxeram.

Venio Parrhisios de via non fessus sed oblectatus, et amicis per famulum significo me adesse. Conuolant ad me frequentes, salutant officiose, gratulantur aduentui.

Conuiuatus sum cum istis, et quidem frequenter et suauiter. Ad mensam tertio verbo sermo statim de te varius, multus etiam sublatis mensis. O mi Erasme, dicerem omnia, si patereris te in epistola ad te laudari. Vtinam ad alium scriberem! Tacendum itaque erit inuito quid illi dicant de Hieronymo tua opera sibiipsi restituto, quid de Nouo Testamento suae integritati reddito, labore longe Christianae pietati vtiliore quam quae sunt intra mille annos in scholis clamata; quantum admirentur Paraphrases, id est Paulum apertius diuina illa sua eloquentem sensa; quantum Adagiis, Copia et aliis prophanis operibus tuis delectentur et proficiant; vt Moria sit omnibus in deliciis, neminem offendat, nimirum quod maiestas illorum theologorum durior et fortior est quam aliorum. O me rusticum et inciuilem quod de his taceam, te durum qui iubeas! Sed erit locus in quo non parebo tibi.

Erasmus wrote back:

Although I have experienced the good disposition of some French people, I am afraid that your last letter was only the expression of your own feelings toward me. I thought that by going to Paris, the capital and fortress of sophistry, you were risking being stoned to death or pierced by the horns of those blockheads . . . Take good care of yourself, my most learned Luis. We want you back as soon as possible, happy and smiling.[26]

In 1520, when this exchange of letters took place, Vives had already secured for himself a central position in the most influential circles of English and Flemish Humanism. *In Pseudo-Dialecticos*, however, was only a token of his future activity. The more mature and influential thought of Vives on the reformation of Logic has to be found in his later works *De disciplinis* (1531), *Censura de Aristotelis Operibus* (1538), *De instrumento probabilitatis* (1537). Paris, on the other hand, had experienced a considerable change. Celaya had left Montaigu College, and Gaspar Lax was about to. The school of Montaigu was on the verge of total collapse. The cause of Humanism had made considerable progress, and Francis I had increasingly nationalized the former academic center of medieval Christianity. Here we want to remind the reader once again that both the most conservative and the most revolutionary expressions of intellectual activity in the Parisian University during those tense decades of quick change were, partially at least, the work of Spanish thinkers.

Illud nunc feres velis nolis, nulla te illos ex parte spectare, vnde non occurras summus, admirabilis, absolutus. Possum tibi pluresquam decem ex hominibus ordinis illius nominare, qui suam tibi omnem operam, diligentiam, fauorem, studium pollicentur et deferunt: nihil se tua causa non facturos, suas esse tibi apertas domos, si illuc ieueris, paratas facultates, familias, opes, amicos." (*EE.* IV, 1108, vv. 5–15, 50–69.)

26 "Porro quod scribis istic plerosque tam magnifice sentire de lucubrationibus meis, equidem vt agnosco candorem Gallicae gentis erga me, ita vereor ne hic sane nonnihil de tuo in me studio sis admensus.

Praesertim Lutetiae, vbi, quod huius disciplinae veluti regnum et arx quaedam esse videbatur, periculum erat ne lapidareris aut crabronum aculeis confodereris.

Bene vale, Lodouice doctissime, et cura vt te quam primum hic hilarem ac lubentem videamus." (*EE.* IV, 1111, vv. 70–73, 6–9, 92–93.)

CHAPTER TWO

VITORIA, SALAMANCA, AND THE AMERICAN INDIANS

Juan Luis Vives and Francisco de Vitoria were, without any doubt, the most outstanding representatives of Spanish intellectual life during the reign of Charles V. The differences between the two men, striking as they are, reveal the inner tension in Spanish thought during the first half of the sixteenth century. Vives the layman, Jewish exile, prolific writer, humanist and pedagogue was, as a good cosmopolitan European, primarily concerned with the cultural crisis of his age. Vitoria the Dominican monk, professor at Salamanca, scholastic theologian, counselor of kings and bishops was, above all, a teacher bent on clarifying the new moral and juridical issues raised by Spain's European and American politics. In many ways Vives was more European than Spanish; Vitoria, on the other hand, belongs entirely to Castile. Vives had no disciples to speak of, but his insights and premonitions recur with increasing clarity in the leading avenues of modern European philosophy. Vitoria's name has become inseparably associated with the University of Salamanca and Spanish Renaissance scholasticism, of which he was, in its early stage, the leading exponent and inspiration. In spite of these obvious differences, Vives and Vitoria had much in common. Both men were extraordinarily aware of the problems and challenges brought about by the changing conditions of the day, and tackled the new realities with a novel outlook and method typical of sixteenth century Renaissance.

The personal background and early education of Vitoria and Vives share certain similarities. As with Vives', the ancestry, date and place of birth of Vitoria have been a matter of much discussion among scholars. German historians of the nineteenth century were inclined in principle to Italianize his name (Francesco de Vittoria), and reputable writers – Ueberweg is a good example – did not hesitate to describe him as a brilliant Italian imported into Salamanca. Classical biographers unanimously referred to the Basque city of Vitoria as the birthplace of Francisco who, upon entering the Dominican Order in his early youth, would have added the name of his home town to his Christian name according to the respectable tradition of the Order – as did Thomas of Aquinas, Albert of Cologne, Peter of Verona, or Luis de Granada. The date of his birth was more controversial, oscillating between 1480 and 1486.[1]

More recent scholarship, however, has reasonably proved that Francisco was born in Burgos, the very heart of Old Castile, and that the date of his birth has to be advanced to 1492. Furthermore, according to the findings of Father Beltrán de Heredia – the outstanding Vitorian scholar of today – Vitoria's maternal ancestry (the Compludos) was Jewish and directly related to Pablo de Santa Marìa and Alonso de Cartagena, the most formidable "converts" of the fourteenth century. Vitoria's bitter attacks against the Inquisition and the diatribes of his brother Diego, also a Dominican, against the statutes of *limpieza de sangre*, seem to confirm Heredia's conclusions. The fact that Francisco assumed a Basque name to disguise his Old Castilian birth might be interpreted as an attempt to hide his Jewish pedigree intimately associated with the city of Burgos, a well-known center of Jewish converts. The Vitoria brothers' membership in the Dominican Order does not at all preclude their Jewish ancestry. The policy of religious orders toward Jewish converts was remarkably fluid at the beginning of the sixteenth century, and most local ordinances permitted their admission, especially – as in Vitoria's case – to second and third generation converts.[2]

Unlike Vives, Vitoria was extremely reticent about his relatives and childhood. The existence of his brother Diego is known to us through

[1] The traditional biographies of Vitoria are: Echard et Quetif, *Scriptores Ordinis Praedicatorum Recensiti*, (Paris, 1719–1721).

L. G. Alonso Getino, *El Maestro Francisco de Vitoria y el Renacimiento filosófico-teológico del siglo XVI*, (Madrid, 1914).

[2] Vicente Beltrán de Heredia, O. P. has written abundantly on this subject: *La Patria del Maestro Francisco de Vitoria a la luz de la crítica histórica*, (Vitoria, 1930).

El Maestro Francisco de Vitoria. Su naturaleza Vitoriana, (Vergara, 1932).

"En que año nació Francisco de Vitoria? Un documento revolucionario." *Anuario de la Asociación Francisco de Vitoria*, VI (1943–1945), pp. 1–29.

"Final de la discusión acerca de la patria del Maestro Vitoria: La prueba documental que faltaba." *Ciencia Tomista*, April–June 1953, pp. 276–289.

See also, Diez de la Lastra y Diaz Güemes, *El Burgalés Francisco de Vitoria*. (Burgos, no date).

Bruno de St. Joseph, "Où naquit François de Vitoria?", *Revue Neo-Scolastique de philosophie*, XXXIV (1932), 247–249.

Luciano Pereña Vicente, *Diario YA*, 24 April 1953 (Madrid).

José Iriarte, S. J., "Fray Francisco de Vitoria, del linaje de los Arcaya de Vitoria-Alava," *Hispania*, XXXVI (1952), p. 43.

a letter from Erasmus to Francisco, and scholars interested in these matters still discuss whether his name was Diego or Pedro, indeed whether there was one brother or two. According to Echard et Quetif, Vitoria studied humanities in Burgos under excellent teachers – *sub optimis magistris* – and Vives recommended Vitoria to Erasmus as a theologian who had cultivated the liberal arts from early childhood – *inde a puero* (EE., VII, p. 255). It is far from clear, however, whether Vitoria's humanistic training took place before or after his admission into the Dominican Order. Although Dominican historians esteem enthusiastically the high academic standards of the Convent of Saint Paul where Vitoria joined the Order, it seems difficult to believe that a monastery of Spanish friars in sixteenth century Burgos was a nest of humanistic endeavors. Unlike Palencia or Valladolid, Burgos had no academic tradition in the Middle Ages, and was also unsuccessful in attracting the generous foundations of Renaissance patrons, foundations which went instead to Alcalá, Sigüenza, and Toledo. Vives' testimony, therefore, must refer to Vitoria's studies in Paris *circa* 1509, the only stage of Vitoria's early career which might possibly have been known to Vives. In that case, Vitoria's education was entirely Parisian. The difference between Vitoria and Vives in this respect is a remarkable one: Vives spent less than three years in Paris, Vitoria fifteen. Vives was a lay student at Montaigu College, Vitoria a young Dominican friar at the Convent of Saint Jacques. Vives' studies were limited to the Arts course; Vitoria studied humanities, philosophy and theology. In Paris, however, their basic human experience was one and the same. There, the *civitas litterarum* of medieval Christianity, Vives and Vitoria came into close contact with the religious, cultural, and political crisis of modern Europe. Their reaction to it and their intellectual quest no doubt went in different directions, but both of them attempted to cope with new facts through the mediation of novel ideas and thus they reached a common title of greatness.[3]

A. VITORIA IN PARIS (1509–1522)

The Dominican Order was extremely careful in selecting the students to be sent to Paris. As a rule, only those who had completed three years of philosophy with honors in their local monasteries, and whose religious life had been exemplary, were exposed to the intellectual challenge

[3] See Getino, "Vitoria y Vives. Sus relaciones personales y doctrinales." *Anuario de la Asociación Francisco de Vitoria,* II (1931), 277–309.

and moral risks of the Parisian University. Vitoria was apparently an exceptional case in that he was sent to Paris right after the end of his Noviciate, before he had even finished his courses in Latin, grammar and rhetoric.[4]

Vitoria's first two years at Paris were dedicated to the study of Latin and Greek. Although the details of Vitoria's humanistic studies at Paris are ignored, to a certain extent the nature and quality of the humanistic movement to which he was exposed can be described and his personal achievements evaluated. Among his contemporaries (Vives, Clenard, Vaseo, Erasmus) Vitoria enjoyed the reputation of an accomplished Latinist, a tribute which humanists lavishly and generously bestowed upon fellow humanists, but which was rarely granted to a Dominican friar and a teacher of scholastic theology (*EE.*, VII, p. 255). As for Greek – a language Vitoria could not have taken in Burgos – evidence enough exists to state that he was able to read Aristotle in the original text and to discuss with reasonable authority the Greek version of the Bible. Much more relevant, however, to the understanding of Vitoria's genius was the process of assimilating the humanistic values he later attempted to infuse into the disreputable methods of scholastic teaching. This process of assimilation – of obvious importance in the early history of Spanish Renaissance scholasticism – was enhanced by the particular intensity the humanistic movement had reached in Paris *circa* 1509. In 1507, the famous French Hellenist Tissard had begun the teaching of Greek at Coqueret College (where Vitoria registered two years later for the Arts Course) and published, for the first time in the history of French printing, the Greek text of Homer and Hesiod. More important to the cause of Parisian humanists was the arrival of Jerome Aleander in 1508, the future Papal legate sent to the Netherlands in 1520 to extirpate the first roots of Lutheranism from the region (*See above*, p. 24). Aleander's teaching of Latin and Greek, both in public and private, was received with extraordinary enthusiasm. The election of Aleander in 1513 as Rector of the University was a landmark in the history of French humanism. The death of Standonck and Gaguin, the benevolence of Francis I toward Budé and other humanists, and the increasing influence of Erasmus, favored

[4] In describing Vitoria's education at Paris, we follow closely the definitive work of Ricardo G. Villoslada, S. J., *La Universidad de Paris durante los estudios de Francisco de Vitoria,* (Rome, 1928).

We have also consulted: Augustin Renaudet, *Préréforme et Humanisme à Paris.*

Villoslada, "Pedro Crockaert O. P., maestro de Francisco de Vitoria," *Estudios Eclesiásticos,* XIV (1935), 174–201.

a turn of the conservative Parisian institution toward a more secular and critical approach to education. These advances, however, were still challenged by two powerful institutions which represented, as a whole, the traditional side of the academic establishment: the College of Montaigu (under the Rectorship of Noel Beda), and the Faculty of Theology. Interestingly enough, the two Spanish thinkers whose intellectual vocation was precisely to arrive at a constructive synthesis of scholasticism and humanism – a noble enterprise doomed to failure because of the religious fanaticism of reformers and counter-reformers – were at that time students at those conservative institutions: Vives was at Montaigu from 1509 to 1512, Vitoria began his theological studies in 1513.

Although conditions at the Parisian Colleges of the monastic orders were obviously not too favorable for the advances of secular humanism, the Convent of Saint Jacques, where Vitoria lived and studied, was remarkably progressive. After all, the Dominican friars from the Dutch province who had reformed the convent at the beginning of the century, had brought to Paris the more enlightened and liberal attitudes of the Brethren of the Common Life and the spirit of Windesheim. When Aleander came to Paris he made a special effort to maintain friendly relations with the friars of Saint-Jacques. In fact, a Spanish dominican and friend of Vitoria, Cipriano Benet, became Aleander's closest follower in Paris. Another friar of Saint-Jacques, Guillaume Petit, was the personal confessor of Francis I, a position he used to protect such controversial figures as Reuchlin, Lefèvre, Budé, and Erasmus. Some of Vitoria's fellow friars went even too far in their liberal pursuits. One of them, Amadeus Meygret – to whom Vitoria was to dedicate one of his first publications – eventually became a devout Lutheran, left the Order, and followed the Reformer to Germany. We have some indications that Vitoria personally knew Lefèvre – whom he called "a nice fellow" (*iste bonus Stapulensis*), and Budé, "a distinguished man of great authority" (*vir egregius magnae auctoritatis*). His personal relations with Erasmus of Rotterdam will be discussed later in some detail.[5]

If Vitoria's intense contact with French humanism gives us the historical background of his humanistic leanings in the reform of scholastic

[5] See M. B. Chenu, *L'Humanisme et la Réforme au Collège Saint-Jacques de Paris*, Archives d'histoire Dominicaine, (Paris, 1946).

The classical work of Imbart de la Tour, *Les Origines de la Réforme*, 4 vols., (Paris, 1905–1935), contains much information about the progress of French Humanism in the first half of the sixteenth century. See especially III, pp. 324–366.

methodology, the prolonged study of philosophy and theology at Paris is even more important to our purpose, since it helps explain the main thrust of his intellectual achievements. Vitoria's academic record can be summarized in the following *curriculum vitae*. From 1510 (or 1511?) Vitoria studied philosophy under Juan de Celaya and Pierre Crockaert (also known as "Bruxellensis"). The names of Antonio Coronel and John Mair have also been suggested, but in his writings Vitoria never calls them *magistri*, a title he reserves exclusively for the names of Celaya and Crockaert. To follow the lectures of Celaya, who was not a member of the Dominican Order, Vitoria had to walk a few blocks from Saint-Jacques to Coqueret College, a practice dear to Parisian students of that time. As a member of the Order, Vitoria was allowed to start his theological studies immediately after the three years of the Arts course, without first obtaining the degree of Master in Arts. Vitoria studied theology from 1513 to 1516, in his own convent, under Pierre Crockaert and Juan de Fenario, official members of the theological faculty. In 1516, Vitoria began the teaching of Theology as "Assistant Bachelor" and, in the best medieval tradition, he lectured on the *Liber Sententiarum* of Peter Lombard. One year later he became a *bacchalaureus formatus*, a title he enjoyed for four years (1517–1521) and during which, according to the rules of the University, he was supposed to participate in all public disputes and preach a public sermon at least once a year. As a Dominican friar, however, Vitoria was also exempt from this long period of testing, but worked instead in publishing the edition of Pedro de Covarrubias' *Sermones dominicales* and the *Summa Aurea* of Saint Antonine of Florence. In March 1522, the Chancellor of the University conferred on Vitoria the *licentiature*, namely the right to teach theology anywhere in the world without previous permission from the local Bishop. The solemn ceremony was preceded by a short theological dispute for which Vitoria – as an indication of his future teaching – selected three problems of moral theology: the obligation of restitution, the duties of Bishops, and the conditions of martyrdom. Three months later, as was customary, Vitoria received the Doctorate, a degree which did not add much to the *licentia docendi* and which some medieval educators compared to the banquet following the wedding itself.

Vitoria's role in the history of Spanish scholasticism – the reform of method and the application of general principles to the pressing issues of the day – demands for its understanding a general knowledge of scholastic philosophy at the beginning of the sixteenth century, and, more specifically, a careful study of the part played by Vitoria's Parisian masters in this complex scenario. It is well known that, during the Renaissance, scholastic philosophy and theology suffered severe attacks from different quarters. Latin Averroism was blooming in Padua under the leadership of Paul of Venice, Gaetano di Thiene, and Nifo. The very core of Christian thought, the individuality and immortality of man's soul, was sacrificed to the conclusions of an Aristotelianism derived from Neo-Platonic sources. Renaissance Platonism, represented by Marsilio Ficino and Pico della Mirandola, although very much indebted to medieval scholasticism, displayed a daring of speculation which was not always mindful enough of the requirements of orthodoxy. The Humanists, led by Valla, derided the barbarian language of scholastic philosophy and the wastefulness of its endless distinctions and disputes, a criticism which Erasmus and his disciples made even more powerful with theological and moral considerations. Pomponazzi made fashionable a materialistic interpretation of Aristotle's *De Anima*, inspired by Alexander of Aphrodisias. The rationalism and naturalism of Telesio, Patrizi, Campanella, and Giordano Bruno – a few decades later – was the logical outcome of these trends of thought. Facing this formidable attack, sixteenth century scholasticism was split into three different branches frequently engaged in mischievous and verbal quarrels: Nominalism, Scotism, and Thomism. The first essay of this book tried to sketch the history of Parisian nominalism and the decline of the Montaigu school of logicians. Precisely the most representative member of this quickly vanishing school, Juan de Celaya (*See above*, pp. 19-20), was Vitoria's teacher of Arts. Nominalism, however, was not only a Parisian fad. Besides Oxford, where it originated back in the fourteenth century (Woddham, Holcott, and others), other European Universities like Heidelberg, Prague, Vienna, and Erfurt, had opened their gates to nominalistic professors, a fact of considerable importance in the intellectual training of some Reformation leaders, including Luther himself. Spain had traditionally denied Nominalism any official recognition, but Alcalá's opening up to Scotism, forced Salamanca to make a liberal gesture in the opposite direction by inviting Fray Alfonso de Córdoba (*See below*, p. 152) to teach Logic *ad modum Parisiense* in 1510. Córdoba's efforts, however, were more than neutralized by Domingo de Soto's merciless opposition to the novel teaching, and Nominalism was soon forgotten in Salamanca.[6]

[6] See Bertrán de Heredia, "Accidentada y efímera aparición del nominalismo en Salamanca," *La Ciencia Tomista*, LXII (1942), pp. 77–78.

Celaya's special brand of philosophy might well have influenced Vitoria in several important directions. It is interesting that both men were often called *Doctor resolutissimus* by their disciples, a clear proof of their independent judgment, and of their total lack of submissiveness to authority and partisanship. Celaya's increasing disinterest in Logic and his late conversion to moral theology made a lasting impression upon Vitoria. Celaya's impetuous attacks against simony and the abuses of ecclesiastical benefits surely impressed the young student of Saint Jacques; fifteen years later, from his chair at Salamanca, Vitoria was to strike repeatedly at the same ecclesiastical abuses.

As for Scotism, we should not forget that both the *Qoudlibeta* and the *Opus Parisiense* of Scotus were printed in Paris in 1519 and 1518, respectively, the former by Tartaret, and the latter by John Mair, during the first two years of Vitoria's teaching at the University. Vitoria's theological writings reveal an extraordinary familiarity with the great masters of the Franciscan Order without the aggressive animosity which characterizes the works of other Dominicans, such as Cajetan and Ferrarense. In fact, Vitoria's benevolent respect for Scotus made possible the incorporation of certain Franciscan traits into the Dominican theology of grace and free will at the University of Salamanca (*See below*, p. 160).

The most vigorous revival of scholasticism in the sixteenth century was, however, signaled by a return to Saint Thomas among the Dominican friars in Italy. The most distinguished Italian disciples of Saint Thomas in the fifteenth century were Natalis, Giovanni di Napoli and, above all, Capreolus (died 1444), whose classical work *Libri Defensionum Theologiae divi Thomae* earned him the title of *Princeps Thomistarum.* Capreolus' work, as the very title of the book indicates, was an apology of the *via Sancti Thomae* against the "modern" criticism of Scotus and his disciples. If Capreolus was the leading exponent of Thomistic dogmatic theology, Saint Antoine of Florenze (died 1459) was beyond any doubt the outstanding moral theologian of his century. Saint Antoine's moral principles were consistently based upon the immortality of the soul, a truth he attempted to prove not only with theological and rational arguments, but also with an extraordinary display of testimonies from classical sources. Together with Saint Bernardine of Siena, Saint Antoine was the champion of a Christian Renaissance, seeking a harmonious synthesis of the classical ideal of beauty and the religious values of revelation. As a prior of the Convent of Saint Marcos in Florence, Saint Antoine opened the first public library of Europe, and his work *Summa Aurea* became the leading manual of spiritual devotion in the Church before the Council of Trent. Saint Antoine's overriding concern with the guidance of a Christian conscience in the midst of new temptations, alternatives, and problems, in time became the unifying principle of Vitoria's entire intellectual activity. An evident proof of the influence of the Italian Saint upon the Spanish theologian was the 1521 publication of the *Summa Aurea* in Paris under the careful direction of Vitoria.[7]

The revival of Thomism in the first two decades of the sixteenth century was further strengthened by two Italian Dominicans and by one of Vitoria's professors at Paris, Pierre Crockaert. The two Italians were Thomas de Vio and Francesco de Silvestri, better known by their place of origin as Cajetan (1468–1534) and Ferrarense (1474–1528). Through their extensive commentaries to the works of Saint Thomas they reinstated Thomistic epistemology and metaphysics against the objections of Scotus, thus carrying further the antagonistic trend inaugurated by Capreolus. The speculative refinements of both authors regarding the Thomistic theory of abstraction, analogy, and the basic principles governing the relations of act and potency, represent a new level of philosophical sophistication in the history of scholastic thought matched only in the sixteenth century by the genius of Suárez – who substituted the medieval partisanship of the Italian Dominicans for the wiser and more cosmopolitan eclecticism of the Jesuit Order. Of these two scholars Cajetan, especially, had a tremendous influence upon Vitoria, although, as we shall see later (*See below*, p. 70), the Spanish moral theologian occasionally had a few scornful remarks about the excessive subtlety of the Italian metaphysician. As a rule, however, Vitoria followed Cajetan very closely in all his lectures, and the name of the distinguished Cardinal appears in almost every page of Vitoria's books. His familiarity with Cajetan's works reflects the latter's high reputation in the University of Paris during Vitoria's years of study. The fearsome ability of Cajetan as a polemist was legendary since his confrontation with Pico della Mirandola in the summer of 1494. Cajetan was also the Pope's champion against the conciliaristic ideas of two Parisian professors, John Mair and Jacques Almain, both personally known to and admired by Vitoria. Finally, we cannot forget that Vitoria's ordi-

[7] See L. Allevi, "Francisco de Vitoria e il rinascimento della scolastica nel secolo XVI," *Rivista di Filosofia Neoscolastica*, XIX (1927), pp. 401–441. Also, G. M. Bertini, *Influencia de algunos renacentistas italianos en el pensamiento de Vitoria*, (Salamanca, 1934).

nation to the priesthood at an exceptionally young age was approved by Cajetan, General of the Dominican Order from 1508 to 1518.

The third outstanding champion of Thomism mentioned earlier was Vitoria's most admired teacher, Pierre Crockaert. The achievements of Crockaert in the field of scholastic theology can only be fairly appreciated if they are compared with the pitiful condition of Theology at Paris toward the turn of the century. Dogmatic theology had been undermined by nominalist theologians, like Gerson and Pierre d'Ailly, chancellors of the University in the fifteenth century, who scorned the abuse of rational speculation in the presentation of the dogma. Vitoria's colleagues and friends at Paris, men like John Mair, Almain, Raulin, and Hangest, belonged entirely to this school of thought. Biblical Theology, on the other hand, was severely handicapped by the low level of linguistic interest at the Parisian University, and by the blind loyalty to old-fashioned medieval textbooks on the subject. Patristic Theology was confined to Carolingian compilations like the *Glossa Ordinaria* of Walafried Lalouche, the disciple of Rhabanus Maurus, or to even more unreliable lexicons like the *Catholicon* or the *Mammoctretus*. The endless and sterile disputes between Dominicans and Franciscans about the Immaculate Conception, the trite and pedestrian commentaries on Peter Lombard, kept Parisian theologians dangerously removed from the pressing religious issues to which Luther would address himself. Even the moderately interesting dispute about the relationship between Council and Pope, involving such complex theological problems as the universal priesthood of all Christians, or the subject of ecclesiastical jurisdiction, degenerated into a legalistic and canonical controversy of little interest to the layman. As the Jesuit theologian Maldonado would later complain, the Parisian theologians had nothing but long sticks to match the modern weaponry of the Lutheran divines.[8]

Against this background of intellectual infertility, the work and name of Pierre Crockaert (also spelled "Crokart," or "Crokaart") acquire an impressive profile.

Born in Bruxelles, around 1470, Crockaert joined Montaigu College as a young student of theology, and became personally acquainted with Standonck, Noel Beda, Erasmus, and Latomus. Crockaert studied under John Mair and later became the teacher of Antonio Coronel

[8] For further study of Renaissance theology, see A. Humbert, *Les Origines de la Théologie Moderne*, 4 vols., Vol. I 'La Renaissance de l'antiquité Chrétienne', (Paris, 1911). Also, Martin Grabmann, *Die Geschichte der Theologie* (Freiburg, 1933).

(*See above*, p. 16). In spite of this strong involvement with the Montaigu school of Logicians, Crockaert joined the Dominican Order in 1503, impressed as he was by the reform of Saint-Jacques and the studious zeal of the friars. The first books of Crockaert after his profession in the Dominican Order were still a tribute to his acknowledged expertise in terminist logic: a wonted commentary on Peter Hispanus (1508), and a long explanation of the Aristotelian *Organon* (1509). The next books, a commentary to Aristotle's *Physics* and *De Anima* and especially an edition of Thomas' *De ente et essentia*, revealed a significant change of interest. Crockaert's final conversion to Thomism was, however, evinced by an event of great significance in the history of Catholic theology: the edition of the *Secunda secundae* (1512) in collaboration with his favorite student of theology, Francisco de Vitoria. It is true that Cajetan, in Pavia, and Conrad Koellin, in Heidelberg, had preceded Crockaert in following the *Summa* as their primary text-book – a practice previously tried by some Dominicans of the fifteenth century in Cologne, Vienna, and Leipzig. Crockaert's novelty, both in this publication and in his teaching until his premature death in 1514, was the emphasis upon Thomas' moral theology – the subject matter of the *Secunda secundae*. Vitoria's introduction to this publication proves that, as a young student of Theology, the Spanish Dominican had already a most definite design of what his own magisterium would be like. Vitoria's twenty-four years of teaching at Valladolid and Salamanca were the most faithful and unwavering fulfillment of the project conceived in Paris under the direction of Crockaert.[9]

Vitoria begins his elegant introduction with an assessment of Thomas' authority. The purpose in following a proved author – Vitoria remarks – is not to deny the freedom of thought (*libertatem ingeniorum opprimi*) nor to constrain the creativity of the thinker (*nec facultas nobis, ut ferunt, adimitur multa excogitandi inveniendique*), but rather to secure a reliable guide in avoiding the temptation of novelty for novelty's sake. Thomas' qualities, Vitoria suggests, are unique in that respect: a comprehensive commentator of Aristotle's work, nobody can surpass him in the order, clarity, and concision of his presentation – three intellectual virtues which Vitoria greatly cherished. In the works of Saint Thomas, Vitoria continues, the reader can find whatever is needed to lead an honest life – (*ut ad juste, pie, caste, sancteque vivendum nullo alio magistro opus sit*). Vitoria's emphasis upon method, moral and positive theology; his

[9] The Latin original of this introduction makes the second Appendix to Villoslada's book *La Universidad de Paris*.

lack of interest in Thomistic epistemology and metaphysics, describe exactly the main features of his future intellectual enterprise.

The last ingredient of Vitoria's Parisian training was the profound impression made upon him by Erasmus of Rotterdam. The relationship between Vitoria and Erasmus has been, to nobody's surprise, a most controversial subject in Spanish scholarship. The very association of Erasmus' name with that of the founder of what is generally known as "Spanish Counter-Reformation scholasticism" was enough to enrage *ad nauseam* some otherwise well deserving Spanish scholars. Getino's introductory remarks on this subject, in the twelfth chapter of his classical book on Vitoria, should be relished by those who want to see an exact twentieth century replica in action of the Spanish monk Erasmus despised four hundred years ago. Surprisingly enough this is not a question to be solved by wishful guessing, for there is more than enough first-hand written evidence to form a precise idea of Vitoria's attitude toward the master from Rotterdam. The first document is a letter from Vives to Erasmus, two weeks before the opening of the conference of Valladolid (June 27 to August 13, 1527 – *See above*, p. 38), assembled together by the General Inquisitor of Spain to pass judgment upon the opinions of Erasmus. In this letter Vives reviews the record of those likely to become Erasmus' judges at Valladolid. After mentioning Pedro de Vitoria, one of Erasmus' most dedicated adversaries, Vives describes his brother Francisco, a totally different man (*admodum dissimilis*) well-trained in humanities from early youth, a professor of great reputation, (*homo maximi nominis*) a man of sharp intelligence (*ingenio acutissimo*), and of quiet dispositions. According to Vives, Francisco de Vitoria was known to have a worshipping admiration for Erasmus (*admirat te ac adorat*); furthermore, on more than one occasion (*non semel*) Francisco had publicly defended Erasmus' cause among his Parisian colleagues (*causam tuam defendit frequenti theologorum collegio Lutetiae*). Vives' testimony, although dated 1527, obviously refers back to Vitoria's years at Paris, and reveals with no ambiguity whatsoever the admiration of the young Dominican for the controversial humanist. Five months later, in November 1527, Erasmus himself wrote to Vitoria after the closing of the Valladolid assembly (*EE.*, VII, p. 255). The letter was addressed to *Theologo cuidam Hispano Sorbonico*, although Vitoria had never been a student of La Sorbonne College and was teaching at the University of Salamanca in 1527. This document which, most likely, Vitoria never read, sheds some extraordinary light into Erasmus' character.[10]

[10] See the curious history of this letter in R. G. Villoslada's article "Erasmo y Vitoria",

The purpose of the letter was clearly to persuade Francisco to take some restraining action against his brother Pedro. In doing this, Erasmus was following Vives' suggestion according to whom Francisco was slightly irresponsible for allowing his brother's tirades against the Dutch scholar. Erasmus' troubles in Spain had been initiated by the accusations of Lee (*See above*, p. 13), and Beda, the Rector of Montaigu College. The Dominicans at the Court of the Emperor and the Franciscans of Salamanca were responsible for the vigorous campaign against the dangerous innovator. Erasmus' letter to Francisco begins with a soft approach: the love that he, Erasmus, felt for Vitoria was in no way threatened by the fact that, unfortunately, Pedro had joined a group of "misinformed people." However, Erasmus hastened to add, "given your intelligence and prudence I have reason to hope that you will in time help your brother to forsake his foolish misconceptions." The rest of the letter consisted of an apology of his doctrine perfectly appropriate for a professor of scholastic theology, one more example of Erasmus' tireless effort to win security and approval from the greatest possible number of people. Its content is of considerable interest to us, not because it defines the Erasmian *philosophia Christi*, but because it attempts to formulate such philosophy in the form most acceptable to a sixteenth century Spanish professor at Salamanca. Erasmus is very careful to point out that he is not entirely opposed to the scholastic method "which has its applications" (*habet et ille suum usum*). Beda and Lee's misunderstandings were based upon misquotations and the neglect of contextual reference. More importantly, Erasmus insists, his adversaries unfairly subject his more rhetorical phrases to the exacting and severe standards of scholastic speculation and definitions. By the same criterion, Erasmus claims, Saint Jerome's sayings on property and marriage, Saint Basile's statements on the right of private property, and even Saint Augustine's passionate words on the efficacy of grace, could also be labeled as heretical and impious. He continued, the most unfortunate consequence of this misdirected anti-Erasmian movement was that Catholic theologians, who were supposed to fight under the same banners (*sub iisdem signis militant*) wasted their time in petty accusations while, at the same time, the "tremendous fire of Lutheranism" (*gravissimum Lutheri incendium*) threatened to destroy Christianity itself. The letter ends in a typically Erasmian manner with a humble word of apology and an arrogant cry of defiance: "It is possible, of course, that in my fight against impiety, I myself might oc-

Razón y Fé, (1935), pp. 19–38, 340–350.

casionally have fallen into an impious dogma. But if such a thing ever happened, my fault was due to ignorance or imprudence, never to bad intention ... I am not, however, going to put up with all these venomous vilifications, not even if six Popes came to share these opinions. Neither the authority of the Pope nor yours (*sic*!) is strong enough to suppress truth and innocence. The same, of course, applies to your brother Pedro."

The words of Erasmus have been quoted at length because, except for the last three lines, Vitoria's behavior at Valladolid proves beyond any doubt that, had he ever received Erasmus' letter, he would have been extremely sympathetic to the humanist's complaints. For some reason unknown to us, Vitoria was asked by the Valladolid assembly to give his written report on only two of the twenty-one objections raised in Spain against Erasmus' works: the mystery of the Trinity, and the divinity of Christ. A possible explanation of Vitoria's restricted participation in the assembly was his reputation of sympathetic benevolence toward Erasmus. His written report on Erasmus' Trinitarian doctrine was by far the most fair, the most learned, and the most relevant of all similar documents presented at Valladolid. The report starts by qualifying as *temerarium et scandalosum* Erasmus' opinion that the words of the Fourth Gospel (Chapter V, vv. 19–30) were neither canonical nor sufficient proof of the unity of nature against Arrius. Erasmus' criticism of theological speculation is encountered by Vitoria with an important distinction: "If Erasmus means that we should avoid useless and trivial controversies, he is absolutely right (*rectum et sanctum dogma*); however, if he condemns the efforts of the Fathers of the Church in defending the unity of nature and the Trinity of Persons in God against the heretics, his opinion would be scandalous ..." Vitoria's distinction between scholastic and Patristic theology cannot be interpreted as an enthusiastic apology of the former, but rather of the latter – a central position of Erasmus. Therefore, Vitoria adds immediately that a Catholic man like Erasmus should not be interpreted as condemning the Church's opposition to Arrius, although it could not be denied that in his answer to Lee Erasmus had given ample excuse, (*occasionem magnam praebuit*) to be thus misunderstood. In the second half of the document, Vitoria becomes more severe toward Erasmus. It was scandalous to say that the mystery of the Trinity could not be proved from the Scriptures; it was an error, condemned by the Church, to maintain that a Christian was not obliged to believe more than what is explicitly stated in the Scriptures; it was dangerous and misleading to praise primitive Christianity for its simple faith and lack of theological speculation. The last paragraph of the document gives us a better insight into Vitoria's attitude toward Erasmus: "Granted that Erasmus is faithful to his Catholic heritage, as it is fair to assume (*ut credere par est*) it is undeniable that some of his statements would not help the ignorant or the weak, and that, therefore, his works ought to be expurgated, a proposal which surely Erasmus himself would welcome (*et haec puto me dixisse Erasmo ipso non invito*)." In the written report on Erasmus' position toward the divinity of Christ, Vitoria is even more harsh and demanding.

From these documents it is possible to reach the following conclusions. Vitoria's youthful admiration for Erasmus in Paris later turned into a benevolent understanding for the intentions and sincerity of the Dutch humanist perfectly compatible with a clear awareness and censure of his dogmatic deviations and ambiguities. It is even possible that Vitoria, alarmed by the quick advances of Lutheranism, later became increasingly severe toward Erasmus. At least in his Theology lectures at Salamanca he did not hesitate to call Erasmus a "dangerous man," and an "advocate of heresies." If some scholars have called Vitoria "a mild Erasmian" (for instance, Menéndez y Pelayo, Bonilla San Martín, or Beltrán de Heredia), such a label must be understood as relative. There is no doubt that in comparison with some of the most fanatic and ignorant Spanish monks assembled in Valladolid, Vitoria's understanding, moderation, and learning, could be called a form of mild Erasmian attitudes. Nor can it be denied that certain characteristics of Vitoria's intellectual career – his disinterest in theoretical speculation, and his passionate concern with moral issues – can be traced back to the fundamental principles of Erasmus. What obviously differentiated the Dutch humanist from the Spanish theologian was their fundamentally divergent attitude toward the role of the Church in the development of the dogma. By this standard Vitoria was clearly a man of the Counter-reformation, worlds apart from Erasmus' *philosophia Christi*.

B. VITORIA AND SALAMANCA (1524–1546)

Towards the end of 1522 or early in 1523 Francisco de Vitoria was recalled to Spain by the superiors of the Dominican Order, and was assigned to the College of San Gregorio in Valladolid.[11]

[11] The history of this institution is recorded in detail by G. de Arriaga, corrected by M. M.

The journey from Paris was the last long trip of Vitoria's life. He would not leave the boundaries of Old Castile anymore, he whose thought was destined to encompass the whole earth in the spirit of a novel internationalism. The Dominican College of San Gregorio (founded in 1486), and "the greater College of Santa Cruz" (founded in 1484), were not only the pride of the University of Valladolid, but also became the institutional model for similar Renaissance colleges in Alcalá, Salamanca, Lisbon, Seville, and El Escorial. The surviving Plateresque *claustro* of San Gregorio has been described as "perhaps the most magnificent collegiate building in Europe" (Rashdall). The reputation of the College at the beginning of the sixteenth century was very impressive; Salamanca had not yet reached its undisputed primacy, and the Convent of San Esteban was not to become the headquarters of the Dominican intellectuals until the fourth decade of the century. The most distinguished scholars of the day were trained at San Gregorio: men like Melchor Cano, Fray Luis de Granada, Astudillo, Medina, Bañez, Fray Bartolomé de las Casas, and Bartolomé Carranza. The College was attached to the University of Valladolid, founded in the middle of the thirteenth century. At the time of the Great Schism, in 1418, a regular faculty of Theology had been established, and it was there that Vitoria taught his courses although we ignore further details about the content of his early teaching. At Valladolid, the normal residence of Charles V, Vitoria came into close contact with the political life of the Imperial Court, where Dominican priests had from time immemorial exercised an extraordinary influence. In fact, from Alfonso XI to the end of the Hapsburg dynasty in the eighteenth century, all the confessors of the Spanish Kings had been Dominican priests. The Dominican García de Loaysa who, as General of the Order in 1523, had brought Vitoria to Valladolid, was chosen to be the Emperor's confessor, and later became President of the "Consejo de Indias." The victory of Pavía in 1525, and the conquest of Perú by Pizarro in 1526 filled the Spanish Court with dreams of a God-given Empire, but provided the theologians with awesome moral problems. The moral theologian trained in Paris under Crockaert, Fenario, Almain and John Mair, was now confronted in his homeland with ethical problems of a magnitude he had never experienced. The unresolved problems of medieval Christianity; the relations between Church and

Hoyos, in *Historia del Colegio de San Gregorio de Valladolid*, (Valladolid, 1928). The classical book on the University of Valladolid is Mariano Alcocer Martínez, *Historia de la Universidad de Valladolid*, (Valladolid, 1918).

State; between Kings and Emperor; between nations; between Christianity and the Gentiles, all converged at Valladolid. There they were given a new urgency and importance through the reports and consultations of missionaries and diplomats, theologians and conquistadores scattered through Charles' vast domains.

In the summer of 1526, Vitoria was summoned to Salamanca to compete for the most prestigious salaried chair of Theology, the Chair of Prima, vacant after the death of Pedro de León. The fact that the Dominicans chose Vitoria for this difficult task was, to say the least, totally unexpected, and speaks better than any other word of praise for the tremendous reputation won by Vitoria during his three years of teaching at San Gregorio. The first to be surprised was Vitoria himself, modest as he was and aware that one of his colleagues at Valladolid, Diego de Astudillo, was a veteran and prestigious theologian known as "the most learned man of the Kingdom." Vitoria was modest enough to admit that Astudillo knew more than he did. But he was also convinced that the old man "could not sell his ware" as well as he could.

In the first quarter of the sixteenth century, the University of Salamanca was being challenged by the younger institution of Alcalá de Henares, the recipient of royal monies and generous foundations. From the very beginning, the Franciscans were clearly in a commanding position at Alcalá; Salamanca, on the contrary, had always been a Dominican monopoly. To keep the Chair of Prima Theology in Dominican hands was a matter of vital importance to the Order. All of Pedro de León's predecessors had been Dominican theologians, with the exception of Pedro de Osma (1463–1477), the master of Nebrija, whose name the University was eager to forget as having spoiled its otherwise immaculate tradition of Catholic orthodoxy with the negation of the sacrament of penance. In fact, the Chair of Prima was occupied by Dominican priests without any interruption until the seventeenth century. Since 1621 two Chairs of Prima Theology had existed at Salamanca: one, the Dominican chair of Royal appointment, and another open to free competition, a tradition which lasted until the middle of the nineteenth century. Among Pedro de León's predecessors were two of the fifteenth century's most distinguished scholastic theologians, Cardinal Torquemada (1388–1468); and Diego de Deza, who held the Chair from 1480 to 1486, and later, as General Inquisitor, tried his very best to neutralize the influence of Nebrija at Salamanca.

Two men were competing for the Chair of Prima, Francisco de Vitoria and Pedro Margallo, a veteran professor of moral theology, author of highly popular scholastic summaries (*Physices compendium, Collectorium omnibus scholasticis utilissimum*), and at that time the Rector of the most prestigious College of the University, the "Colegio Mayor de San Bartolomé." His reputation among the students was a serious handicap to Vitoria, totally unknown in Salamanca. More than in any other European university of that time, election to the salaried chairs at Salamanca was mostly in the hands of the students. Each Theology student had a vote for each course he had successfully completed, provided he had attended the trial lectures of the candidates for as long as five weeks of thorough testing. The excitement, intrigues and even bloody fights between the followers of opposing candidates, revealed the passionate participation of the student body in those decisive episodes of the University's academic life. Vitoria's mastery of teaching proved decisive in the final count and, although we ignore the exact numbers, we know that he won the Chair "by a large number of votes." At the approximate age of thirty-two Francisco de Vitoria took possession of the most prestigious, and best paid Chair of theology in the University of Salamanca.

Educated Spaniards are used to saying that the University of Salamanca was the oldest Spanish University, and one of the first in medieval Europe. The truth is that they are wrong on both counts. In Spain both Palencia and Valladolid were founded earlier. There was a considerable number of older institutions in Europe: Vicenza, Padua, Naples, Montpellier, Salermo, Bologna, Paris, Oxford, and Cambridge. Still no other Spanish name can compare to that of Salamanca as a symbol of traditional Spanish thought.[12]

The real founder of the University of Salamanca was the King of Castile, Ferdinand III, the Saint, who issued the charter of privilege in 1243 – generously endowed later by his son, Alfonso X, the Wise. In spite of its close connection with the Crown, Salamanca, like most Spanish universities, developed as a *studium* of the Cathedral under the authority of the local Bishop, who appointed a capitular master (*scholasticus, magister scholarum*) to supervise the administration of the school. From the very beginning, the academic degrees of the University were granted in the name of both the King and the Pope; *auctoritate Apostolica et Regia*. The rectorship was introduced in the fourteenth century: the rector was elected by students and teachers and was in charge of disciplinary matters. The influence of Alfonso X, the Papal policy of preserving the theological monopoly of the University of Paris, account

12 The bibliography on the University of Salamanca is extremely large. The classical

for the fact that, until the time of the Great Schism, the reputation of Salamanca was that of a school of Law, both civil and ecclesiastical, rather than that of a center of medieval Theology. The increasing Gallicanism and conciliarism of the Parisian theologians, however, forced the Popes into becoming more generous toward Salamanca, always a staunch patroness of ultramontane claims. The statutes still being enforced at Salamanca in 1524 when Vitoria joined the prestigious *claustro*, were those of 1422, promulgated by Pope Martin V toward the end of the Great Schism. According to those regulations, the Rector had to be assisted by eight *consiliarii*, elected by students of various dioceses; the powers of the *scholasticus* – or as he was now called, the "chancellor" of the University – were considerably enlarged at the expense of the judiciary authority previously held by the rector of the University. The democratic basis of the University was preserved by the creation of a governing body, or executive committee, made up of the following members: the Rector, the Chancellor, and thirty deputies: twenty of them elected by students and ten elected by tenured professors. It was up to this executive committee to appoint the Chancellor of the University with the approval of the Archbishop of Toledo (not the Bishop of Salamanca!). Three weeks after winning the Chair of Prima, Vitoria was elected to this formidable *Claustro de Diputados*, and had therefore a magnificent opportunity to become actively involved with the internal problems of the University: the threat of Royal interference; the constant dependence upon Papal decisions and favors; the tension between religious and secular priests; the restlessness of the students; the Inquisitorial vigilance; the endless intrigues of the professors themselves and the serious financial troubles of the Institution. The most troublesome spot in the organization of the University was the friction between the Chancellor – a life-long position of ecclesiastical origin – and the Rector, elected every year (until 1854!) by the students themselves. The Royal inspectors occasionally appointed by the Crown did not help much to simplify the cumbersome structure of the University.

In spite of these administrative setbacks, Salamanca, spurred by the competition of Alcalá, was an intense intellectual center at the time Vitoria joined its Theology faculty. Besides Nebrija, Torquemada and Deza, some of Vitoria's immediate predecessors had been men of great

works are: Enrique Esperabé Arteaga, *Historia de la Universidad de Salamanca*, 2 vols., (Salamanca, 1914–1917). Pedro Chacón, *Historia de la Universidad de Salamanca*, (Salamanca, 1569), ed. Antonio Valladares de Sotomayor, *Semanario Erudito*, VIII (1789), pp. 3–67. *See also* Rashdall, *Medieval Universities*, II, pp. 74–90.

learning. It would be preposterous to affirm that Salamanca's golden era was the result of Vitoria's exclusive inspiration. It was rather the work of an impressive group of theologians, jurists and humanists, who laid the foundations of Counter-reformation scholasticism, the political thought of Spain under Philip II, and the literary splendor of the Spanish baroque. Although most of these men paid their tribute of respect and admiration for Vitoria, historical fairness demands that their names be mentioned here on account of their own merits and achievements. We should start with those who were never Vitoria's disciples, but rather his colleagues in the faculty. Juan Martínez Guijarro (1486–1557) had been trained in Paris by Celaya, who persuaded him to change his rough Castilian name into the Latin version of *Siliceo*, as history knows him. In 1517, Siliceo was called to Salamanca to teach philosophy *ad modum Parisiense*. Still in Paris, Siliceo had published a commentary on Aristotle's *Organon*, and two books of mathematics, *De usu Astrolabi compendium*, and *Arithmetica*, the latter published several times in the Parisian presses. In Salamanca, Siliceo published Suiseth's *Liber calculationum*, a clear proof that he had lost no interest in logic. As a former friend and fellow-student in Paris, Siliceo (already a professor of moral philosophy in 1526) was a close partner and admirer of the new professor of Prima. When Vitoria took his inaugural oath in the University, Siliceo and Córdoba, another Parisian, attended the ceremony with Vitoria's brother, Pedro. Siliceo was later chosen to be preceptor of the Crown Prince, the future Philip II, and finally became Cardinal Archbishop of Toledo.

Another of Vitoria's fellow students in Paris was also teaching at Salamanca *circa* 1526: Fray Alfonso de Córdoba, whose short-lived attempt to introduce nominalism into the traditionally Thomistic University has been mentioned above. Vitoria's most distinguished colleagues, however, were not members of the Art and Theology faculties, but rather – as befitting Salamanca's tradition – masters of Civil and Canon Law: Diego de Covarrubias y Leyva (1512–1577) and Martín de Azpilcueta (1492–1586). Vitoria, Covarrubias and Azpilcueta (known also as "Doctor Navarro") were the great architects of Spanish political and legal thought in the first half of the sixteenth century – a project to be systematized by Soto; thoroughly discussed by a second and powerful generation of theologians and jurists (Medina, Báñez, Cano, among others); and, finally, reduced to an impressive synthesis by the genius of Suárez.[13]

[13] The bibliography on Covarrubias and Azpilcueta is disproportionately meager and

Martín de Azpilcueta had been trained at Alcalá and Toulouse, the most prestigious French University in Jurisprudence, where he also began his teaching career. His reputation in France was such that he was offered a seat in the Parisian Parliament. However, in 1524 he joined the University of Salamanca, and soon became a legend among students and fellow teachers. Azpilcueta introduced the practice of holding extraordinary lectures (*re-lectiones*) on relevant problems of the day as they related to the subject matter of his courses, an exercise which Vitoria took over and which attracted national attention. In 1528, and in the presence of Charles V, Azpilcueta held the first of these extraordinary lectures on the topic: "The Kingdom belongs to the Community, not to the King," a direct attack on the Burgundian tradition of feudal ownership represented by the young Emperor and fiercely opposed by his Castilian subjects. At the request of the Portuguese King, Azpilcueta was sent to Coimbra in 1538, where he held the Chair of Prima until 1555. Like many other distinguished scholars of that time, Azpilcueta was brought back to the Spanish Court by Philip II, and in time became the most enthusiastic apologist for the King's policy toward the Popes and other European Princes. In his teaching Azpilcueta blended in unique fashion his comprehensive knowledge of civil and canonical law with moral theology and natural ethics. His final work *Enchiridion sive manuale confessorarium et poenitentium* (Rome, 1573), printed more than fifty times, earned him the pompous title of *Communis Hispaniae Magister*, and constitutes, even today, an unforgettable monument to the religious, political, and moral concerns of Vitoria's generation.

Diego de Covarrubias, on the other hand, was entirely a product of Salamanca, where he studied under El Pinciano, Azpilcueta, and Vitoria himself. In 1538 Covarrubias became a doctor of Canon Law, a discipline he taught at Salamanca from 1539 to 1549. Later he was consecrated Bishop of Ciudad Rodrigo, and returned shortly to Salamanca as a Royal Inspector of Philip II. A man most typical of the Spanish Counterreformation, Covarrubias played an important part in the Council of Trent where he helped to write the decrees of *De Reformatione*. Covarrubias was an easy and prolific writer. His books on the

almost exclusively Spanish. See, however, Luciano Pereña Vicente, *La Universidad de Salamanca, forja del pensamiento español en el siglo XVI*, (Salamanca, 1954), pp. 25–38; Constancio Gutiérrez, *Españoles en Trento*, (Valladolid, 1951); Fernández Montana, *Los Covarrubias*, (Madrid, 1935); Mariano Arigita y Lasa, *El Doctor Navarro Martín de Azpilcueta y sus obras*, (Pamplona, 1895); María Luisa Larramendi de Olarrea, *Miscelánea de noticias romanas acerca del D. Martín de Azpilcueta*, (Madrid, 1943).

sacrament of marriage, testaments, contracts, ecclesiastical immunities, treaties, taxes, lending, slavery, war, numismatics, legal procedure, penal law, commentaries to the *Fuero Juzgo*, right of asylum, hunting and fishing, bear witness to an incredible familiarity not only with the historical sources of civil and ecclesiastical law (such as the Constitution of Athens, the Laws of Lycurg, the Codex of Justinian and the *Codex Theodosianus*), but also with modern legislation (such as the Constitution of Naples, the Decrees of the French Parliament, and the Decrees of Councils and Popes). With unequivocal Renaissance passion for textual criticism, Covarrubias did not spare any effort to define the original text of any given legal document, making constant use of the latest findings of all the philologists of his time – such as Budé, Beathus Rhenanus, Nebrija and Antonio Agustin, among others. To complete this amazing picture we must add a trait not very common in those days: a comprehensive knowledge of the medieval legal tradition and a constructive synthesis of late scholasticism – Cajetan and John Mair more specifically – and the humanist criticism of Valla, Joannes Vasee, and Juan Luis Vives. Covarrubias was much more than a jurist, a philologist, or a canonist; his work constitutes a pioneer effort in the philosophy of law, in comparative jurisprudence, and in legal sociology. Together with Azpilcueta, Covarrubias formulated the historical role of sixteenth century Spain as it was, for better or worse, understood by the men of his age and carried out with meticulous care by Philip II. Because of his intense nationalism, however, Covarrubias remained a local actor – albeit a leading one – of the Spanish national stage during the decisive years of the first Hapsburgs, without ever reaching the higher cosmopolitanism and significance of Francisco de Vitoria.

The revival of Salamanca in the first decades of the sixteenth century was not only the work of philosophers and theologians, but of humanists as well. The glorious tradition of Nebrija and Arias Barbosa (also known as "el Maestro Griego") was faithfully continued in the sixteenth century by Nebrija's disciple Hernán Nuñez ("El Pinciano"), a teacher at Salamanca since 1527. His commentaries on Seneca and his collections of medieval proverbs were a significant contribution to the revival of stoic and sapiential literature, which attracted the attention of Justus Lipsius and Francisco Sánchez, el Brocense. Another man of letters teaching at Salamanca in Vitoria's days was Fernán Pérez de Oliva, a former disciple of Siliceo in Paris and later a protégé of Pope Leo X in Rome, where he was powerfully influenced by Italian humanism. Oliva became the Rector of the University of Salamanca in 1529. To his name we must add those of two Flemish professors of Humanities: Joannes Vasee and Nicolaus Clenard, whose admiration for Vitoria proves the good taste and refined diction of the scholastic theologian.

In the company of these distinguished philosophers, theologians, jurists and humanists, Vitoria began his teaching career where he was to spend the rest of his life until his death in 1546. Vitoria looked on teaching as a truly priestly and sacred vocation: "Farmers and workers," he said to his students," can have their free time. We cannot take a single break in our life of constant study." Each one of his lectures was preceded by extensive reading – *lectione pene infinita* in the words of Vasee – by lengthy meditation and careful writing. In his twenty years of teaching he attempted never to repeat himself: "You are very wrong," he said to his students at the beginning of the 1539–1540 academic year, "if you think that in this course I am going to repeat the same old story (*eandem cantinellam recantaturum*). That is not my style; on the contrary, I shall try my very best to find new words and new energies in doing this job as though today were the very beginning of my teaching career." After fifteen years of lecturing on the subject those words speak for themselves. Vitoria's delivery was calm, persuasive, dramatic, incisive, and occasionally humorous. He never used any book or written reminder in his lectures (it was strictly forbidden by the rules of the University), a charming mixture of admittedly loose quotations and the most thoughtful and precise formulations in substantial matters. In open rebellion against the tradition of the University of Salamanca, Vitoria imported the Parisian practice of dictating his lectures, although, prudent and accommodating as he was, he waited several years to take a public stand in the matter. At the beginning of the 1539–1540 academic year, Vitoria announced in class that those who refused to take notes had better go to another teacher. But he added: "As for myself, I shall try to make things easier for you by speaking more slowly than I used to in the past." In fact, practically everything we know about Vitoria's thought has been transmitted to us by the notes of his disciples. The success of Vitoria's teaching at Salamanca was incredible. His audience included not only theology students – between seven and eight hundred – but also other students of the University (the student body at that time numbered over five thousand), and a large number of colleagues and other distinguished visitors among whom, more than once, was the Emperor himself. Azpilcueta prided himself on having attracted to his own classes as many students as Vitoria, and contemporary writers place that number at close to a thousand. This extraordinarily large audience forced Vitoria to teach in the Old Cathedral, where students were supposed to follow the dictation of the master for almost two hours each lecture, standing in a dense crowd (*de pie e muy apretados*). When Vitoria's health failed in 1540, the students themselves carried the veteran professor on their shoulders to and from the classroom, a dramatic symbol of the intense religious and intellectual restlessness of the subjects of Charles V.

Vitoria's teaching can be divided into two groups: the ordinary and the extraordinary lectures (*relectiones*). Except for three years dedicated to the IV book of Peter Lombard's *Liber Sententiarum* (sacramental theology), Vitoria's ordinary teaching was a commentary to the *Summa Theologica* of Saint Thomas, a methodological innovation to be discussed later (*See below*, pp. 75-76). Seven years were assigned to the second part of the *Summa*, namely to moral theology. One academic year (1533–1534) dealt with the *Prima Secundae* (morality, grace, original sin, law); six years (1526–1529, and 1534–1537) were spent in discussing the *Secunda Secundae* (theological and moral virtues). Vitoria "read" twice his commentaries to the first part of the *Summa* (God, Trinity, Creation, Man) (1531–1533, and 1539–1540); and once (1537–1538) he lectured on the third part (Christ, the Sacraments). He refused to publish any of these lectures himself. The text we have today was written by his disciples who tried – not always successfully – to reproduce faithfully the words of their dictating teacher. Only in one case did Vitoria himself proof-read one of the manuscripts, the commentary on the fourth book of Peter Lombard (*Summa Sacramentorum Ecclesiae*), put together by his student Tomás de Chaves and published in all probability before Vitoria's death. The name of Vitoria was such a recommendation to the book that it was published thirty-four times in a period of seventy years (1560–1529). The manuscripts to the *Secunda Secundae* have been published recently, but the rest remains unedited in the Vatican Library.[14]

14 See *Francisco de Vitoria, O. P., Comentarios a la Secunda secundae de Santo Tomás*, Ed. R. P. Vicente Beltrán de Heredia (Biblioteca de Teólogos Españoles), (Salamanca, 1932–1935). Also by the same editor, *Summa Sacramentorum Ecclesiae ex doctrina Francisci a Vitoria*, (Salamanca, 1566).

The study of Vitoria's manuscripts was inaugurated by Cardinal Ehrle in his article "Die Vaticanischen Handschriften der Salmantizenser Theologen des 16. Jh.", *Der Katholik* (Mainz), II (1884), from p. 495. Ehrle's work has been completed by Getino, *op. cit.*; by F. Stegmueller, "Die Spanischen Handschriften der Salmantizenser Theologen," *Theological Revue*, XXX (1931), pp. 361–365, and "Zur Literaturgeschichte der Salmanticenser Schule,"

Although these manuscripts –which, if printed would make several impressive volumes – incorporate the hard core of twenty years of complete dedication to the teaching of scholastic theology, Vitoria's reputation among later historians of Spanish Renaissance thought is mostly based upon the thirteen short extraordinary lectures, which he held practically every year from 1527 to 1540 in the style of those introduced by his colleague Azpilcueta. Their subject matter was ordinarily a relevant moral problem of the day related to, but not directly dealt with in his normal teaching. The style was more informal and less scholastic than the rather dry, technical presentation of his commentaries on the *Summa*. Still Vitoria preserved the fundamentally scholastic device of stringing together his talk with a number of precisely formulated conclusions, preceded or followed by proving arguments and solutions to possible objections. These lectures – held in the presence of the entire University community – immediately acquired an extraordinary popularity. Never before had a scholastic theologian spoken about such controversial matters with Vitoria's precision, commanding authority, and persuasiveness. The *relectiones* were published soon after Vitoria's death in frequent editions (1565, 1571, 1580, and 1587) and translations.[15]

It is rather unfortunate that Vitoria's ordinary teaching remained mostly unpublished and that it was soon forgotten, because it is absolutely certain that in the eyes of his contemporaries and immediate disciples it was considered at least as important as the extraordinary lectures. To judge Vitoria exclusively on the basis of the latter would obviously produce a distorted impression of his thought, style, and role.

The first *relectio* was held in December 1528 on the origins and limitations of civil authority (*De potestate civili*), a topic probably suggested by questions 57 and 59 of the *Secunda secundae*, the content of Vitoria's

ibidem, XXIX (1930), pp. 55–59. Beltrán de Heredia has written an informative book on the same subject, *Los Manuscritos del Maestro Francisco de Vitoria*, (Madrid, 1928).

[15] The first edition of Vitoria's *Relectiones* was published outside of Spain, in Lyon (France) by Jacques Boyer (1557), an audacity which irritated the Dominicans of Salamanca. In 1565 they published their own edition under the supervision of Domingo de Soto and Melchor Cano. The critical modern edition was prepared by Luis G. Alonso Getino, *Relecciones teológicas del Maestro Vitoria*, 3 vols. (Madrid 1933–1935). The first seven lectures are given in Latin and Spanish, the rest only in their Spanish translation. There is also an incomplete Spanish translation of the *Relectiones* by Jaime Torrubiano Ripoll, 3 vols., (Madrid, 1917). The *Relectio De Indis* was translated into English by Pawley Bate in 1917. The classical book of James Brown Scott, *The Spanish Origin of International Law, Francisco de Vitoria and his Law of Nations*, (Oxford, 1934), includes the English translation (to be used in this book) of the lectures *De Indis*, *De iure belli*, *De potestate civili*, *De potestate Ecclesiae*, and Vitoria's commentaries on Saint Thomas', *Summa Theologica*, II, 2, q. 57, art. 3 (*De iure gentium et naturali*) and I, 2, q. 40 (De bello).

curriculum in the fall of that same year. In June 1530 Vitoria lectured on homicide (*De homicidio*). This lecture, which begins with a humanistic description of man's individuality and value, has been fairly interpreted as Vitoria's response to the depreciation of human life brought about by religious persecutions, Inquisitorial cruelties, nationalistic wars, and colonial abuses. The fourth lecture, on matrimony, in June 1531, was Vitoria's answer to the Emperor's consultation regarding the threatened marriage of his aunt, Queen Catherine of Aragon, with Henry VIII, a subject he dealt with in a more theoretical vein in his commentaries to the sacramental theology of Peter Lombard in the academic years of 1529–1531. In 1532 and 1533 he gave two lectures on ecclesiastical authority (*De potestate Ecclesiae*), in which he discussed two fundamental questions: the relations of Church and State, and (against Luther) the universal priesthood of all Christians. In June 1534 Vitoria tackled one of the most delicate questions in the history of Canon Law, the relationship of the Pope's and the Council's authority (*De potestate Papae et Concilii*). Vitoria's excessive benevolence toward the conciliar leanings of his former Parisian professors, and the boldness of certain conclusions about possible Papal abuses and mistakes, were too much for the Roman Inquisitors, and Vitoria's *relectiones* shared the glory of many other classical documents of the Spanish Counter-reformation by being included in the Papal *Index* of Sixtus V, together with Cardinal Bellarmin's *Controversiae* (!). The *relectio* corresponding to the academic year 1533–1534 took up a particular point of the *Summa* he was teaching then, the augmentation and diminution of spiritual habits (I, 2, questions 49–54). This theological minutiae, which amazingly enough excited the students of those days beyond belief, gave Vitoria an opportunity to display a bold independence from Thomas' authority to the enormous irritation of other fiery Dominicans, such as Bañez. The lecture of 1535 had for its title "The obligations of those who reach the use of reason" (*De eo ad quod tenetur veniens ad usum rationis*), a practical moral issue related to questions 1–7 (on Faith) of the *Secunda Secundae* Vitoria was then teaching. In 1536, Vitoria chose to speak about ecclesiastical abuses (*De simonia*), a subject of pressing actuality in the face of the accusations of the reformers. This particular *relectio* reveals more than any other Vitoria's Parisian background. The names of Cajetan, John Mair, and Peter de la Palm ("Paludanus") – the favorite author of Crockaert and Saint Antonine of Florence – appear constantly in Vitoria's passionate lecture. In 1538 – after one year of interruption due to his poor health – Vitoria spoke on temperance (*De temperantia*), a virtue Saint Thomas discussed thoroughly in the *Secunda Secundae*, questions 141–154, Vitoria's text for that year. This lecture, of which we have only an incomplete version, deals with several practical problems such as the obligation of preserving one's own health and the unnatural character of anthropofagia. In 1539 Vitoria held the two most outstanding and famous of all his lectures dealing with the moral issue of the American *conquista*. The first, entitled *De Indis*, reviewed and discussed the false and possibly right claims of the Spanish Crown over the American natives; the second, *De iure belli*, explored the conditions of a just war and the rights of the participants. Vitoria's conclusions in those lectures – the subject of detailed analysis discussed further below – were terribly resented by Charles V who immediately directed the Prior of the Convent of San Esteban in Salamanca to silence such "scandalous and harmful" talk, to forbid any further oral or written discussion of the matter, and to send to the Court without any delay all extant written copies of Vitoria's lectures, so that they could be "disposed of, as the urgency of the situation requires." There are no indications, however, that Vitoria was in any way impressed by the angry reaction of the Emperor, and the discussion about the morality of the *conquista* remained for a long time an integral part of the Spanish University in the sixteenth century. No Imperial edict was powerful enough to silence the moral restlessness to which Vitoria gave such articulate expression. The last extraordinary lecture, in 1540, centered around a theme of great interest to the people of that confused age, magic (*De magia*). Vitoria's approach in this lecture was a charming combination of modern common sense, amazing gullibility, and medieval dogmatic hair-splitting.

The phenomenal success of Vitoria's teaching immediately attracted a great deal of attention, not only within the boundaries of the local University, but also on every level of Spanish society. Men of strong and clear ideas could not remain unknown in a society bursting with new energies, challenged by new situations, unaccustomed to power, proud and self-incriminating at the same time. Thought ranked high in Spanish society of that time, and because of their ideas and beliefs men were burned or raised to high dignities, persecuted or flattered. In spite of all the narrow-mindedness of a small circle of zealots, in spite of all the cruelties of Inquisitors and Royal agents, the society of Charles V, as a whole, makes the strong impression of a close-knit community of startled human beings, desperately seeking guidance from each other, longing for advice and intellectual leadership. The royal *consultas*, the intense mail between the Court and the Universities, the constant seeking of opinion (*pareceres*), the assemblies, the national controversies, the public disputes, all reveal an ebullient society attempting to cope with new realities in some reasonable manner. Gross misconceptions and auspicious insights into new avenues of thought alternate freely in the documents of the age. The partial failure of the final result does not in the least diminish the excitement and pathetic beauty of this intellectual struggle in the Spain of Charles V.

Unlike many of his distinguished colleagues, Vitoria was never tempted by the prospect of ecclesiastical or royal emoluments through which, especially under Philip II, both the Church and the Crown sought to tame critical or rebellious thought. On the contrary, the more he felt repelled by the atrocities of the American *conquista*, the less he felt inclined to sell "the possession of his conscience" (*la hacienda de la conciencia*). In 1534, soon after the conquest of Perú and the execution of Atahualpa, Vitoria wrote to the Provincial of the Dominicans in Andalucía:

> If the Peruvian natives were monkeys instead of human beings, I would recognize that they could not be victims of 'injustice.' However, being our fellow-men and subjects of the Emperor (sic!), I cannot see how to excuse the *conquistadores* from the worst kind of cruelty and tyranny (*última impiedad y tiranía*) . . . Even if I desired the Archbishopric of Toledo, which is vacant now, very badly, supposing they offered it to me under the condition that I proclaimed the innocence of those Peruvian adventurers (*destos Peruleros*), I could never bring myself to do such a thing. I would rather lose my tongue and my hand than to say or write such an inhuman and anti-Christian statement. They can keep the seat of the Archbishop for themselves; all I want is to be left in peace (*allá se lo hayan, y déjennos en paz*). They will surely find somebody ready to go along with their plans; even among our Dominicans, they would find somebody ready to excuse them, to praise their deeds, their massacres, and their pillages.[16]

Because of his intelligence and robust independence of character, Vitoria's advice was constantly sought by people of all social ranks. As a counselor Vitoria was an intriguing personality. His natural inclination was to avoid personal conflicts or any threat to his academic immunity or personal security. The last two lines of the letter just quoted could give the false impression that he was a man of dramatic gestures or vociferous protests. Nothing is further from reality. He him-

[16] This remarkable letter, worth reading in its entirety, is printed in Beltrán de Heredia's article, "Ideas del Maestro Francisco de Vitoria anteriores a las Relecciones *De Indis* acerca de la colonización de América, según documentos inéditos," *La Ciencia Tomista*, 122 (March–April 1930), pp. 145–165.

self confesses in the same letter: "My normal attitude toward these people (the Peruvian conquistadores) is simply to avoid them. I do not like to scream or to put on a big act (*non exclamo nec excito tragoedias*). I confess my weakness: I try my very best not to break up with these fellows. However, if they force me to give an unequivocal answer, in the end I always say exactly what I feel." ("*Pero si omnino cogor a responder categóricamente, al cabo digo lo que siento.*")

As a deputy of the University executive committee, as a consultant to merchants, bishops, and kings, Vitoria became in his day one of the leading artificers of Spanish moral standards and sensibility. Vitoria's record as deputy sheds much light on the internal organization of the University, especially upon the tense relations between the University and the Church-Crown establishment, between the theologians and the policy makers, between the men of thought and the men of action.

Vitoria's attendance record to the meetings of the *claustro de diputados* speaks highly of his professionalism and total involvement in the life of the institution. The very first day of his appointment he was faced with a typical case of royal interference which the University passionately resented. The Emperor had announced his intention of sending to England, as personal physician to Queen Catherine of Aragon, one of the young and more promising members of the Faculti of Medicine, Doctor Parra. Furthermore, it was His Majesty's desire that the University give Doctor Parra an indefinite leave of absence without declaring his chair at Salamanca vacant. Knowing that the student body was strongly opposed to this scheme, the *Claustro* rejected the Emperor's petition. When, a few years later, Charles V asked the University to exonerate Azpilcueta from his academic contract to make possible his transfer to Coimbra, Vitoria stated bluntly that he was not willing to approve such a deal (*que él no es parte para ello*").

In 1527 Vitoria was particularly involved in a small incident of some historical significance. The ecclesiastical authorities of Salamanca were extremely alarmed by the presence in the city of a middle-aged man who, without any theological degree or previous study, was bold enough to discuss in public such complicated theological matters as the difference between a mortal and a venial sin – implying of course that he had had such knowledge *via* a special divine illumination. Such a claim to an immediate contact with the Divinity without any ecclesiastical mediation, was an open invitation to Inquisitorial action in sixteenth century Spain. The Bishop of Salamanca consulted on the matter with the Dominican friars of San Esteban Convent, where this strange man used to beg for his food. Vitoria concurred with most of his colleagues in urging the Bishop to silence him until he had completed at least four years of scholastic theology. What nobody could envision in 1527 was that such an ignorant person, Saint Ignatius from Loyola, would in a no distant future become the founder of the religious order destined to champion the intellecual movement of the Catholic Counter-reformation. Vitoria's advice to the Bishop, however, should not be interpreted as a forecast of the intense rivalry between Jesuits and Dominicans which – especially at Salamanca – enlivened the theological arena with noble emulation on some rare occasions, and with opinionated, parochial clannishness most of the time. On the contrary, when the first two Jesuits reached Salamanca in 1545, they received from Vitoria, according to their own testimony, "all the protection they could desire." Two of Vitoria's closest friends in the Dominican Order, Siliceo and Melchor Cano, in time became the most fanatic antagonists to the Order of Loyola.

Vitoria's most intense participation in the administrative life of the University probably took place during the visitation of Juan de Córdoba, a royal inspector appointed by Charles V in 1538, under whose supervision new rules were formulated in important disciplinary and academic matters.[17]

Several features of those new regulations clearly reveal Vitoria's influence. Title XI, for instance, insists upon constant compliance with the obligation of using Latin in the classroom, "except in the elementary teaching of grammar, in the Music courses (a traditionally powerful department in Salamanca!), and in the Astrology courses." Vitoria's faith in Latin did not exclude, however, an occasional and colorful use of certain Spanish phrases in his lectures, in the same way as Latin idioms were scattered through his private correspondence in the vernacular (*See above*, p. 64). Even Vitoria's most dry and technical Latin commentaries to the *Summa* abound in Spanish proverbs, colloquialisms, humorous descriptions, and idioms which his audience probably echoed with uproars of approval and amusement destined to encourage those pioneering incursions into the vernacular. Vitoria obviously enjoyed the student reaction to his use of Castillian and, occasionally at least, he utilized such devices to strengthen the persuasiveness of his talk. Dealing with the proverbial theological ignorance of contemporary Bishops (he made only one exception, John Fisher), and well aware that his young students of theology were more than eager

[17] See Getino, *El Maestro*, Appendix X, pp. 220–237.

to display their disrespect for the ecclesiastical hierarchy, Vitoria descended more often than ever into the green pastures of the vernacular: "*Revera maior pars episcoporum se contentan con lo que sabe el labrador ... Porque ¿quién hizo alcalde? Quia quasi nullus est qui sciat Bibliam ... Tertio dico, quod si excusantur, est quia si ipsi non faciunt, per alios faciunt, porque si no veo por los ojos veo por anteojos ...*"

Another serious abuse Vitoria tried to eradicate from University life was the debauchery and excessive expenses of graduation exercises,, which in those days included a wild bull fight. Vitoria's opposition to luxury and wastefulness was a constant trait of his character. When, in September 1543, the city and University of Salamanca were planning the festivities to follow the wedding of Prince Philip (the future Philip II) to his cousin Isabel of Portugal – an important maneuver in the Emperor's dynastic policy – Vitoria did not hesitate to write a strong letter to the Emperor protesting the exorbitant expenditures: "In conscience I cannot approve this waste ... it creates the impression that this Nation has so much wealth that we do not know what to do with it." (*parescerá que tenemos los doblones atesorados y no sabemos qué hacer de ellos.*) We must add in behalf of Charles V that apparently Vitoria's outburst was accepted with grace: two years later Charles V still invited Vitoria to be the Imperial theologian at the Council of Trent. Unfortunately, as Vitoria himself wrote back to the Emperor, his health was so poor at that time that "it was more likely for him to travel soon to the other world than to any region of this one." A few months later Vitoria died in Salamanca.

Vitoria's counsel and guidance were not confined to the narrow boundaries of Salamanca's ivory tower. Contemporary testimonies bear witness to the fact that he was constantly besieged by men of all ranks and trades seeking his moral advice. Among them there were two important groups: the local merchants and the American settlers, whose presence in the Dominican Convent of San Esteban clearly proves that modern mercantilism and colonialism did not prevail without a heavy tribute of moral anguish and remorse. Finally, the Crown itself approached Vitoria on repeated occasions to have his *parecer* in spiritual matters related to Imperial policy. In November 1539, the Emperor, distressed by Las Casas' charge that the American Indians were being baptized without previous instruction, brought this matter to the Royal Council. The Council, however, refused to deal with this problem, and advised the Emperor to seek advice on this theological issue from theologians themselves (*por ser como es cosa teologal, ha parecido que conviene sea visto y examinado por personas teólogas*). Naturally, the professor of Prima Theology at Salamanca was then asked to report the opinion of the University to the Crown, and Vitoria complied without delay. Furthermore, on his own initiative Vitoria felt obliged more than once to let the Emperor know his private opinion on political matters clearly bearing upon the religious crisis of European Christianity. Such was, for instance, the Emperor's war policy against the King of France, a policy which Vitoria viewed as a calamity to Europe. Like many other Parisian students before him – Vives, Azpilcueta and Siliceo, among others – Vitoria always kept a dear affection for France. Knowing well that Charles V was not inclined to listen to a theologian on international politics, Vitoria found it more expedient to use the influence of a good friend of his, Pedro Fernández de Velasco, Condestable de Castile, and a powerful figure in the Court of the Emperor. Although there are indications of a frequent correspondence between Vitoria and Velasco, only two letters from the former to the latter are known to us. The first was written in 1536 after the death of Antonio de Leyva, the hero of Pavia and scourge of France. Vitoria's scarce sympathy for this national celebrity was more than just a matter of personal taste: Leyva was a symbol of a senseless warfare to him. "I read a letter," Vitoria wrote to Velasco, "about Leyva's death; apparently he died more as a soldier than as a good Christian. I seem to remember that he did not even have time to make a good confession ..." The second letter is much more important. "Sometimes," Vitoria wrote, "I wonder whether it would be as foolish for theologians to speak out on political matters as it would be for a prince to give philosophical opinions" (*si los señores fablasen en nuestras filosofías*). But when I realize that powerful men are also made of flesh, and that it might very well be possible for some outsiders to be as wise as the insiders themselves think they are, I come to the conclusion that it is not total madness to think that they, too, can make terrible mistakes." After this preamble Vitoria goes directly into the matter. If Spain and France were at peace with each other "there would be no heretics nor Moors, and the Church could be reformed with or without the help of the Pope" (*sic!*) (*y la Iglesia se reformaría quisiera el Papa o no*). Without peace between Spain and France there is no hope for Christianity, and even an ecumenical Council would be totally worthless (*ni daré un maravedí por Concilio*). Vitoria's letter to Velasco was not forgotten. In the Cortes of Toledo two years later, the Condestable led the Spanish nobility in the opposition to the Emperor's war policy. Charles V was so irritated by Velasco's attitude that he threatened to throw the Condestable down the balcony of Toledo's Alcázar, a threat Velasco answered with the following words: "Beware Your Majesty, short as I am I carry a lot of weight (*que si bien soy pequeño, peso mucho*).

The death of Vitoria in August, 1546, after long years of poor health and intense physical suffering, was mourned by the entire Spanish nation as an irreparable loss. No other Spanish thinker of the Renaissance can be compared with Vitoria in the number, the quality, and the respect of those who proclaimed him as a master and an inspiration. A survey of Spanish Renaissance thought would be, in many respects, the only worthy eulogy of Vitoria's genius.

C. VITORIA AND SPANISH RENAISSANCE SCHOLASTICISM

The incredible reputation of Vitoria among his contemporaries authorizes us to blame the editors of his lectures for most of the obvious shortcomings of the existing manuscripts. The lack of consistency and perspicuity in certain passages, the occasional disarray of argumentation, and even the doubtful orthodoxy of the doctrine exposed, are probably the results of the unfavorable circumstances under which these classnotes were recorded by well-intentioned students. Textual criticism can, in most cases, corroborate this suspicion. The text of Vitoria's commentaries to the *Secunda Secundae* is full of mistakes based upon homophony more than justified by the poor acoustic conditions of Salamanca's Old Cathedral. Typical cases are, for instance, *omnes* instead of *homines*, *istorum* instead of *sanctorum*, or *petitiones* for *positiones*. Other errors can be attributed to a mistaken transcription of the original notes. Such is the case of *dementes* instead of *clementes*, *audirem* for *auderem*, and *substantia* for *constantia*. Obviously there are certain limitations to our liberal desire of absolving Vitoria from any imperfection whatsoever, but the reader can rest assured that the ensuing evaluation of his merits takes into consideration the facts just recorded, and is, to say the least, an optimal one.

Vitoria's biographers have consistently described him as being the indisputable Patriarch of Spanish Renaissance scholasticism. Such stereotyped characterization – obviously unfair to the distinguished predecessors and colleagues of Vitoria at Salamanca – needs to be qualified in more detail. What we want to know is, firstly, what are the basic differences (if any) between Vitoria's scholasticism and that of his immediate predecessors; and, secondly, how many of Vitoria's innovations were incorporated into the main body of Spanish scholasticism in the sixteenth century.

The overriding feature of Vitoria's teaching was his concern with moral questions at the expense of theological or philosophical speculation. Metaphysical issues traditionally "stolen" from the Arts courses by the scholastic theologians of the religious orders, such as the proofs of God's existence, or the aprioristic construction of divine attributes from the metaphysical essence of the Supreme Being, were practically sidestepped by Vitoria. Not even the fiery contemporary controversies about the immortality of the soul – an issue where even Cajetan's otherwise immaculate orthodoxy paid excessive tribute to Pomponazzi's fideism – occupied much of Vitoria's time. As for the other disciplines of the Arts course, besides ethics, namely logic and physics, Vitoria had the naive idea that they had reached such a degree of perfection that no further effort was warranted. In this respect his influence upon Spanish scholasticism was considerable. Most of the Dominican theologians who followed him shared his lack of interest in the great metaphysical questions of the Aristotelian-Thomistic system, although dialectical and physical problems were discussed at length by Domingo Soto, Domingo Bañez, and Tomás de Mercado. It was left to a Professor of Alcalà, Gaspar Cardillo de Villalpando, and especially to the Jesuits Pedro de Fonseca, Gabriel Vázquez, and Francisco Suárez to renew in Coimbra, during the second half of the century, the speculative tradition inaugurated in Italy by Cajetan and the Ferrarense.

As for Theology itself, it is clear that Vitoria felt much more at home in its moral and positive branches than in a purely rational comprehension and systematization of dogmatic data – a fact evidenced by the choice of his courses' subject matter (*See above*, pp. 59-60). Only the close connection between moral problems and certain domains of dogmatic theology – such as the doctrine of grace, or the nature of the act of Faith – forced him occasionally to deal at length with those matters. It cannot be denied, however, that the man who has pompously been called "the Father of International Law" wasted his promising talents on too many occasions in such theological trifles as whether the demons could make an act of faith (*Secunda secundae*, q. 5, art. 2), or whether servile fear was "substantially" the same as filial fear (*Ibidem*, q. 19, art. 5). In the domain of Theology Vitoria's influence upon the Dominicans was minimal. His detachment from rational Theology contrasts vividly with the exorbitant display of speculative subtlety provoked by the disputes over the harmony of grace and free will between

Dominicans and Jesuits in the second half of the century. Vitoria's achievements in the field of Patristic and Biblical studies were also very meager both in quantity and quality. The Chair of Scripture at Salamanca – held only by three Dominicans between 1400 and 1700 – had never been and never was to become a Dominican, but rather an Augustinian stronghold (*See below*, p. 151).

Where Vitoria excelled above all his contemporaries and immediate followers was in applying the basic principles of scholastic methodology to the relevant moral and juridical problems of the day: war, colonialism, Imperial and Papal rights, consiliarism, simony, astrology, rights of rebels against tyrants, obedience to unfair laws, human sacrifices, social relations between Christians and non-Christians, suicide and violent repression of heresy. Vitoria's moral theology at its best, manages to rise from the concrete moral or legal case to the consideration of general principles of natural ethics or revealed theology. Thus, the discussion of simony provides an occasion for dealing with the more pervasive problem of the relationship between the material and the spiritual levels of the Church; the legalistic issue of the relations between the Pope and the Council ends with a theological inquiry into the universal priesthood of all Christians; the *relectio* on homicide begins with a summary of individual rights and a humanistic eulogy of man's value and nature. Occasionally, however, Vitoria gets miserably lost in a jungle of casuistics, with no traceable path or direction; the exasperating final pages of the same *relectio* on homicide dealing with suicide, or the endless qualifications of the Pope's institutional limitations *versus* the Council, are good examples of such abuse. Except for these (and similar) relapses into casuistry and legalism, Vitoria's concern with the momentous problems of his age, and the high level of his lucid discussions, paved the way for a whole generation of moral, legal, and political writers who are the special pride of Spanish Renaissance scholasticism.

Vitoria's indifference toward purely speculative matters can be construed as a mild form of scepticism of a certain Erasmian flavor. One of the most striking features of Vitoria's intellectual attitude was his constant disdain for excessive subtlety and for the abuse of philosophical jargon. Referring to some scholastic theologians of the past, Vitoria wrote: "They think that they are very sophisticated, but the truth is that they do not say anything" (*Putant se subtiliter dixisse, sed nihil dicunt*). Cajetan, especially, was one of Vitoria's most likely victims: "I do not even know whether he himself (Cajetan!) understands what he is talking about" (*Nescio an ipse intelligat omnia quae dicit*). And again: "Here

Cajetan indulges in metaphysics. I do not understand what he is trying to say. See for yourselves, if you want." (*Cajetanus hic metaphysicat. Nescio quid dicat; videte, si libet*). Or: „Here Cajetan uses many words which are unintelligible" (*Cajetanus dicit ad hoc multa verba unintelligibilia*). Like Juan Luis Vives before him, Vitoria was strongly inclined to dismiss traditionally "respectful" controversies as purely verbal disputes – *in verbis differunt tantum*, a frequently recurrent attitude in the long history of Spanish theoretical eclecticism. Whether this intellectual posture grew out of a deeply rooted fideism, from some blunt intellectual laziness, or from a combination of both, is difficult to say. Vitoria's final words on the torturing problem of predestination betray even a supercilious disrespect for the theologian's attempt at solving the puzzles of Faith: "We shall say no more on this problem, because if what we have just said is not enough, nothing that we could add would ever do it. I hope God has predestined all of us, otherwise it would have been better not to have been born." (*Et ideo haec sufficiat . . . que si esto no basta, no bastará cuanto pudiéramos decir ogaño; plega a Dios que estemos predestinados, si no mal acá nascimos*). The long (and unlawful!) use of the vernacular on this occasion, underscores the sardonic tone of the phrase.

The brighter side of Vitoria's dedication to moral theology was an optimistic humanism diametrically opposed to Luther's ideas about man's total corruption by sin. Vitoria's faith in the basic goodness of man's individual and social nature permeates all his moral and political thought; "Man is not a wolf to man, as Ovid said, but a human being" (*Non enim homini homo lupus, ut ait Ovidius, sed homo*). In this respect Vitoria leads the legal and social philosophy of Spanish Renaissance scholasticism against the pessimistic trends of late medieval thought inherited by Luther. Vitoria and his disciples joined the naturalistic, almost Pelagian direction of the Christian humanist in asserting the exclusively supernatural character of Adam's punishment and loss. The introduction to the lecture on homicide is a brilliant summary of his humanistic credo, and – as we shall see later – a significant departure from the Augustianian "confusion" of the natural and the supernatural.

All the distinguishing features of Vitoria's methodology are clearly derived from the moralizing bent of his intellectual aims. Persuasiveness takes the place of subtle reasoning; guidance substitutes for speculation, and moral wisdom rather than explanatory theory becomes the final goal. Scholastic order and perspicuity was used by Vitoria more as an educational device than as a reasoning scheme. Vitoria's total dedication to oral teaching rather than to voluminous writing was not mere accident. His lectures were a rare blend of the scholastic ideal of orderly rational sequence and the rhetorical pursuit of persuasive communication. Both ingredients are present in all of Vitoria's teaching, but while the former prevails in the ordinary lectures, the latter is more obvious in the solemn occasion of the extraordinary *relectiones*. The general scheme of Vitoria's presentation preserves the fundamental lines of the scholastic method: a clear definition of the terms involved in the dispute, a careful profile of the issue under discussion, the fair representation of the proposed solutions, the syllogistic proof of his own thesis and, finally, the rebuttal of pending objections. Vitoria had no qualms with this scholastic "order." The main reason for substituting Peter Lombard for Aquinas as the central textbook of his courses was precisely the fact that the latter *optimum servat modum scribendi*. It was to Vitoria's credit to have made a clear distinction between the abusive and often grotesque departures from this intellectual strategy on one side and the basic virtues of scholastic methodology on the other – a distinction which the banal sloganeering of at least some humanists of his age totally ignored to the general detriment of European intellecttual history. Vitoria's respect for orderly presentation did not degenerate, however, into an artificial and bookish assortment of interrelated parts. Here, also, the dialectic of oral discourse prevailed over the theoretical demands of reflective thinking and the tempting symmetry of the printed word. More than by the architectural wholeness of the *Summa Theologica*, the lectures of Vitoria are characterized by a progressive linearity strung together by a series of increasingly concrete conclusions. In spite of this general design, partial areas of the total process are at times entangled and confusing, although it is difficult to say whether this defect was the fault of the student (or students) who recorded the lectures, or a weakness of Vitoria's own style. In any case, there is no doubt that Vitoria's execution never reached the sophistication and clarity theoretically formulated by Melchor Cano in his book *Loci Theologici*. In some not unimportant instances, Vitoria's expression forced his interpreters into a painful exegetical effort aimed at preserving the consistency of the master's thought.

It has been said by Menéndez y Pelayo, with obvious exaggeration, that Vitoria succeeded in reconciling Renaissance humanism and scholastic theology into an harmonious synthesis.[18]

[18] Marcelino Menéndez y Pelayo, *Ensayos de crítica filosófica*. "Algunas consideraciones sobre Francisco de Vitoria y los orígenes del Derecho de Gentes". (Madrid, 1918), p. 236.

If such a high-flown statement is interpreted to mean that Vitoria "humanized" theology by shifting gears from specialized, technical, and jargonistic speculation into the down-to-earth task of guiding man's moral choices, we have no objection to it, provided we accept the fact that on more than one occasion the Master paid his own generous tribute to theological nonsense. If it means, however, that Vitoria's literary style was a paragon of formal beauty and classical elegance, Menéndez y Pelayo's pompous phrase needs to be carefully toned down. There is no doubt that in comparison with the barbarous jargon of the Montaigu logicians, Vitoria's Latin diction was a model of lucidity and syntactical propriety. It is also true that on some occasions Vitoria's style could rise to the fashionable Atticism of well-rounded periods and the loftiness of colorful expression. These occasions include not only the early Parisian writings – slightly pretentious as they sound – but also some of the introductions to the relectiones, such as the first pages of the lecture *De potestate civili*. However, the bulk of Vitoria's writings (as transmitted to us!) is as distant from classic Latin as the scholastic idiom of Aquinas or Cajetan – graceless, dry, gramatically incorrect at times, and full of medieval concoctions and neologisms. Phrases like *Et Magister videtur dicere quod non* or *Videtur ex Doctore quod sic*, are constantly used by Vitoria with no apparent sign of remorse. In spite of these limitations, Vitoria's lectures stand out in the scholastic traditions of all times on account of their dramatism and depth of verbal analysis. Vitoria's famous *relectiones* – all thirteen of them – make up a short volume, one fifth the size of Suárez's *Disputationes Metaphysicae*. No words are wasted in artificial introductions. The rhetorical recommendation of *in medias res* was kept by Vitoria with almost religious scrupulosity. The commentary on the *Secunda Secundae* begins as follows: "Although in all my lectures I purposedly avoid any words of introduction, I intend now to say a few words ... I do not intend to abuse your patience with a long talk. And so, without further delay, I shall begin talking on the assigned subject" (*Cum ab omni prologo et praefatione in meis studiis ex consulto abstinuerim, nunc tamen, ut veterem demum conciliem benevolentiam quam erga me sensi vos habuisse, ea licet paucissimis utar. Non enim animo duxi vos mea perlonga oratione gravare. Et ideo, rumpendo morulas omnes, ad lectionem mihi assignatam accedo.*)

Vitoria's direct concern with his audience is further revealed by the vivacity and liveliness of his delivery. To enhance the dramatization of the issues under discussion, his lectures were frequently sparked by dialogues with an imaginary adversay, a rhetorical device seldom used by scholastic authors. Finally, the extent and wealth of Vitoria's analysis of key words reveals a linguistic concern which was new in the tradition of scholastic theology. The analysis of the word "Faith" at the beginning of his commentary on Thomas' *Secunda Secundae*, (q.1, art. 1,) is a magnificent example of Vitoria's familiarity with the textual issues raised by biblical scholars of Erasmian persuasion and also by the sharp criticism of Lutheran reformers. Cicero, Saint Paul, Saint Thomas, Valla, Budé, Tertullian, Erasmus, Virgil, and Homer, are quoted by him to strengthen the traditional Catholic interpretation of the word. Without ever surrendering to the literalism of the *theologi gramatici*, Vitoria introduced into the main stream of Spanish Renaissance scholasticism a great respect for the propaedeutic value of textual criticism previously missing in scholastic circles.

D. VITORIA'S THOUGHT

Vitoria begins his lecture *De potestate civili* with the following words: "The duties of a theologian are so widespread that there is no argument no controversy, no topic, alien to his profession." This same idea reappears in his introduction to the commentary on the first part of the *Summa Theologica:* "Theology has no boundaries whatsoever, no final limit." (*Theologia tamen sacra nullum habet terminum, nullam metam*). Vitoria's understanding of Theology, involving such fundamental issues as the relation between Faith and Reason and the distinction between the Natural and the Supernatural dimensions of man, was the most original and influential feature of his thought. *Prima facie* Vitoria's words appear to be a profession of strict Augustinism, but actually their meaning is exactly the opposite. Vitoria's thought is based upon a constant and sharp distinction between the Natural and the Supernatural. When dealing with the ecclesiastical abuse of simony, he differentiated between simoniac violations in the state of natural religion and the same violations as sanctioned in the Church by divine positive Law and canonical rules. In the lecture *De potestate Ecclesiae* Vitoria rejected the Protestant idea of universal priesthood by pointing out the limitations of the analogy between the Aristotelian notion of organic unity (restricted to the natural organisms) and the hierarchical constitution of Christ's mystical body as the revealed Law of God. According to Vitoria, then, Theology comprehends both the Natural and the Supernatural, not because it ignores their differences, but rather because it emphasizes the fact that both proceed from the same First Cause through two different channels: the Natural by way of Creation, the Supernatural as a result of Redemption.

The distinction between Natural and Positive Law (either human, divine, or ecclesiastical), which is fundamental to Vitoria's legal and political theory, is only a concrete example of the more comprehensive antithesis he sees between the natural attributes which men share in common, and the specific rights and duties of those who have been incorporated into the supernatural body of the Church or are members of a concrete political community. Vitoria's claim that defining the Natural was a legitimate theological endeavor was historically induced by the American discoveries and by the threatening pressure of Asiatic culture on the eastern flank of Christian Europe. The moral, political, and legal dilemmas aroused by the confrontation of the old, narrow and inoperative structures of medieval Christianity with those of people and races whose existence had not even been suspected before, made imperative the need to seek a definition of the Natural foundations upon which mutual obligations and the rights of all men could be grounded. This explains the extraordinary fact that the most enlightened literature of the sixteenth century regarding Natural rights and International Law was indeed written by those Spanish theologians who followed Vitoria's lead and inspiration. Except for a few accidental references to revealed or ecclesiastical sources, their efforts were by contemporary standards, more philosophical than theological; and, in conflict with their own expectations, these efforts paved the way for the galloping secularization of political thought in the century to follow.

The second outstanding feature of Vitoria's thought was an extraordinary display of independent judgement, which earned him, among his contemporaries, the title of *Doctor resolutissimus*. The selection of the *Summa Theologica* for his main textbook – an accepted practice before him in several European Universities – should not be taken as an indication of servile surrender to Saint Thomas' authority. In more than one occasion Vitoria did not hesitate to profess his disagreement with an opinion of Aquinas. On the fundamental matter of Aquinas' theory of predestination Vitoria wrote: "This is the opinion of Saint Thomas, an opinion which, to tell you the truth, I have never understood." (*Ista est propositio de mente Sancti Thomae, quae tamen nunca me avia encajado hasta ahora, ut verum fatear;* [I, q. 23, a. 6]). In the lecture *De homicidio* Vitoria was even more blunt: "I totally dislike the opinion of Saint Thomas." (*Neque mihi omnino per omnia placet opinio Sancti Thomae recitata*). The same fierce independence of thought applied to Cajetan, whose authority, however, Vitoria greatly respected. Vitoria's commentaries on the *Summa* were much more than a literal hermeneutics, as was frequently the practice among his contemporaries. The *Summa* was only Vitoria's frame of reference, the organizing structure, and the accepted point of departure for an original and novel approach.

Another characteristic of Vitoria's thought was his consistent fairness and serene appraisal. His wise eclecticism was enriched by a careful and non-partisan presentation of different suggested solutions to a problem under discussion, virtues which unfortunately fell from view in the partisan polemics of his followers. As a dogmatic theologian Vitoria was not a man of novel ideas, an exhaustive or subtle thinker, or the founder of a particular school of thought. Where he excelled was in the moderation of his theological speculation, in his mature desire to ponder with equanimity the acceptable ingredients of conflicting opinions, and in elucidating the groundwork for sketching constructive and mediating solutions. Vitoria's theology of Grace was a model of such restraint, fairness, and erudition.[19]

In his explanation of God's knowledge of possible future events (*praescientia futurorum contingentium*) Vitoria adheres basically to Cajetan without the Cardinal's fiery opposition to Scotus' theory of divine decrees – a fact of no minor importance to an understanding of Bañez and other Salamanca Dominicans in the second half of the century. On the other hand, and in conflict with the opinions of Almain (his former professor at Paris) and Gabriel Biel, Vitoria insisted upon the traditional Dominican theory of God's "irresistible motion of the will," a theory which Bañez would later on tenaciously defend against the advances of the Jesuit Molina.

Vitoria's claim to fame in the history of Spanish and European thought is, however, more solidly based upon his contribution in the fields of political and legal theory. Two historical events of undeniable importance prepared the ground for radical changes in political thought: the emergence of the modern State in Europe and the discovery of the Americas. The growth of nationalist sentiment and organization, the confrontation between secular and ecclesiastical authorities, the decline of the Empire and the Papacy as unifying structures, the centralization of power under the new monarchies (especially in England, France, and Spain), were the more obvious landmarks of the new political landscape which the political thinkers of the day were

[19] See F. Stegmueller, *Francisco de Vitoria y la doctrina de la Gracia en la Escuela Salmantina*, (Barcelona, 1934).

attempting to map and to justify. The theories of royal supremacy (Hooker), absolute monarchy (L'Hopital and Machiavelli), the divine right of Kings (Barclay), and State sovereignty (Bodin), provided the convenient paradigms. The more or less medieval assumptions of many of these theoretical constructions were further shattered by an entirely new state of affairs in European political life: the emergence of powerful enclaves of religious dissent. Puritans and Catholics in England, the Huguenots in France, the Anabaptists in Germany, Jews and Moors in Spain, raised the question of religious toleration to the forefront of political discussion. The constitutional and democratic theories of Buchanan and Salamonius, Mariana's defense of the right to rebellion, the Huguenot proclamation of the "divine right of resistance"(considered by most historians as a preliminary to the more modern vision of the political body) were no doubt sparked by the debate on toleration.

The continuing discussion of the rights of religious dissenters within the State brought also a new perspective to the medieval controversy about the relations between secular and ecclesiastical powers, a problem of capital importance not only in the history of the Spanish Inquisition, but also to the development of Calvinism, Lutheranism, and Anglicanism.

The dicovery of new continents, primitive societies, and exotic rituals, raised fundamental questions about the value of civilization itself, the absolute validity of Christianity, and the limitations of political power. For Spain the conquest of the Americas, carried out as a deliberate and self-conscious extension of the Crown's sovereign power, produced an imposing administrative and legal structure without parallel in the history of any Empire. Soon the profound moral and religious issues arising out of the conquest began to attract the attention of Spanish theologians. It was Vitoria's historical vocation to raise the claim that the problems of the conquest ought to be brought to the Tribunal of the theologians and the priests: "Being a moral problem, its solution belongs formally to the priests" (*Cum agatur de foro conscientiae, hoc spectat ad sacerdotes*).

Vitoria's response to the problems of the conquest and Spanish policy in Europe was over time incorporated into a complete body of legal and political theory to which we will now dedicate our attention. Vitoria's political and legal thought can be divided into three parts: the individual and the State, the State and the Church, and relations between sovereign States.

1. The Individual and the State

Vitoria's conception of the State is the cornerstone of his political theory, and as such it has been the object of serious and extensive studies.[20]

In its essential features Vitoria's political theory coincides basically with the Aristotelian-Thomistic synthesis. For him the State is neither an artificial human convention nor the necessary product of human evolution or divine ordination, but rather a unique combination of Nature and man's free initiative. Nature dictates the needs of social life in a communal organism, but man's reflection and will create by mutual consent the concrete social organization of each political body. According to this scheme the State must have certain fundamental and necessary features derived from its very nature (Natural Law), but also some accidental determinations (Positive Law) resulting from historical contingencies and free human choices. The essential characteristics of the State are dictated by its final purpose and the means which are indispensable to its fulfillment. The goal of the State is to satisfy the needs of man which neither isolated individuals nor domestic or tribal societies can satisfy.

Vitoria draws freely from Aristotle's *Ethics* and *Politics* to prove the natural sociability of man: the need for mutual aid and fellowship, the perfection of the understanding through shared experience and instruction, the full use of the human privilege of speech, and the crowning of the will with the virtues of justice and charity. More emphatically than Aristotle himself he reiterates his conviction that in solitude man could perhaps satisfy his basic needs to survive, but could never reach the perfection and happiness he is capable of: "And even if it were agreed that human life was sufficient unto itself, nevertheless, it could not fail to be bitter and unpleasant when passed in solitude." (*Et si*

[20] Brown Scott, *The Spanish Origin of International Law*; J. T. Delos, *La société internationale et les principes du droit public*, (Paris, 1929); H. Beuve-Mery, *La théorie des pouvoirs publics d'après François de Vitoria et ses rapports avec le Droit contemporain*, (Paris, 1928); D. L. Recasens Siches, *Las teorías políticas de Francisco de Vitoria*, Anuario de la Asociación Francisco de Vitoria, vol. II, pp. 165–222, (Madrid, 1931); H. F. Wright, *Vitoria and the State*, (Washington, 1932); Emilio Naszalyi, *El Estado según Francisco de Vitoria*, (Madrid, 1948); Alois Dempf, *Christliche Staatsphilosophie in Spanien*, Chapters 1 and 2, (Salzburg, 1937); Eustaquio Galán, "La teoría del poder público según Francisco de Vitoria," *Revista general de Legislación y Jurisprudencia*, (Madrid), July–August, 1944; Bernice Hamilton, *Political Thought in XVIth Century Spain*, (Oxford, 1963); Roger Labrousse, *Essai sur la philosophie politique de l'ancienne Spagne*, (Paris, 1938); Salvador Lisarraga, "Un texto de Francisco de Vitoria, sobre la potestad política," *Revista de Estudios Políticos*, (Madrid), April, 1941; Juan Antonio Maravall, *Carlos V y el pensamiento político del Renacimiento*, (Madrid, 1960); Pierre Mesnard, *L'essor de la philosophie politique au XVIe siècle*, (Paris, 1936), pp. 454–472.

constaret humana vita et sibi sufficeret, tamen in solitudine non nisi iniocumda et inamabilis esset. De pot. civ. 4). Vitoria tries very hard to prove the qualitative discontinuity between domestic and civil societies. His main contention is that the end and the means of both societies are specifically different, since the needs which the body politic aims at fulfilling are qualitatively superior to and different from the needs which the family naturally attempts to satisfy.

Therefore since human societies have been established for this purpose – namely, that we should bear one another's burdens – and since civil society is of all societies that *which best provides for the needs of men*, it follows that the community is, so to speak, an exceedingly natural form of communication, that is, a form thoroughly in accord with Nature. For even though the various members be of mutual assistance, nevertheless a single family is not self-sufficient least of all for the resistance of violence and injury.[21]

The thrust of Vitoria's argument was not directed toward the refutation of an evolutionary theory of the genesis of civil society (a typically nineteenth century view) but rather to emphasize the radical difference between paternal and civil authority. In the case of the father, the authority resides in a concrete individual on the basis of a biological fact which is not the result of free consent or choice, but (especially in the case of Adam, the first father) a providential event ultimately referring back to God Himself. Vitoria's opposition to a paternalistic theory of civil authority represents a typical Castilian reaction against the absolutist tendencies of the French and English patrons of the Divine Right of Kings (Barclay, Pierre de Belloy, etc ...). Furthermore, by insisting upon the natural character of the State without any reference to Adam's fall, or Christ's redemptive work, Vitoria was able to proclaim the fundamental homogeneity of the Christian and the non-Christian States, a cornerstone of his Law of Nations.

The nature of the State is specified exclusively by its final purpose, which cannot be other than the satisfaction of the needs, which make it a natural and necessary institution. The origin, the purpose, and the nature of the State are in this purely Aristotelian framework three different aspects of one and the same reality. Nevertheless, Vitoria discusses in more detail the *causa finalis* of the State because it was at this

[21] "Cum itaque humanae societates propter hunc finem constitutae sint, scilicet, ut alter alterius onera portaret, et inter omnes societates societas civilis ea sit in qua commodius homines necessitatibus subveniant, sequitur, communitatem esse (ut ita dixerim) naturalissimam communicationem naturae convientissimam. Quanquam enim mutua officia sibi praestent, non tamen familia una sufficiens est sibi, et maxime adversus vim injuriamque propulsandam." (Luis G. Alonso Getino, *Relecciones Teológicas del Maestro Fray Francisco de Vitoria*, tomo II, Madrid: 1934, pp. 178–179.)

juncture that he decided to engage two doctrines of noble pedigree which he nevertheless considered highly fallacious. The first was the political moralism of Plato. Plato maintained that the State was primarily an educational institution aimed at the ethical training of its citizens. This error was made fashionable again in the sixteenth century by Humanists of Erasmian inspiration, including Juan Luis Vives. The second error Vitoria wanted to impugn was the medieval confusion between the earthly destiny of the State and the eternal vocation of man, a confusion of Augustinian origin which had complicated for centuries the relations between civilian and ecclesiastical authorities and was being reiterated at that time by Lutheran Princes and Calvinist magistrates. In spite of some hesitations in his commentaries to the *Summa Theologica*, (*See for instance* I, II, 92, 1: "Every human law aims at making man virtuous") Vitoria constantly emphasized the mundane and pragmatic character of the State's ultimate goal, an end which he described as "peaceful coexistence among men," "human peace and order," "civil partnership," "order," "public utility" (*utilitas*), "welfare" (*commoditas*), and "the government of the temporal city." From this clear definition of the aims of the State Vitoria derived his doctrine of the proper relationship between Church and State, a subject we shall consider later (*See below*, pp. 85ss.) more in detail. This earthly and natural end of the State is also described as "the common good of the community." This common good transcends the private good of each citizen just as the good of the body transcends the good of each member of the body. On the other hand, the common good is immanent to each individual in the sense that it responds to its needs. For this reason the State can ask an individual citizen to risk his life in the defense of the common good (for example, in the case of a "just war") and is entitled to enforce the sale of private property against the will of the individual owner for the benefit of the community. The common, good, as the *entelechia* of an organism, is *not* the sum total of the individual goods of its members, but superior to it. Vitoria asserts the same organic conception of the State by bluntly proclaiming that "man belongs to the republic more than to himself." (II, II, art. 104. q. 6).

As a natural institution the State must be endowed with the necessary means to achieve its essential purpose. This Stoic-Christian-optimistic persuasion adequately correlating natural ends and natural means was the foundation of the medieval notion of "sufficientia" which Vitoria assumed as the cornerstone of his own political thought. The republic – he writes – is a "perfect community" (*perfecta communitas*), a "totality" (*per se totum*), "entirely self-sufficient" (*sibi sufficiens*). In his lecture *De Indis* Vitoria suggests that the requirements of political autarchy belong entirely to the natural order and can therefore be found among the American natives. These include certain specifications concerning adequate economic resources, size of population and territory, language, traditions, etc. However, the primary and necessary condition of political self-sufficiency was the existence of a public power capable of enacting and executing laws directed to the common good of the body politic. Public power (*potestas civilis*) is more than physical power alone. It includes the idea of a "legitimate, authoritative, and permanent right to rule the community." Public power is so essentially connected with the political body that, according to Vitoria, "not even by the consent of the whole world can it be destroyed or annulled." (*De pot. civ.* 1).

Since public authority is a necessary condition of political life proceeding from man's very nature, the "efficient cause" of public authority must be the author of nature, God himself. Vitoria subscribes without hesitation to this fundamental position of all Christian thinkers, and with them he makes the routine recommendations of willing obedience to the equitable laws of a legitimate Prince. The second half of the lecture *De potestate civili* is a casuistic treatment of the moral problems which had as their origin marginal cases of obedience or rebellion to unfair laws, to illegitimate princes or tyrants, etc.

Much more complicated and debatable was the question about the "material" cause of public authority. Vitoria clearly rejected the opinion of those who maintained that God immediately confers authority to the ruler designated by the community. The basic difference between the body politic and the Church resides primarily in the fact that in the former power is *inalienably* conferred upon the multitude itself, while in the Church individual members have only the right to choose the recipient of power and jurisdiction. The material cause or subject of political power is, then, according to Vitoria, the people themselves, the community of citizens. The people in fact hold this power and cannot transfer it to the ruler. On the other hand, the people cannot exercise such power by themselves. Although they cannot "transfer" it they must delegate its authorized exercise to the ruler or rulers they freely choose. Vitoria's statement that the power of the ruler and the power of the Republic are one and the same must therefore be understood in the sense that the people have the power and the ruler its legitimate use. The contract or agreement among the people is exclusively the normative specification of public authority, never – as later contractual theories would assert – its constitutive principle. These are the words of Vitoria on this important matter:

The State, then, possesses this power by divine disposition; but the material cause in which, by Divine and Natural Law, power of this kind resides, is the State itself, which by its very nature is competent to govern and administer itself, and to order all its powers for the common good. The proof of this fact is as follows: since by Natural and Divine Law there must be a power for the government of the State, and since – if common, positive and human Law are laid aside – there is no reason for depositing that power in one person rather than in another; it necessarily follows that the community is self-sufficient and that it has the power to govern itself.[22]

The problem with this theory is that it seems to imply a chronological sequence which is difficult to visualize, an interval of time in which people are already the members of a political body as the material cause or subjects of civil authority without having yet authorized any ruler to exercise such power. Such a situation is not a figment of the imagination surrounded by the halo of prehistorical reveries, but a frequent event in the case of a popular revolt against a tyrannical ruler. Vitoria seems to think that a multitude assembled with the common intention of organizing themselves into a concrete form of government is in fact a political body even before the designation of the ruler (or body of rulers!) and the choice of a particular set of governing relationships. This seems to imply, furthermore, that according to him it was possible for an indefinite length of time to have a State wherein the legitimate use of public power was not yet authorized. One would have to accept the amazing conclusion that people attempting to agree upon an organization they want to impose upon themselves would be already members of the very society they are trying to create.

Although Vitoria's political thought on this particular point leaves much room for improvement, the fundamental principles remain clear: the ruler administers the power which the people hold in their possession. The choice of both the ruler and the concrete political organization – whether it be democratic, aristocratic, or monarchic rule – is to

[22] "Constitutione ergo Divina, Respublica hanc potestatem habet; causa vero materialis, in qua hujusmodi potestas residet Jure Naturali et Divino, est ipsa Respublica, cui de se competit gubernare seipsam, et administrare, et omnes potestates suas in commune bonum dirigere. Quod sic probatur: Nam cum de Jure Naturali et Divino sit aliqua potestas illa sit in uno, quam in altero, necesse est, ut ipsa communitas sit sibi sufficiens, et habeat potestatem gubernandi se." (*Ibid.*, pp. 181–182.)

be made by the majority of the people. That the majority has a natural right to impose its will upon the dissenting minority was assumed by Vitoria without further discussion as a self-evident truth. The majority can authorize a ruler in two different ways: under certain conditions previously agreed upon, or unconditionally. Vitoria's "horror of absolutism" (Parry) – a common trait of all Spanish political thinkers of the sixteenth century – becomes evident in his insistence on the limitations imposed by Nature upon any designation of authority, even the unconditional one. The ruler has no dominion over the *res publica* – and cannot under any circumstances abrogate the reason for his own existence – the common good. The ruler, therefore, is only a "minister" of the people and remains, even as a ruler, a member of the community, subject to the laws of the State exactly in the same manner as the people are subject to the laws they have enacted through public plebiscite:

It is more probable that kings and legislators are bound by the laws. The proof of this is, first: that a legislator of this sort injures the State and the other citizens if, being himself a member of the State, he does not bear a part of the burden – in a manner that accords, to be sure, with the person, his quality, and his rank. But since this obligation is indirect, we shall offer another proof. The laws which are made by kings have the same force – a fact we have already expounded – as if they were made by the whole State; but the laws made by the State are binding upon all; therefore, even those laws which are made by the King, are binding upon the King himself. This argument is confirmed as follows: Under an aristocratic form of government, the decrees of the Senate are binding upon the very senators who issued them; under a popular government the plebiscite is binding upon the whole people; and therefore laws made by the King are in like manner binding upon the King himself. Moreover, although the act of creating the law be voluntary on the part of the King; nevertheless, the fact that he is thereby bound or not bound, does not depend upon his own will: just as in the case of pacts; for he who enters a pact of his own free will, is nevertheless bound thereby.[23]

[23] "Quaeritur tandem: *An leges civiles obligent Legislatores, et maxime Reges.* Videtur enim aliquibus quod non, cum sint supra totam Rempublicam, et nullus possit obligari, nisi a superiore; sed certius, et probabilius est, quod obligentur. Quod probatur primo: Quia hujusmodi Legislator facit injuriam Reipublicae, et reliquis civibus, si cum ipse sit pars Reipublicae, non habeat partem oneris, juxta personam tamen suam et qualitatem, et dignitatem.

Sed ista obligatio est indirecta. Ideo aliter probatur. Nam eandem vim habent latae leges a Rege, ac si ferrentur a tota Republica, ut supra declaratum est. Sed leges latae a Republica obligant omnes; ergo etiam si ferantur a Rege, obligant ipsum Regem.

Et confirmatur: Quia in Aristocratico Principatu senatusconsulta obligant ipsos Senatores, authores illorum, et in populari regimine plebiscita obligant ipsum populum; ergo similiter leges regiae obligant ipsum Regem; et licet sit voluntarium Regi condere legem, tamen non est in voluntate sua non obligari, aut obligari. Sicut in pactis. Libere enim quisquis paciscitur, pactis tamen tenetur." (*Ibid.*, p. 206.)

One section of Vitoria's *De potestate civili* (6 to 9) has been occasionally misrepresented as a profession of anti-democratic absolutism.[24] Vitoria's careless expression is partly responsible for such interpretation. After having stated that the material cause of public power is the community itself, Vitoria proceeds to discuss kingly power, and to defend it against those who assert that "all kings, rulers, and princes are tyrants and plunderers of our liberty," and who reject any form of domination and power "with the sole exception of democratic power." Against these extreme defenders of democratic rule Vitoria declares:

Not only is monarchy, or royal power, just and legitimate; but, in addition to this, the power of kings is derived from divine and natural law, not from the State itself, nor directly from men (*et non ab ipsa republica, aut prorsus ab hominibus*).[25]

In spite of the faulty expression, the meaning of the author is clear enough: all public power comes from God as the efficient cause of all authority. Since "this power cannot be exercised by the multitude, it is, therefore, necessary that the administration of the State be entrusted to some person, and it matters not whether this power is entrusted to one or to many." (*et nihil refert, uni an pluribus commendetur*). To "entrust" power to the King is not to create power. In this sense Vitoria can safely emphasize that kingly power is not derived "directly from men." What is misleading in this expression is that its negative aspect – "not derived from men" – applies not only to kingly power but precisely to *all* forms of political power. Such power, be it monarchical, aristocratic, or democratic, is not derived from an agreement among individual citizens, "like that which the members of a religious order confer upon their abbot." On the contrary, public power is derived only from God and "entrusted" to one or many rulers by the choice of the majority of the people.

Such are the general contours of the political theory of Francisco de Vitoria. Basically he offered a solid profession of Jus Naturalism, universally applicable, steering a course between the past confusions of medieval Augustinism and the crude positivism of Machiavelli and his disciples. Furthermore, his political philosophy was a bold and excep-

[24] See, for instance, Salvador Lisarraga in his article "Un texto de Vitoria." Lisarraga is persuasively refuted by Eustaquio Galán in his article "La teoría del poder político según Vitoria." (*See* note 20).

[25] "... Monarchiam, sive regiam potestatem non solum justam esse, et legitimam, sed dico Reges etiam a jure divino et naturali habere potestatem, et non ab ipsa Republica, aut prorsus ab hominibus." (*Relecciones Teológicas*, pp. 184–185.)

tional profession of faith in the inalienable power of the people to govern themselves against the growing threat of abolutist rulers and theoreticians. Finally, he was a passionate advocate of constitutional and representative government by majoritarian rule, typically Spanish in pedigree, and extremely modern in sound and style.

2. *The Church and the State*

Vitoria's theory of the State as a secular and organic body is closely related to his liberal views on Church-State relations. The solution to this artificially complex problem is based upon a far-reaching premise: the final purpose and the means of both societies belong to two entirely different human dimensions. The political body aims by natural means at the earthly and temporal happiness of its members. The Church uses supernatural means to lead man to his eternal and heavenly reward. As self-sufficient bodies (*societates perfectae*) both societies are adequately endowed with all the means required to reach their respective ends. The difference in purpose and the availability of commensurate means explains the mutual independence of both societies. The State has no spiritual power of any kind, and the Church lacks purely temporal power. National churches headed by temporal Kings are as absurd as the Pope's claim to administer civil authority beyond the boundaries of the Papal territories.

To clarify the distinction between both societies, Vitoria proclaimed that the existence of civil society – unlike the Church – was totally unrelated to the "historical" fact of Adam's fall. The need for a directing and supervisory organic structure overlaying man's communal life is an ingredient of his own nature, rather than a consequence of man's exile from paradise. In the hypothetical case of a human nature neither raised to the supernatural order nor fallen from it by a parental sin, man would still have had the same natural exigency for a civil society without the supernatural complement of a Church. Obviously, in such a case the coercive power of the State might have been qualitatively different from the one we know in our historical condition.

If civil society is a natural fact, independent of man's fall and salvation, it follows with stringent consistency that neither the right of private property nor the right to erect a sovereign civil society are dependent upon man's spiritual condition. Against John Wycliffe and the Waldensians Vitoria vigorously rejected the opinion that "those in mortal sin have no dominion over anything" (*De Indis*, I; also *In 2, II*,

62, 1); an amazing conclusion previously condemned by the Council of Constance and tenaciously upheld by such medieval moralists as Richard Fitz-Ralph, and Richard of Mediaville. The doctrine of Constance applies equally to the pagans: "It is manifestly indefensible to take the possessions of either Sarazens, Jews, or other unbelievers, just because they are unbelievers; to do so would be theft or robbery exactly as if it were done to Christians." (*De Indis*, 7) Vitoria's reasoning in this matter is a clear profession of the natural origin of private ownership and civil dominion: "Man is entitled to ownership because he is an image of God; man, however, is an image of God because of his rational nature, which mortal sin does not destroy; therefore, the right of ownership is not destroyed by mortal sin." (*De Indis*, 6) Only in the case of heresy does Vitoria's thinking become hesitant, erratic, and casuistic – a heavy tribute to the religious crisis of his day.

Having established the exclusively temporal character of civil society, Vitoria proceeds to explain the purely spiritual dimension of Papal authority. The rejection of the Pope's direct temporal power was a traditional Thomistic teaching which Cajetan had abundantly elaborated in his massive commentaries. The historical context, however, in which Vitoria again proclaimed the old doctrine conferred upon it a novel poignancy. In 1493 a Spanish Pope, Alexander VI, had granted to the Spanish Crown the so-called "Bulls of Demarcation" which confirmed Spanish sovereignty over discoveries already made and the right to make new discoveries within a given zone of influence. Although this unequivocal grant was considered invalid by some Spanish and by most foreign jurists, and was soon superseded by the Treaty of Tordesillas to which the Pope was no party, the very fact that a Pope would dare to claim such a right had put severe pressure on Catholic theologians and canonists.

The issue was passionately debated at the Juntas de Burgos, called by Ferdinand of Aragón in 1512 to investigate the alleged abuses of the Conquistadores made known in the metropolis by two dominican friars, Fray Pedro de Córdoba and Fray Antonio de Montesinos. The practical outcome of that assembly was the so-called "Laws of Burgos" which forbade personal servitude, restricted the amount of labor to be exacted from the Indians by the encomenderos, but unfortunately, legalized the system of the *encomienda*. The historical significance of Burgos was enormous: for the first time in a public document the very right of the Spanish Crown to the lands and the possessions of the American Indians became a matter of national dispute. To settle this important question the King asked a jurist and a theologian to write down their respective opinions (*pareceres*) on the subject. The treatise of the Jurist Palacios Rubios, *De Insulis Oceanis*, has been lost; the work of the theologian Matías de Paz, a dominican, has been partially printed under the title *De dominio regum Hispaniae super Indos*, and deserves our attention for awhile.[26]

Paz attempted to justify the Spanish enterprise in America on the basis of the Papal grant which abrogated the "natural rights" of the Indians. The conclusion reached stemmed from two premises which Vitoria would reject twenty years later: first, that non-believers are endowed with political rights (*dominium praelationis*) only inasmuch as the Church allows them (*nisi quantum Ecclesia permittit*); second, that the Pope, as the Vicar of Christ the King, has temporal jurisdiction over the entire earth. Paz' constant demand for a humanitarian policy toward the American Indians does not diminish in the least his mistaken endorsement of the basic injustices inherent in the colonial undertaking. To add insult to injury, Paz attributed the same doctrine to Saint Thomas, entirely forgetting the contrary opinion of his own brother in the Dominican Order, Juan de Torquemada, whose thought was clearly formulated in his treatise *Summa de Ecclesia* in the following words: "The Pope does not have temporal power on account of his spiritual jurisdiction, and should not be called 'Lord of the Earth,' " (*Papa non sic dicendus est habere iurisdictionem in temporalibus iure papatus, ut dicendus sit totius orbis dominus*). Furthermore, Paz reinstated the old-fashioned Caesaropapism of Henricus from Segusia, Cardinal of Ostia in the thirteenth century.

Paz' "solution" was slightly moderated by Gregorio López, the official spokesman for the Spanish Crown during the transitional years between the "Laws of Burgos" and the teaching of Vitoria at Salamanca. According to López the intervention of the Spanish armed forces in America was justified only to protect the Catholic missions and to prevent the killing of innocent victims in certain ritual sacrifices among the Indians. López, however, denied the Ostiensian doctrine of universal Papal jurisdiction in temporal matters. His explanation was an attempt to build a secular justification for Spanish imperialism, an approach similar to that of Vitoria's professor at Paris, John Mair. López and Mair's theories were based not upon the

[26] See Beltrán de Heredia, "El Padre Matías de Paz, O. P., y su tratado *De dominio regum Hispaniae super Indos*," *Ciencia Tomista*, XL (1929), pp. 173–190. See also J. H. Parry, *The Spanish Theory of Empire in the Sixteenth Century*, (Cambridge, 1940), pp. 11–21.

Pope's direct temporal jurisdiction, but more indirectly upon the temporal consequences of his spiritual powers, and upon consideration of the natural relations among States, two aspects of Vitoria's teaching we shall investigate later. The names of López and Mair deserve to be mentioned here because Vitoria's juridical system owes to them a great deal of its inspiration. In his denial to the Pope of any temporal jurisdiction Vitoria was more consistent than any of his predecessors. One of the reasons why Vitoria's *De potestate Ecclesiae* was included in Sixtus V's *Index* was the doctrine that the Pope was not entitled to mediate in civil lawsuits, to depose or to appoint civil magistrates, to ratify or to invalidate civil laws.

According to López and Mair the spiritual power of the Pope entails serious consequences in the temporal realm which need to be taken into consideration. Although the Church and the State are mutually independent and self-sufficient societies, their inter-action is necessitated by the fact that their memberships coincide at least partially. Some human actions are clearly and exclusively directed to a temporal goal, some to a spiritual end, others, however, partake of both in some inseparable manner. Following the inspiration of López and Mair, Vitoria saw clearly that the two first categories were easy to ascribe to their proper domain: the Church has nothing to do with temporal action, the State is indifferent to the spiritual behavior of man. A problem arises with the third type of behavior. The problem here, which Vitoria did not fully recognize, was to define in theory and circumscribe in practice the character and range of those "mixed actions" (*actiones mixtae*). Many historical invasions of one jurisdiction into the domain of the other were based on exorbitant claims about the impact of civil legislation upon "conscience rights," or conversely. Vitoria attempted to clarify this problem, first, by coming forth with some basic theoretical guidelines; and secondly, by dealing directly with the most pressing cases of his time.

The relations between Church and State are, first of all, unlike the relations between two sovereign States, e.g., France and England. Nor can it be doubted that the end and the means of the Church are far superior to those of the political body. As a theologian Vitoria was most concerned about those civil laws which could serve the temporal aims of the State, but at the same time, could endanger the spiritual welfare of its citizens. In case of such conflict Vitoria did not hesitate to proclaim that the temporal order should yield to the supernatural power, and that, if needed, the Church might in some exceptional occasions (*casu*) intervene in the civil domain to secure the spiritual salvation of its members. Only in this restricted sense can we interpret some of the most ultramontane expressions of Vitoria: "The Church has some temporal jurisdiction and authority over the whole earth." (*De potestate Ecclesiae*, 1)[27]

In spite of these and similar protestations – which ironically enough did not save the document from Papal wrath – Vitoria was extraordinarily anxious to edge his thought with well-pondered limitations. The final result was a theory practically equivalent to Cardinal Bellarmin's famous doctrine of the Church's "indirect power" (*potestas indirecta*) over the State, although without the felicitous accuracy of the Jesuit Cardinal's writings. Civil authority is not subject to the Pope in the same way as the Bishops or the Parish Priests are dependent upon him, nor even in the manner Christian Kings are subordinate to the Emperor. If a Christian Prince promulgates a law which is harmful to the spiritual welfare of his Christian subjects, the Pope cannot immediately invalidate such a law, but has the authority to order the King to invalidate it. Only in that case when the secular ruler refuses to do so, can the Pope act on his own authority. Similarly, if a Christian society should choose a pagan ruler who is intent upon destroying the faith of his subjects, the Pope is authorized to depose him with or without the consent of the citizens. In the case of a war between States resulting in obvious detriment to the spiritual well-being of the people, the Pope can declare such war unlawful, and, as an extreme measure, he is authorized to judge the issue and pronounce sentence among the contenders. In no case, however, may the Pope pass judgement on a purely temporal matter, and if the Pope dares to do precisely that, then "nobody is obliged to listen to him"

Although Vitoria deals in great detail with those actions of the civilian ruler which might fall under the spiritual jurisdiction of the Pope on the basis of their spiritual consequences, he is much less explicit in his explanation of the rights and limitations of civil authorities toward Church policies which clearly infringe upon the temporal power of the State. Still, he discusses at length three concrete issues of no minor historical significance: the privilege of clerical exemption, the relations between colonialism and evangelization, and, finally, the secular executive power of the Inquisition.

The exemption of the clergy from the judicial power of the State is

[27] See Joseph Biederlack, "Das Verhaeltnis von Kirche und Staat by Franz von Vitoria, O. P." *Zeitschrift fuer Katholische Theologie*, Innsbruck, LI (1927), pp. 548–555.

discussed in the lecture *De potestate Ecclesiae* (question 7). In the Council of Constance the Church had stated, in opposition to Wycliffe that members of the clergy could not rightfully be brought to a civil or criminal court of the State. Vitoria accepted without discussing this dogmatic statement, but attempted to specify the character of the exemption. He said that the clergy is exempt from secular courts in purely ecclesiastical matters and that this is a divine right implied by the supernatural and self-sufficient character of the Church itself. It is also clear that the clergy is not entirely exempt from all secular authority because as members of a republic they are subject to its laws. However, inasfar as the proper administration of the Church makes it necessary or even convenient, the Pope is authorized to exempt the members of the clergy from their subordination to secular rulers, provided that the republic is not thereby seriously threatened. The entire discussion has a strong medieval character. Not even for one moment did Vitoria take into account the possibility of a multidenominational society, in spite of the sweeping advances of Lutheranism in central Europe, and the pressing character of the religious tolerance issue.

Regarding the political consequences of the missionary work in the Americas, Vitoria was not much more enlightened. Although he emphatically denied the right of the Pope to grant any discovered land to any Prince he was more than generous in making special allowances to the Spanish Crown for the sake of protecting the purely religious tasks of the colonial Church. In this respect the Spanish professor proved himself unduly dependent upon the teachings of his Parisian professor John Mair and totally oblivious to the requirements of egalitarian internationalism he had championed on other occasions. Mair had taught that if the American Indians resisted peaceful missionaries by force of arms, the Spaniards would be justified in deposing the native rules and in seizing power themselves. Caught between his own national pride and the demands of his Christian conscience, Vitoria attempted both to justify the particularly Spanish right to protect the Gospel in America and to foreclose all possible abuses of such a right. The final result was a baffling concoction of noble thoughts and chauvinistic claims which bespeaks with touching eloquence the enormous spiritual confusion of his age. Vitoria agreed with Mair that the Pope should be granted a regulatory authority by virtue of which a single Prince might be commissioned with the task of protecting the work of the missionaries by armed intervention, if necessary. Such authority was not based upon any alleged temporal jurisdiction of the Pope, but only upon his spiritual power which in some extraordinary cases could "ordain temporal matters for the sake of spiritual aims." Unless a particular nation be chosen by the Pope to perform this special task, the ensuing strife could prove disastrous to the missionary work itself.

Although this (the preaching of the Gospel) is a common task permitted to all, yet the Pope might entrust it to the Spaniards and forbid it to all others. The proof is in the fact that, although the Pope is not the temporal Lord, yet he has power in matters temporal when this would subserve spiritual matters. Therefore, as it is the Pope's concern to bestow special care on the propagation of the Gospel over the whole world, he can entrust it to the Spaniards *to the exclusion of all others*, if the sovereigns of Spain could render more effective help in the spread of the Gospel in those parts; and not only could the Pope forbid others to preach, but *also to trade there* if this would further the propagation of Christianity; for he can order temporal matters in the manner which is most helpful to spiritual matters... But it seems that in this case this is the course most conducive to spiritual welfare, because if there was to be an indiscriminate inrush of Christians from other parts to the part in question, they might easily hinder one another and develop quarrels to the banishment of tranquility and the disturbance of the concerns of the Faith and of the conversion of the natives.[28]

Vitoria was not naive enough to ignore the fact that the spiritual monopoly of patronizing the missions was closely linked to the possibility of considerable material profit. Thus, in attempting to justify the fact that the sovereigns of Spain had actually been chosen by the Pope to perform this task, he enumerated a series of reasons wherein spiritual and material considerations became strangely intermingled: the Kings of Spain were better able to render effective help to the missionaries than any other European Princes; the Spaniards had been "the first to patronize and pay for the navigation of the intermediate ocean"; finally, because the Spaniards "had the good fortune to discover the

[28] "Secunda conclusio: Licet hoc sit commune et liceat omnibus, tamen Papa potuit hoc negotium mandare Hispanis et interdicere omnibus aliis. Probatur, quia, licet (ut supra dictum est) Papa non sit dominus temporalis, tamen habet potestatem in temporalibus in ordine ad spiritualia. Ergo, cum spectet ad Papam specialiter curare promotionem Evangelii in totum orbem, si ad praedicationem Evangelii in illis provinciis commodius possent principes Hispani dare operam potest eis committere et interdicere omnibus aliis, et non solum interdicere praedicationem, set etiam commercium, si hoc ita expediret ad religionis Christianae propagationem, quia potest ordinaire temporalia, sicut expedit spiritualibus. Si ergo hoc ita expedit, ergo spectat ad auctoritatem et potestatem summi Pontificis. Sed omnino videtur ita expedire eo, quod, si indiscriminatim ex aliis provinciis Christianorum concurrent ad illas provincias, possent se invicem facile impedire et excitare seditiones; unde et tranquillitas impediretur et turbaretur negotium fidei et conversio barbarorum ..." (Franciscus de Victoria, *De Indis et de Ivre Belli Relectiones*, English translation by John Pawley Bate, edited by Ernest Nys in *The Classics of International Law*, (Washington, 1917) pp. 262–263.) (Hereafter quoted as *Bate Translation.*)

new world ... they should therefore *alone* enjoy the fruits of their discovery."

In more detail than Mair had attempted, Vitoria hastened to specify under which conditions armed intervention could be justified, and the legitimate limitations on the same. The simple and peaceful refusal of the Indians to accept the Faith preached to them was not a lawful title for occupying their lands. In fact, their very refusal to accept Christianity without proof of miracle was not even sinful; nor when instead of miracles, or signs, or exemplary patterns of life, the preaching of the Gospel in the Americas had been tainted "by many scandals and cruel crimes and acts of impiety."

> Before the barbarians heard anything about Christianity they did not commit the sin of unbelief by not believing in Christ. ... The proof of it is as follows: Such as have never heard anything, however much they may be sinners in other respects, are under an invincible ignorance, therefore their ignorance is not sin.
>
> The Indians in question are not bound to believe the Christian faith announced to them, in such a way that they commit mortal sin by not believing it, merely because it has been declared and announced to them that Christianity is the true religion and that Christ is the Savior and Redeemer of the world, without miracle or any other proof or persuasion. ... From this proposition it follows that, if the faith be presented to the Indians in the way named, and they do not receive it, the Spaniards cannot make this a reason for waging war on them or for proceeding against them under the law of war.[29]

Vitoria then proceeds to emphasize that the Indians would not be excused from mortal sin if they refused to enter into consultation and listen to the missionaries in religious matters. Furthermore, if the Christian faith be put before the aborigines "with demonstrable and reasonable arguments, and this be accompanied by an upright life, well ordered to the law of nature, and this be done not once and perfunctorily, but diligently and zealously," the Indians would be bound to accept the faith of Christ under penalty of mortal sin. However, Vitoria adds with solemnity:

[29] "Secunda propositio: Barbari non ad primum nuntium fidei Christianae tenentur credere, ita quod peccent mortaliter non credentes solum per hoc, quod simpliciter annuntiatur eis et proponitur quod vera religio est Christiana et quod Christus est Salvator et Redemptor mundi, sine miraculis aut quacumque alia probatione aut suasione ...

Ex qua propositione sequitur quod, si solum illo modo proponatur fides barbaris et non recipiant, non hac ratione possunt Hispani inferre illis bellum neque iure belli contra eos agere." (*Bate Translation*, p. 248 and p. 249.)

It is not sufficiently clear to me that the Christian Faith has yet been so put before the aborigines and announced to them that they are bound to believe it or commit fresh sin . . . Now I hear of no miracles or signs or religious patterns of life; nay, on the other hand, I hear of many scandals and cruel crimes and acts of impiety. . . .[30]

In any case, he concluded that even if the Indians refused to accept the Faith, the Spaniards would not be entitled to make war on them and deprive them of their property. And in general, "Christian Princes cannot, even by the authorization of the Pope, restrain the Indians from sins against the law of nature or punish them because of their sin," not even to prevent the most flagrant violations of natural law such as incest and bestiality. The example of Israel should not be misinterpreted:

Even in the Old Testament, where much was done by force of arms, the people of Israel never seized the lands of unbelievers, either because they were unbelievers or idolaters or because they were guilty of other sins against nature (and there were people guilty of such sins, in that they were idolaters and committed many sins against nature such as sacrificing their sons and daughters to devils), but because of either a special gift from God or because their enemies had hindered their passage or attacked them.[31]

The use of force, then, was exclusively restricted to cases where the rights of Christian missionaries to peacefully preach the Gospel (*See below*, p. 120) were violently impaired by the natives. Under those circumstances, any Christian Prince could resort to war "until he succeeded in obtaining facilities and safety for preaching the Gospel." War could also be lawful against those natives who tolerate the peaceful preaching of the Gospel, "but make conversion extremely difficult with their threats or simply proceed to kill the converted Christians." Having said so much, however, Vitoria was very anxious to emphasize that this extreme right might in practice prove totally self-defeating to the very purpose it was intended to serve – spreading the Gospel. If that

[30] "Quinta conclusio: Non satis liquet mihi an fides Christiana fuerit barbaris hactenus ita proposita et annuntiata, ut teneantur credere sub novo peccato. Hoc dico, quia (ut patet ex secunda propositione) non tenentur credere, nisi proponatur eis fides cum probabili persuasione. Sed miracula et signa nulla audio nec exempla vitae adeo religiosa, immo contra multa scandala et saeva facinora et multas impietates . . ." (*Bate Translation*, p. 250).

[31] "Et confirmatur quod nec iste titulus nec praecedens sit sufficiens, quia etiam in Veteri Testamento, ubi tamen armis res gerebatur, unquam populus Israël occupavit terras infidelium, vel quia essent infideles et idololatrae vel quia haberent alia peccata contra naturam (qui multa habebant, quia erant idololatrae et alia peccata contra naturam habebant, ut quia sacrificabant filios suos et filias suas daemoniis), sed vel ex speciali dono Dei vel quia transitum impediebant vel eos offenderant . . ." (*Bate Translation*, pp. 253–254.)

should prove to be the case, the awfulness of such armed intervention would be superseded by a higher norm, that of procuring always "the welfare of the aborigines rather than the gain of the discoverers." Needless to say, if war had to be waged, Christian Princes should proceed with utmost "moderation and proportion." Vitoria seemed convinced that as a matter of historical fact, the Spaniards had been often justified in the employment of force in order to continue their missionary work, but that too often "the measures adopted were in excess of what it was allowed by human and divine law."

The third and final issue discussed by Vitoria regarding Church policies which resulted in political decisions was the repression of heresy by the "secular arm" of the Inquisition. This frightening matter is discussed in the commentaries to the *Secunda Secundae* (q. 11, art. 3). Vitoria asserts firstly, that heretics fully deserve death by fire; secondly, that in special cases, and for the sake of the Christian Faith, the Church should decide to tolerate heresy. The first proposition is proved by the history of Civil Law and Canon Law, as well as by the dispositions of Papal Law which "delivers the heretics to the secular arm" (*tradit hereticos relapsos brachio seculari*). The authority of Saint Augustine and the Holy Scripture (*Deuter.* 13, 1; *Ad Galatas*, 5, 12; *Ad Rom.*, 4, 13) confirms it. The second proposition is proved in a more dialectical manner: to force right beliefs upon the population can easily lead to hypocrisy and pretended orthodoxy. Furthermore, the Church has no power to deal with interior acts which are judged exclusively by God Himself. Still, Vitoria thought that if a very small minority insisted upon heresy, the majority had the right to demand from them a formal retraction.

3. *The Law of Nations*

Protestant and Catholic scholars have passionately discussed the significance of the so-called Spanish School of International Law in the sixteenth century. Kaltenborn, for instance, in his classical book *Lehrbuch der Rechtsphilosophie* denies the Spanish scholars any historical relevance because of their stubborn medievalism, their primitive methodology, and especially because of their dogmatic prejudice. According to Welzel and Battaglia, the honor of having envisioned a Natural Law among nations apart from any theological reference belongs, not to the Spanish scholastics of the Renaissance, but rather to the Protestant jurists of the Baroque. Madariaga explains the "failure" of the school of Salamanca as the fateful outcome of "its dogmatic fragility."[32] In sharp oppostion to these unflattering remarks, another group of equally respectable scholars has not hesitated to proclaim that the glory of having pioneered the modern concept of a community of nations bound by a universal law of reason belongs entirely to the Spanish Jurists and Theologians of the sixteenth century. Thus, among many others, Joseph Kohler: "Wenn sich daher heutzutage ein Naturrecht bilden soll, so muss es an diese Spanier anschliessen aus Spanien grosser Zeit, nicht an Hugo Grotius, noch weniger an jene philisterhafte Verflachung Wolff's, welche das Grotianische Naturrecht zu Grabe getragen hat."[33] With similar undisguised enthusiasm, the famous American jurist, James Brown Scott, claimed that "Hugo Grotius . . . is to be considered a member of the Victorian, or as it is usually termed, the Spanish School, in that he derived his doctrine on the Law of Nature and of Nations from members of the Spanish School, which doctrine formed the basis of his treatise *On the Law of War and Peace* of 1625." Lange, Barthelemy, Conning, Nys, de Giorgi, Salvioli, and most Spanish scholars concur in this opinion.[34]

There can be no doubt whatsoever that such disparity of judgement is but one more case of exaggeration and prejudice on both sides. For some strange reason the study of Spanish intellectual history has frequently invited these extreme reactions. Our contention is that, as a whole, the Spanish School of the sixteenth century made important and novel contributions to the modern conception of international and lawful relations between sovereign States; that in their massive Latin works later (and better known) jurists and philosophers of Law found the central ideas they were able to systematize; and finally that the novelty of their guiding principles was not always obliterated either by

[32] Kaltenborn, *Lehrbuch der Rechtsphilosophie*, (Leipzig, 1848); Hans Welzel, *Derecho Natural y Justicia Material*, trans. Felipe González Vicen, (Madrid, 1957), pp. 131–141; F. Battaglia, *Cursos de Filosofía del Derecho*, trans. F. Elías de Tejada and P. Lucas Verdú, (Madrid, 1951), I, pp. 215–218; Salvador de Madariaga, Diario *El Sol*, November 11, 1927, "Francisco de Vitoria, Salamanca y Ginebra."

[33] Joseph Kohler, "Die Spanischen Naturrechteslehrer des 16. und 17. Jahrhunderts," *Archiv fuer Rechts- und Sozialphilosophie*, (1927), pp. 235–263.

[34] J. B. Scott, *The Spanish Origin of International Law*, pp. 9–10; Herman Conning, *Opera Omnia* (Brunswich, 1730), IV, *De Republica Hispanica*, p. 77; Ernest Nys, *Les Origines du Droit International* (Bruxelles, 1894), pp. 102 and 126; A. de Giorgi, *Della vita e delle opere di Alberico Gentili*, (Parma, 1876), p. 92; J. Salvioli, *Il concetto de guerra justa negli scrittori anteriori a Grocio* (Naples, 1915), p. 93.

Among the Spanish scholars the following deserve special mention: J. Larequi, "El Derecho Internacional en España durante los siglos XVI y XVII," *Razón y Fé*, LXXXI (1927), pp. 222–232; "Del *Ius Gentium* al Derecho Internacional," *Ibidem*, LXXXIII (1928), pp. 21–37; Avelino Folgado, "Los tratados *De Legibus* y *De iustitia et iure* en los autores españoles del siglo XVI y primera mitad del XVII," *La Ciudad de Dios*, CLXXII (1959), pp. 225–302.

the requirements of their Catholic orthodoxy or by the undeniable medieval atavisms into which they frequently relapsed.

The increasing number of Spanish colonies in the Americas and Charles' European *politik* presented to conscientious Spaniards of the sixteenth century an entire complex of problems entirely without precedent in their historical past. The first attempts to regulate and order the tumultous stream of events reflected the importance and social prestige of the Spanish legal profession. Spanish jurists, in close collaboration with the Crown and the Church, set out in deliberate manner to promulgate an entirely new body of legislation aimed at controlling under the canon of the Law the bold initiatives of warriors, adventurers, discoverers, conquistadores, and *encomenderos*. Their achievements were not the result of quick improvisation, but rather the crowning of a glorious legal tradition borne out of the Middle Ages. As early as the thirteenth century Castile had promulgated *Las Siete Partidas* a legal code which "was centuries ahead of the rest of Europe" (Nys), and contained the first draft of a modern Law of war. The works of Saint Raymond of Peñafort, Alfonso Tostado, Gonzalo de Villadiego, and Juan López, demonstrated the creativity of the Spanish legal mind. Spanish scholars of today are fond of relating this legal tradition to the "Roman heritage of the Iberian peninsula," but fairness demands that Spanish Jews be recognized as the major contributors to this glorious task.

In the case of the boisterous interference in European affairs by Charles V – an entirely new experience for the Kingdom of Castile – the legal battle was fought at two different levels. On the practical side, it was left to the Spanish Cortes to veto as often as possible the Emperor's constant demands for war monies. On the theoretical side, the Spanish jurists discussed at length two themes of pressing relevance: the applicability of the medieval conception of the Empire to the newly emerging national States; and, the laws of war. Their contributions to these two subjects will be discussed later when we deal with Vitoria's thoughts on these matters.

The American *Conquista* was a much more complicated affair. The Papal Bulls of Demarcation (1493), the treaty of Tordesillas between Spain and Portugal (1494), the legal recognition of the *Encomienda* in the instructions sent to the Governor of the Hispaniola Nicolás de Ovando (1503), and the formal drawing of the *Requerimiento* by the Council of Castile in 1510, bear eloquent witness to the deeply-felt need for legal sanctions and controls over the zealous activities of the discoverers and settlers. We have mentioned before the Laws of Burgos (1513), the opinions of López, Matías Paz, and John Mair on the morality of the American enterprise. To those we must add the name of Sepúlveda, according to whom the *Conquista* was a noble attempt to bring civilization to a barbarous and inferior people born to be natural slaves. Fourteen years after the Juntas of Burgos Vitoria became a professor at Salamanca (1526). The ideas of John Mair, Covarrubias, López, Sepúlveda, and Palacios Rubios, were well known to his students. The American issue, Vitoria wrote, "is a solemn question which is discussed in our schools year after year." From 1526 to 1537 Vitoria worked hard to define his own positions and lay down the foundations for his practical recommendations. The lectures *De potestate civili* (1532), and his lessons *De fide* (1534–1535), were but solemn introductions to the lectures *De Indis* (1539) where Vitoria expounded the entirety of his thought on the matter.

During those long years of silent and thoughtful preparation, the events themselves were crying for some radical solutions. In 1530, the second *Audiencia* arrived in New Spain and started out to replace the authority of the *Conquistadores* with that of royal justices and officials. In 1534, Spain was both amazed and shocked by the exploits of Pizarro in Perú, by the rebellion and execution of the Inca Prince Atahualpa. In 1537, the new Pope Paul III issued three bills concerning the treatment of the Indians. In the first, *Altitudo Divini Consilii*, he placed the spiritual guidance of the natives under the ordinary jurisdiction of the local Bishops; the second, *Veritas Ipsa*, was a valiant condemnation of Indian slavery; the third, *Sublimis Deus*, declared as heretical the opinion that the Indians were less than human, and incapable of receiving the Faith. Now the time had clearly arrived for Vitoria to proclaim from his Salamanca chair a moral pronouncement about the *Conquista* itself.

The opening questions of the first lecture *De Indis* seem to restrict the ensuing discussion to a purely canonical matter, namely whether the children of unbelievers might be baptized against the wish of their parents. The situation in America demanded a quick and decisive answer to this problem. The answer was, however, based upon a thorough discussion of three related matters: first, by what right (if any) were the American natives placed under Spanish jurisdiction; second, which rights did the Spanish Crown obtain over the Indians in temporal and civil matters; and, finally, which rights did the Spanish King or the Pope obtain over them in the spiritual domain? Thus, a canonical issue was placed within a much larger frame of reference involving not only theological but also exclusively philosophical considerations. Vitoria's explicit intention of dealing with the three aforementioned issues might, however, lead the reader into some confusion. Although Vitoria deals in detail with them, the formal structure of this lecture is organized along different lines.

The lecture opens up with a short but profound methodological inquiry into the need for a theological discussion of the matter. The first part discusses whether the American natives were capable of private and civil ownership before the arrival of the Spaniards. The second part deals with the illegitimate titles for the reduction of the American natives under Spanish rule. The third and final part presents the lawful titles whereby the American Indians *could have* come into the power of the Spanish Crown.

By way of introduction, Vitoria rhetorically asks his audience whether there is any justification to open up once again for discussion the issue of the American *Conquista* by the Spaniards. Forty years of *bona fide* occupation and "peaceful" (?) possession seemed to have settled the question in a definitive manner. No ruler could be obliged to constantly reexamine his original titles to power and certainly not such Princes as Ferdinand and Isabella, "who were most Christian," and the Emperor Charles V, "a most just and scrupulous sovereign." Still, Vitoria argued that it is always the case that whenever a man plans to do something "concerning which there is reasonable doubt whether it be good or bad, just or unjust, one is obliged to take advice from others, to deliberate, and to abstain from premature action before finding out and determining how far it is or is not lawful." Furthermore, to act in such matters without proper consultation, or against the advice of the wise, is always sinful. Vitoria's conclusions – which he openly avows to be different from those of Cardinal Cajetan – are in fact slightly exaggerated and misleading, but the intention of the theologian is absolutely clear: in all reasonably doubtful matters, all Christians – be they private citizens or rulers – are obliged in their conscience to listen and follow the advice of "the teachers approved by the Church." Such, he proclaimed, was indeed the case of the American *Conquista*, "not in itself so evidently unjust that no question about its justice can arise, nor again so evidently just that no doubt is possible about its injustice." It is true that the administration of the new lands was in most cases entrusted to men of honesty and decency; nevertheless "we hear of many massacres, so many plunderings of otherwise innocent people, so many native princes evicted from their possessions and stripped of their rule, "that a thorough discussion of the entire Spanish enterprise does not seem at all superfluous." Furthermore, these problems were not to be settled by jurists, or at any rate not by jurists alone, but by priests and theologians since the laws under which the native Americans live were not human positive laws but divine and natural laws which bind primarily in the *forum* of conscience. The purpose of this valiant introduction is absolutely clear: to silence those who were already in 1539 convinced that the primitive rights of the Indians had been prescribed under more than forty years of Spanish rule; and that, consequently, the moral issue of the *Conquista* had to be set aside in favor of a more pragmatic and legalistic approach.

After this solemn introduction, Vitoria proceeded to determine whether the special circumstances of the pre-Colombian aborigines did in any way deprive them of the right of private ownership or the right to erect legitimate political jurisdictions. As explained above (*See* pp. 85-86) neither mortal sin nor unbelief precluded such rights. Much more interesting is the discussion of what eventually, a few years after Vitoria's death, would become the central issue in the attempt to justify colonialism. The theory that the American natives were men of unsound mind, barbarous people incapable of any ownership, destined by nature to be slaves of those races which had reached a far superior degree of civilization, was not the concoction of a chauvinistic Spaniard, but the suggestion of a man personally detached from the American enterprise itself, the Scottish Dominican Priest, John Mair. That his ideas were familiar to Vitoria can be taken for granted, although the Spanish Dominican prudently avoided in his lectures any direct confrontation with his former professor at Paris, a respected member of his own religious Order. It is more difficult to say whether Mair's thoughts were literally known in 1539 to those Spaniards who enthusiastically supported the American Conquest. There is no doubt, however, that the conflicting reports from the colonies themselves prepared the ground for the great controversies to follow.

The *encomenderos* described the Indians of the New World as barbaric savages with no culture to speak of; the missionaries – at least most of them – emphasized their achievements, their good natural manners, and their inalienable rights. The historians of the *Conquista* were equally divided in their opinions. Columbus insisted upon the exotic and the fantastic; Hernan Cortés wrote admiringly of the natives he conquered; Gonzalo Fernández de Oviedo described the Indians with detached and scientific objectivity; López de Gómara was more eager to write a eulogy of Cortés than a narrative of the enterprise; Bernal Díaz del Castillo was convinced that the Spanish adventure was also a divine and providential mission; Francisco de Jerez and Pedro Cieza de León, the historians of Perú, disclosed to the old world the marvels of the Inca Empire. The controversy about the natural aptitudes of the Indians became most fiery three years after Vitoria's death. In 1542, Cardinal Loaysa, President of the Council of Indias, completed a legislative code known as *The New Laws* which forbade slavery, even in the mines; made illegal the employment of Indians as carriers or in personal service; and, finally, abolished the deeply rooted institution of the *encomienda*. Whether Vitoria's lectures had a direct impact upon the new legislation is difficult to prove. That it did help, cannot be doubted. Loaysa, a Dominican, was a great admirer of Vitoria; more importantly, the man who at that time was already known as the champion of Indian rights, the Bishop of Chiapa (Mexico), Fray Bartolomé de las Casas, also a Dominican, discussed the entire matter with Vitoria at the Convent of San Esteban in Salamanca before pressing the Council for the New Laws which Loaysa enacted a few months later. The promulgation of those laws provoked a terrible reaction among the colonists who saw themselves threatened by misery and rebellion when deprived of Indian labor. The theoretical defender of the colonists in the metropolis was Juan Ginés de Sepúlveda who in his book, *Democrates Alter* (1542), formulated in unequivocal terms a full theory of sixteenth century colonialism. Although Sepúlveda's book was written three years after Vitoria's lectures, his thought deserves at least a summary presentation because it obviously reflected opinions and attitudes which the professor of Salamanca could not have ignored in 1539.

According to the author of *Democrates Alter*, Natural Law in the physical sense of "what nature has taught all animals" (*quod natura omnia animalia docuit*) is obviously shared by all mankind. However, in its rational dimension, namely, Natural Law as Reason, it is to be found only among the "*gentes humaniores*" and not among those outside the civilized portion of humanity. The conclusion of this theory of natural aristocracy was, in Sepúlveda's terms, the Aristotelian doctrine of natural servitude: civilized nations had the right *and the duty* to subdue by force those people "who require, by their own nature and in their own instincts, to be placed under the authority of civilized and virtuous princes and nations so that they may learn from the mighty, wisdom, and from the laws of their conquerors better morals, worthier customs, and a more civilized form of life."[35] That such a mandate was incumbent upon the Spanish Crown to the exclusion of others Sepúlveda proved with three irresistible arguments: the natural superiority of the Spaniards over other European races, the right of discovery, and the "Bulls of Alexander."

Four years after Vitoria's death Sepúlveda faced las Casas in the second Junta de Valladolid (1550), where, under the chairmanship of one of Vitoria's disciples, Domingo de Soto, and by explicit order of Charles V, the two extreme opinions were publicly and thoroughly discussed. As a result of this confrontation Sepúlveda's book was left unpublished and his theories lost all appeal to the Spanish intelligentsia. The practical results of the dispute were much more dismal: the *encomienda* was never abolished; the *Conquista* itself became progressively a "fait accompli"; and deflected from engaging in ethical controversy the Spaniards turned their attention to the task of administering the new territories. The conscience-stricken Spaniards of Vitoria's day became progressively desensitized by the routine of administering the gigantic Empire with all its problems. Las Casas and Vitoria represent the highest moment in the history of Spain's self-criticism regarding the conquest of the Americas. Las Casas supported the missionaries in the conquered lands; Vitoria spoke for the Spanish University. Las Casas' knowledge of the Indians was that of an eye witness; Vitoria depended entirely upon written and oral reports; the strength of Las Casas was his passion and sincerity; Vitoria excelled in the articulation of theoretical principles and clear guidelines.

With typical composure and serenity, Vitoria sets out to discuss with short powerful arguments the imperialistic contentions of Sepúlveda and Mair, according to whom the lower condition of the Indians had placed them naturally under the dominion of the Spanish conquistadors. "It remains to ask whether the Indians lacked ownership because of want of reason or unsoundness of mind." The answer to this question involves a theoretical principle and a matter of fact. Theoretically it is questionable whether the use of reason is a precondition of ownership. It is true that "irrational creatures" are not capable of dominion or any other "right." So let us focus the discussion on children and those suffering from unsound mind to test this assumption. That children can have dominion, even before they have the use of reason, is proved, firstly, by the fact that they can suffer wrong; secondly, because they

[35] The Spanish translation of *Democrates Alter* was published by Marcelino Menéndez y Pelayo in *Boletín de la Real Academia de Historia*, vo. XXI (Madrid, 1892).

can be heirs; and lastly, because "the basis of dominion is in the possession of the image of God, and children already possess that image." More important still is the necessity to decide the factual question about the soundness of mind of the American natives.

The true state of the case is that they are not of unsound mind, but have, according to their kind, the use of reason. This is clear, because there is a certain method in their affairs, for they have polities which are orderly arranged, and they have definite marriage laws and magistrates, overlords, workshops, and a system of exchange, all of which call for the use of reason; they also have a kind of religion. Further, they make no error in matters which are self-evident to others; all this is witness to their use of reason.[36]

It is true, Vitoria concedes, that some of those Indians seem sometimes "unintelligent and stupid." The fault lies in a bad and barbarous upbringing"; for the same reason, "even among ourselves we find many peasants who differ little from brutes."

The section ends with an explanation of the Aristotelian theory of natural servitude, a theory which does not call for "a civil and legal slavery" of entire nations, but only reminds us of the obvious fact that some individuals are more naturally gifted to rule than others. All these valiant declarations end with a mysterious conclusion which deserves our attention:

Accordingly, even if we admit that the aborigines in question are as inept and stupid as alleged, still dominion cannot be denied to them, nor are they to be classed with the slaves of civil law. *True, some right to reduce them to subjection can be based on this reason and title, as we shall show below.* Meanwhile the conclusion stands sure, that the aborigines in question were true owners, before the Spaniards came among them, both from the private and the public point of view.[37]

At the end of the entire lecture, Vitoria discussed a final and doubtful title whereby the aborigines of America could have come into the power of Spain. The thought of Vitoria is so carefully pondered that any discussion of its meaning should be prededed by the reading of the text itself:

[36] "... Probatur, quia secundum rei veritatem non sunt amentes, sed habent pro suo modo usum rationis. Patet, quia habent ordinem aliquem in suis rebus, postquam habent civitates, quae ordine constant, et habent matrimonia distincta, magistratus, domin s, leges, opificia, commutationes, quae omnia requirunt usum rationis; item religionis specien . Item non errant in rebus, quae aliis sunt evidentes, quod est indicium usus rationis ..." (*Bate Translation*, p. 231.)

[37] "... Et sic, dato quod isti barbari sint ita inepti et hebetes, ut dicitur, non ideo negandum est habere verum dominium, nec sunt in numero servorum civilium habendi. Verum est quod ex hac ratione et titulo posset oriri aliquod ius ad subiciendum eos, ut infra dicemus. Restat conclusio certa quod, antequam Hispani ad illos venissent, illi erant veri domini, et publice et privatim." (*Bate Translation*, p. 232.)

There is another title which can indeed not be asserted, but brought up for discussion, and some think a lawful one. I dare not affirm it at all, nor do I entirely condemn it. It is this: although the aborigines in question are (as has been said above) not wholly unintelligent, yet they are little short of that condition, and so are unfit to found or administer a lawful State up to the standard required by human and civil claims. Accordingly they have no proper laws nor magistrates, and are not even capable of controlling their family affairs; they are without any literature or arts, not only the liberal arts, but the mechanical arts also; they have no careful agriculture and no artisans; and they lack many other conveniences, yea necessaries, of human life. It might, therefore, be maintained that, in their own interests, the sovereigns of Spain might undertake the administration of their country, providing them with prefects and governors for their towns, and might even give them new lords, so long as this was *clearly for their benefit.* I say there would be some force in this contention; for if they were all wanting in intelligence, there is no doubt that this would not only be a permissible, but a highly proper, course to take; nay, our sovereigns would be bound to take it, just as if the natives were infants. The same principle seems to apply here as to people of defective intelligence; and indeed they are worse or little better than that of beasts. Therefore, their governance should in the same way be entrusted to people of intelligence. There is confirmation hereof, for if by some accident of fortune, all their adults were to perish and there were to be left boys and youth indeed of a certain amount of reason, but of tender years and under the age of puberty, our sovereigns would certainly be justified in taking charge of them and governing them *so long as they were in that condition.* Now, this being admitted, it appears undeniable that the same could be done in the case of their barbarian parents, if they be supposed to be of that dullness of mind which is attributed to them by those who have been among them and which is reported to be more marked among them than even among the boys and youths of other nations. And surely this might be founded on the precept of charity, they being our neighbours and we being bound to look after their welfare. Let this, however, as I already have said, be put forward without dogmatism and subject also to the limitation that any such interposition be for the welfare and in the interest of the Indians and not merely for the profit of the Spaniard. For this is the respect in which all danger to the soul and salvation lies.[38]

[38] "Alius titulus posset non quidem adseri, sed revocari in disputationem et videri aliquibus legitimus, de quo ego nihil affirmare audeo, sed nec omnino condemnare, et est talis: Barbari enim isti, licet (ut supra dictum est) non omnino sint amentes, tamen etiam parum distant ab amentibus; ita videtur quod non sint idonei ad constituendam vel administrandam legitimam Rempublicam etiam inter terminos humanos et civiles. Unde nec habent leges convenientes neque magistratus, immo nec sunt satis idonei ad gubernandam rem familiarem. Unde etiam carent et litteris et artibus, non solum liberalibus, sed etiam mechanicis, et agricultura diligenti et opificibus et multis aliis rebus commodis, immo necessariis ad usus humanos. Posset ergo quis dicere quod pro utilitate eorum possent principes Hispani accipere administrationem illorum et constituere illis per oppida praefectos et gubernatores, immo etiam illis dare novos dominos, dummodo constaret hoc illis expedire. Hoc, inquam, posset suaderi, quia, si omnes essent amentes, non dubium est quin hoc esset non solum licitum, sed convenientissimum, immo tenerentur ad hoc principes, sicut si omnino essent infantes. Sed videtur quantum ad hoc eadem ratio de illis et de amentibus, quia nihil aut paulo plus valent ad guber-

The first part of this long paragraph presents the argument in a conditional manner, assuming namely a factual interpretation which itself was a matter of discussion. The emphasis here is not upon the rationality of the aborigines, but rather upon that degree of rationality without which it is impossible to have "proper" laws, "careful" agriculture, the "conveniences" of life, and "the standards" required by human and civil claims. Should the Indians lack that degree of rationality, so the argument goes, the sovereigns of Spain could and might be obliged by charity to undertake the administration of those countries; provided, firstly, that it be done *mainly* for the welfare of the Indians, and secondly, "so long as they were in that condition." Vitoria does not approve the argument, but neither does he "entirely condemn it." In fact, he grants that "there could be some force in such contention," although he never volunteered the admission that the facts about *all* American natives warranted in any way this temporary and altruistic form of guardianship or protectorate. Much less did he ever suggest that the brutal abuses of many Spanish conquistadores could in any remote way be described as such charitable wardenship. Still, notwithstanding the property and fairness of the antecedent remarks, we must confess that Vitoria's sketch of an international tutelage theory remains – even in its hypothetical form – highly incomplete, historically naive, and grossly biased. The shabby and frequently scandalous record of nineteenth century European colonialism, justified as it was upon theoretical principles very similar to those in which Vitoria saw "some force," has clearly revealed to contemporary men the tragic consequences of those patterns of thought. Vitoria's argument leaves aside entirely a condition of tutelage for which the American representative to the African Conference of Berlin in 1885 valiantly but unsuccessfully fought: the "free consent," or at least, the willing non-resistance of the potential

nandum se ipsos quam amentes, immo quam ipsae ferae et bestiae, nec mitiori cibo quam ferae, nec paene meliori utuntur. Ergo eodem modo possent tradi ad gubernationem sapientiorum. Et confirmatur hoc apparenter. Nam, si fortuna aliqua omnes adulti perirent apud illos et manerent pueri et adulescentes, habentes quidem aliqualem usum rationis, sed intra annos pueritiae et pubertatis, videtur profecto quod possent principes recipere curam illorum et gubernare illos, quamdiu essent in tali statu. Quod, si hoc admittitur, videtur certe non negandum quin idem fieri posset circa parentes barbaros, supposita hebetudine, quam de illis referunt qui apud eos fuerunt, quae multo, inquiunt, maior est quam apud alias nationes sit in pueris et adulescentibus. Et certe hoc posset fundari in praecepto caritatis, cum illi sint proximi nostri et teneamur bona illorum curare. Et hoc (ut dixi) sit sine assertione propositum, et etiam cum illa limitatione, ut fieret propter bona et utilitatem eorum, et non tantum ad quaestum Hispanorum. In hoc enim est totum periculum animarum et salutis, et ad hoc posset etiam prodesse illud, quod supra dictum est, quod aliqui sunt natura servi; nam tales videntur omnes isti barbari, et sic possent ex parte gubernari ut servi." (*Bate Translation*, p. 267.)

protegés. Furthermore, Vitoria's only Court of Appeal to safeguard the rights of primitive societies was postponed to the final decision of the Divine Justice in the great Hereafter, a solution obviously consistent with his own religious beliefs, but hardly helpful to the victims during their earthly pilgrimage. Vitoria's hope that the profits of the Spanish administration in America could ever become secondary to the interests of the aborigines themselves, was not a realistic expectation, but betrays a painful compromise between the demands of his Christian ideals and the hard realities of sixteenth century commercialism. Last but not least, Vitoria's ambiguous position reveals a complete lack of criticism with respect to some basic value judgements assumed in the argument: the assumption that human happiness depends upon the complexity of civilization, and the assumption that entire nations can be forced to accelerate their own historical cultural pace.

The second part of the lecture discusses the illegitimate means used by the Spaniards to reduce the aborigines of the New World to their tutelage. The author strikes his first and lethal blow at two medieval institutions which still claimed the right to a universal mastership over the entire earth: the Papacy and the Empire. Having already explained Vitoria's thought on the alleged temporal jurisdiction of the Pope, we can now turn our attention to the claims of the Emperor. Vitoria puts forward two fundamental propositions: first, the Emperor is *not* the master of the whole world; second, even if he were, that would not entitle him to seize the possessions of the Indians, to levy taxes, or to erect new rulers among the Indians. These clear-cut statements were an important contribution to the passionate and complex controversy about the Empire in Spain during the reign of Charles V. This controversy was of great significance to the history of European political thought because it unequivocally signalled the transition from a narrow and medieval conception of Christianity and the European States to a more secular, universalistic, and pluralistic understanding of mankind's political realities. Furthermore, the controversy about Charles V's imperial claims shed light on one of the most crucial moments in the history of Spain as a colonial power and as a full participant in the European affairs of the century.

Vitoria's rejection of Charles V's lordship over the entire world was one of the most dramatic moments in the history of the political confusion which prevailed in Spain during the first half of the sixteenth century, a confusion brought about by the flagrant contradiction between the medieval Spanish tradition toward the Empire and the expectations of the young Charles V. From as early as the twelfth century the Kings of the Christian Kingdoms in the Iberian peninsula – busy as they were with their own crusade against the Moslem invaders – had steadily proclaimed their total exemption from the Holy Roman Empire of the German Nation. Gregorio López, Vitoria's friend in Salamanca, formulated the traditional theory in his commentary to Alphonse XII's *Las Siete Partidas:* "Some Kings are exempt from the jurisdiction of the Emperor. The King is God's Vicar in his kingdom, exactly as the Emperor is in the Empire." (*Sunt enim reges aliqui exempti a jurisdictione Imperatoris. Rex est vicarius Dei in temporalibus in regno suo, sicut Imperator in Imperio.*)[39]

In the summer of 1517, the grandson of Maximilian and the Catholic Kings arrived in Spain to be crowned King of Castile and Aragon. Born in Flanders and educated in Brussels, the new King was a complete foreigner to the nation he was supposed to rule. His language was French and Flemish, his education a singular mixture of Hapsburg and Burgundy, his political counselors a team of Flemish ministers with more greed than wisdom. The death of Maximilian in 1519 left vacant the Imperial title, coveted by Henry VIII of England and Francis I of France. The German princes, however, and also Pope Leo X elected Charles, who thus became Charles I, King of Spain, and Charles V, Emperor of Germany. The entire reign of Charles (1516–1556) was an attempt to overcome the internal contradictions expressed in his own title. Historians have discussed at length the imperial ideas of Charles. Brandi and Rasow seem convinced that those ideas did not take any definite shape until 1528, and that, even then, the Emperor was merely following the inspiration of his minister Gattinara, an Italian humanist and diplomat whose final ambition was nothing less than Dante's *monarchia universalis.*[40]

Spanish historians, however, present a more complex picture of Charles' frame of mind, a picture in which the attitudes of the Emperor and the reactions of his Spanish subjects interplay with rich variations and oscillations. In 1520, during the "Cortes of Santiago-Coruña," the Bishop of Badajoz, Pedro Ruiz de la Mota, proclaimed the fundamental conception of a universal Empire centered in Spain under Charles' rule. The historical speech of the Spanish Bishop contained

[39] Quoted by G. Parry, *The Spanish Theory of Empire* (Cambridge, 1940), p. 15.

[40] See John Brandi, *The Emperor Charles V; The Growth and Destiny of a Man and of the World-Empire*, Eng. trans. C. V. Wedgwood (London, 1960).

Also, G. Rassow, *Die Kaiser-idee des Karls V dargestellt an der Politik der Jahre 1528–1540* (Berlin, 1932).

six fundamental claims: that Charles, the descendant of more than seventy Kings, was by birth a unique sovereign, a true King of Kings; that Castile, "the foundation, the protection and strength" of all the other regions, was his central Kingdom; that, therefore, the Emperor ought to live and to die in Castile; that the obligations of the Empire, the unity namely of Christianity and the war against the gentiles, were exactly those recommended by his grandmother, Queen Isabella; that Spain, the "mother of Trajan, Adrian, and Theodosius," had inherited from Rome the divine vocation of the Empire; and, finally, that Charles' journeys through Europe were only the inevitable consequence of his Imperial duties. That Mota's eloquence was not enough to appease Castilian pride became evident a few months later, when the communities of the Kingdom took arms against the foreign ministers of the Emperor for levying taxes against them to finance Charles' European ambitions. The short but bloody wars known as the *Comunidades* in Castile and the *Germanías* in Valencia, had a double effect: the nobility, threatened by the republican leanings of the *comuneros*, turned their loyalties with increased enthusiasm toward the monarchic rule of Charles; and the young Prince himself, especially after his confrontation with Luther in Worms (1521), became more resolved than ever to make Mota's speech the political program of his reign. The address of the Emperor to the Cortes of Valladolid (1523), the sack of Rome (1526), and, finally, the solemn proclamation of Madrid before his journey to Italy to be crowned by the Pope (1528), marked the highest moments of that process by which the Hapsburg Prince gave to Spain the illusion of an Empire for a tragically short time. Spanish men of letters reflected in their writings the buoyancy of the historical opportunity. Ulzurrum wrote the *Catholicum opus imperiale regiminis mundi* (1525), a treatise of pure medieval flavor; Pedro Mexía related in his *Historia Imperial* the feats of the Imperial legions; Alfonso de Valdés, in his dialogues *Lactancio con un arcediano* forged his Erasmian scheme of a universal peace under the aegis of Charles; Fray Alonso de Guevara formulated in his masterpieces *Reloj de Príncipes* and *Libro Aureo del Emperador Marco Aurelio* the very ideas proclaimed solemnly by the Emperor in his Madrid speech of 1528; and even the sober and detached Juna Luis Vives succumbed for awhile to the fascination of a unified Europe under the leadership of a Spanish Emperor.

With the crowning of the Emperor in Bologne, a time of frustation and deep questioning began. The protracted absence of the Emperor, the wars in Tunisia and Oran, the disintegration of European unity and the failure to control the progress of the Reformation, the terrible financial burden brought about by this massive intervention in the affairs of remote lands, were too much for the restless subjects of Charles. The American colonies and the claims of the Conquistadores provided the only hope to make possible in the New World what the Old so stubbornly refused to the Spanish Crown. The Imperialistic overtones of the American *Conquista* were a compensatory side-effect of the political ideals formulated in the Spanish Court of Charles V. A strange mixture of medieval conceptions, Renaissance ideals, humanistic universalism, Erasmian irenism, and, finally, political machiavellism, explain the words of Hernan Cortés (1522) in one of his letters to the Emperor: "Your Majesty is entitled to be the Emperor of this land (México) no less than Emperor of Germany, by the grace of God."

Against this tense background, Vitoria's solemn words acquire their historical significance: "Let our first conclusion be: the Emperor is not the lord of the whole earth." The refutation of this claim proceeds in great detail. Natural Law excludes any dominion and pre-eminence, except paternal and marital dominion. As for Divine Law, a sharp distinction needs to be made between the providential character of some of the old empires, such as the Roman Empire, and the divine institution or grant of imperial claims. Christ's kingship was not temporal, but spiritual; and if temporal in any way, it would be "guesswork to say that He bequeathed that power to the Emperor, there being no mention of such thing in the entire Bible." As for human law, Vitoria claimed it to be manifest that there was no such law nor any jurisdiction capable of enacting it. To this conclusion Vitoria added a second one of manifest historical significance: "Granted that the Emperor were the lord of the world, still that would not entitle him to seize the provinces of the Indian aborigines." The proof of this is that even those who attribute to the Emperor lordship over the entire earth, do not claim that he is lord in ownership (*in dominio*), but only in jurisdiction (*in iurisdictione*), and this latter right does not go so far as to warrant the conversion of provinces to his own use, or giving towns or even states away at his pleasure. This second conclusion was directly opposed to the Burgundian background of Charles where the feudal confusion of civil authority and public ownership attempted to survive under the deceitful mask of royal chivalry and dynastic patrimony.

The denial of a world-wide jurisdiction – be it Papal or Imperial – is central to Vitoria's philosophy of International Law. Historically speaking, it signifies a total break with the medieval political tradition based upon a misinterpretation of Saint Augustine and precariously maintained within the narrow horizons of European Christianity. To Vitoria the community of nations was not limited to the States of Christendom, but was coextensive with mankind as such: a plurality of perfect societies bound together by their mutual needs and subject to the same International Law. This community of Nations included as perfectly equal partners the Christian and the non-Christian States, and also those States and nationalities at different levels of cultural achievement. The plurality of political bodies within the totality of humanity as such, was, in Vitoria's mind, a historical matter of fact reasonably consistent with certain biblical revelations such as the myth of the Tower of Babel and the confusion of languages. Natural geographical boundaries, cultural differentiation, historical processes, practical demands of manageability and intercommunication, and other natural factors, explained the convenience, if not the necessity, of the division of mankind into independent political communities.

Vitoria's thought oscillated between an emphasis upon the "self-sufficiency and autarchy" of single States – the Aristotelian and medieval tradition – and their mutual need and interdependence, echoing the voice of the rising mercantilism ethic among at least one small section of mankind, Christian Europe. Had Vitoria consistently applied to the relations among states his own clear principles governing the relations between individuals and the State, he could have reached the conclusion that all nations should become members of a Republic of republics, a society of nations empowered to legislate, to judge, and to execute International Law. Unfortunately Vitoria's drive toward internationalism stopped short of this conclusion, and remained rigidly medieval in its relegation to the forum of conscience and to Divine Justice in Heaven the redress of international grievances among secular States and nationalities. In one section, however, of his lecture *De potestate civili*, Vitoria suggested a possibility which sheds enormous light over his entire political thought. Among the corollaries to his theory of civil authority we find the following conclusion regarding the justice of war:

The third corollary is as follows: No war is just the conduct of which is manifestly more harmful to the State than it is good and advantageous; and this is true regardless of any other claims or reasons that may be advanced to make of it a just war. The proof is: That if the State has no power to make war except for the purpose of defending itself, and protecting itself and its property, it follows that any war will be unjust, whether it be begun by the King or by the State, through which the latter is not rendered greater, but rather is enfeebled and impaired. Nay more, since one nation is part of the whole world, and since the Christian province is a part of the whole Christian State, if any war should be advantageous to one province or nation but injurious to the whole world or to Christendom, it is my belief that, for this very reason, that war is unjust. If, for example, the Spanish should undertake against the French a war which, in other respects, was just, and which was, besides, advantageous to the Spanish kingdom, but which involved Christendom as a whole in still greater harm and loss (suppose, for instance, that the Turks in the meantime take possession of Christian provinces), then the Spanish should cease from waging that war.[41]

The welfare of each single State is then subordinated and directed to the universal welfare of mankind exactly in the same way that the welfare of the individual citizen is subordinated to the common good of the State. This thought leads to the second conclusion or corollary which follows immediately: "Just as the majority of the members of one State may set up a King over the whole State, although other members are unwilling, so the majority of Christians, even though there be some who are opposed, may lawfully create a monarch whom all provinces and princes are obliged to obey." Vitoria's proof of this startling conclusion is a baffling mixture of rich suggestion and misleading prejudice. The first part of the proof deals with a marginal issue, the right of the majority to impose upon a dissenting minority a ruler of its choice. The second part attempts – without much success – to explain why the right to set up a universal monarchy belongs, not to men in general, but to "the majority of Christians." Vitoria begins by saying that since the Church, as a whole, is "so to speak, a State and one Body" (*Rom.* XII, 5), she must have the power to take any shape or form which she deems most convenient to protect herself against the enemy. Therefore, if the spiritual hierarchy of the Church came to the conclusion that a universal temporal monarch among Christians was the most convenient structure for the defense and propagation of the Catholic

[41] "Nullum bellum est justum, si constat geri majori malo Reipublicae, quam bono, et utilitate, quantumvis aliunde suppetant tituli et rationes ad bellum justum.

Probatur: Quia si Respublica non habet potestatem inferendi bellum, nisi ad tuendum se, resque suas, atque se protegendum; ergo ubi ipso bello attenuatur potius, atque atteritur, quam augetur, bellum erit injustum, sive a Rege inferatur, sive a Republica.

Imo cum una Respublica sit pars totius orbis, et maxime Christiana Provincia pars totius Reipublicae, si bellum utile sit uni Provinciae, aut Reipublicae cum damno orbis, aut Christianitatis, puto eo ipso bellum esse injustum, ut si bellum Hispaniarum esset adversus Gallos, alias ex causis justis susceptum, et alioqui Regno Hispaniarum utile; tamen cum majori malo et jactura geritur Christianitatis, puta quia Turcae occupant interim Provincias Christianorum, cessandum esset a tali bello ..." (*Relecciones Teológicas*, pp. 191–192.)

Church, such a hierarchy would *oblige* all Christians to set up a universal King. The assumption of this shaky argument was, of course, that the "majority of Christians" and the "majority of mankind" were one and the same, an assumption obviously unwarranted, even in 1539. The third part of the argument is by far the most interesting. Here Vitoria seems to break down all the boundaries of his medieval background and writes without hesitation:

It is evident that, since the human race did at one time (long before all these divisions took place) possess this power to elect a universal monarch, it is still able to do so; for the power of which we speak, being derived from Natural Law, does not pass away.[42]

According to Vitoria, then, mankind is "in some sense a universal republic," and could by majoritarian rule elect a universal monarch over the entire community of nations. Furthermore, such a right is, in fact, an inalienable right of Natural Law, and remains intact even in the present condition of a plurality of separate states. On this particular point, however, Vitoria's position is not entirely self-consistent. If the common good of mankind is itself superior to the particular good of each single State, then an international body endowed with legislative, judicial, and executive powers, could not be described as a contingent, free choice of individual States, but rather as an institution necessary for their perfection, as the State itself is a necessary complement to the needs of individual citizens. What is truly important about the words quoted above is that the possibility of a universal ruler therein described is not limited to a choice of Christian nations, but a natural possibility of all mankind based, not upon dogmatic argument, but rather derived from purely natural premises. There is no doubt, however, that Vitoria's vision of internationalism stopped short of these extreme logical consequences, the same consequences which today, four hundred years later, still remain utopian and hardly reconcilable with the proved inefficiency of both the Society of Nations and the United Nations Organization. On the other hand, Vitoria's assertion of mankind's natural right to erect a universal monarch is intimately connected with the most original part of his thought regarding the nature of International Law. Toward the end of his lecture *De potestate civili* we find the following conclusion:

[42] "Item, quia aliquando genus humanum habuit istam potestatem ,scilicet, eligendi Monarcham, ut patet a principio antequam fieret divisio; ergo, et nunc potest; cum enim illa potestas esset juris naturalis, non cessat." (*Relecciones Teológicas*, p. 194.)

From all that has been said, a corollary may be inferred, namely: that International Law has not only the force of a pact and agreement among men, but also the force of law; *for the world as a whole, being in a way one single state,* has the power to create laws that are just and fitting for all persons, as are the rules of International Law. Consequently, it is clear that those who violate these international rules, whether in peace or in war, commit a mortal sin; moreover, in the gravest matters, such as the inviolability of ambassadors, it is not permissible for one country to refuse to be bound by International Law, the latter having been established *by the authority of the whole world.*[43]

Before we discuss further Vitoria's doctrine of International Law, we intend to present several concrete cases of its application: first, the specific case of the relations between the Spanish Nation and the American political communities; and, second, the generic problem of the Law of War. Both sets of examples were closely related in Vitoria's mind since the *Conquista* was a war the righteousness of which was far from clear. In fact the lecture known as *De iure belli* was conceived by Vitoria as the second and complementary lecture on the American problem.

Having denied a world-wide jurisdiction to both the Pope and the Emperor, the case of American colonization was squarely discussed by Vitoria in terms of those provisions of International Law which regulate the relations among equally sovereign states. On the basis of such rules it was possible to dismiss as totally invalid two alleged titles which served to justify the Spanish enterprise: the right of discovery, and the voluntary choice of the aborigines.

Although by Natural and International Law "those regions which are deserted become the possession of the first occupant," in America "the object in question was not without an owner"; therefore this title "in and of itself gives no support to a seizure of the aborigines, *any more than if it had been they who had discoverd us.* With equal incisiveness and energy Vitoria rejects the attempt to justify an extension of Spanish sovereignty in the Americas on the basis of a "voluntary choice of the aborigines." Such choice, if it ever took place, would be vitiated from the very beginning by fear and ignorance of "an unwarlike and timid crowd" in the face of "the armed array or the Spaniards." Furthermore, "the populace could not procure new lords

[43] "Ex omnibus dictis infertur corollarium, quod jus gentium non solum habet vim ex pacto et condicto inter homines, sed etiam habet vim legis. Habet enim totus orbis, qui aliquo modo est una respublica, potestate ferendi leges aequas et convenientes omnibus, quales sunt in jure gentium. Ex quo patet, quod mortaliter pecant violantes jura gentium, sive in pace, sive in bello, in rebus tamen gravioribus, ut est de incolumitate legatorum. Neque licet uni regno nolle teneri jure gentium; est enim latum totius orbis authoritate." (*Relecciones Teológicas,* p. 207.)

in defiance of their own rulers, nor could the rulers themselves appoint a new prince without the assent of the populace." Theoretically speaking, however, Vitoria accepted the possibility that if the majority of the Indian citizenry would knowingly – "aware of the prudent administration and the humanity of the Spaniards" – and freely – "of their own volition" – accept the King of Spain as their ruler, "this could be done and would be a lawful title of sovereign expansion." It goes without saying that the lawfulness of this "possible" title was based upon hypothetical conditions totally denied by the historical facts, as Vitoria saw them.

In the third section of his lecture *De Indis*, Vitoria investigated in detail the provisions of International Law "whereby the aborigines of America could have come into the power of Spain." The titles discussed were the following: the title of natural society and fellowship; the right to preach the Gospel; the right to protect new converts; the right to rescue innocent people from tyrannical laws; the right to voluntary choice among the majority of both rulers and subjects: the right of mutual alliance; and finally, the right of international patronage. Of these titles some have already been fully discussed, and others partially touched upon in our previous discussion. The second, third, and fourth titles were previously examined in as far as they related to the temporal consequences of the Pope's spiritual jurisdiction. It was Vitoria's contention that the legitimacy of those titles, especially the second and third, was based not only upon Divine Positive Law, but also upon the rights and duties guaranteed by Natural Law, a claim we must now probe more in detail.

The right to preach the Gospel in America and to protect the newly converted Christians was based upon the following provisions of Natural Law: the right of the Spaniards to travel and to trade among the Indians; the duty of brotherly correction among neighbors; and the demands of human friendship and alliance. These rights, duties, and demands can be summarized in the first title under discussion, "that of natural society and friendship." It amounts in fact to a solemn declaration of the most fundamental rules governing the relations among States: the right of communication and trade, the right of intervention, and, finally, the right of international alliances and agreements. These three rights are but the legal expression of the international solidarity which binds the whole human race into "a universal Republic."

The right of communication and trade is expanded in several propositions backed by a whole array of different arguments. The first proposition reads: "The Spaniards have a right to travel into the lands in question and to sojourn there, provided they do no harm to the natives, and the natives do not prevent them." Obviously this proposition might be understood as a concrete application of a general rule: men of all races have the right to travel and to live in foreign lands, provided they respect the rights of their hosts. Vitoria accumulates no less than fourteen different proofs of this basic rule of International Law:

Proof of this may in the first place be derived from the Law of Nations, which either is Natural Law or derived from Natural Law: 'What natural reason has established among all nations is called the *jus gentium.*' (*Inst.*, I, 21, 1). For congruent herewith, it is recognized among all nations that it is inhumane to treat visitors and foreigners badly without some special cause, while, on the other hand, it is humane and correct to treat visitors well; but the case would be different, if the foreigners were to misbehave when visiting other nations.

Secondly, it was permissible from the beginning of the world (when everything was held in common) for anyone to set forth and travel wheresoever he would. Now, this was not taken away by the division of property, for it was never the intention of peoples to destroy by that division the reciprocity and common use which prevailed among men, and indeed in the days of Noah it would have been inhumane to do so.

Thirdly, everything is lawful which is not prohibited or is not injurious or hurtful to others in some other way. But (so we suppose) the travel of the Spaniards does no injury or harm to the natives. Therefore it is lawful.

Fourthly, it would not be lawful for the French to prevent the Spanish from travelling or even from living in France, or vice versa, provided this in no way enured to their hurt and the visitors did no injury. Therefore it is not lawful for the Indians.

Fifthly, banishment is one of the capital forms of punishment. Therefore it is unlawful to banish strangers who have committed no fault.

Sixthly, to keep certain people out of the city or province because they are considered to be enemies, or to expel them after they have arrived, are acts of war. Inasmuch then, as the Indians are not making a just war on the Spaniards (*it being assumed that the Spaniards are doing no harm*), it is not lawful for them to keep the Spaniards away from their territory.

Further, seventhly, there is the Poet's verse:

Quod genus hoc hominum? quaeve hunc tam barbara morem
Permittit patria? hospitio prohibemur arenae.

Also, eighthly, 'Every animal loveth its kind.' (*Ecclesiastes*, 17). Therefore, it appears, that friendship among men exists by Natural Law and it is against nature to shun the society of harmless folk.

Ninthly, there is the passage (*Matthew*, 25): 'I was a stranger and ye took me not in.' Hence as the reception of strangers seems to be by Natural Law, the judgment of Christ will be pronounced with universal application.

Tenthly, 'by Natural Law running water and the sea are common to all, so are rivers and harbours, and by the Law of Nations ships from all parts may be moored there,' and on the same principle they are public things. Therefore it is not lawful to keep anyone from them. Hence it follows that the aborigines would be doing a wrong to the Spaniards, if they were to keep them from their territories.

Also, it is evident that these very persons admit all other barbarians from all parts. Therefore, they would be doing a wrong if they were not to admit the Spaniards.

And, if it were not lawful for the Spaniards to travel among them, this would be either by Natural Law or by Divine Law or by human law. Now, it is certainly lawful by Natural and by Divine Law. And if there were any human laws which without any cause would take away rights conferred by Divine and Natural Law, it would be inhumane and unreasonable and consequently would not have the force of law.

Next one must decide whether the Spaniards are subjects of the Indians or whether they are not. If they are not, then the Indians cannot keep them away. If they are, then the Indians ought to treat them well.

Finally, the Spaniards are the neighbors of the Indians, as illustrated in the Gospel parable of the Samaritan (*Luke*, 10). But they are bound to love their neighbors as themselves (*Matthew*, 22). Therefore, they may not keep them away from their country without cause: when it is said 'Love thy neighbor,' it is clear that every man is our neighbor. (Saint Augustine, *De doctrina Christiana*).[44]

44 "... Probatur primo ex iure gentium, quod vel est ius naturale vel derivatur ex iure naturali (*Inst.*, De iure naturali et gentium): "quod naturalis ratio inter omnes gentes constituit, vocatur ius gentium." Sic enim apud omnes nationes habetur inhumanum sine aliqua speciali causa hospites et peregrinos male accipere; e contrario autem humanum et officiosum se habere bene erga hospites; quod non esset, si peregrini male facerent, accedentes in alienas nationes.

Secundo, a principio orbis (cum omnia essent communia) licebat unicuique, in quamcumque regionem vellet, intendere et peregrinari. Non autem videtur hoc demptum per rerum divisionem; nunquam enim fuit intentio gentium per illam divisionem tollere hominum invicem communicationem, et certe temporibus Noë fuisset inhumanum.

Tertio, omnia licent, quae non sunt prohibita aut alias sunt in iniuriam aut detrimentum aliorum. Sed (ut supponimus) talis peregrinatio Hispanorum est sine iniuria aut damno barbarorum. Ergo est licita.

Quarto, non liceret Gallis prohibere Hispanos a peregrinatione Galliae, vel etiam habi-

The atypical verbosity of this passage – not to mention the disorder of the argumentation – is a clear sign of the momentum of the issue under debate. Vitoria's thought can be summarized in the following propositions. Before the division of property (which apparently took place after Noah's ark) Natural Law guaranteed to all men the right to set forth and sojourn anywhere in the world. The division of property has in no way cancelled this right, provided that visitors respect the property rights of their hosts. Furthermore, it is clear that in setting up a plurality of nations mankind did in no way intend to prevent the exchange of ideas and resources which prevailed before. To mistreat a peaceful and harmless visitor, is, therefore, inhumane, unlawful, and, if sanctioned by civil authority, an unjustified act of war. Finally, the division of property has in no way affected the seas, rivers, and harbours which the Law of Nations has everywhere preserved as "public things."

In the second proposition Vitoria asserts the right of the Spaniards not only to travel, and to sojourn among the aborigines, but especially to trade among them, "so long as they do no harm to their country."

tatione, aut e contrario, si nullo modo cederet in damnum illorum nec facerent iniuriam. Ergo nec barbaris.

Item quinto, exsilium est poena etiam inter capitales. Ergo non licet relegare hospites sine culpa.

Item sexto, haec est una pars belli, prohibere aliquos tanquam hostes a civitate vel provincia vel expellere iam exsistentes. Cum ergo barbari non habeant iustum bellum contra Hispanos, supposito quod sint innoxii, ergo non licet illis prohibere Hispanos a patria sua.

Item septimo, facit illud poetae,

Quod genus hoc hominum? quaeve hunc tam barbara morem
Permittit patria? hospitio prohibemur arenae.

Item octavo, "Omne animal diligit sibi simile" (*Eccle.*, 17). Ergo videtur quod amicitia inter homines sit de iure naturali, et contra naturam est vitare consortium hominum innoxiorum.

Item nono, facit illud *Matth.*, 25, "Hospes eram, et non collegistis me." Unde, cum ex iure naturali videatur esse recipere hospites, illud Christi iudicium statuetur cum omnibus.

Decimo, "iure naturali communia sunt omnium, et aqua profluens et mare, item flumina et portus, atque naves iure gentium undecumque licet applicare" (*Inst.*, De rerum divisione); et eadem ratione videtur publice. Ergo neminem licet ab illis prohibere. Ex quo sequitur quod barbari iniuriam facerent Hispanis, si prohiberent illos a suis regionibus.

Item undecimo, ipsi admittunt omnes alios barbaros undecumque. Ergo facerent iniuriam non admittentes Hispanos.

Item duodecimo, quia, si Hispanis non liceret peregrinari apud illos vel hoc esset iure naturali aut divino aut humano. Naturali et divino certe licet. Si autem lex humana esset, quae prohiberet sine aliqua causa a iure naturali et divino, esset inhumana nec esset rationabilis et per consequens non haberet vim legis.

Decimo tertio, vel Hispani sunt subditi illorum vel non. Si non sunt subditi, ergo non possunt prohibere. Si sunt subditi, ergo debent eos bene tractare.

Item decimo quarto, Hispani sunt proximi barbarorum, ut patet ex Evangelio (*Luc.*, 10) de Samaritano. Sed tenentur diligere proximos (*Matth.*, 22) sicut se ipsos. Ergo non licet prohibere illos a patria sua sine causa: (Augustini, *De doctrina Christiana*) "Cum dicitur, 'Diliges proximum tuum,' manifestum est omnem hominem proximum esse.'" (*Bate Translation*, pp. 257–258.)

Spaniards, therefore, are entitled to bring into Indian lands merchandise the natives lack in exchange for those natural resources (like gold or silver!) the Indians have in excess. This right is a rule of the Law of Nations which applies to the Indians exactly in the same way it applies to trade relations among Christians themselves. Furthermore (and this is the third proposition) if there are among the Indians things which are treated as common, inasmuch as they belong to nobody and are acquired by the first occupant who "digs for gold in communal land, or fishes for pearls in the sea or in a river," the Spaniards cannot be prevented from a communication and participation in them, *nor any other foreigners*. This right to acquire property in a foreign country has the force of law, if not as a conclusion of Natural Law, at least as a majoritarian consensus of mankind, and is therefore valid "even though the rest of mankind objects thereto."

In the fourth proposition Vitoria attempts to clarify the basic concepts of 'native' and 'foreigner' which are central to the above discussion. His doctrine of nationality coincides basically with the fourteenth amendment to the Constitution of the United States – all persons born or naturalized in the United States are citizens thereof. This limits citizenship to children born of foreigners having their *habitual* domicile in the land, and excludes the children of foreigners *in transit*. Vitoria quotes the Code of Justinian as one of the foundations of the Law of Nations, and then proceeds to a rational proof: "Man is a civil animal. Whoever is born in any one State is not a citizen of another State. Therefore, if he were not a citizen of the State referred to, he would not be a citizen of any State, to the prejudice of his rights under both Natural Law and the Law of Nations." The second way of acquiring citizenship is by naturalization, either because of marriage "or by virtue of any other fact whereby other foreigners are wont to become citizens," provided they are willing to submit to all the burdens others have accepted.

The first four propositions have spelled in detail the rights of the Spaniards in America under the universal provisions of the Law of Nations, given certain hypothetical conditions not warranted by historical facts. In the same conditional and hypothetical manner Vitoria proceeds to define in the next three propositions the means by which the Spanish could have asserted those rights if the Indian natives had without any justification decided to prevent them from enjoying such rights. Before we specify those means, however, we must attempt to answer a possible objection of our readers. It could be said that Vitoria's theoretical construction toward the end of this lecture becomes increasingly irrelevant to the concrete problem he was trying to deal with. To say that the Spaniards *could* have been entitled to fight the native Indians if they had been prevented by them from enjoying rights they in fact never had, seems a finicky platitude in the face of the historical indictment against the massive brutality of the *Conquista*. To this serious censure a double answer is possible. First, it is very well possible that Vitoria's intention was precisely to question the legality of the whole enterprise by raising the fundamental issue of the debate: namely, whether the actions of the Spanish Conquistadores had in effect harmed the American Indians and violated their natural rights. It is true that in this most questionable section of his lecture, Vitoria did not have the courage to come forth with an outright condemnation of Spain's colonial policy. But his reiterated emphasis on the basic condition of preserving the natural rights of the Indians was an open invitation to those who were aware of the facts to draw the inescapable conclusion. In fact, in the very last paragraph of his lecture Vitoria tackled the fundamental conclusion:

> Now, it seems from all this discussion that, if there be no force in any of the titles which have been put forward, so that the native Indians neither gave cause for just war nor wished for Spanish rulers, etc. . . . all the travel to, and trade with, those parts should be stopped, to the great loss of the Spaniards, and also to the detriment of the royal treasury (a thing intolerable).[45]

In his answer to this implicit question Vitoria draws a sharp distinction between private trade and royal administration. If all the titles whereby the aborigines of America could have come into Spanish jurisdiction proved to be invalid, Spanish merchants would still be entitled to trade with the Indians, but without ever attempting to reduce them to civil subjection. In such a case, however, the Crown, responsible for the maritime discovery and the safety of the sea routes, would be entitled to a tax – "as much as a fifth or even more" – placed upon all the gold and silver which would be brought away from the Indians. Had the lecture finished at this point, we would be under the impression that Vitoria was simply suggesting the cancellation of any political expansion of Spain in America, and substituting for it a peaceful and reciprocal trading agreement between American Indians and Spanish

[45] "Sed ex tota disputatione videtur sequi quod, si cessarent omnes isti tituli, ita quod barbari nullam rationem iusti belli darent nec vellent habere Hispanos principes, etc., quod cessaret tota illa peregrinatio et commercium cum magna iactura Hispanorum et etiam proventus principum magnum detrimentum acciperent, quod non esset ferendum . . ." (*Bate Translation*, p. 268.)

merchants. On purely natural grounds there is no doubt that Vitoria had indeed reached such a revolutionary conclusion. However, the last three lines of this lecture read as follows: "It is evident, now that there are already so many converts that it would be neither expedient nor lawful for our sovereign to wash his hands entirely of the administration of the lands in question." This advice personally directed to Charles V, betrays more eloquently than any other word ever pronounced by Vitoria the blinding and deleterious effect of religious prejudice upon an otherwise enlightened mind. It is hard to measure the historical impact of such a recommendation. Some documents of the time suggest that precisely around 1539 Las Casas had almost succeeded in persuading the Emperor to give up entirely any Spanish sovereignty in the Americas, and that the Emperor abandoned such a drastic plan because of Vitoria's warning about the future of Christianity in the newly discovered territories. Although some scholars doubt the veracity of such documents, it is still evident that in Vitoria's eyes the political subjection of the American Indians was justified in 1539 by the obligation of the Spanish Crown to protect the new Christians, even if, as Vitoria strongly suggested, the whole enterprise had initially been an unjust war against the aborigines.[46]

We mentioned before that two answers are possible against the charge of irrelevant speculation on Vitoria's part. So far we have suggested that behind the subtleties of his distinctions one can detect the historical conclusion of the author. Equally important is a second point. The discussion of the Spanish right to use force against the Indians provided Vitoria with an ideal test case to outline his theory about the Law of War. Propositions five, six, and seven (*See below*), together with titles five and seven, are in fact a short treatise on the legitimacy of war. That Vitoria considered this sketch highly deficient is obvious from the fact that his second lecture *De Indis* one year later was entirely dedicated to the subject "on the law of war made by the Spaniards on the barbarians." These documents make up the most comprehensive study on the Law of War written in Europe during the sixteenth century, and are the most remarkable parts of Vitoria's theory on the Law of Nations.

Propositions five, six, and seven on the character of "natural society

[46] Among those who doubt the documents mentioned, see M. Bataillon, "Charles-Quint, Las Casas, et Vitoria," in *Charles Quint et Son Temps*, Colloques Internationaux du Centre National de la Recherche Scientifique, (Paris, 1949). The opposite opinion is held by Alfonso García Gallo, Juan Manzano, Juan Pérez de Tudela, and by Ramón Menéndez Pidal. (See *ibidem*, p. 79, footnote 5).

and friendship" deal with the alternatives available to the Spaniards in the event the Indians wished to prevent them from exercising their natural right to travel, to sojourn, and to trade in the new lands. Proposition five says:

If the Indian natives wish to prevent the Spaniards from enjoying any of the above-named rights under the Law of Nations, for instance, trade, or other above-named matter, the Spaniards ought in the first place to use reason and persuasion in order to remove scandal and ought to show in all possible methods that they do not come to hurt the natives, but wish to sojourn as peaceful guests without doing the natives any harm; and they ought to show this not only by word, but also by reason, according to the saying, 'It beloveth the prudent to make trial of everything by words first.' But, if after this recourse to reason, the barbarians decline to agree and propose to use force, the Spaniards can defend themselves and do all that is consistent with the maintenance of their own safety; it being lawful to repel force with force. And not only so, but, if safety cannot otherwise be had, they may build fortresses and defensive works, and if they have sustained a wrong, they may follow it with war on the authorization of their sovereign and may avail themselves of the other rights of war.[47]

The striking severity of this proposition is soon tempered with a most humane consideration. It is very well possible, Vitoria warns, that no matter how sincerely the Spaniards attempt to remove the fears of the Indians, they might not succeed in their efforts. Being by nature "timid, dull, and stupid," the Indians might excusably continue to be afraid of "men, strange in garb, armed, and much more powerful than themselves." If, then, under the influence of those fears, the natives tried to drive out the Spaniards, these could indeed defend themselves, but only within the limits of permissible self-defense, and it would not be right to enforce against the natives "any of the rights of war." Such a purely defensive war would be the typical case of a just war on both sides, where the right of one party and the invincible ignorance of the other collide against each other. The distinction is important, because "the right to make war against men who are really guilty and lawless differs from one which may be invoked against the innocent and ignorant."

[47] "Si barbari velint prohibere Hispanos in supra dictis a iure gentium, puta vel commercio vel aliis, quae dicta sunt, Hispani primo debent ratione et suasionibus tollere scandalum et ostendere omni ratione se non venire ad nocendum illis, sed pacifice velle hospitari et peregrinari sine aliquo incommodo illorum, et non solum verbis, sed etiam ratione ostendere, iuxtra illud, "Omnia sapientes prius experiri decet." Quod si, reddita ratione, barbari nolint acquiescere, sed velint vi agere Hispani possunt se defendere et omnia agere ad securitatem suam convenientia, quia vim vi repellere licet. Nec solum hoc, sed, si aliter tuti esse non possunt, artes et munitiones aedificare, et, si acceperint iniuriam, illam auctoritate principis bello prosequi et alia belli iura agere ..." (*Bate Translation*, p. 260.)

The sixth proposition defines the "extremities" which might become lawful in a defensive war, such as "seizing the cities of the Indians and reducing them to subjection." Furthermore, indicates proposition seven, if the Indians persist in their hostility to the Spaniards, no matter how diligently the latter have tried to persuade the natives of their peaceful intentions, then "they can make war on the Indians, no longer as an innocent folk, but as against forsworn enemies, and may enforce against them all the rights of war, despoiling them of their goods, reducing them to captivity, deposing their former lords, and setting up new ones."

The reader might find these words terribly appalling. We must, however, once again remind him that Vitoria is here drawing conclusions from a hypothetical premise: "provided the seizure be without guile or fraud and they do not look for imaginary causes of war. For if the natives allow the Spaniards to traffic peacefully among them, the Spaniards could not allege in this connection any just cause for seizing their goods any more than the goods of other Christians." Still, Vitoria's reasoning seems based upon a highly controversial assumption, the legitimacy of backing with armed intervention the right to live, to travel, to seize unoccupied territory and natural resources in a foreign nation.

The fifth title, alleged by some Spanish jurists to justify the reduction of American aborigines into the Spanish domain, discusses the brotherly obligation to rescue innocent people from tyrannical rulers who subscribed to ritual sacrifices, cannibalistic practices, or the killing of children. Vitoria deals with this title in surprisingly simple terms. After quoting the Bible (*Ecclesiastes* XVII, 12; *Proverbs* XXIV,) in favor of man's responsibility to his neighbor, he concludes that "even if all the Indians in question assent to these rules and sacrifices, and do not wish the Spaniards to champion them," still "we might find a lawful title here." The right to intervention and the principle of human solidarity were held with admirable conviction; nevertheless, the simplistic manner in which he dealt with this complex problem leaves the reader with more questions than answers.

The seventh title relates to another momentous problem of International Law: the right to enter into agreements and alliances between nations. Vitoria considers the case of an Indian nation engaged in a lawful war against another Indian nation which summons the Spaniards to help and to share the rewards of victory. Such was the case in the war of the Tlaxcaltecs "against the Mexicans" (*sic*). The Spanish theologian accepts this as a possible title, and confirms it with the example of the Roman Empire – "approved by Saint Augustine and Saint Thomas" – which by bringing aid to their allies and friends came "by right of war" into possession of new territories.

Vitoria's lecture on war stands out as a masterpiece in the vast literature produced on the subject during the sixteenth century. The repeated conflicts between the Habsburgs and the Valois (no less than six different wars between 1521 and 1559), the constant defensive war against the Turks in Eastern Europe and the Mediterranean, the civil wars in Germany and Spain, and lastly the war-like adventures of the Portuguese and Spanish were more than enough to make war an obsessive topic of Renaissance consciousness. The new use of gun powder, the refinement of strategy and technique as reflected in the combined utilization of infantry, cavalry, and artillery, the reinforcement of military discipline and preparation, the complexity of maritime warfare, the growing impact of armed hostilities upon civil population and trade relationships, the increased need and progressive establishment of permanent national armies, all of these circumstances revealed both a heightened tension between national States and a progress in technology which was disturbing to the more enlightened and humane thinkers of Vitoria's age. Erasmian humanists decried the evils of war in the name of man's higher values while others seemed to relish the new exploits and risks of warfare. No other century in the history of Europe has produced such exuberant war literature: the war histories of Guichardin, Jove, Santo, Cerezeda, Brantôme, Rabutin, Pedro Mexía, Luís de Avila, Francesillo de Zúñiga, Bernal Díaz del Castillo, Francisco de Jerez, Diego Hurtado de Mendoza; the memoires of Bellay, Fleuranges, Monluc, Hernan Cortés, Gonzalo de Córdoba; the *ars belli* of Louis XI (toward the end of the fifteenth century), Philippe de Clèves, Machiavelli, Raymond de Fourquevaux, Gianbattista della Valla and Tartaglia; all these, and other less known writers, betray in eloquent terms the concern with war in Renaissance Europe.

Vitoria's treatment of the subject was purely legal and theological. As such his work was not a revolutionary innovation, but had many remote and immediate predecessors in traditional Christian thought. The basic theological directives of his thinking were drawn from Saint Augustine – especially as embodied in the *Decretum* of Gratian – and from the *Summa Theologica* of Saint Thomas (especially *Secunda secundae*, art. 29). Legal treatises on the correctness of war had been written before and during Vitoria's life. One cannot forget Giovanni da Legnano's *De bello* (XIV century), Paide de Puteo's *De Re militari* (XV century), Martino Gariati di Lodi's *De confederatione, pace, et conventionibus principum*, Francisco Arias' *De bello et eius justitia* (1533), Gonzalo de Villadiego's *Tractatus de legato* (1490), and Juan López' *De bello et bellatoribus* (1488). To these names we should add those of Baltasar de Ayala, Fernando Vásquez de Menchaca, and Diego de Covarrubias, all of whom were Vitoria's contemporaries. Scholars, however, unanimously agree in placing Vitoria's lecture on war far above these and similar works because of its thoroughness, conciseness, clarity, and equanimity.[48]

In Vitoria's own words the lecture on war deals with four principal questions: "first, whether Christians may make war at all; second, where does the authority to declare war repose?; third, what may and ought to furnish just cause for war?; fourth, what extensive measures may be taken in a just war against the enemy?" The first, introductory, question deals with a purely theological problem: the reconciliation of the evangelical counsel of forgiveness and meekness – "Whoever shall smite thee on the right cheek, turn to him the other cheek also," (*Matthew*, V) – with the alleged Christian right to serve in war and to make war. In a way, however, Vitoria tackles here a more comprehensive issue, one of constant relevance: the conflict between high principles and realistic practicality, utopian irenism and political expediency. Both sides were abundantly represented in Vitoria's day. Wycliffe, Luther, Melanchthon, Erasmus, Colet, Thomas More, and even Juan Luis Vives appealed to the example of early Christians and also to the words of the Fathers, especially Cyprian, Chrysostomus, Ambrose, Basil, and Tertullian to condemn all wars, even the 'holy war' against the Turks. Others invoked the authority of Saint Augustine

48 The bibliography on the subject is very rich. Here are the most important titles. Camilo Barcia Trelles, *Francisco de Vitoria. Fundador del Derecho Internacional Moderno*, third part, "El derecho y la guerra," pp. 131–218, (Valladolid, 1923); J. Kosters, "Les fondateurs du Droit des Gens," *Bibliotheca Visseriana*, vol. 4, (The Hague, 1925); E. Nys, *Le Droit de la Guerre et les Précurseurs de Grotius*, (Bruxelles, 1882); Pillet, *La Guerre et le Droit*, (Louvain, 1922); Alberic Rollin, *Le Droit Moderne de la Guerre*, 3 vols., (Bruxelles, 1920); L. Vanderpol, *Le Droit de la Guerre d'après les Théologiens et les Canonistes du Moyen Age*, (Paris, 1911); also, *La Doctrine Scolastique du droit de la Guerre*, (Paris, 1918); Herbert F. Wright, *Francisco de Vitoria 'De iure belli' relectio*, (Washington, 1916); Wheaton, *Histoire du progrès du droit des gens*, (Leipzig, 1841); A. Carrión, "Los maestros Vitoria, Báñez, y Ledesma hablan sobre la conquista y evangelización de las Indias," *La Ciencia Tomista* (Salamanca), XLII (1930), pp. 34–57; J. T. Delos, "La doctrine de Monroe, la politique Américaine et les principes du droit public de Vitoria," *La Vie Intellectuelle*, I (1928), pp. 461–475; Hinojosa y Navarro, "Los Precursores españoles de Grocio," *Anuario de Historia del Derecho Español*, (Madrid), VI (1910), pp. 220–236; L. Urbano, "La Sociedad de Naciones y los principios tomistas del Maestro Francisco de Vitoria," *La Ciencia Tomista* (Salamanca), XXIX (1929), pp. 37–59, 348–369; R. Regout, *La doctrine de la guerre juste de S. Augustin à nos jours, d'après les théologiens et les canonistes catholiques*, (Paris, 1935).

and Saint Thomas to insist that a literal interpretation of the New Testament's text would lead to a world-wide anarchy and to the very destruction of Christianity itself. In this controversy Vitoria sided with the latter group.

Passing over outside opinions, however, let my answer to the question be given in the single proposition: Christians may serve in war and make war. This is the conclusion of Saint Augustine in the many passages where he thoroughly considers the question, such as: (a) in his *Contra Faustum*, (b) in his *Liber 83 Quaestionum*, (c) in his *De verbis Domini*, in his *Contra Secundinum Manichaeum*, (d) in his sermon on the Centurion's son, and (e) in his letter to Boniface. And, as Saint Augustine shows, this is proved by the words of John the Baptist to the soldiers (*Luke*, III), 'Do violence to no man, neither accuse any falsely.' But, says Saint Augustine. 'if Christian doctrine condemned war altogether, those looking for the counsel of salvation in the Gospel would be told to throw away their arms and give up soldiering altogether'; but what is said to them is 'Do violence to no man and be content with your wages.'

Secondly, there is proof in the reason of the thing (*Secunda Secundae*, quaest. 40, art. 1). To draw the sword and use arms against internal wrongdoers and seditious citizens is lawful according to *Romans*, ch. 13, 'He beareth not the sword in vain, for he is the minister of God, a revenger of wrath upon him that doeth evil.' Therefore, it is lawful also to use the sword and arms against external enemies. Princes, accordingly, are told in the *Psalms* (41), 'Deliver the poor and needy, rid them out of the hand of the wicked.'

Thirdly, this was allowable by the Law of Nature, as appears in the case of Abraham, who fought against four Kings (*Genesis*, ch. 14) and also by the written law, as appears in the case of David and the Maccabees. But the Gospel Law forbids nothing which is allowed by Natural Law, as is well shown by Saint Thomas (*Prima secundae*, quaest. 107, last art.) and that is why it is called the law of liberty (*Saint James*, ch. 1 and 2). Therefore what was lawful under Natural Law and in the written law is no less lawful under the Gospel Law.

Fourthly, since there can be no doubt that in a defensive war force may be employed to repel force (*Digest*, I, i, 3), this is also the case with respect to an offensive war, that is, a war where we are not only defending ourselves or seeking to repossess property, but also where we are trying to avenge some wrong done to us. This, I say, is proved by the authority of Saint Augustine (*Liber 83 Quaestionum*) in a passage also found in can. *Dominus*, C 23, qu. 2, 'Those wars are described as just wars which are waged to avenge a wrong done, and where punishment has to be meted out to a city or state because it has itself neglected to exact punishment for an offence committed by its citizens or subjects, or to return what has been wrongfully taken away.'

A fifth proof of the righteousness of an offensive war is that even a defensive war could not be waged satisfactorily, were no vengeance taken on enemies who have tried to do a wrong. For they would be emboldened to make a second attack, if the fear of retribution did not keep them from wrong doing.

A sixth proof is that, as Saint Augustine says (*De verbo Domini* and *Ad Bonifacium*), the end and aim of war is the peace and security of the State. But there can be no security in the State unless enemies are made to desist from wrong doing by the fear of war. For the situation would be glaringly unfair if all that a State could do when enemies attack it unjustly was to ward off the attack and did not follow this up by further steps.

A seventh proof comes from the end and aim and good of the whole world. For there would be no condition of happiness for the world, nay, its condition would be one of utter misery, if oppressors and robbers and plunderers could with impunity commit their crimes and oppress the good and innocent, and these latter could not in turn retaliate.

My eighth and last proof is one which in morals carries the utmost weight, namely, the authority and example of good men. Such men have not only defended their country and their own property in defensive wars, but have also in offensive wars sought reparation for wrongs done or attempted by their enemies, as was shown in the case of Jonathan and Simon (*I Maccabees*, ch. 9), who avenged the death of their brother John on the sons of Jambri. And in the Christian Church we have the conspicuous examples of Constantine the Great and Theodosius the Elder and other renowned Christian Emperors, who made many wars of both kinds, although their councils included bishops of great sanctity and learning.[49]

[49]. "Sed, relictis extraneis opinionibus, sit responsio ad quaestionem unica conclusione: Licet Christianis militare et bella gerere. Haec conclusio est Augustini in multis locis. Nam *Contra Faustum* et *Libro 83 Quaestionum* et *De verbis Domini* et *Libro contra Secundinum Manichaeum* et in sermone de puero Centurionis et ad Bonifacium epistola diserte astruit. Et probatur conclusio, ut probat Augustinus ex verbis Ioannis Baptistae (*Luc.*, 3) ad milites, 'Neminem concutiatis, nemini iniuriam feceritis.' 'Quod si Christiana disciplina,' inquit Augustinus' 'omnino bella culparet, hoc potius consilium salutis petentibus in Evangelio daretur, ut abicerent arma seque militiae omnino subtraherent. Dictum est autem eis, Neminem concutiatis, contenti estote stipendiis vestris.'

Secundo, probatur ratione (scilicet, *Secunda Secundae*, qu. 40, art. 1). Licet stringere gladium et armis uti adversus interiores malefactores et seditiosos cives, secundum illud *ad Rom.*, 13: 'Non sine causa gladium portat. Minister enim Dei est, vindex in iram ei, qui male agit.' Ergo etiam licet uti gladio et armis adversus hostes exteriores. Unde principibus dictum est in *Psalm.*, 'Eripite pauperem et egenum de manu peccatoris liberate.'

Tertio, in lege naturae hoc licuit, ut patet de Abraham, qui pugnavit contra quattor reges (*Gen.*, 14). Item in lege scripta, ut patet de David et Machabaeis. Sed lex Evangelica nihil interdicit, quod iure naturali licitum sit, ut S. Thomas eleganter tradit (*Prima Secundae*, qu. 107, art.ult.); unde et dicitur lex libertatis (*Iac.*, 1 et 2). Ergo quod licebat in lege naturae et scripta, non minus licet in lege Evangelica.

Et quia de bello defensive revocari in dubium non potest, quia vim vi repellere licet (ff., De iustitia et iure, 1. *ut vim*), quarto probatur etiam de bello offensivo, i. e., in quo non solum defenduntur aut etiam repetuntur res, sed ubi petitur vindicta pro iniuria accepta. Probatur, inquam, auctoritate Augustini (*Libro 83 Quaestionum*) et habetur can. *Dominus*, 23, qu. 2: 'Iusta bella solent diffinire, quae ulciscuntur iniurias, si gens vel civitas plectenda est, quae

The second issue discussed by Vitoria was the specification of a proper authority to declare and make war. The different candidates to such a doubtful honor make up a colorful picture of the complicated and rapidly changing political realities of the sixteenth century: private citizens, petty rulers (such as "the Duke of Alba or the Count of Benevento"), States and principalities under one prince (such as "the Kingdom of Castile and Aragon and the Republic of Venice"), the rulers of those States and Principalities, or, finally, their common Lord or Prince (such as the Emperor). The first proposition states that a private person, can "accept and wage a defensive war" not only for the defense of his own person, but also for the defense of his property and goods. This right of self-defense was upheld by Vitoria in uncompromising terms. Armed resistance in defense of life and property is lawful even if flight is possible. Furthermore, civil law (in this case the *Digest*) allows even killing by both laymen and clergymen in defense of their property, "so long as scandal is not caused." The only limitation imposed by Vitoria upon the right of self-defense has to do with the case where "*time* has been allowed to go by since the seizure." But even in this case Vitoria generously allows the victim to immediately strike back "in order to avoid infame and disgrace."

The basic difference between the right of private self-defense – which Vitoria, unlike Grotius, refuses to classify as a "private" war – and the right to declare war by a sovereign authority, is clearly expressed in the second proposition: "Every State has the authority to declare and to

vel vindicare neglexit quod a suis improbe factum est vel reddere quod per iniuriam ablatum est.'

Probatur etiam quinto de bello offensivo, quia bellum etiam defensivum geri commode non potest, nisi etiam vindicetur in hostes, qui iniuriam fecerunt aut conati sunt facere; fierent enim hostes audaciores ad iterum invadendum, nisi timore poenae deterreantur ab iniuria.

Probatur sexto, quia finis belli est pax et securitas Reipublicae, ut Augustinus inquit (*De verbis Domini* et *ad Bonifacium*). Sed non potest esse securitas in Republica, nisi hostes coërceantur metu belli ab iniuria. Esset enim omnino iniqua condicio belli, si, hostibus invadentibus iniuste Rempublicam, solum liceret Reipublicae advertere hostes nec possent ulterius prosequi.

Probatur septimo ex fine et bono totius orbis. Prorsus enim orbis consistere in felici statu non posset, immo esset rerum omnium pessima condicio, si tyranni quidem et latrones et raptores possent impune iniurias facere et opprimere bonos et innocentes, nec liceret vicissim innocentibus animadvertere in nocentes.

Probatur octavo et ultimo, quia in moralibus potissimum argumentum est ab auctoritate et exemplis sanctorum et bonorum virorum, qui non solum bello defensivo tutati sunt patriam resque suas, sed etiam bello offensivo prosecuti sunt iniurias ab hostibus acceptas vel attentatas, ut patet de Ionatha et Simone (I *Machab.*, 9), qui vindicaverunt mortem Ioannis fratris sui contra filios Iambri. Et in Ecclesia Christiana patet de Constantino Magno, Theodosio maiore, et aliis clarissimis et Christianissimis Imperatoribus, qui multa bella utriusque generis gesserunt, cum haberent in consiliis sanctissimos et doctissimos episcopos." (*Bate Translation*, pp. 272–275.)

make war." In explaining this proposition Vitoria makes it clear that the rights of the State transcend those of the private citizen acting in his own self-defense because the State is entitled not only to redress wrongs, but more importantly, to engage both *preventive* and *punitive* measures. This right of every State is also available to the lawful Princes of the State (third proposition). The main difficulty, however, is to define precisely "what is a State, and who can properly be called a sovereign State, since the Prince can easily be identified as the lawful ruler of a sovereign State. Vitoria characterizes the State as a perfect society – the Aristotelian-medieval tradition of autarchy and self-sufficiency – having two fundamental features. The first is a negative one: a State is a complete community which "is not a part of another community"; the positive feature consists in the possession of "its own laws and its own Council and its own magistrates." Unfortunately Vitoria's examples did not help to define the basic concept. The Kingdoms of Castile and Aragon did in fact satisfy the second condition but not the first: having their own laws, councils and magistrates, they were in fact "parts of another community." Vitoria's confusion reveals the unresolved tension in his thought between the medieval notion of "self-sufficiency" and the modern demand for interrelatedness and expanding internationalism.

From his own definition of the State, which makes it possible to have many perfect States under one Prince, Vitoria drew the logical conclusion that those States may make war without previous authorization of their common Lord, "just as the Kings who are subordinated to the Emperor can make war on one another without waiting for the Emperor's authorization." Petty rulers, however, who are not at the head of a perfect State, but are parts of another State, have no right to declare war, unless custom or necessity makes it lawful. An example of the latter might be a case where the King neglects to exact redress for the wrongs that have been done to his state. More importantly, however, than these specific distinctions is Vitoria's marked emphasis upon the notion of sovereignty as the fundamental condition of the legal authority to declare and wage war.

The third part of his lecture deals with the central problem of war: "What may and ought to furnish causes of *just* war?" The issue is approached from two different directions: first, Vitoria deals with the objective causes of a just war in a purely theoretical manner; then, after a misplaced discussion of the material consequences of war, he discusses at length the moral problems which confront citizens regarding the just nature of their tacit or implicit involvement in a war.

The theoretical discussion is extremely concise, having been fully treated in the first lecture *De Indis* in connection with the *Conquista.* The invalid causes of war are a difference of religion, extension of Empire, and the personal glory of a Prince. The only "just" cause for commencing a war must always be without exception "a wrong received," a wrong of such severity and magnitude as to justify "the severe and atrocious character of war." Much more comprehensive and original is Vitoria's discussion of war as a problem of conscience for both rulers and individual citizens. Here the juridical approach recedes for a while in favor of the pastoral and moralistic. As a skillful director of conscience Vitoria attempts to reckon with the complicated casuistic of an individual's response to the emergency of war.

The first section examines the obligations of princes and rulers. Princes cannot be satisfied with the belief that a war is just, because such a belief might very well be a vincible and inexcusable error. Were such a belief a sufficient justification for war, most wars, including the war of the Turks against the Christians, would be justified on both sides. The Princes are therefore obliged to make "an exceedingly careful examination of the righteousness and causes of war", and to listen to those "who on grounds of equity oppose it." If after this close and sincere scrutiny "there are still apparent and possible" reasons on both sides, the Prince should abide by the following norms. First of all, it is not lawful to dispossess the possessor in a doubtful case.

For example, suppose the King of France to be in lawful possession of Burgundy, and it be doubtful whether he has the right thereto. The Emperor may not try to oust him by force of arms; nor on the other hand may the French King seize Naples or Milan, if there be doubt who is entitled to it. The proof is that in doubtful matters the party in possession has the better position. Therefore it is not lawful to dispossess the possessor in a doubtful case. Further, if the matter were being heard by a lawful judge, he would never in case of doubt dispossess the party in possession. Therefore, if we postulate that those princes who are asserting a right are judges in their own cause, they may not lawfully eject a possessor so long as there is any doubt about the title. Further, in the suits and causes of private persons it is never permissible in a doubtful matter to disposses a lawful possessor. Therefore, if by human law it is not permissible in a doubtful matter to dispossess the lawful possessor, it can validly be objected to Princes, 'Obey the law thyself hast made, seeing that a man ought to adopt for himself the same law he has enjoined on others.' Also, were it otherwise, a war could be just on both sides and would never be settled. For if in a doubtful matter it were lawful for one side to assert his claim by force the other might make armed defence, and after the one had obtained what he claimed, the other might afterwards claim it back, and so there would be war without end, to the ruin and tribulation of peoples.[50]

The second rule establishes that if the city or province about which the doubt arises has no lawful possessor – as it frequently happens in cases of doubtful inheritance – both sides are bound to accept a compromise, even the party which is stronger and "is able to seize the whole by armed force." The four proofs of this conclusion are typical of Vitoria's argumentation throughout this lecture: "The proof is that when the merits of a quarrel are equal one side does no wrong by claiming an equal part of the thing in dispute. Further, in private disputes where the matter is in doubt, one party may not seize the whole thing. In the same sense, war is not just on both sides. A judge would not decree and award the whole thing to either party." The first part of this proof is then a rational argument; the second, an analogy with private litigations; the third, a *reductio ad absurdum;* the fourth, an analogy between princes and judges.

The third and final norm concerns the obligations of the lawful possessor whose titles are contested by others. In doubtful matters princes, who are judges of their own actions, are obliged to examine their own cases exactly in the same way the judge is bound to examine a case when an objection is raised against a lawful possessor. However, after due examination of the merits of the allegation the lawful possessor is not bound to quit possession as long as the doubt reasonably persists.

The last part of the third proposition has to do with the responsibilities of individual citizens. Vitoria opens up this section with a valiant and unqualified defense of the rights of conscientious objectors: "If a subject is convinced of the injustice of a war, he ought not to serve in it, even on the command of a prince." Otherwise, he would sinfully and inexcusably kill innocent people. Furthermore, the subject whose conscience is against the war is not only *allowed* but morally *obliged* to refuse military service.

50 "... Ut, e. g., si Rex Francorum est in legitima possessione Burgundiae, si etiam est dubium an habeat ius ad illam necne, non videtur quod Imperator possit armis repetere; et e contrario nec Rex Francorum Neapolim aut Mediolanum, si dubium est cuius iuris sint. Probatur, quia in dubiis melior est condicio possidentis. Ergo non licet spoliare possessorem pro re dubia. Item, si res ageretur coram iudice legitimo, nunquam in re dubia spoliaret possessorem. Ergo dato quod illi principes, qui praetendunt ius, sint iudices in illa causa, non possunt licite spoliare possessorem, manente dubio de iure. Item in rebus et causis privatorum

As a moralist, however, Vitoria was much more concerned with the problems of a doubtful case, rather than with the certainty of clear-cut choices. The rest of this section, therefore, is dedicated to the case of a doubtful war. Vitoria makes here a sharp distinction between political leaders – "senators and petty rulers, and in general all those who are admitted to the public or the Prince's Council," and private citizens, or as he puts it "lesser folk, who have no place or audience in the Prince's council or in the public council." The former are clearly bound to examine into the causes of an unjust war, first because they are powerful enough to avert it; secondly, because otherwise they would be consenting parties to an injustice. Furthermore, Vitoria strongly recommends that war should not be made on the sole judgment of the King, "not capable by himself of examining into the causes of war," but rather "on that of many wise and upright men."

With respect to the "lesser folk," Vitoria's teaching becomes more controversial and vulnerable. The general theme of his thought is that such people are under no obligation to examine the causes of war, "but may serve in it on reliance of their betters." The reasons brought in favor of this conclusion are three: first, because it is both impossible and inexpedient to give reasons for all acts of State to every member of the political body; second, because these people "of the lower orders" could not in fact stop the war even if they perceived its injustice; third, because "for men of this sort" the fact that the war is waged after public council and by public authority should normally be proof enough of its justice. However, Vitoria hastens to warn, it is very well possible that the proofs and tokens of the injustice of war may be such that even those "lesser people" would be totally inexcusable if they agreed to serve in it. The most frequent and morally excruciating problem concerns the case where the subjects are doubtful regarding the righteousness of the war. Here Vitoria had to reckon with the opinion of Pope Adrian VI – the friend of Juan Luis Vives and the last non-Italian Pope – according to whom those subjects who doubted the justice of any war should not serve in it, even at the command of their Princes. Vitoria disagrees with such opinion, and relying heavily upon

nunquam in causa dubia licet spoliare possessorem legitimum. Ergo nec in causis principum; leges enim sunt principum. Si ergo secundum leges humanas non licet in causa dubia spoliare legitimum possessorem, ergo merito potest obici principibus, "Patere legem, quam ipse tuleris; quod enim quisque iuris in alios statuit, ipse eodem iure uti debet." Item alias esset bellum iustum ex utraque parte, et bellum nunquam componi posset. Si enim in causa dubia licet uni armis repetere, ergo alteri defendere, et, postquam unus recuperasset, posset iterum alius reposcere, et sic nunquam esset finis bellorum cum pernicie et calamitate populorum." (*Bate Translation*, pp. 283–284.)

Saint Augustine's authority (*Contra Faustum*, Book 22, ch. 75) maintains that as long as the citizen cannot reach moral certainty about the injustice of the war, he is obliged to follow his Prince and fight exactly in the same way as the lictor is bound to carry out the decrees of the judge, even though he might have some doubts about their legal justification. The reason behind Vitoria's opinion was that no State could even survive if a single doubt could excuse its members from obedience to the ruler, especially in a state of national emergency. It is true, Vitoria concedes, that when the lawfulness of a given action is doubtful a man would be committing a sin if he proceeded to take such action without first attempting to overcome such doubt. Here, however, the doubt of the individual is neutralized and even offset by his obligation to obey. A husband, for instance, is bound to render to his wife her conjugal rights even if he doubts the validity of his marriage. Vitoria's position might seem today highly undemocratic and hawkish: ordinary citizens, unless utterly convinced of the injustice of the war, must rely upon the judgment of their rulers, ignore their own doubts, and fight. In practice, however, even the most democratic governments of the world expect as much from their citizens and practically abide by Vitoria's realistic policy with perhaps only one significant difference. In our era of mass communication politicians are more efficient in publicly advertising and "selling" to the "lesser folk" their reasons (real or not) for going to war. Furthermore, in spite of his apparent severity, Vitoria was obviously aware of the nebulous boundaries between certainty and doubt, and was therefore deeply moved by the fate of millions of "lesser folk" who, in good faith, followed their natural leaders into highly questionable and bloody war adventures. The sincere compassion of Vitoria for those innocent victims of their princes' follies – one of the recurrent themes of Erasmian irenism – will become manifest later on when we discuss the consequences of war upon human beings.

The section about the righteousness of war closes with two related doubts. The first deals with the question whether a war can be just on both sides? Logically consistent with his own objective standards of justice Vitoria denies that the case could ever occur, except where on one side there is true justice and on the other invincible ignorance. The second doubt is whether one who has in ignorance gone to an unjust war and is subsequently convinced of its injustice is bound to make amends. According to Vitoria, princes and subjects are in this case obliged to give back what they have taken away and not yet consumed, but need make no amends for what they have already consumed.

At the very end of this section Victoria makes a remark of considerable importance. It is very well possible, he warns, that a war may be just and lawful in itself, and yet, owing to some "collateral circumstances," may be unlawful. The "collateral circumstances" enumerated by Vitoria in this lecture and in *De potestate civili* are two. The first is scandal; the second is the case when the conduct of war is manifestly more harmful than it is advantageous. The latter can happen when the State itself is enfeebled and impaired by war, or when the war might prove useful to one single Kingdom of Christianity but injurious to the world or to Christendom. Vitoria gives two examples of those circumstances.

Inasmuch as wars (according to what has been said before) ought to be waged for the common good, if some one city cannot be recaptured without greater evils befalling the State, such as the devastation of many cities, great slaughter of human beings, provocation of Princes, occasions for new wars, the destruction of Christianity (in that an opportunity is given to pagans to invade and seize the lands of Christians), it is indubitable that the Prince is bound rather to give up his own rights and abstain from war. For it is clear that if the King of France, for example, had a right to retake Milan, but by the war both the Kingdom of France and the Duchy of Milan would suffer intolerable ills and heavy woes, it would not be right for him to retake it. This is because that war ought to take place either for the good of France or for the good of Milan. Therefore, when, on the contrary, great ills would befall each side by the war, it could not be a just war.[51]

The other example is given in the lecture *De potestate civili:*

The State has no power to make war except for the purpose of defending itself, and protecting itself and its property; it follows, then, that any war will be unjust, whether it be begun by the King or by the State, through which the latter is not rendered greater, but rather is enfeebled and impaired. Nay more, since one nation is part of the entire world, and since the Christian province is a part of the whole Christian State, if any war should be advantageous to one province or nation but injurious to the world or to Christendom, it is my belief that for that very reason, that war is unjust. If, for example, the Spanish should undertake against the French a war which in other respects, was just, and which was, besides, advantageous to the Spanish kingdom, but which involved Christendom as a whole in still greater harm

[51] "... Cum enim, ut supra dictum est, bella geri debeant pro bono communi, si ad recuperandam unam civitatem necesse est quod sequantur maiora mala in Republica, ut vastatio multarum civitatum, caedes magna mortalium, irritatio principum, occasiones novorum bellorum in perniciem Ecclesiae, item quod paganis detur opportunitas invadendi et occupandi terras Christianorum, indubitatum est quin teneatur princeps potius cedere iuri suo et abstinere se bello. Clarum est enim quod, si Rex Gallorum, v. g., haberet ius ad recuperandum Mediolanum, ex bello autem et Regnum Galliae et ipsa provincia Mediolanensis paterentur intoleranda mala et calamitates graves, non licet ei recuperare, quia

and loss (suppose, for instance, that the Turks in the meantime take possession of Christian provinces), then the Spanish must cease from waging that war. And these are the points which pertain to the exposition of the first conclusion.[52]

The fourth and final proposition discusses the measures which may be taken against the enemy in the case of a just war. The fundamental principle in this matter is that in war everything is lawful which is required to defend and preserve the state. More specifically, whether the measures taken against the enemy are lawful is determined by the four aims of war: the defense of self and property; the recovery of goods taken away; the redress of wrongs suffered; and the protection of future peace and security. In determining the gravity of those measures the prince should further keep in mind the following rules of behavior. First, the prince has the obligation to see that greater evils do not arise out of war than those the war itself is intended to avert. Therefore, the severity of the measures taken in war must be proportionate to the effect those measures will have upon the ultimate issues of the war. Second, the Prince must keep the extent of the punishment entirely proportionate to the magnitude of the offense, "according to the estimate of a good man," knowing that according to the rules of Natural and Divine Law "punishments should be awarded restrictively, and rewards extensively." Thirdly, the Prince should constantly keep in mind, that although the war be unjust on the other side, in the majority of cases the troops engaged in it are innocent and their punishment therefore, unjustifiable. Furthermore, in some cases even the princes of the enemy who in reality have no just cause of war, may nevertheless be waging war in good faith, and therefore, (beyond the limits of just satisfaction) the victor is not entitled to other punitive measures. Fourthly, the prince must always respect what "the use and custom of war" has constituted as the Law of Nations. More important, however, than

bellum ipsum aut fieri debet vel propter bonum Galliae aut Mediolani. Quando ergo e contrario utriusque magna mala ex bello futura sunt, non potest bellum iustum esse." (*Bate Translation*, p. 287.)

[52] "Nullum bellum est justum, si constat geri majori malo Reipublicae, quam bono, et utilitate, quantumvis aliunde suppetant tituli et rationes ad bellum justum.

Probatur: Quia si Respublica non habet potestatem inferendi bellum, nisi ad tuendum se, resque suas, atque se protegendum; ergo ubi ipso bello attenuatur potius, atque atteritur, quam augetur, bellum erit injustum ,sive a Rege inferatur, sive a Republica.

Imo cum una Respublica sit pars totius orbis, et maxime Christiana Provincia pars totius Reipublicae, si bellum utile sit uni Provinciae, aut Reipublicae cum damno orbis, aut Christianitatis, puto eo ipso bellum esse injustum, ut si bellum Hispaniarum esset adversus Gallos, alias ex causis justis susceptum, et alioqui Regno Hispaniarum utile; tamen cum majori malo et jactura geritur Christianitatis, puta quia Turcae occupant interim Provincias Christianorum, cessandum esset a tali bello." (*Relecciones Teológicas*, pp. 191–192.)

these formal rules of conduct, are Vitoria's recommendations concerning the moral attitude of the Prince. His leading assumption is that by the law of war the Prince is put in the position of a judge mediating between the two States. It will be "as judge *and not as accuser* that he will deliver the judgment whereby the injured State can obtain satisfaction." As a judge the Prince should, first of all, abstain from seeking occasions of war, but should, if possible, live in peace with his neighbors, love them as brothers, and only come to the necessity of war "under compulsion and reluctantly." Secondly, after the war has broken out he should seek not to devastate the people against whom it is directed, but should seek only the defense and security of his own country.

Having made clear these noble rules of conduct and attitude we will present the concrete guidelines of warfare policy specified by Vitoria. To prepare the reader for the occasional harshness of his "law of war," we should first make some preliminary remarks. Vitoria has often been criticized for the oversimplified laconism of his principles and recommendations. It is unquestionably true that Vitoria's lecture lacks the comprehensiveness and methodological thoroughness of Grotius' *De iure belli*, and that in this respect our sketch of the Spanish theologian does not bear comparison with the treatise of the Dutch jurist. No wonder, therefore, if some concrete pasages of Vitoria's lecture, taken literally and without further qualifications, sound today extremely harsh and severe. Furthermore, although the basic guidelines of Vitoria's thought are, in my opinion, of unremitting actuality, some specific rules are directly related to old-fashioned patterns of sixteenth-century warfare, and consequently totally irrelevant to the problems of our atomic age. Nor can we forget that Vitoria proceeds constantly on the naive assumption that in any war there is always in reality a "just" and an "unjust" cause, and is entirely oblivious to the pathetic mixture of the right and the wrong in human affairs. He calmly proceeds to dictate his rules of behavior for the rare case where the victorious prince is also the immaculate champion of a righteous war. Finally, it is important to note that the natural jurist and the Catholic exegete make a rather uncomfortable alliance. The interpretation of the Old Testament (especially some passages from *Deuteronomy*) haunts Vitoria with an image of a God who does not seem to abide by the most fundamental requirements of the Law of Nations. Those sections where Vitoria's discrimination against pagans appears most eloquently are not by any means the most enlightened and respectable parts of this otherwise memorable document.

The discussion is clearly divided into two parts: in the first Vitoria specifies the measures which may be lawfully taken against an enemy's property; in the second, the measures which may be directed against the people themselves. As far as property is concerned Vitoria allows the victorious side in a just war to recapture lost property, to extract from enemy property all expenses of the war, and all the damages wrongfully caused by the enemy. It is also lawful to destroy the enemy's fortresses and to build new ones on the enemy's soil, provided future peace and security justify these precautions. Finally, as a deterrent and preventive measure, the victorious side can exact proportionate punishment from the enemy. These measures may lead to the destruction of weaponry (even that which belongs to innocent folk), to the spoliation of agricultural produce if the war cannot be otherwise effectively carried out or the enemy sufficiently weakened. The exaction of tributes from the enemy is justified on the same grounds. The property, however, of neutral foreigners and travellers ought to be respected. At the end of this section Vitoria asks himself whether captured property belongs entirely to the captor. Here he makes a sharp distinction between movable and immovable property. The former goes to the victor according to the Law of Nations, even if it exceeds in amount what would compensate for damages sustained. Vitoria even thinks that to give a city up to the soldiery to sack is not "unlawful in itself," although it usually results in so many horrors and cruelties that it should be allowed only "in the greatest necessity and weightiest reason," provided the generals do whatever is possible to prevent those crimes. In dealing with immovable property Vitoria is much more generic: the victorious prince is allowed to seize as much as the right to compensation, the security of the State, and the punishment of the enemy makes necessary.

Concerning those measures directed against human life Vitoria forbids the deliberate killing of the innocent "such as children, women, harmless agricultural folk, peaceful civilian populations: guests and foreigners, clerics and professed persons, and even the children of the Turks." It is lawful, however, in some circumstances to kill the innocent together with the guilty in the conduct of the war itself. Another question is whether the killing of innocent people is lawful when – as in the case of the Saracens – they may be reasonably expected to cause danger in the future.

Here a doubt may arise whether the killing of guiltless people is lawful when they may be expected to cause danger in the future; thus, for example, the children of Saracens are guiltless, but there is good reason to fear that when grown up they will fight against Christians and bring on them all hazards of war. Moreover, the adult male civilians of the enemy who are not soldiers are presumed to be innocent, yet they will hereafter carry a soldier's arm and cause the hazard named. Now, is it lawful to slay these youths? It seems so, on the same principle which justifies the incidental killing of guiltless persons. Also (*Deuteronomy*, Ch. 20) the sons of Israel were ordered when assaulting any city to slay 'every adult male.' Now, it cannot be presumed that all of these would be guilty.

My answer is that although this killing may be possibly defended, yet I believe that it is in no wise right seeing that evil is not to be done even in order to avoid greater evil still, and it is intolerable that any one should be killed for a future fault. There are moreover other available measures of precaution against their future conduct, namely, captivity, exile, etc., as we shall forthwith show. Hence it follows that, whether victory has already been won or the war is still in progress, if the innocence of any soldier is evident and the soldiers can let him go free, they are bound to do so.[53]

Therefore, when the conduct of a war justifies the indiscriminate spoliation of all enemy subjects it is also justifiable to carry all enemy subjects into captivity, whether they be guilty or guiltness. This rule, however, applies only to the war against pagans, since "it is a received rule of Christendom that Christians do not become slaves according to the rights of war, but only captives in exchange for ransom." The next question concerns the rights of hostages. Vitoria maintains without hesitation that guilty hostages, "those, for instance, who have borne arms," may rightfully be killed. Furthermore, in a just war it is lawful to kill all the guilty, not only in the actual heat of battle, but also when victory has been won and no danger remains, although the punishment has to be inflicted without cruelty, in proportion to the wrong suffered, and with due consideration to the possible good faith of the enemy.

[53] "Sed circa haec potest dubitari an liceat interficere innocentes, a quibus tamen in futurum imminet periculum. Puta pueri Saracenorum sunt innocentes, sed timendum merito est ne facti adulti pugnent contra Christianos et inferant bellum cum periculo. Et praeterea etiam togati puberes apud hostes, qui non sunt milites, praesumuntur innocentes, sed isti armabuntur postea in milites et inferent periculum – an liceat tales interficere. Et videtur quod sic eadem ratione qua per accidens licet interficere alios innocentes. Item (*Deut.*, 20) praecipitur filiis Israel, ut, cum expugnaverint aliquam civitatem, interficiant omnes puberes. Non est autem praesumendum quod omnes essent nocentes.

Respondetur ad hoc, licet posset fortasse defendi quod in tali casu possint interfici, tamen credo quod nullo modo licet, quia non sunt facienda mala, ut vitentur etiam alia mala maiora, et intolerabile est quod occidatur aliquis pro peccato futuro. Et praeterea sunt alia remedia ad cavendum in futurum ab illis, ut captivitas, exilium, etc., ut statim dicemus. Unde sequitur quod, sive iam parta victoria sive in actu bellum geratur, si constat de innocentia alicuius militis et milites possunt eum liberare, tenentur." (*Bate Translation*, p. 289.)

This rule applies without reservation to those who have unconditionally surrendered, but not to captives whose lives are protected by the use and custom of war "received into the Law of Nations." The final issue to be decided is whether it is lawful to depose the enemy's princes and to appoint new ones, or even to keep the princedom for the victor. These "utterly savage and inhuman measures," Vitoria claims are not always permissible, even assuming that the enemy's offense was a sufficient cause for war. Nevertheless, the number and enormity of the wrongs which were wrought, and the protection of the State's security, might deem it necessary to seize the enemy's sovereignty.

Such is the substance of Vitoria's theory of the law of war, a noble combination of high ideals and realistic appraisals, a laconic sketch of fundamental guidelines, a pioneering document in the history of International Law, and still a baffling mixture of political philosophy and theological constructions. It is on the basis of these two lectures, *De Indis* and *De iure belli*, that Vitoria has frequently been called *the* father of International Law.

We cannot close our study of Vitoria's thought without at least a short discussion of the legitimacy of this title – father of International Law. To achieve this purpose we shall investigate his thought regarding the nature of the Law of Nations, and we shall compare Vitoria's work with Grotius' *De iure belli ac pacis*, the classical monument of International Law traditionally seen as the stepping stone in the field.

Having so far presented the reader the specific rules of the Law of Nations concerning war and the Spanish *Conquista* of America in particular, it is time now to turn our attention to a discussion of the nature of that law. Even the most enthusiastic admirers of Vitoria have to recognize that the highly pastoral and casuistic approach of these lectures prevented Vitoria from making a comprehensive theoretical scrutiny of the basic concept. In fact the reader will find only a few passing remarks on this all-important subject. These remarks are extremely important, but a complete understanding requires a much more extensive background which is only to be found in Vitoria's scholastic teaching, especially in his commentaries to questions 52 and 57 of the *Secunda secundae*. Without reference to those commentaries it is practically impossible to assess Vitoria's thought in this matter, and any attempt to rely exclusively upon the extraordinary *relectiones* – as has been frequently done – will lead to inconclusive results.[54]

[54] Besides the authors mentioned in footnote 48 (Barcia Trelles, Kosters, Nys, Wheaton, Hinojosa y Navarro) one should consult the following titles regarding Vitoria's Law of

In the introductory remarks to the third section of his lecture *De Indis*, Vitoria gives the following definition of the Law of Nations: "What natural reason has established among all nations (*inter omnes gentes*) is called the *Ius Gentium.* Vitoria's definition is taken from Gaius: "*Quod ratio inter omnes homines constituit, id apud omnes populos paraeque custoditur, vocaturque ius gentium, quasi quo iure omnes gentes utuntur.*" Most scholars generally agree that by substituting his own *gentes* for Gaius' *homines* Vitoria fundamentally changed the Roman conception of *Ius Gentium* from a universal common law founded upon the unity of man's rational nature and made up of both public and private elements into the modern concept of International Law as a public juridical order between sovereign States. Other scholars, however, accepting the significance of this change cast some doubts about its total implications and point out that the preposition *inter* in this context could be understood in the sense of universality – the very essence of the Roman conception of *Ius Gentium* – rather than in the sense of legal reciprocity between States, which is the fundamental trait of modern International Law. The fact that in the same context Vitoria also used the preposition *apud* seems to reinforce the power of this objection. To say, therefore, that Vitoria "created the modern concept of international law" (Truyol Serra) by just introducing this questionable linguistic alteration into the traditional definition of *Ius Gentium* seems an exaggeration. Furthermore, the same alteration had already been introduced into the same definition by Saint Isidore of Seville (*eo iure omnes fere gentes utuntur*) and had at least implicitly been suggested by Saint Augustine in *De Civitate Dei*, Book 4, Chapter 5. Still it is doubtless true that the paternity of the expression *ius inter gentes* should not any more be attributed to the English jurist Zouch (author of *Iuris et iudicii ferialis, sive iuris inter Gentes et quaestionum de eodem explanatio*, Oxford 1650) as Oppenheim, Fauchille and Lange have falsely claimed.

Nations: Jean Baumel, *Le droit international public, la découverte de l'Amérique et les théories de Francisco de Vitoria,* (Montpellier, 1931); Joseph Berthélemy, *Les fondateurs du droit international,* (Paris, 1904); J. Castán Tobenas, "El Derecho y sus rasgos en el pensamiento español," *Revista general de Legislación y Jurisprudencia,* 97 (1949), pp. 646–707; 98 (1950), pp. 153–204; A. de la Pradelle, *Maîtres et doctrines du droit des gens,* (Paris, 1939); J. Larequi, "El derecho internacional en España durante los siglos XVI y XVII," *Razón y Fé,* 81 (1927), pp. 222–232; "Del 'ius gentium' al Derecho internacional. Francisco de Vitoria y los teólogos españoles del siglo XVI," *Ibidem,* 83 (1928), pp. 21–37; G. Goyau, *L'Eglise Catholique et le Droit des Gens,* (Paris, 1922); M. Goergner, *L'Influence de la Réforme sur le Développement du Droit International,* (Paris, no date); I. G. Menéndez Reigada, "El sistema ético-jurídico de Vitoria sobre el Derecho de Gentes," *La Ciencia Tomista,* Salamanca, 39 (1929), pp. 307–330; N. Pfeoffer, *Doctrina Iuris Internationalis iuxta Franciscum de Victoria,* (Zug, 1925); L. V. Pereña, "El concepto del Derecho de Gentes en Francisco de Vitoria," *Revista Española de Derecho Internacional,* 5 (1952), pp. 603–628.

A serious study of Vitoria's theory of International Law has to deal first, with its nature; secondly, with its origin; and, finally, with its end or purpose. The sources for this study are larger than merely a linguistic analysis of its definition, and include, as we noted before, the scholastic theories expounded in the commentaries to Saint Thomas, the fundamental assumptions of the practical lectures *De Indis* and *De iure belli* and, finally, the short remarks on the subject throughout Vitoria's lectures.

In the commentaries to the *Summa Theologica* Vitoria discusses at length the nature of the *Ius Gentium*. *Ius* for the Spanish Jurist is an analogous term which in its original and primary meaning is used objectively as "that which is due to another" (*debitum alteri*). It is only in a derivative manner that we speak of *ius* as the juridical norm which dictates what is due to another. The fundamental difference between Natural Law and the Law of Nations is that the former, of itself, declares that there is a certain equality of justice, while the latter does not posit equality (*propter se non importat equalitatem*), but only declares that some thing is equal to another in relation to a third term. In other words, the Law of Nations does not of itself declare what is just but declares only what ought to be done in order to achieve what is naturally just.

Here are Vitoria's words:

2.2.q.57,a.3: Whether the Law of Nations may be distinguished from the Natural Law. Saint Thomas marks a distinction, to wit: that right is a natural right which, from its very nature, as it were, balances the right of another. And this can happen in two ways: firstly, that Natural Law of itself declares that there is a certain equality and justice – as it were to return a deposit – or, because no wrong is done to you, you do no wrong to another; and in another way (i.e., according to the *Ius Gentium*), some thing is made equal to another in relation to a third thing, just as property be private – one may not say in equity or justice – but such division of property is ordered for the peace and concord of men which cannot be preserved unless everyone should have his property clearly defined. And, therefore, it is the *Ius Gentium* that property should be private. Therefore, having posited this, the first proposition is that which is, in the first way, equal and absolutely just, is called Natural Law; that is, it is of natural right. The second proposition is that which is equal and just in the second way, as it were a certain disposition of things with relation to a third just thing, it is *Ius Gentium*. And so that which is not in itself just, but is derived from human statute firmly established in reason, is called *Ius Gentium*, so that, on its own account it does not imply equity, but on account of something else, as in the matter of war, and other things.[55]

If the *Ius Gentium* is thus distinguishable from Natural Law, it follows, according to Vitoria, that "it is contained more under Positive than under Natural Law." The formulation of this conclusion is puzzling and hazy. Why does not Vitoria clearly say that *Ius Gentium* is under Positive Law without further qualifications? Why does he weaken the conclusion with the expression "*more* under Positive Law *than* under Natural Law"? Behind this apparent hesitation there are some serious considerations. First of all, Vitoria had to reckon with a long and confusing tradition on the subject. Medieval jurists, as Vitoria reminds his readers in the next paragraph, had extended the *Ius Gentium* to include all those things which are common to man alone – a clear residue of the Roman version of *Ius Gentium*. Vitoria, on the other hand, had envisioned it as a juridical order binding equally independent and sovereign States, an order resulting however from a contingent and historical fact, namely, the division of mankind into a plurality of political communities. This is precisely the fundamental assumption of the lecture *De Indis* upon which the entire political thought of Vitoria was built. The Indian nations were sovereign and independent States comparable to the Kingdoms of Christendom. Consequently the assessment of the Spanish enterprise in America was really a problem of international relations between equal partners, subject to regulation by an international code of laws. Those laws, however, could not be a part of Natural Law since the pluralism of nations in itself was not a necessary, natural condition of man, but only a contingent choice, made by humanity in its historical past. On the other hand, Vitoria felt impelled to emphasize the close relationship between Natural and International Law in order to avoid the uni-

[55] "Utrum jus gentium sit idem cum jure naturali.

Sanctus Thomas ponit distinctionem, scilicet jus naturale est quod ex natura sua est alteri commensuratum. Et hoc dupliciter contingere potest. Uno modo, ut de se dicit aequalitatem quamdam et justitiam, ut reddere depositum, Quod tibi non vis fieri alteri non facere, etc. Alio modo aliquid est alteri adacquatum in ordine ad allud. Sicut quod possessiones sint divisae non dicit aequalitatem nec justitiam, sed ordinatur ad pacem et concordiam hominum quae non potest conservari nisi unusquisque habeat bona determinata; et ideo jus gentium est quod possessiones sint divisae, etc.

Hoc ergo supposito, est prima propositio: Illud quod primo modo est adaequatum et absolute justum, vocatur jus naturale, id est de jure naturali.

Secunda propositio: Illud quod est adaequatum et justum secundo modo ut ordinatur ad aliud justum, est jus gentium. Itaque illud quod non est aequum ex se, sed ex statuto humano in ratione fixo, illud vocatur jus gentium; ita quod propter se non importat aequitatem, sed propter aliquid aliud, ut de bello et de aliis, etc." (*Comentarios a la Secunda Secundae de Santo Tomás*, ed. Beltrán de Heredia, III, p. 12.)

lateral character of the later rationalistic approach, and the concomitant dangers of juridical positivism. We must confess that Vitoria's attempt to explain this relationship between the two orders met with only partial success.

Natural Law includes three kinds of rules: rules which are self-evident and universally known; the necessary and valid conclusions from those rules; and, the moral consequences of those rules which are known as highly probable. This division, which Saint Thomas had made traditional in the School, was clearly inspired in the Aristotelian trilogy of first principles, apodictic conclusions, and dialectical reasoning. The *Ius Gentium* cannot follow necessarily from Natural Law because it would, therefore, be Natural Law. Vitoria writes: 'However necessary the *Ius Gentium* is to the conservation of Natural Law, it is not wholly necessary, but *nearly necessary* (*propinque et paene neressarium*), because Natural Law can be but badly preserved without the *Ius Gentium.*" To explain this "near necessity" Vitoria gives one example "Indeed the world could go on if possessions should be in common ... however, it would be with great difficulty for men would be likely to rush into discords and wars." Thus, Vitoria agrees with the later rationalistic school in proclaiming the *Ius Gentium* as a contrivance of human reason; he also would have agreed with juridical positivism in maintaining that this contrivance of reason is made into law by the will of man – the majority of mankind. He disagrees, however, with the former, in the matter of establishing a close relationship between what reason finds and what the nature of man dictates for his own preservation, thus linking man's rational constructions to the plans of the Creator of Nature. He also disagrees with the latter because the dictates of the will are not to him the constitutive elements of the *Ius Gentium*, but rather the connections between what is in itself naturally just and the means agreed upon by mankind's choice.

It is in the light of Vitoria's commentaries on Saint Thomas that other unclear statements of the extraordinary *relectiones* ought to be interpreted. In the first paragraph of the third section of the lecture *De Indis* Vitoria describes the *Ius Gentium* in the following manner:

I will now speak of the lawful and adequate titles whereby the Indians might have come under the sway of the Spaniards. The first title to be named is that of natural society and fellowship. And hereon let my first conclusion be: that Spaniards have a right to travel into the lands in question and to sojourn there provided they do no harm to the natives, and the natives may not prevent them. Proof of this may be in the first place derived from the

Law of Nations *which is either Natural Law or derived from Natural Law* (*Inst.* I, 2, 1): 'What natural reason has established among all nations is called the *Ius Gentium*.'"[56]

The interpretation of these words requires a few introductory remarks. In the Commentaries to the *Summa* Vitoria explicitly writes that the dispute over whether the Law of Nations be distinguished from Natural Law is "a matter of words." The only interesting problem to him as a moralist was the issue whether it was a sin to violate the precepts of the Law of Nations. In the lecture *De Indis* Vitoria was intent upon reminding his students of the obligatory and binding character of the Law of Nations, and was therefore reluctant to enter into any theoretical discussion centering on a "dispute of words." Furthermore, the burden of proving the morally obligatory character of the *Ius Gentium* lay precisely upon those who, like Vitoria himself, were obviously inclined to distinguish it from Natural Law. The sense of the previous quotation can be paraphrased in the following way: the Law of Nations obliges under penalty of sin even if such law is only a derivation from Natural Law; it would be *a fortiori* obligatory to those who classify it under the Natural Law. That this is the most likely interpretation of Vitoria's words is further evidenced by Vitoria's emphatic proof of the obligatory character of the Law of Nations as distinct from Natural Law, a proof presented in the following quotation:

And indeed there are many things in this connection (the right of the first occupant) which issue from the Law of Nations, which, because it has a sufficient derivation from Natural Law, is clearly capable of conferring rights and creating obligations. And even if we grant that it is not always derived from Natural Law, yet there exists clearly enough a consensus of the greater part of the whole world, especially in behalf of the common good of all. For if after the early days of the creation of the world or its recovery from the flood the majority of mankind had decided that ambassadors should everywhere be reckoned inviolable, and that the sea should be common, and that prisoners of war should be made slaves, and that strangers should not be driven out, it would certainly have the force of law, even though the rest of mankind objected thereto.[57]

[56] "Nunc dicam de legitimis titulis et idoneis, quibus barbari venire potuerunt in dicionem Hispanorum.

1. Primus titulus potest vocari naturalis societatis et communicationis.

2. Et circa hoc sit prima conclusio: Hispani habent ius peregrinandi in illas provincias et illic degendi, sine aliquo tamen nocumento barbarorum, nec possunt ab illis prohiberi. Probatur primo ex iure gentium, quod vel est ius naturale vel derivatur ex iure naturali (Inst., De iure naturali et gentium): 'quod naturalis ratio inter omnes gentes constituit, vocatur ius gentium.'" (*Bate Translation*, p. 257.)

[57] "... Et quidem multa hic videntur procedere ex iure gentium, quod, quia derivatur sufficienter ex iure naturali, manifestam vim habet ad dandum ius et obligandum. Et, dato

This agreement or consensus of the majority of mankind has in fact the force of law, "for the world as a whole, being in a way a single State, has the power to create laws ... and it is not permissible for a country to refuse to be bound by International Law, the latter having being established by the authority of the whole world." (*De potestate civili*, 21). There is no doubt in Vitoria's mind that the Law of Nations obliges even those who actually have not explicitly participated in the consensus and those in the minority who disagree with it. Still a specific nature of the Law of Nations does not clearly emerge from Vitoria's words. Is it possible for mankind to proclaim a law binding in conscience which is "not derived from Natural Law" in some form or shape? Are there two kinds of international law, Natural International and Positive International Law? Several answers are possible to these troublesome questions. First of all, it seems undeniable that Vitoria never worked out a clear theory about the relationship between Natural and International Law – a task he left to his followers Vázquez de Menchaca, Domingo Soto, Pedro de Valencia, and especially to Francisco Suárez. On the other hand, it is also certain that according to Vitoria the connection between Natural and International Law can be more or less explicit, in the same way that the precepts of Natural Law itself are dependent upon a few self-evident principles. Thirdly, the argument by analogy between Municipal Law (Civil Positive Law) and International Law, which dominates the reasoning of *De Iure belli*, clearly shows that Civil Law is to each State precisely what International Law is to the universal society of mankind.[58] Finally, whether a particular rule of International Law is clearly derived from Natural Law or not – in any case it never follows *necessarily* from it – its morally binding force is based upon the legislative power of mankind, "being in a way a single State," to create laws that are just and fitting for all people.

This last point brings us to the second aspect of International Law discussed by Vitoria: its origin. The origin of International Law is a consensus of the majority of mankind. Such consensus can be explicit or formal, implicit or interpretative. The former is either public or

quod non semper derivetur ex iure naturali, satis videtur esse consensus maioris partis totius orbis, maxime pro bono communi omnium. Si enim, post prima tempora creati orbis aut reparati post diluvium, maior pars hominum constituerit, ut legati ubique essent inviolabiles, ut mare esset commune, ut bello capti essent servi, et hoc ita expediret, ut hospites non exigerentur, certe hoc haberet vim, etiam aliis repugnantibus." (*Bate Translation*, pp. 259–260.)

[58] Because of this analogy Vitoria is frequently numbered among those of the 'monistic' school of International Law. According to this school "International Law is part of the Law of the Land"; an interpretation which prevails in American and British jurisprudence and is defended by such jurists as Brown Scott, Leon Duguit, and Hans Kelsen. See J. Larequi, *Del Jus Gentium al Derecho Internacional* p. 31.

common, private or particular. Common, formal, International Law is found in legal compilations and digests such as Justinian's *Institutiones*. Particular, formal International Law is expressed in international treaties between single States. Interpretative International Law begins with unconscious accretions through isolated acts of usage, grows with conscious practice, and finally becomes unwritten, customary International Law. The consensus of mankind is established by majoritarian principles and the dissenting minority cannot refuse to be bound by it. The Law of Nations, therefore is truly a universal constitutional law of the society of nations. The consenting parties are not the individual citizens but the single independent States. This point is of capital importance in Vitoria's thought and is occasionally obscured by such misleading expressions as *ex condicto hominum sancitum est*, and *ex consensu hominum*.

The end or purpose of International Law is the common good of mankind, *bonum totius orbis*, exactly in the same way as the goal of Civil Law is the good of the State. The common good of mankind is seen primarily as peace and concord among men. War is just a means to achieve and secure peace; the inviolability of legates is ordained to make possible the end of a particular threat of war or war itself; private property attempts to secure human harmony and peace. International Law is a human device to make possible the natural aspiration for peace. Precisely because historical events dictate the convenience of international rules, International Law can be abrogated in various ways as the history of slavery abundantly proves.

We will conclude our study of Vitoria's thought with a brief comparison with Hugo Grotius. We are forced into this uncomfortable and somewhat artificial task by the frequent and highly rhetorical claims of some scholars – mostly Catholic and/or Spanish – that the "foundation" of International Law as a science ought to be attributed to our sixteenth century Spanish Theologian rather than to the seventeenth century Dutch jurist. That in these claims and counter-claims religious and chauvinistic prejudices have played an important and unglorious role is a familiar fact in the history of ideas. The formulation of the issue itself is a gross oversimplification. The origins of International Law are far too complex to justify the attribution of the pompous title of "founder" to any single individual. Vitoria was indeed a daring pioneer while Grotius' special gift was that of systematizing previously scattered insights. But between then one should add a long list of names such as Covarrubias, Soto, Vásquez, Suárez, Ayala, Arias, Menchaca,

Mariana, Bodin, Connan, Dumoulin, Decio, Gentili, Menocchio, Mazzolini, Everard, Lessius, Selde, Zouch, and many others whose works paved the way to the classical formulations of later times.

A comparison between Vitoria and Grotius should first of all take into consideration their radically different background and personal character. Grotius (1583–1645) was a Dutch Calvinist, jurist, poet, theologian, historian, philologist, and above all a pragmatic diplomat whose main concern was to defend the rights of his countrymen to take part in the East Indian Trade against the claims of Portuguese, Spanish and English merchants, and to formulate universally acceptable rules of conduct between sovereign States, especially in times of war. His ideas and principles were neatly suited to the secular needs of an international society of burgeoning States which had already, for all practical purposes, discarded the two Medieval pillars of unity and order, the Empire and the Church.

In the prolegomena to his massive treatise *De iure belli ac pacis* (1625) – which together with *Mare liberum* (1609) contains most of Grotius' thought – the Dutch Jurist claims for himself the glory of having been the first to present the problems of International Law in a comprehensive and systematic manner. With regard to the first part of this claim Grotius wrote that his predecessors in the field – and he mentions Vitoria, Gorkum, Matthaei, Juan López, Francisco Arias, Giovanni de Legnano, and Martin de Caraziis – had "said *next to nothing* upon a most fertile subject"; an obviously arrogant and unfair characterization. Limiting ourselves to Vitoria it seems undeniably true that Grotius deals in his works with many aspects of International Law neglected by the Spanish theologian, and that in discussing the same problems Grotius is much more thorough and exhaustive. To the first category belong Grotius' chapters on usucaption, arbitration, postliminy, truces, and many others; to the second kind we can refer the reader to the thirty three pages of *De iure belli ac pacis*, Book I, Chapter 2 where Grotius discusses at length whether war is in conflict with the Law of the Gospel, a matter disposed of by Vitoria in three laconic paragraphs of his lecture *De bello*.

Another obvious difference between the work of Grotius and that of Vitoria is the range of their erudition. *De iure belli ac pacis* is studded with literally thousands of references to an immense variety of classical, medieval, and modern scholars: Greek and Roman philologues, poets, historians, and jurists; medieval canonists, scholastic philosophers and theologians; Biblical and Ecclesiastical sources; Byzantine historians;

Fathers of the Church; and Rennaisance jurists from Spain, Italy, France, Germany and the Low Countries. By way of example let it suffice to say that the book contains one hundred and fifteen references to Thucydides, more than two hundred to Livy, more than three hundred to Plutarch, fifty to Saint Jerome, eighty five to Euripides, more than four hundred to the *Institutiones* of Justinian; altogether an extraordinary display of bookish learning and scholarship unknown in the sixteenth century.

The second half of Grotius' claim is even much more relevant to a comparison with Vitoria: "Most of them," Grotius wrote in the aforementioned passage, "have done their work without *system* and in such a way as to intermingle and utterly confuse what belongs to the Law of Nature, to the Law of Nations, to Civil Law, and to the body of law which is found in the canons." Grotius' concern with method is an eloquent testimony to the intellectual trends of the Baroque. The revival of Platonism and idealism found its universal medium and instrument in the mathematical method whereby the intellect, independent from experience, creates a system of deductions drawn from self-evident axioms. This apriority of the Law upon which is based the universal validity and unchangeable character of legal norms is the cornerstone of Grotius' philosophy of Law: "I have made it my concern to derive the proofs of things touching the Law of Nature from certain fundamental conceptions *which are beyond question*, so that no one can deny them without doing violence to himself." And even more explicitly: "With all truthfulness I confess that, just as mathematicians treat their figures as abstracted from bodies, so in treating Law I have withdrawn my mind from every particular fact." To make the science of law more detached from facticity Grotius even denied that in writing *De iure belli ac pacis* he had ever had in view the actual controversies of his own time, a claim hardly admissible but highly revealing. A critical aspect of Grotius' concern with method was his careful and discriminating use of the argument from authority in drawing the conclusions which make up the deductive science of International Law. In the "Prolegomena" to his book *De iure belli* Grotius painstakingly explains the general value and the particular weight of the different authoritative sources accumulated with extraordinary generosity throughout the treatise. After proclaiming his basic respect for Aristotle, Grotius pays fervent homage to history, the illumination of which he found especially lacking in his immediate predecessors, Alberico Gentili and Baltasar Ayala. The views of poets and orators are frequently presented, not because they add much weight to the argument, but because they add "some embellishment" to the discussion – a humanistic trait which Grotius inherited from the Renaissance, especially from his beloved master, Erasmus of Rotterdam. The most important qualification, however, concerns the theological argument. Grotius makes extraordinary use of theological data: Old and New Testament, Hebrew writers, Fathers of the Church, synodical canons, medieval digests, scholastic theologians. Nevertheless, in the "Prolegomena" he carefully explains the value and limitations of his procedure. First of all, Grotius separates carefully the rational from the theological argument. Secondly, Grotius justifies the use of the New Testament "in order to explain that Christians are invited to a higher degree of perfection than the one enjoined upon all men by the Law of Nature." Thirdly, and this is the most interesting remark, because although "what we have been saying would have a degree of validity even if we should concede that which cannot be conceded without the utmost wickedness, *that there is no God*," still the essential traits of man upon which the Law of Nature is actually based have in fact been willed by God, and the divine will be considered as "another source of law." Important as these words are their significance and novelty in the history of ideas have been grossly exaggerated. It has repeatedly been said that Grotius' main contribution to the science of International Law was precisely its secularization, that following the advice of his master Gentili – *desinant Theologi in opere alieno* – he proceeded to separate jurisprudence from any dogmatic entanglement. Scholars seem to forget that medieval scholasticism had long before Grotius accepted the hypothetical possibility of a natural order independent from God's existence, a position defended by such authors as Gregory of Rimini in the fourteenth century, Hugh of Saint Victor, Gabriel Biel, Iacob Almain, and Antonio de Córdoba in the fifteenth and sixteenth centuries. The Spanish jurists and theologians of the sixteenth century – well known to Grotius as we shall show later, discussed the issue in a thorough manner. Medina and Soto proclaimed that if God did not exist a violation of Natural Law would be an evil (*ratio mali*), but not a sin (*ratio culpae*). Suárez went even further and wrote that such a violation would indeed be a sin (*peccatum morale*), but not a theological sin (*peccatum theologicum*). Vázquez, finally – one of Grotius' favorite theologians – asserted that the immediate and sufficient foundation of Natural Law was man's nature – in itself – without any explicit reference to the Creator. Vitoria himself in his lecture *Ad quod tenetur homo veniens ad usum rationis* firmly established that if God did not exist the violation of the natural order would be a sin "in the same way there is a sin in nature and in art" (*licet posset esse peccatum, sicut est in natura et in arte*). All these distinctions and qualifications do not proclaim the independence of morality from God, but are not basically different from Grotius' vague assertion that "what we have been saying *would have a degree of validity* . . . if there is no God."

To compare Grotius' methodological sophistication with Vitoria's is to compare early Renaissance thought with early Enlightenment attitudes. Vitoria's achievement was to purge late Medieval scholasticism from gross abuses and deviations. Grotius' scientific systematization reflects the Cartesian concern with unquestionable principles, mathematical order, and rational procedure. Vitoria's indiscriminate and at times confusing usage of theological and rational argument was carefully avoided by Grotius, who in so doing prepared the way for a totally secular science of jurisprudence. A comparison of Vitoria and Grotius cannot be completed without assessing the possible influence of the former upon the latter. That Grotius was familiar with the work of Vitoria and other Spanish jurists and theologians of the Sixteenth Century is obvious from the extraordinary number of references to their work which we can find in *De iure belli ac pacis*. The names of José de Acosta, Miguel de Aguirre, Francisco Arias, Domingo Báñez, Pedro Belluga, Juan de Cartagena, Alfonso de Castro, Fernandez Messía, García de Erzilla, Antonio Gómez, Bartolomé de Medina, Pedro de Navarra, Tomás Sánchez, Domingo Soto, Francisco Suárez, Francisco de Toledo, Torquemada, Alfonso Valdés, Vazquez, and Menchaca appear frequently in Grotius' footnotes. His favorites among them seem to have been Covarrubias (fifty-four references), Mariana (fifty-three), Molina (twenty-one), Azpilcueta (thirteen), Soto (thirty), and Menchaca (thirty). Grotius' attention to Spanish jurists was not only a tribute to their merits, but also a historical and dialectical necessity. In his attempt to demonstrate the rights of the Dutch against the claims of the Portuguese and the Spanish, Grotius was especially anxious to prove his conclusions from those premises already accepted by Spanish and Portuguese scholars. The theme "not even the Spanish jurists cast any doubt about it" (*ipsi doctores Hispani non dubitant . . .*) is a recurrent one in Grotius' first book *Mare liberum*. There is no doubt, then, that Grotius' devotion to Vitoria was founded upon his admiration for the liberal ideas of the Spanish Dominican. The first chapter of *Mare liberum* mentions Gentili and Vitoria as the outstanding defenders of the right to travel and to trade everywhere in the world. *De iure belli ac pacis* mentions Vitoria twice by name and contains fifty-six references to his works.

A perusal of Vitoria's and Grotius' works gives ample evidence of their close relationship. The structure of *De iure belli* corresponds exactly to the three parts of Vitoria's lecture *De bello*. The first book discusses "Those who wage war"; the second "On what grounds war is waged"; the third "What is permissible in war." The number of coincidences and similarities is also very striking: the same severity regarding personal reprisals, the same distinctions between movable and immovable property, the same approach to the problem of whether a war might be just on both sides, the same refutation of alleged causes of a "just war," and many others. The basic and fundamental conceptions of the book are clearly inspired by Vitoria's thought: the same universalistic vision of a society of States ruled by norms of behavior agreed upon by majoritarian consent, the same exclusive justification of war as essentially a defensive war against wrongful injury, the same analogy between the Municipal Law of each State and the International Law of mankind, the same faith in the universal and normative value of man's rational and social nature. The differences in their thoughts are in most cases a matter only of degree and emphasis. Grotius insisted more on reason than on divine order to derive the postulates of Natural Law, thus following closer in the steps of the Stoics than in those of the Medieval scholastics. If Vitoria tended to color Natural Law with his theological prejudices, Grotius on the other hand could not resist the temptation to project political laws of his own time into immutable principles of order. Thus he exaggerated the importance of the postulate of freedom of the seas, condemned as unnatural the right of rebellion against autocratic governments, exaggerated the natural character of private property, and accepted severe forms of personal punishment in war. Vitoria's thought might very well be considered an unsuccessful but progressive attempt to liberate man's reasoning from religious prejudice in matters of law; Grotius, almost a hundred years later, was not yet able to build a geometrical science of jurisprudence without paying his personal tribute to the demands of mercantilism, nationalism, and individualism.

CHAPTER III

FRAY LUIS DE LEON AND THE CONCERN WITH LANGUAGE

At Paris, Padua, Bologna, and Naples the Hermits of Saint Augustine had been since the second half of the thirteenth century constantly involved in the intellectual life of the medieval universities. In September 1377 they arrived in Salamanca to open a center of studies attached to the University where Dominicans and Franciscans held unchallenged control over the teaching of Theology. The active participation of the Augustinians in the academic life of the University, however, was delayed for over a century by the obscurantism of a monastic reform from Salamanca which spread to all the monasteries of the Order in Castile and Aragón, and which by 1504 finally achieved a unity under the strict observance of a new rule. Soon thereafter the Augustinians returned to the University, and in 1510 a member of the Order, Fray Alfonso de Córdoba, had the dubious privilege of introducing into Salamanca the teaching of nominalist logic *ad modum Parisiense*. The decisive step toward full participation of the Spanish Augustinians in the intellectual life of Spain was taken in 1541 at the Chapter of Dueñas by the General of the Order Girolano Seripando, a typical man of the Counter-Reformation and a Papal Legate at Trent from 1545 to 1552. The Convent of Saint Augustine in Salamanca was chosen by the Order to provide the courses of Philosophy to all the friars of the Spanish Provinces. As for Theology, the young Augustinians were expected to attend the regular courses of the University. From the very beginning Biblical studies were given top priority by the Order, and soon Augustinian professors competed with members of other religious Orders for the prestigious chairs of the University. Thus Salamanca became the center of Augustinian life in Spain, a position held up to that date by the Convent of Saint Augustine in Valencia.

The Chapter of Dueñas signalled the beginning of an Augustinian Renaissance comparable only to the vigor of the Order in the fourteenth century under the inspiration of Thomas of Strasbourg and Gregory of Rimini. It is important to understand the special characteristics of this Salamanca school of Augustinian thought for several reasons. First of all, we should not forget that Augustinian monks played an important role in the history of the Reformation. The authority of Saint Augustine, whom Augustinian scholars naturally claimed to understand better than anyone else, was widely invoked by the Reformers to support their theories of man's corruption by sin, and of the irresistible power of Grace. Those who made a special profession of following the authority of the Saint were obviously more vulnerable to the persuasive arguments of the Reformers. In fact the Augustinian Congregations of Germany and the Low Countries became powerful centers of Reformation thought and activity. Erasmus was an Augustinian Canon; Luther, Zwingli, John Eck and Henry Voes were Augustinian friars. The Augustinian monks at Erfurt were the first to abandon monastic life, soon to be followed by their brothers at Wittenberg and Karlstad. In sharp contrast with the fragile orthodoxy of the Augustinian monks in Northern Europe, the Spanish friars were always, if not above any suspicion, (an almost impossible ideal when confronted with the Inquisition) free at least from any serious breach of loyalty toward the Catholic Faith.

In the history of the Spanish Renaissance, the Augustinians played an important role as a mediating force between the two mendicant Orders (the Franciscans and Dominicans) and the newly founded Jesuits. Like the latter, the Salamanca Augustinians challenged the theological establishment of the former. In the lengthy and painful struggle for the coveted Chairs of Theology the Augustinians became an independent third force which helped to preserve the balance of power. Their autonomy was not only a matter of personal policy, but also a traditional doctrinal position. According to the official regulations of the Order, the Augustinians were supposed to follow the *via Aegidiana,* the teaching namely of Giles (Aegidius) of Rome, a General of the Order in the thirteenth century, together with the commentaries of the great Augustinian theologians Thomas of Strasbourg and Gregory of Rimini (*Doctor authenticus*). The *via Aegidiana* was not a body of doctrine nor even a radical departure from Thomistic doctrines, but rather a critical and independent version of Thomism itself. The eclectic and independent character of the Spanish Augustinians manifested itself in their almost complete detachment from the very traditional positions held by their own Order. In spite of official regulations the

Augustinians from Salamanca never became the champions of the *via Aegidiana*. The course of Theology "according to Gregory of Rimini", given by Alfonso de Córdoba, failed entirely to arouse the enthusiasm or loyalty of the young students of Theology. Rimini's association with Nominalism was indirectly attacked by another Augustinian professor of Theology, Fray Juan de Guevara, the author of an *Index* of thirty three "false and dangerous" propositions taken from Durandus' works (1560). Giles' insistence upon the affective character of Theology, the priority of the Good above the True, the superiority of Love over Knowledge, and other theories of clear Neo-Platonic inspiration, were either ignored or denied by the Augustinians of Salamanca. In only two concrete doctrinal points did they unanimously agree: in defending the Immaculate Conception of Mary, and in maintaining that Christ would have come to the world even if Adam had never sinned. These two dogmatic positions the Augustinians had borrowed from the Franciscan School. On the whole, however, the teachings of the Augustinians in Salamanca proved to be much more enlightened than the provincial and shortsighted regulations of their Order. By refusing to repeat the opinions of Giles of Rome, and by approaching Saint Thomas with loyal criticism, the Salamanca Augustinians took a significant step toward cancelling the ridiculous doctrinal partisanship between the medieval religious orders and prepared the way for the erudite and eclectic syntheses of the Spanish Jesuit thinkers in the last decades of the century.[1]

A. FRAY LUIS DE LEÓN: THE MAN AND HIS WORK

The most notable figure from the Convent of Saint Augustine in Salamanca was no doubt the impressive Fray Luis de León. The name of Fray Luis, as Spaniards of all times and creeds have affectionately called him (there are many other Fray Luises, but they need a surname to be identified), will not be found in any general history of Philosophy. Those who are exclusively interested in the history of philosophical systems, and investigate the founders of new schools or radical pioneers, or rebels, might not find in Fray Luis a great deal of interest. Those, however, who seek to understand the complexities

[1] For the history of the Spanish Augustinians in the sixteenth century, see P. David Gutiérrez, "Del origen y carácter de la escuela teológica hispano-augustiniana en los siglos XVI y XVII," *La Ciudad de Dios*, vol. 153, n. 2 (1941), pp. 227–255; also P. E. Dominguez Carretero, "La escuela teológica Agustiniana de Salamanca," *La Ciudad de Dios*, vol. 169 (1956), pp. 638–685.

and richness of Spanish intellectual life during the central years of Philip II' reign cannot bypass his name, because Fray Luis, like his own statue in front of the Plateresque facade of the old University of Salamanca, stands precisely at the very center of the Spanish Renaissance.

Fray Luis was born in Cuenca in 1527, the same year Philip II was born and Rome was sacked by the troops of Charles V. Fray Luis died in 1591 in Avila, the birth place of Saint Teresa, a few months before the death of Saint John of the Cross. He joined the Augustinian Order at the Salamanca Convent in 1543, three years before Vitoria's death, and two years after the historical Chapter of Dueñas. In 1560 he obtained the license to teach Theology and was chosen to pronounce the funeral eulogy of Soto. One year later he won the Chair of Saint Thomas by a large margin of votes. From 1572 to 1576 he was jailed by the Inquisition, a victim of a famous process. In 1583 he published *La Perfecta Casada* and *De Los Nombres de Cristo*, two books which together with Ribadeneira's *Vida de San Ignacio* and Saint Teresa's *Camino de Perfección* (all of them published the same year) elevated Spanish prose to a new level of maturity. Fray Luis studied in the best Spanish Universities of his time, Salamanca, Alcalá, and Toledo. In Salamanca he heard Guevara on Durando, Soto on Saint Thomas, and Melchor Cano (*De Locis Theologicis*). In Alcalá he studied the Bible (*Book of Job*, *Psalms*, *The Song of Songs*) with one of the best exegetes of that time, Fray Cipriano de la Huerga. During his thirty years of teaching at Salamanca he came in contact with the most interesting men of that century. He was a personal friend of Arias Montano, el Brocense, Grajal, and Martínez de Cantalapiedra, all of them, like Fray Luis himself, converted Jews, men of liberal ideas, and, for those noble reasons, victims also of the Inquisition. Fray Luis was a teacher of Suárez and a disciple of Domingo de Soto; he published for the first time the books of Saint Teresa and had among his disciples Saint John of the Cross. He defeated Báñez in an open competition for a Chair of Theology at Salamanca and listened to Molina on the Controversy *De auxiliis*. He wrote against the Jesuit Ribera, but shared with another Jesuit, Father Jorge de Montemayor, the condemnation of theological opinions on Grace. At Salamanca Fray Luis "read" Saint Thomas (1561–1565), Durandus (1565–69), Moral Philosophy (1578–79), and the Holy Scripture (1579–91), thus bridging the traditional gap between scholastic and biblical theology and breaking the Dominican control over the Chairs of dogmatic theology.

Fray Luis wrote abundantly, with the typical eloquence of a humanist and the natural loquaciousness of a Spaniard. His books, both in Latin and in Spanish, can be divided into the following categories: a.) Latin treatises of dogmatic theology (*De Incarnatione*, *De Fide*, *De Creatione*, *De Predestinatione*), b.) Theological essays in Spanish (*Un quodlibeto sobre el pan y el vino que Melchisedec ofreció a Abraham*, *De las diferencias entre la Ley Vieja y la del Evangelio*, and others), c.) Latin commentaries on the Scripture (*In Ecclesiastem*, *Canticum Moysis*, *In Epistulas Pauli ad Galatas*), d.) Spanish commentaries on the Scripture (*Comentario al Profeta Abdías*, *Exposición del Salmo Treinta y Seis*, *Comentario al Génesis*, *Exposición del Libro de Job*, *Exposición del Cantar de los Cantares*), e.) Moral and theological treatises in Spanish (*La perfecta casada*, *De Los Nombres de Cristo*), f.) Several works of Spanish prose (*La Vida de Santa Teresa*, *Apología de los Libros de Santa Teresa*), g.) Original poems in Latin and Spanish, h.) Imitations of classical poetry, i.) Translations of Virgil and Horace, j.) Poetical translations of the Scripture.

Prolific as he was Fray Luis displayed a bewildering detachment from his own writings. His Latin treatises of dogmatic theology – which embody the main efforts of his life at Salamanca – remained unpublished for nearly three hundred years. Only five of his biblical commentaries in Latin were published before his death. In 1631 Quevedo published for the first time the poetry of Fray Luis. The only books published by Fray Luis himself were *La Perfecta Casada* (1583, 1585, 1586, 1587), *De Los Nombres de Cristo* (1583, 1585, 1586, 1587), a Spanish commentary on Psalm 26 (1581), the Latin commentaries on *The Song of Songs* (1580, 1582), *Abdías* (1589), *ad Galatians* (1589), and the Latin commentary to *Psalm 26* (1580, 1582).[2]

This short bibliographical note suffices to explain why Fray Luis' reputation has been built mostly upon the literary, popular, and Spanish portion of his writings, rather than upon the academic, theological, and Latin treatises. The poet and the master of the Castilian

[2] The Latin works of Fray Luis were published by the Augustinians of Salamanca between 1891 and 1895 under the title *Magistri Luysii Leogonensis Augustiniani divinorum librorum primum apud Salmaticenses Opera* in seven volumes (here called *opera*). This *editio princeps*, however, does not contain the treatise *De Legibus*, which was first published by Luciano Pereña in 1963 (Madrid), nor many other manuscripts of great importance (such as *De libero arbitrio*, *De Gratia et Justificatione*) which remain unpublished in the libraries of Valladolid, Evora, Coimbra, Pamplona, the Vatican, and others. The edition of the Spanish works of Fray Luis (here called *Obras Completas Castellanas*) made by Felix García O.S.A., two volumes (Madrid, 1957), leaves out only minor documents such as sermons, letters, *quodlibeta*, and their like. A complete bibliographical information on Fray Luis can be obtained in Karl Kottman's book *Law and Apocalypse: The Moral Thought of Fray Luis de León* (1527–1591), vol. 44 of the International Archives of the History of Ideas (The Hague, 1972), pp. 134–138.

prose has clearly overshadowed the theologian and the philosopher. This characterization, however, does not square with the historical reality of Fray Luis' life. His energies, his struggle, his intellectual efforts were dedicated, day after day, to the teaching of theology. His theological lectures – which he dictated in violation of University regulations – were the solid basis of his reputation in the University and the pretext for his persecution. Although most of them were only posthumously published, unauthorized manuscript copies circulated among the University students in large numbers. In those lectures Fray Luis took a very active part in the great theological and philosophical controversies which swept the Spanish Universities in the wake of the Reformation.[3]

The significance of Fray Luis' theological teaching consists primarily in its pervasive eclecticism. Situated between the Dominicans and the Jesuits, a follower of Saint Thomas with some Scotist persuasion, trained by Soto and Melchor Cano in a balanced synthesis of speculative and positive theology, imbued by the independent spirit of his religious Order, Fray Luis reflects and combines all the trends of that moment into a harmonious and flexible synthesis. The three great issues of the Counter-Reformation, (the Scripture, the Law, and Grace), were the focal points of his theological writings. The first Inquisition's trial against Fray Luis (1572) was directed at his opinions on the value of the Vulgate and the Mosaic Law; the second trial (1582) investigated and condemned his theological opinions on Grace and predestination. Leaving aside for a moment (*See below* p. 160). Fray Luis' contribution to Biblical hermeneutics, we shall consider

[3] The publication of Fray Luis' Latin works, together with the discovery of the second Inquisition's legal proceedings against Fray Luis in 1582, published by Blanco García O.S.A. in *La Ciudad de Dios*, vol. 41 (1896), sparked the discussion of Fray Luis' theological opinions. The Dominican Fathers Getino and Beltrán de Heredia on one side, and the Augustinians Vela, Blanco García, and Pinta Llorente on the other, have engaged in lengthy and somehow tedious debates which even now give a pretty realistic idea of the rivalry between religious orders which plagued the academic life of Fray Luis. The best book on Fray Luis' theological thinking is Salvador Muñoz Iglesias' *Fray Luis de León. teólogo* (Madrid, 1950), although it deals almost exclusively with the problem of predestination. Other titles include: Ursino Dominguez, "Fray Luis de León. Su doctrina Mariológica," *La Ciudad de Dios*, vol. 154 (1942), pp. 413–437; "Fray Luis de León. Su doctrina acerca de la predestinación y reprobación," *Ibidem*, vol. 154 (1942), pp. 65–84. David Gutiérrez, "La doctrina del Cuerpo Místico de Cristo en Fray Luis de León," *Revista Española de Teología*, II (1942), pp. 727–753. Rafael García de Castro, *Fray Luis de León, teólogo y escriturario* (Granada, 1928), Vicente Beltrán de Heredia, *Las corrientes de espiritualidad entre los dominicos de Castilla en la primera mitad del siglo XVI*, (Salamanca, 1941). Ursino Domínguez del Val, "La teología de Fray Luis de León," *La Ciudad de Dios*, vol. 164 (1952), pp. 163–178. Miguel de la Pinta Llorente, "En torno al proceso de Fray Luis de León," (Contestando al R. P. Beltrán de Heredia), *Archivo Agustiniano*, XLIV (1950), pp. 53–66.

now the issues of Law and Grace in the context of the American colonization and the advances of the Reform.

Fray Luis' treatise *De legibus* was unknown to the editors of the *Opera Omnia* in 1891, and was first published in 1963 by Victor Pereña.[4] This short book, which contains the lectures Fray Luis dictated to his students (among them Francisco Suárez) in the academic year 1570–1571, is a beautiful example of sixteenth century scholasticism. The harmony of content and form, and the balance of elegant and technical Latin, bespeaks the teaching of Vitoria and Melchor Cano. More importantly, the book reveals to us the significant role played by Fray Luis in the momentous debate about Justice and Law. Fray Luis' task was to reduce to a harmonious unity the different trends he had learned from his predecessors – Vitoria, Soto, Covarrubias, Miguel de Palacios, and Juan de la Peña. The central inspiration of his thought was a recognition of the unity of the human race to which the welfare of each particular State must be subordinated in order to reflect the hierarchical harmony of God's creation. "The common good of mankind is ordained to the good of the entire Universe" (*Bonum proprium et commune generis humani ordinatur ad bonum totius universi*). Fray Luis incorporated Vitoria's legal cosmopolitanism into his own Platonic scheme of Unity and Order, and separated himself from Soto's organic conception of the individual States. Fray Luis' insistence upon the hierarchy of the common good is the primary source of Suárez's opinions on that subject. Through Suárez his influence spread to the Universities of Coimbra and Evora. More emphatically than Vitoria, Fray Luis emphasized the mediation of the people in the designation of the *potestas civilis*, although in this particular respect his was not an original contribution, but rather an echo of a central thesis of Spanish political thought in the sixteenth century introduced by Soto and Covarrubias, confirmed by Azpilcueta, Menchaca, Fox Morcillo, Báñez, and Molina, and given a definite formulation by Francisco Suárez.

A further manifestation of Fray Luis' eclecticism was his conception of the Law, a mixed product of Dominican rationalism and Franciscan voluntarism. According to Fray Luis reason judges and selects the good

[4] The contributions of the Augustinians to the study of the Law have been presented by B. Diferman in his articles "Estudio específico del Derecho Natural y Derecho Positivo según los clásicos agustinos españoles del siglo XVI," *La Ciudad de Dios*, vol. 169 (1956), pp. 253–285; and "La orden agustiniana y los estudios jurídicos en la época clásica española," *Anuario de Historia del Derecho Español*, XXV (1955), pp. 775–790. See also the third chapter of Kottman's *Law and Apocalypse*, (pp. 42–65).

and the right, but it is the will of the lawgiver that formally establishes the Law by enacting it (*imperium*). On this point, however, Fray Luis was somewhat hesitant and ambiguous; once again it was reserved to the genius of his disciple Francisco Suárez to find the exact words to express a clear synthesis of these two medieval traditions in the definition of the Law.

On one particular point of legal philosophy did Fray Luis clearly go beyond the teachings of Vitoria. Against Soto (whose opinions in this respect were not very firm) and against Palacios, Fray Luis definitively maintained that the *ius gentium* belonged to the domain of Positive rather than Natural Law. According to him the *ius gentium* shares with Natural Law its universal character; but it is similar to Positive Civil Law in that it derives its legal binding force from the consent of the people. Furthermore, the conclusions of the *ius gentium* were not absolute but conditioned by concrete historical circumstances. This opinion, maintained in Salamanca by Pedro de Aragón and in Coimbra by Bartolomé de Medina, was also adopted and elaborated by Francisco Suárez, and thus became the general position of Jesuit thinkers. It was probably through Suárez that Fray Luis' progress in the conceptualization of International Law could have had some indirect influence upon the work of Hugo Grotius.

The real test of this legal theorizing was to be found in the pressing problem of racial discrimination at home and the rights of the American natives in the newly discovered continent. Both issues were tackled by Fray Luis from a very personal angle, without parallel in Spanish thought at that time. As a Jewish convert (*cristiano nuevo*) Fray Luis was displeased with Soto's contention (Soto was a *cristiano viejo*) that Judaism had entirely lost its significance after Jesus' death. According to Soto the Mosaic Law included three kinds of precepts: ritual precepts, judicial precepts, and moral precepts (the Decalogue). The first two prefigured Christ's Kingdom, and were consequently cancelled by the fulfilment of the prophecies in Jesus Christ. Soto did not hesitate to say that the observance of those Mosaic ceremonies was, after Christ's death, sinful and heretical. As a practical example, Soto criticised the practice of circumcision among the baptized Indians in Mexico. Soto's rationalistic definition of Law – a definition which saw the Law formally constituted by its objective content rather than by the *imperium* of the lawgiver in enacting and prescribing it – led him to classify the Decalogue as Natural Law, a binding force which in the new order of the Church had nothing to do with the Mosaic proclamation but rather with its necessary connection with natural reason. Thus, according to Soto, Mosaic Law in its triple manifestation was a thing of the past. Fray Luis accepted of course the temporary and transient character of Moses' ritual and judicial prescriptions, but he strongly disagreed with Soto in his opinions about the relationship between the Decalogue and Natural Law. According to Fray Luis the Decalogue was Divine Positive Law reinforcing Natural Law with the revelational proclamation and enactment through Moses. The Ten Commandments were different from Natural Law, not because they prescribed anything unknown to natural reason, but because they prescribed it in a different manner. This view corresponds exactly to Fray Luis' definition of the Law as formally constituted by the very act of the legislator's will, binding an inferior to the performance of a particular act. According to Fray Luis, then, the Mosaic proclamation of the Decalogue constituted a Divine Positive Law still valid as such after the foundation of the Church. That meant in more practical terms that mankind as a whole had to obey a Law revealed with precision and indubitability through the mediation of the Jewish Nation. Consequently it was wrong to say that Judaism had been "phased out" by Christianity, on the contrary the Church itself was only "a new Israel". This doctrine – which was obviously more Pauline and Patristic – had been side-tracked in medieval theology and constituted in sixteenth century Spain a yardstick by which to measure the pro or anti-Semitism of a given thinker. The new Christians themselves moved in two opposite directions. Some, like the rabbi of Burgos, Salomon ha Levi, better known by his Christian name of Pablo de Santa María after his conversion in 1390, remained loyal to the Jewish heritage and proclaimed the unbroken continuity of Judaism and Christianity. Others, like Alfonso de Espina toward the end of the fifteenth century, denied any significance to his Jewish ancestry. The former type sooner or later became the victims of the Inquisition, while some of the latter became in time the most cruel Inquisitors. It was Fray Luis' distinction to have belonged without compromise to the first group, a fact which brought to his life the bitter envy and hatred of all the bigots around him.[5]

Fray Luis' emphasis on the significance of Judaism and Mosaic Law became evident in two different fields. As a biblical scholar Fray Luis upheld the primacy of the original Hebrew text of the Bible and the

[5] See Luciano Serrano, O.S.B., *Los conversos D. Pablo de Santa María y D. Alfonso de Cartagena* (Madrid, 1942).

value of the rabbinical tradition in hermeneutics, an aspect of his thought we shall consider later (*See below*, pp. 195–97) Here we are primarily concerned with his eschatological views which combine into an amazing apolalyptic vision two historical facts of his time: the supposed conversion of the Spanish Jews after 1492 and the preaching of the Gospel in the Americas by Spanish missionaries. That the end of the world would be immediately preceded by the conversion of the Jews to Christianity was a widespread belief based upon a rather fanciful interpretation of some biblical quotations. On the other hand, Fray Luis' characterization of the American Indian was much closer to Sepúlveda's notion of a wild beast than to the noble savage of Bartolomé de Las Casas. Consequently, without scruple, Fray Luis accepted the opinion of those who maintained that the American Indians could and should be coerced into civilization and Christianity by the power of Spain. And, although on repeated occasions he solemnly deplored the greed and unnecessary cruelty of the Conquistadores, there is no denying that in passing judgement upon this crucial event in man's history our Augustinian monk succumbed tragically to the bias of his historical environment. To make things worse Fray Luis came out with an almost ridiculous interpretation of some Biblical texts to "prove" that the Spanish conquest of the Americas had been clearly revealed (*sic!*) by God through Isaiah and Job. Furthermore, it was his contention that in the book of Abdias God Himself had revealed the choice of Spain for this formidable task of discovering, colonizing, and converting the American Indians, a choice which was dependent upon and based on the conversion of the Spanish Jews to Christianity. This misleading effort of the new Christian to blend in one revealed word the historical destiny of Spain with his own victimized and persecuted race culminated in the supreme folly of engaging in detailed Bibliomancy with the solemn prognostication of the end of the world by, exactly, 1656. Fray Luis' obviously unfulfilled prophecy is perfectly in tune with all the apocalyptic, cabalistic, messianic, magical, and astrological fads of his age, and reveals the strange combination of enlightenment and naiveté which characterizes the sixteenth century in Europe.[6]

[6] Fray Luis' thought on this matter can be found in his Latin commentaries on *The Song of Songs* (*Opera*, II, pp. 1–472); *In Abdiam Prophetam Explanatio* (*Ibidem*, pp. 423–481); *Tractatus de Fide* (*Ibidem*, V, pp. 384–387). Also, in the Spanish commentaries on the *Book of Job* (*Obras Completas Castellanas*, III, pp. 155–156) and, finally, in the Chapter "Brazo de Dios" of *De Los Nombres de Cristo*.

Fray Luis' attitude toward the *Conquista* is discussed by Luciano Pereña Vicente in "El

Three years after the conclusion of the Council of Trent (1543–1563) found Fray Luis lecturing from the Chair of Durandus in Salamanca on the most controversial of all the theological issues of the Counter-Reformation: Grace and Freedom. The discovery in 1882 of the legal proceedings initiated by the Inquisition in the second trial against Fray Luis revealed for the first time the significant part he played in the dispute between the Dominican and the Jesuit theologians. In January 1582 the faculty and students of Theology at the University of Salamanca congregated for a public discussion (*disputatio*) in which a Jesuit theologian, Father Jorge de Montemayor, was selected to defend some fine points of theology concerning the Incarnation. In the face of everyone's expectations (*praeter omnium spem*) the discussion shifted to the hot issue of predestination. Opinions on the matter were expressed with much passion and little refinement. To the delight of the student audience, the competing professors soon began to accuse each other of heresy and theological error. To make things worse the glamorous athletes of that theological arena represented different religious Orders. There were two Jesuits (Montemayor and Enrico Enríquez), one member of the Order of Saint Benedict (Juan de Castañeda), one fiery Dominican (Domingo Báñez), and finally, one Augustinian, Fray Luis de León. The turmoil which followed this debate was too much for the Spanish Inquisition. A few weeks later a "process" was started against all the participants in the public debate. The process was exceptionally short and expeditious, by the standards of that time. As a result Montemayor and Fray Luis were severely censured by the Holy Tribunal; Castañeda, Báñez, and Enríquez (who later left the Jesuit Order, became a Dominican, and a loyal servant of the Inquisition) were generously absolved. This debate of 1582 is a landmark in the history of Theology at Salamanca because it revealed the profound doctrinal gap between the theological establishment – the Dominicans – and the newly arrived Jesuits over the central issue of Counter-Reformation theology: the reconciliation of man's freedom and God's Providence. Caught in the middle, Fray Luis de León maintained a rather imprecise and blurry position which avoided the extreme solutions clearly defined by Báñez O. P. and Molina S. J. in the next two decades. Although Fray Luis failed to open new theological avenues for the mo-

descubrimiento de América en las obras de Fray Luis de León," *Revista Española de Derecho Internacional*, VII (1955), pp. 587–604. Sandalio Diego in his article "Fray Luis de León y Francisco de Ribera en el Comentario de Abdías," *Estudios Eclesiásticos*, VIII (1929), pp. 5–22, explains the disagreement between the two theologians regarding the interpretation of the prophet.

ment, he was able to sketch a typically Augustinian view of Grace and can therefore be considered as one of the forerunners of the so-called Augustinian school of the seventeenth century (Novis, Berti, Belleli), a school whose relations with Jansenism are still a matter of dispute among Catholic scholars.[7]

Fray Luis' intense participation in these theological disputes tends to obscure the most outstanding characteristic of his theology and the backbone of his devotion and piety: the supreme central position of Christ as the converging point of the Finite and the Infinite, of the Temporal and the Eternal, of the Cosmos and God. Both in his scholastic treatise *De Incarnatione* and in the first chapter of *De Los Nombres de Cristo* ("Pimpollo"), Fray Luis defended with extraordinary eloquence and vigor Scotus' opinion that the Incarnation of the Son of God had been decreed by God before and independently from the foreknowledge of Adam's fall. Although no translation can convey the unique quality of Fray Luis' Castilian prose, the following paragraphs from *Los Nombres de Cristo* give an idea of his thought:

> That is the reason why Christ is called by various names that signify flower or fruit, and when Scripture refers to Him in such terms it is to make us understand that Christ is the end of all things. Even as in the tree the roots do no exist for themselves, and much less the trunk which rises from the roots, but both of these, together with the flowers, the branches, and the leaves are directed to the fruit which the tree will produce, so also the vast heavens with their brilliant stars, especially that principal luminary of surpassing beauty which gives light to the world, the earth adorned with flowers and the waters filled with fish, the animals and men, and the entire universe have as their end and purpose the Incarnation. Christ is, so to speak, the Fruit or Offspring of all creation.[8]

7 The debate of 1582 is presented in detail by Muñoz Iglesias in his book *Fray Luis, Teólogo*, pp. 130–183. The second trial of Fray Luis before the Inquisition was published in *La Ciudad de Dios*, vol. 41 (1896), pp. 15–37, 103–112, 182–191, 273–283. Báñez' trial is discussed by V. Beltrán de Heredia, O. P., in his article "El maestro Fray Domingo Báñez y la Inquisición Española," *La Ciencia Tomista*, 37 (1928), pp. 289–309; 38 (1928), 35–38, 171–186.

8 The English translations of *De Los Nombres de Cristo* which appear in the text are by Edward J. Schuster, *The Names of Christ* (Binghamton: Herder Book Co., 1955).

"– Pues – dijo entonces Marcelo – esto es ser Cristo fruto; y darle la Escritura este nombre a El, es darnos a entender a nosotros que Cristo es el fin de las cosas, y aquel para cuyo nacimiento feliz fueron todas criadas y enderezadas. Proque así como en el árbol la raíz no se hizo para sí, y menos el tronco que nace y se sustenta mas y la flor y la hoja, y todo lo demás que el árbol produce, se ordena y endereza para el fruto que de él sale, que es el fin y como remate suyo; así por la misma manera, estos cielos extendidos que vemos, y las estrellas que en ellos dan resplandor, y entre todas ellas esta fuente de claridad y de luz que todo lo alumbra, redonda y bellísima; la tierra pintada con flores y las aguas pobladas de peces; los animales y los hombres, y este universo todo, cuan grande y cuan hermoso es, lo hizo Dios para fin de hacer Hombre a su Hijo, y para producir a luz este único y divino fruto que es Cristo, que con verdad le podemos llamar el parto común y general de todas las cosas." (*Obras Completas Castellanas*, p. 413.)

The highly technical and forbidding distinctions in the treatise *De Incarnatione* concerning the different stages (*signa*) of God's knowledge and decisions – a pathetic effort of Christian theology to rationalize God's behavior in strongly anthropomorphic and self-defeating language – should not mislead the reader into minimizing this issue as another scholastic trifle. Behind this apparently harmless theological issue, never officially sanctioned by the Church, lies a conception of nature and grace, of cosmos and history, much closer to the Neo-Platonic idea of Divine communication than to the Christian emphasis upon the historical and supernatural character of the redemptive act. In fact, the reasoning of Fray Luis in *De Los Nombres de Cristo* is entirely cast in this Neo-Platonic mold. God's creation cannot be directed toward the procurement of perfection because as Infinite, Self-subsisting Perfection God cannot desire nor move toward any good outside of Himself. The only purpose, therefore, of God's operations *ad extra*, is the communication of His Own perfection, a purpose which admirably fits with God's own nature since the Good tends always to communicate itself (*bonum diffusivum sui*). God's final cause in creating the world cannot be but the highest possible communication of Himself through the hypostatic union of the Son of God and the human nature in the Person of Christ. Jesus Christ then is the central point of history, of the cosmos, of both the natural and the supernatural order. In Christ God communicates and gives Himself to man, the microcosmos, and through this union the Creator and His creature converge into the highest and purest form of Unity and Harmony. Christ is accordingly the beginning and the end, the Alpha and the Omega of Creation. Everything in the Universe, the trees, the stars, the animals, men, were all created only to make possible the supreme beauty of the God-Man, Jesus Christ. If Adam had never sinned the Incarnation would have been deprived of any sacrificial and soteriological character, but it would have taken place any way as the supreme form of divine communication. Like those of Teilhard de Chardin in our own time, the opinions of Fray Luis' were viewed with suspicion by the bigots of his day. In fact, in his first Inquisitorial process Fray Luis was unfairly accused of having denied the messianic character of Christ:

León de Castro testified also that Fray Luis Enríquez, a Dominican priest in Salamanca, had told him the following story. At a lunch meeting of several faculty members, one of those present had used the expression "he came", to which Fray Luis had remarked, "Whenever He comes we shall be obliged to believe in Him; the doubt is whether He has come or not." According to the witness Enríquez everyone present understood that Fray Luis was speaking about the advent of Christ.[9]

Fray Luis' answer to the investigators of the Holy Tribunal was most revealing. It was true, he confessed, that on this particular point he had abandoned the opinion of Saint Thomas, which is "one of the reasons the Dominicans are so incensed against me." But no one in the last hundred years of Salamanca history had honored the humanity of Christ as much as he had, a fact which even the Jesuits could corroborate with their testimony. Furthermore, the same opinion had been upheld for a long time by the Franciscans, and was considered a respectable theological position; "although," he added, "in my lectures I proved it to be true and most probable with Biblical arguments and theological proofs no theologian before had ever brought to light in such a manner that it had become a common opinion among the professors of theology in Salamanca." The last two lines of Fray Luis' self-defense are obviously exaggerated, but they betray the intensity of his feelings in this matter. Fray Luis' originality in defense of the thesis was exhibited in his rich exegesis of biblical testimony. In addition to the classical quotations (*Colossians*, L, 15–20; *Ephesians*, L, 4: *Proverbs*, VIII, 22–31) he found in the original Hebrew text of the Old Testament the following passages to confirm his views:

This message thou shalt give him from the Lord God of hosts: Here is one who takes his name from the Dayspring, where his feet have trodden; spring there shall be.

Zachariah 6, 12.

When that day comes, bud and fruit there shall be of the Lord's fostering; burgeoning of glory made manifest, harvest of our soil, the trophy of Israel's gleanings.

Isaiah, 4, 2.

Behold, he says, a time is coming when I will make good my promise to Israel and Juda; the day will dawn, the time will be ripe at last for that faithful scion to bud from David's stock; the land shall give a King to reign over it, giving just sentence and due reward.

Jeremiah, 33, 15,

9 "Item dijo que un día después de señor san Bastian próximo, que agora pasó, estando en esta ciudad en el convento de señor San Augustin, hablando con fray Luis Enriquez, de la órden dicha, y profeso en el convento de Salamanca, sobre la prisión del maestro fray Luis de León, catedrático de Salamanca, el dicho fray Luis Enriquez dijo á este quél ha oído decir que, estando un día en un convite el dicho fray Luis de León y otros maestros, había el uno dellos dicho *vino*, y el dicho fray Luis había respondido: 'Cuando viniere obligados somos á creerle, aunque se dubda ó hay dubda si es venido;' y que todos habían entendido que lo había dicho por el advenimiento de Cristo." (*Biblioteca de Autores Españoles*, vol. 37, part II, Real Academia Española: Madrid, 1950, p. XXI.)

Through his efforts this venerable Franciscan tradition was not only kept alive in the stormy days of the Counter-Reformation, but also transmitted with new freshness to the Jesuit theologians among whom it has prevailed ever since.

If Fray Luis' significant participation in the theological revival of Salamanca in the second half of the sixteenth century has only recently become evident, the popular impact of his Spanish treatises *La Perfecta Casada* and *De Los Nombres de Cristo* upon the religious life of his contemporaries has never been doubted. This is not the place to discuss the importance of the use of the vernacular in spiritual books (*See below* p. 193); nor do we intend to go beyond our own purpose and self-imposed limitations to pass judgment on the quality of Fray Luis' inimitable prose. But the student of Spanish culture ought to understand that these books – together with the Spanish commentaries to the Bible we will discuss later – are classic landmarks in the history of the Spanish language. And no one should imagine himself to have mastered the Castilian idiom until he has been able to experience a pervasive and overpowering aesthetic pleasure in reading the elegant, restrained, solemn, classical, musical, harmonious, persuasive, serene, and intense prose of Fray Luis de León. "*Más alto no ha culminado la lengua castellana*" ("The Spanish language has never scored a higher mark") wrote Azorin, himself a master of words and style.

The two books, published by Fray Luis in 1583, opened a new era in the history of Spanish spiritual literature in the vernacular. The Roman Index of 1558, promulgated by Paul IV, and the Spanish *Index* of 1559, – the special pride of the General Inquisitor Valdés, – were instrumental in curbing the magnificent blossoming of spiritual writing during the first years of Philip II's reign. Fray Luis de Granada, Saint Juan de Avila, Saint Francis a Borgia, Jorge de Montemayor, the translations into Spanish of the Bible and the German mystics, were among the victims of Valdés' incredible zeal. The black market of forbidden books, the constant censorship of University libraries, the prohibition of importing books printed abroad, reached during those sad years tragic proportions. Any vernacular publication stressing the inner character of religious life or making available the Bible to the masses of the faithful was considered dangerous, and was consequently labeled as Lutheran, Calvinistic, or at least, Erasmian. Acccording to the exact boundaries of orthodoxy defined by Melchor Cano in Salamanca the Tribunal of the Inquisition went to work with amazing enthusiasm. El Brocense and Arias Montano, both of them personal friends of Fray Luis, were constantly harassed by the Inquisition. The deaths of Paul IV and of Valdés brought some temporary relief, but the situation remained tense for a number of years. The publication of the writings of Saint Teresa and Saint John of the Cross was considered a serious risk by their editors, Fray Luis de León and Fray Basilio Ponce de León respectively, and both of them had to make public and extensive apologies. Fray Luis de León wrote:

> I shall conclude by saying that those who speak about her (Saint Teresa's) books with no respect are obviously possessed by the devil . . . And the proof is that if they were inspired by God they would first of all condemn such books as *La Celestina*, *Libros de caballerías*, and similar documents full of vanity, obscenities and poison to the souls.[10]

Up until 1601 the University of Salamanca had to fight the attempt of some Dominican theologians to forbid without exception the publication of any vernacular book dealing with any religious matter whatsoever. The Jesuits themselves became tame and conservative. The accusations of Melchor Cano and the initial involvement of Salmeron in the legal proceedings against Carranza led to an extreme concern with the reputation of the Order. The two great Jesuit masters of spiritual prose, Luis de la Puente and Alonso Rodriguez, belong already to the reign of Philip III. Fray Luis de Granada (whose books Fray Luis de León requested while in jail during his first process before the Inquisition) expurgated the later editions of his two well-known books, *Libro de Oración* and *Guía de Pecadores*, from any Erasmian overtones. The book of his late years, *Introducción al Símbolo de la Fé*,was a typical orthodox summary of Counter-Reformation theology and devotion, and as such it was soon translated into several European languages and highly recommended by Saint Francis of Sales in his *Introduction to the Devout Life*. The Franciscan Fray Diego de Estella wrote two popular books in Spanish between 1570 and 1580, but the most daring and original of his writings, a commentary to the Gospel of Saint Luke, was in Latin, and was repeatedly 'cleansed' by the theologians of Alcalá and the Inquisitors from Seville.[11]

10 "Y así concluyo, diciendo que tengo por sin duda que trae el demonio engañados a los que de estos *Libros* no hablan con la reverencia que deben; y que sin duda les menea la lengua, para, si pudiese por su medio, estorbar el provecho que hacen. Y vese claramente por esto: porque si se movieran con espíritu de Dios, primero y ante todas cosas, condenaran los libros de *Celestina*, los de *Caballerías*, y otras mil prosas y obras llenas de vanidades y lascivias, con que cada momento se emponzoñan las almas." (*Obras Completas Castellanas*, p. 1363.)

11 See Marcel Bataillon, *Erasmo y España*, trans. Antonio Alatorre, 2 vols. (México, 1950), pp. 715–724, 750–760. The *Index* of Valdés has been published by the Real Academia Española, *Tres índices expurgatorios de la Inquisición española en el siglo XVI* (Madrid, 1952). The

Only against this somber background of constant censorship and mutual suspicion can one measure the enormous significance of Fray Luis' work. *La Perfecta Casada* was written by Fray Luis after his Spanish commentary to *The Song of Songs*. The very title of the book, *The Perfect Married Woman*, was in the sixteenth century a bold profession of the controversial thesis that Christian perfection was not the exclusive patrimony of monastic life, but also a duty of married men and women. The fact that each chapter of the book was introduced as a commentary on *Proverbs*, Chapter 31, was also a risky maneuver to bypass the existing regulations concerning vernacular books dealing with the Bible. The book was written for women, who, with rare exceptions, were not able to read Latin, and dedicated to a woman, María Osorio, a distant relative of Fray Luis. The author was immediately criticized for having written on a subject he was not supposed to know much about by reason of his own celibacy vows. The accusation was obviously ill-founded. Fray Luis' treatise was only the last title in a long series of traditional books on the subject, a series which began with Saint Augustine and Saint Ambrose and included in Spain such representatives as Alvaro de Luna, Juan Rodriguez del Padrón, and more recently, Juan Luis Vives, the Augustinians Orozco, Saint Tomás de Villanueva, and Martín de Córdoba. *La Perfecta Casada*, however, is practically the only book of this kind which has retained its enormous popularity in Spain through the centuries. Those who want to know something about the Spanish ideal of womanhood in the age of Vittoria Collonna, Caterina Sforza, and Marguerite of Navarre, should read Fray Luis' book, a book which Gregorio Marañón still recommends as the best possible gift to every Spanish bride. The central thesis of the book is that women are by nature "the weakest and most abject of all animals" (*De su natural flaca y deleznable más que ningún otro animal*); that, therefore, for a woman to be good she ought to be "more than just good" (*No es buena la que es no es más que buena*); and that, finally, a good woman, more so than in the case of a good man, is "a masterpiece of art, an incomparable blessing, and the acme of perfection" (*Artificio puro y bien incomparable, o por mejor decir, un amontonamiento de riquísimos bienes*). The perfection of the wife and the mother is then the indispensable condition to a harmonious and mutually enriching partnership which Fray Luis considered the very essence of the institution of marriage. The list of perfections

works of Fray Luis de Granada can be found in Biblioteca de Autores Españoles, vol. 6. The *Archivo Ibero-Americano* has published a special issue (Madrid, 1924) under the title *Estudio histórico-crítico sobre la vida y obras de Fray Diego de Estella.*

which should adorn the wife is the traditional one: the woman should be a prudent administrator (Chapter 3), a diligent worker (Chapter 5), a good house-keeper (Chapter 6), generous toward the poor and the servants (Chapter 11), modest in her attire (Chapter 12, the longest chapter!), restrained in speaking (Chapter 16), clean in appearance and reserved toward strangers (Chapter 17). Fray Luis does not deal with the intellectual education of women, a very controversial subject previously discussed by Juan Luis Vives in his book *De institutione feminae Christinae;* nor does he recognize for a moment the right of women to any professional activity beyond the narrow limits of the home. The charm of the book is not based upon this conservative statement of traditional values, a clearly anti-feminist position, but rather upon some marginal qualities and aspects. In the tradition of *La Celestina* Fray Luis delights in colorful sketches of different types of women which excel in fine psychological insights and in a mastery of the language. These unforgettable portraits give us a first hand acquaintance with Spanish society of the sixteenth century, and are, like *El Corbacho*, *La Celestina*, the picaresque or Lope's dramas, an integral part of Spain's national folklore. Here are some examples:

If a married woman does not keep herself busy at home, what is she going to do? She will fatally involve herself in the problems of other people, she will waste her life leaning out of the window, visiting friends, on the streets, in parties, away from her own little corner, oblivious of her household, prying into the affairs of strangers. She will spread gossip, invent stories, and will end as a chatterer, a busybody, source of intrigues, given to gambling, to laughter, to idle talk, to luxury, and to everything else that naturally flows from such behavior but I will not mention here being too obvious to the reader.

When I say that a married woman ought to rise early in the morning I do not mean that she should spend three hours, surrounded by bottles and chests, attempting to sharpen her eyebrows, coloring her face, or persuading the mirror to lie and to call her 'pretty'. Besides all the evils brought about by this kind of artificial cosmetics, she will inevitably achieve nothing thereby, and neglect her household. In a way it would have been better for her to stay in bed and sleep.[12]

[12] "Y demás de esto, si la casada no trabaja ni se ocupa en lo que pertenece a su casa, qué otros estudios o negocios tiene en que se ocupar? Forzado es que, si no trata de sus oficios, emplee su vida en los oficios ajenos, y que dé en ser ventanera, visitadora, callejera, amiga de fiestas, enemiga de su rincón, de su casa olvidada y de las casas ajenas curiosa; pesquisidora de cuanto pasa, y aun de lo que no pasa inventora, parlera y chismosa; de pleitos revolvedora, jugadora también y dada del todo a la risa y a la conversación y al palacio, con lo demás que por ordinaria consecuencia se sigue, y se calla aquí ahora por ser cosa manifiesta y notoria." (*Obras Completas Castellanas*, pp. 259–260.)

"Porque no se entiende que, si madruga la casada, ha de ser para que, rodeada de botecillos y arquillas, como hacen algunas, se esté sentada tres horas afilando la ceja, y pintando la

The popular flavor of *La Perfecta Casada* is maintained throughout the book despite the severity of its ethical attitudes, and in amazing harmony with the solemn Biblical inspiration and display of rich erudition. The style, both dignified and entertaining, reflects with delightful immediacy the typically Spanish mixture of the transcendent and the familiar, the grave seriousness of the churchman and the humorous observations of the humanist.

Still more significant to the history of Spanish thought was Fray Luis' masterpiece *De Los Nombres de Cristo*. The theologian and the poet, the Biblical scholar and the humanist, the mystic and the philosopher, conspired together to write this extraordinary book which, as a symbol of the Spanish Counter-Reformation, has fittingly been compared to Philip the Second's Monastery of El Escorial. *De Los Nombres de Cristo* is properly speaking a treatise of Christology built around the Biblical Names of Christ: Fruit, Face of God, Path, Shepherd, Mountain, Father of the Future, Arm of God, Prince of Peace, Spouse, Son of God, the Beloved, Jesus. The theme of the book will not arouse today the enthusiasm of most readers. Some contemporary critics have described it as "abstruse" (Getino), "tedious" (Ticknor), and "drawn out with theological voluptuousness" (Ortega y Gasset). As a recapitulation, however, of Spanish Renaissance thought during the reign of Philip II, *De Los Nombres de Cristo* had no equal in its century. As a theological treatise the book represents the most harmonious synthesis of Biblical, Patristic and speculative theology ever written by the disciples of Vitoria and Melchor Cano. Through this book Biblical poetry, primitive Christianity, and solid scholastic theology became the spiritual nourishment of Spanish Catholics outside the University classrooms, the simple Christian folk uninformed and uninterested in the annoying theological controversies of rival professors. Bataillon has seen in *De Los Nombres de Cristo* one of the last echoes of Spanish Erasmianism, a manual of inward Christianity directed against the institutional and sacramental structure of the Church.[13] There is no doubt that in some enigmatic passages Fray Luis severely attacked the false prophets of ceremonial sanctity:

These words of St. Macarius teach us how to recognize which doctrines and rules of life are the rules and teachings of Christ . . . However much it

cara, y negociando con su espejo que mienta y la llame hermosa. Que demás del grave mal que hay en este artificio postizo, del cual se dirá en su lugar, es no conseguir el fin de su diligencia, y es faltar a su casa por ocuparse en cosas tan excusadas, que fuera menos mal el dormir." (*Ibid.*, pp. 253–254.)

[13] *Erasmo y España*, I, pp. 762–768.

is proclaimed in the name of Christ, it is not of Christ, because Christ our Health works interiorly while those practices merely work externally. The work of Christ is the renewal of the spirit and the restoration of justice; the result of those external practices is only the appearance of health and justice. The name Christ means anointed; hence, Christ is an unction, and an unction penetrates to the bones. Those other practices may varnish or embellish, but they do not anoint. Christ destroys the power of uncontrolled passions, but merely external practices only cover them over and give them the appearance of goodness. Indeed, they concentrate attention on the passions and even direct them to their own advantage. Thus, any doctrine which does not look primarily to man's health is not the true teaching of Christ.[14]

Fray Luis repeatedly emphasized the inner transformation of the redeemed soul through Christ's grace as the essential part of man's religious life, but such emphasis could be interpreted in two different ways: as a criticism of Catholic piety and devotion, or also as an attack against Luther's theory of external justification through faith. The reader should judge for himself:

. . . In this way grace, entering into the soul and taking possession of the will, makes the soul by participation that which the will of God is in itself: a law and an inclination for whatever is good and just. When this has been accomplished, the soul becomes serene and tranquil, for it has been put in order and has banished whatever has disturbed its peace.[15]

It would be fair to conclude that Fray Luis' position in this matter was slightly ambiguous, and that, maybe on purpose, he never formulated the relation between Nature and Grace, man's good works and

[14] "Que, cuanto a lo primero de las enseñanzas y caminos de vida, habemos de tener por cosa certísima que la que no mirare a este fin de *salud*, la que no tratare de desarraigar del alma las pasiones malas que tiene, la que no procurare criar en el secreto de ella, orden, templanza, justicia, por más que de fuera parezca santa, no es santa; y por más que se pregone de Cristo, no es Cristo. Porque el *nombre* de Cristo es *Jesús y salud*, y el oficio de ésta es sobresanar por defuera. La obra de Cristo propia es renovación del alma y justicia secreta; la de ésta son apariencias de salud y justicia. La definición de Cristo es *ungir*, quiero decir, que Cristo es lo mismo que *unción*, y de la unción es ungir, y la unción y el ungir es cosa que penetra a los huesos; y este otro negocio que digo, es embarnizar, y no ungir. De solo Cristo es el deshacer las pasiones; esto no las deshace, antes las sobredora con colores y demostraciones de bien. Qué digo no deshace? Antes vela con atención sobre ellas, para, en conociendo a do tiran, seguirlas y cebarlas y encaminarlas a su provecho. Así que la doctrina o enseñamiento que no hiciere, cuanto en sí es, esta *salud* en los hombres, si es cierto que Cristo se llama *Jesús* porque la hace siempre, cierto será que no es enseñamiento de Cristo." (*Obras Completas Castellanas*, pp. 776–777.)

[15] "Queda, pues, concluído que la gracia, como es semejanza de Dios, entrando en nuestra alma y prendiendo luego su fuerza en la voluntad de ella, la hace por participación, como de suyo es la de Dios, ley e inclinación y deseo de todo aquello que es justo y que es bueno. Pues, hecho esto, luego por orden secreta y maravillosa se comienza a pacificar el reino del alma, y a concertar lo que en ella estaba encontrado, y a ser desterrado de allí todo lo bullicioso y desasosegado que la turbaba; y descúbrese entonces la paz, y muestra la luz de su rostro y sube y crece, y finalmente queda reina y señora." (*Ibid.*, p. 614.)

God's supernatural help, with the accuracy of Saint Ignatius in the *Spiritual Exercises*. However, to see in Fray Luis an underground agent of Erasmus of Rotterdam, seems an enormous misinterpretation of history. One should not forget that in many respects most of the victims of the Spanish Inquisition represented the main stream of Catholic life more faithfully than the Inquisitors themselves. Loyola, Saint Teresa, Saint John of the Cross, Estella, and Fray Luis himself were not Erasmian illuminists; their emphasis upon inner life was basically more Pauline and Augustinian than Erasmian, more authentically Christian than indulgences, candles, and relics. For this reason the victims of the Inquisition have become canonized Saints and Doctors of the Church, while the names of their persecutors have fortunately been forgotten by everyone except a few scholars and historians.

De Los Nombres de Cristo, nevertheless, is much more than a popular treatise of Counter-Reformation theology. The book is also a splendid display of humanistic jewelry. Through this book the Castilian language reached the dignity and position of a classical language, a theme we intend to discuss later in more detail (*See below*, pp. 190ss). The balance of form and content, the perfect equilibrium of artful finesse and natural wit, the unique blend of classical and Biblical inspiration with an inextinguishable Castilian popular flavor, were unmatched in that century. The book manifests a classical erudition. The dialogue is perhaps closer to the Ciceronian than to the Platonic model. A delight in the external world is combined in attractive proportions with the simplicity of Franciscan devotion, the contagious charm of the Virgilian bucolic, the lifting effect of Neo-Platonic contemplation, and the withdrawing intimacy of Stoic naturalism.[16]

In spite of Fray Luis' merits as a theologian and spiritual writer, his name and reputation have been almost exclusively linked with his achievements as a poet. Américo Castro has bluntly written: "Luis de León was immortalized in his poetry, but the ideas in his head, which were imprisoned with him in the jails of the Inquisition, and which he might have given to his century, he took with him into eternity."[17]

[16] On *La Perfecta Casada* see José Martinez Ruiz Azorín, *Los dos Luises y otros ensayos* (Madrid, 1961); also the introduction to *Obras Completas Castellanas* (Madrid, 1944), pp. 187–203. Gregorio Marañón in his book *Tres ensayos sobre la vida sexual*, 3rd edition, (Madrid, 1927), p. 114, discusses Fray Luis' ideas on marriage. As a summary of the literary merits of Fray Luis in *La Perfecta Casada* see A. Valbuena Prat, *Historia de la literatura española* 6th ed. (Barcelona, 1960), pp. 596–603.

On the aesthetic values of *Los Nombres de Cristo* see Marcelino Menéndez y Pelayo, *Historia de las Ideas Estéticas en España* (Madrid, 1940), II, pp. 101–103.

[17] *The Structure of Spanish History* (Princeton, 1954), p. 635.

Fray Luis' active role in the theological disputes at Salamanca and his leading influence on the spiritual life of sixteenth century Spaniards proves beyond any doubt the obvious exaggeration of this uncritical remark. It remains true, however, that since Quevedo published Fray Luis' poetry in 1631, the brilliance of the poet has almost eclipsed the reputation of the thinker. To present this undeniable fact, as Américo Castro does, as another tragic proof of the Inquisition's power to repress new ideas, would give only a partial explanation of a complex situation. Perusal of Fray Luis' books shows indeed that the fear of the Inquisition often forced the writer to express with extreme circumspection his personal opinions in matters religious, social, and political. The same books, however, display other features of Fray Luis' thought which would make it very difficult to find an exact profile of his opinions. As a thinker Fray Luis was much more an eclectic synthetizer than an original innovator. His theological ideas – relevant as they are to the intellectual history of the University of Salamanca – were in most cases transitional solutions between well-defined doctrinal schools, and, in some critical problem areas, they were ill-formulated and poorly-conceived. In fact, the most interesting characteristic of Fray Luis' thought has nothing to do with scholastic distinctions nor with any particular book, but rather with his comprehensive view of reality, both natural and supernatural, which defined in every moment his attitude toward existence and reduced to an admirable harmony all the extraordinary gifts of his mind. The study of Fray Luis' poetical work gives us the most reliable insight into the cultural climate of his epoch and at the same time provides us with the master key to understand "the ideas in his head." It goes without saying that a close, formalistic analysis of text and context, goes well beyond our limitations. Others – especially Dámaso Alonso, Gerardo Diego, and Federico de Onís – have done a masterful job in this direction.[18]

The poetical production of Fray Luis can be divided into several categories: a) original poems (some of them of uncertain attribution), b) translations of classical authors (Virgil, Horace, Pyndarus, Tybullus), c) Biblical translations (*Psalms*, *Proverbs*, *Book of Job*), and d) imitations (Horace, Martial, Bembo, Ansonio, Garcilaso, Petrarch). This simple catalogue of Fray Luis' poems is enough to suggest the vast and rich background of his inspiration, Greek and Latin, Biblical and modern. Literary critics have indicated the different sources of this

[18] See, for instance, Dámaso Alonso, *Poesía Española*, 4th edition (Madrid, 1962), pp. 121–205.

literary work. Menéndez y Pelayo is mainly responsible for the association of Fray Luis' name with that of Horace; José María Millás Vallicrosa has convincingly shown the dependence of Fray Luis' intense lyrical expressions upon medieval Jewish poets such as Ibn Gabirol, Yehuda ha Levi, and others; Rafael M. Hornedo has collected all the Petrarchian echoes from the early poems of Fray Luis; Montolín has underlined the overpowering impact of Biblical inspiration; others have pointed to the Virgilian character of Fray Luis' bucolic flavor.[19] Most critics, however, have recognized that what has made Fray Luis de León one of the greatest poets of Spain has been precisely the unique blending of all these materials into an extremely personal work of art. Fray Luis' short poems might very well have some Horatian contours, but the transcendent horizons of his Christian vision of the created cosmos cannot be compared with the narrow naturalism and the *Aurea Mediocritas* of the Latin Poet. Fray Luis' youthful poetry had no doubt some artificial Petrarchian flavor, but the mystic and Neo-Platonic élan of his mature thirst toward the Supreme Good clearly surpasses the flirtatious character of erotic literature. Virgil's love for the simplicity of country life and Fray Luis' delight in the created beauty of nature belong to two different levels; even his Biblical and Jewish poetry – which is in my opinion the main offspring of his inspiration, cannot adequately explain the unique fascination of Fray Luis de León. All the beauty of his Hebraic soul, all the tension of his Christian Faith, all the classical refinement of his Greek and Roman education, all the trappings of his humanistic erudition, converge into his poetry to produce a final melody which is at the same time a work of art transcending all limitations of space and time, and also a poetical confession of his inner soul and a plastic expression of his world-view.[20]

[19] Marcelino Menéndez y Pelayo, *Discurso leído en la Universidad Central* (Madrid, 1889); also *Mística Española* (Madrid, 1956).

J. M. Millás Vallicrosa, "Probable influencia de la poesía sagrada hebraico española en la poesía de Fray Luis de León," *Sefarad*, XV (1956), pp. 261–285.

Rafael María Hornedo, "Algunos datos sobre el petrarquismo de Fray Luis de León," *Razón y Fé*, 85 (1928), pp. 336–353.

Manuel Montolín, *El alma de España y sus reflejos en la literatura del siglo de Oro* (Barcelona, no date).

The position of Menéndez y Pelayo is discussed by Felipe Mellizo in his article "Fray Luis de León, en Menéndez y Pelayo," *La Ciudad de Dios* 170 (1957), pp. 464–471.

[20] In *Obras Completas Castellanas* Feliz García O.S.A. reviews the critical editions of Fray Luis' poetry, starting with Quevedo's edition (pp. 1432–1440). To these we must add the extensive and authoritative critical edition of Father A. C. Vega L. S. A. (Madrid, 1955) enriched with an introduction of Menéndez Pidal and an epilogue of Dámaso Alonso.

Besides the general histories of Spanish literature (Ticknor, Vossler, Valbuena, Alborg, Díaz Plaja, and others) one should consult the following titles on Fray Luis' poetry:

Angel González Palencia, *Fray Luis de León en la poesía castellana* (Madrid, 1942).

It is then through the poet that we try to discover the thinker and the philosopher. Fray Luis de León never wrote a book of philosophy proper, and the philosophical insights scattered throughout his theological work are mostly concerned with detailed matters of scholastic theology (analogy of being, essence and existence, plurality of forms, etc.) in which he merely reflected the doctrinal fluctuations of his colleagues.

Literary critics of all times have passionately disputed the alleged central theme of Fray Luis' poetry. Menéndez y Pelayo and his disciples (or rather his imitators) have made it a cliché that the outstanding feature of Fray Luis' poetry was precisely the serenity, harmony, and *sophrosine* of his verses. Other critics, – among them Dámaso Alonso, Azorín, and the main editor of Fray Luis' poetry, Father Vega O.S.A. – have emphatically rejected this evaluation in favor of exactly the opposite view. For them Fray Luis was the poet of inner tragedy, violent sublimation, and intense lyrical effusion. Fray Luis' aggressive character, his obvious connection with a long Jewish tradition of poetical withdrawal and despair, his sad vision of contemporary events – "*ésta triste y espaciosa España*" –, the intrigues of academic life and the constant harassment by the Inquisition, were more than enough – these critics claim – to poison the soul of the poet with intense bitterness and to justify the constant attempt to escape from reality his poetry betrays. What this sharp disagreement between these two judgments points to is precisely the secret of Fray Luis' creativity, the intense (almost neurotic) contrast between the painful experience of the daily struggle for survival, and the enlightened, educated, inspired longing for Unity, Harmony, and Love. The therapeutic *sophrosine* Fray Luis creates in his work of art is not the result of some pagan *ataraxia*, but a painful victory constantly threatened from within and from outside. It is true that most of his verses are permeated by a lukewarm transparency of self-restraint and moderation. But, occasionally, in the most unexpected moment, the rhythm breaks into a staccato of intense lyrism, loud exclamation, unrepressed feeling, which has nothing to do with Horatian *mediocritas*, but reveals the deeper levels of his magnificent soul, partly Hebrew and partly Christian, both serene and tortured, living constantly in the twilight of hope and despair.

This melancholy and sadness shows forth in the *Commentaries to the*

M. M. Arjona, "Crítica de las Obras poéticas de Fray Luis de León," *La Ciudad de Dios*, 15 (1888), p. 469–486.
Audrey F. G. Bell, "The Chronology of Fray Luis' Lyrics," *MLR* 21 (1926), pp. 168–177.

Book of Job and to Psalm 26, both of which he published during his lifetime in Latin and in Spanish.

> "Those who lived in my own house, my servants, treated me as a stranger".
> When the tree falls, people run away from it. Job fell, and God threw him down to the ground and stepped on him. And, as the Book says, his friends left him behind. When Fortune changes, friends are always absent. This is the bitterest part of it all: your own relatives ignore you. Man quickly understands that one should not rely upon other human beings, that no one is loved because of what he is but because of what he *seems* to be, that nothing is firm and solid, least of all your own friends.[21]

The confessional character of the first part of Job's commentaries (up to chapter 33) deeply touched the intense and split personality of Quevedo, who in 1799 published part of the book. The very text of Psalm 26, one of Fray Luis' favorite prayers, unveils the secret depths of our poet: "The Lord is my light and my deliverance, whom have I to fear? Vainly the malicious close about me, as if they would tear me to pieces ... all at once they stumble and fall. One request I have made of the Lord ... to dwell in the Lord's house my whole life long... In His royal tent he hides me ... safe from peril ... I long, Lord, for Thy presence. ... Lord, do not give me over to the will of my oppressors, when false witnesses stand up to accuse me ..." Fray Luis' inner life was a relentless search for peace, away from division, struggle, and hatred. In this respect his personality was typical of the century. Cusanus' coincidence of opposites, Ficino's NeoPlatonic contemplation of the One, Vives' central idea of *Concordia*, the pacifism of More's circle, the irenic impulse of the Erasmian middle way, were parallel reactions of different noble souls to the divisive trends of nationalism and religious controversy which marked an end to the medieval aspiration for unity and solidarity. Fray Luis' central word, the epitome of his thought, is the word *concierto*. The musical inner harmony of Salinas, the silent cosmic peace of the stars above the cold Castilian plateau, the surrender of the lower passions to the enlightened command of reason through the irresistible attraction of Christ's grace,

21 "*Moradores de mi casa y mis siervos por extraño me contaron; extraño fuí en sus ojos.* A la caída de un árbol se sigue que huyan y se aparten los que la ven. Cayó Job, y derrocólo el Señor y batióle como ha dicho, y púsole por el suelo; y así sucedió lo que dice, que le huyeron todos y le dejaron solo. Que es uno de los accidentes que, cuando la fortuna se vuelve, causan mayor sentimiento el faltar luego los amigos, y el desconocerse los deudos, y el ver el hombre por la misma experiencia lo poco que puede fiar de los hombres, y el engaño grande que pasa en la vida, que nadie es querido por lo que es en sí, sino por lo que representa de fuera, que como no es suyo ni firme, así no lo son los amigos." (*Obras Completas Castellanas*, p. 1059.)

are visible or invisible manifestations of that Unity in plurality which signals the return of the creation to its *concierto* with the One and the Creator.

"When this time shall come, the arrogant pride of the mountains shall be cast down to the earth and all mortal strength, pleasure, and wisdom shall disappear like smoke. With them Thou shalt bury all tyranny and the kingdom of the new earth shall belong to Thy faithful ones. Then shall they sing Thy praises without ceasing and it shall be exceedingly pleasing to Thee to be thus praised. They will live in Thee and Thou in them. They shall be kings, and Thou the King of kings."[22]

On the natural level Fray Luis sought unity and inner *concierto* through the contemplation of created Beauty. His pastoral nostalgia, his love of solitude, a withdrawal into the self, a delight in the harmony of numbers and sounds, was much more than an erudite synthesis of Virgilian poetry, Stoic resignation, Neo-Platonic contemplation, and Pythagorean proportions. It was rather a form of sublimation for a man whose luxurious humanistic education had added to the archetypal quest for peace and order the beauty and the form of Renaissance culture and taste.

"Cuándo será que pueda,
libre de esta prisión, volar al cielo,
Felipe, y en la rueda
que huye más del suelo,
contemplar la verdad pura, sin duelo?
Allí a mi vida junto
en luz resplandeciente convertido,
veré distinto y junto
lo que es y lo que ha sido,
y su principio propio y escondido."[23]

On the supernatural level Fray Luis sought unity in Christ, the point of convergence of God's Infinite Perfection and Man's contingent misery. And it was precisely in Christianity where Fray Luis desper-

[22] "Cuando viniere este tiempo (ay amable y bienaventurado tiempo, y no tiempo ya, sino eternidad sin mudanza!), así que, cuando viniere, la *arrogante soberbia de los montes, estremeciéndose, vendrá por el suelo; y desaparecerá hecha humo*, obrándolo tu Majestad, toda la pujanza y deleite y sabiduría mortal; y sepultarás en los abismos, juntamente con esto, a la tiranía; y el reino de la tierra nueva será de los tuyos. Ellos *cantarán entonces de continuo tus alabanzas, y a Ti el ser alabado por esta manera te será cosa agradable.* Ellos vivirán en Ti, y Tú vivirás en ellos dándoles riquísima y dulcísima vida. Ellos serán reyes, y Tú Rey de reyes. Serás Tú en ellos todas las cosas, y reinarás para siempre." (*Obras Completas Castellanas*, p. 515.)

[23] *Ibid.*, p. 1464.

ately attempted to find the synthesis of his past Jewish heritage and his present Spanish reality, the fulfillment of past promises and the prophecy of future grandeur. Finally, the inner harmony of the natural and the supernatural, can be glimpsed through the pervasive mystical overtones of his poetry, Fray Luis' journey from the miseries of earthly life to the final Union with the source of all Being and Beauty.[24]

B. THE CONCERN WITH LANGUAGE DURING THE RENAISSANCE

The pervasive interest in language which characterizes so much of today's intellectual endeavor is not by any means a discovery of this age. No historian would deny that the Renaissance was a critical period in shaping the linguistic attitudes of Western man. The central issues of contemporary linguistics, philosophy of language, linguistic philosophy, hermeneutics, and literary criticism were also the problems with which the early Humanists and the thinkers of the sixteenth century were concerned. It is true that linguistic problems are treated today with a sophistication and explicitness unknown to the generations between Petrarch and Guillaume du Vair. For this reason it would sound preposterous to call Ramus a precursor of Saussure's structuralism or Erasmus the founder of historical criticism; to see in the speculative grammarians of the late middle ages the forerunners of Chomsky's generative grammar and in the Renaissance cabalists a mystical conception of language similar to the symbolic functions of Cassirer. Pico's belief in a universal tradition of thought can hardly be resolved into Jung's collective unconscious or into an archetypal perspective of literary criticism. Valla's defense of ordinary language against the jargon of the schools does not cover all the philosophy of language exposed by Wittgenstein. Still, there is obviously something in common to both historical occasions. When established patterns of thought threaten to become stagnant and inoperative the language in which they are imbedded becomes naturally the immediate object

[24] Fray Luis de León's thought is the object of Marcelino Gutierrez' book *Fray Luis de León y la Filosofía Española del Siglo XVI* (Madrid, 1885). See also Aubrey Bell, *Luis de León. A Study of the Spanish Renaissance* (Oxford, 1925); A. Coster, "Luis de León, *Revue Hispanique*, 53 (1921), pp. 1–468; Guillermo Fernández Quintana, "Las bases filosóficas de la teología de Fray Luis de León," *Revista de la Universidad de Madrid*, 13 (1963), pp. 346–367. Karl Vossler, *Luis de León* (Munich, 1943).

Crisógono de Jesús has made a special study of Fray Luis' mysticism, "El misticismo de Fray Luis de León," *Revista de Espiritualidad*, I (1942), pp. 30–52; also P. F. Marcus del Rios, "La doctrina mística de Fray Luis de León," *Religión y Cultura*, 2 (1928), pp. 531–543; 3 (1928), pp. 205–220; 4 (1928), pp. 47–67, 224–236, 417–430.

of attention and criticism. A strong emphasis on linguistic issues denotes always the quickening of intellectual change, and betrays a sharp increase in man's old struggle between empiricism and rationalism, between skepticism and belief. Obviously from a different perspective and under the unique colors of Renaissance dilemmas and choices the intellectuals of the fifteenth and sixteenth centuries were in fact dealing with the central problems of language: the relation between speech and thought, form and content, syntax and meaning, subject and object. Two late medieval movements, speculative grammar and nominalistic terminism, prepared the ground, albeit in a negative manner, for the linguistic attitudes of early Humanism. Speculative grammar was a fourteenth century attempt to integrate the purely descriptive and teaching-oriented categories of Priscian and Donatus into the world-view of scholastic philosophy. By seeking philosophical explanations of grammatical rules those thinkers developed the original notion of a universal grammar underlying the superficial differences of national languages. The semantic distinctions of Peter Hispanus, *significatio* and *suppositio;* the refinements of his disciples, – first and second order language or metalanguage, plus a special emphasis upon syntactic theory and sentence structure, were the most significant achievements of this school. The nominalists (See the first Chapter of this book) stripped speculative grammar of its commitment to any form of realism and used it as a point of departure for a body of formal logic (dialectic) based upon supposition theory and the study of inferential operations between propositions (*consequentiae*). Previously we emphasized the merits (formalization, quantification) and the weaknesses (lack of proper symbolism, neglect of propositional calculus) of terminist logic. What is important for us now is to make clear that the purely formal character of terminist logic with its contempt for rhetoric, epistemology and psychology, its aridity and highly technical jargon, were precisely the point of departure for the rebelion of fourteenth and fifteenth century Humanists. The opposition of rhetoric to dialectic we shall consider later was basically a linguistic problem. Both, the terminist dialecticians and the Ciceronian rhetors agreed that the study of language was the foundation and the core of the Liberal Arts. Their disagreement was a matter of their divergent approaches to the study of language itself.

A series of events at the beginning of the modern era helped further to rekindle man's interest in language. The fall of Constantinople in 1543 – an event which according to many scholars marks the "official" end to the Middle Ages – pushed many Greek scholars toward Italy. Hundreds of manuscripts of classical texts were brought to Western Europe. Chrisolorus wrote the first Greek grammar of the West, and for the first time learning Greek became an imperative of higher education. The rediscovery of ancient Greek and Latin manuscripts opened the eyes of modern men to the beauty of classical form and encouraged the diachronic study of romance languages. The discovery of the press and the rise of an urban middle class increased in fantastic proportions the availability of the written word. The discovery of America dramatically broadened the linguistic horizons of Europeans. The publication of native American grammars (Quechua in 1560; Guaraní in 1639) was the seed for a comparative linguistics. This field of study increased in scope and importance with the accrued knowledge of Indian, Chinese, and Japanese amassed by missionaries and explorers (Marco Polo). Finally, the two most important developments of that age – the rise of the modern State and the Reformation – brought about two fundamental changes in the linguistic temper. Nationalism was one of the most powerful allies of the vernacular in its struggle against the supremacy of Latin. The details of the contest varied from nation to nation. In spite of Dante's defense of the vernacular in his *De vulgari eloquentia*, and notwithstanding the powerful impulse given to Tuscanese by the Florentines Petrarch and Bocaccio together with Pietro Bembo (a superior Latinist himself), the regional divisions of Italy, the opposition to Tuscanese by Castiglione, and the prejudice of the Humanists against the Romance dialects as derivative forms of plebeian Roman speech, delayed for a while the recognition of an Italian national language. In France and in England, the lack of competitive dialects facilitated such recognition. Du Bellay in France and Mulcaster in England were the champions of French and English as proper tools of serious intellectual endeavor.

As for the Reformation, with its emphasis upon the right of the individual to a personal understanding of the Biblical text, its rejection of oral tradition and authoritative interpretation, it is clear that it encouraged the vernacular translations of the Holy Scripture and the writing of vernacular treatises of Theology. Luther's German translation of the Bible in 1534 was an event of great significance not only in the religious history of Europe, but also in the very history of the German language. The incredible achievements of Erasmus of Rotterdam – who among other things fixed the pronunciation of Greek in European Universities – were inspired by a desire to master the language in which the *philosophia Christi* had first been spoken. The intensified study of the Biblical text gave Hebrew a place along side Latin and Greek in sixteenth century education. The ideal of the *homo trilinguus* was fostered not only by such institutions as the Trilingue College of Louvain but also by polyglot editions of the Bible (Alcalá de Henares, Antwerp) and by the outstanding Hebrew grammars of Reuchlin (1506) and Clenard (1529). Through Hebrew western scholarship was introduced for the first time to a non Indo-European language and to a linguistic tradition of Semitic ancestry. Finally, the works of Pico della Mirandola, Ricci, Agrippa, and Thenaud (among many others) redirected the attention of the Renaissance man toward such medieval cabalists as Abraham Gikatilion (died in 1305) and Shenahem Benjamin of Recanati (died in 1350), whose highly esoteric work was based upon a different and extremely interesting philosophy of language we shall consider later.[25]

These events we have just summarized are well known, but their significance upon the history of philosophy of language deserves closer study. The opposition of the Humanists to the barbaric jargon of scholastic Latin was more than a simple matter of taste, it was a clear rebellion against thought itself. The Humanist ideal was not to rewrite medieval thought in Ciceronian Latin, but rather to rethink it in a new idiom and expression. The Humanist rebellion, therefore, was based upon the assumption that the style is at least part of the message; that language was not a neutral and transparent tool of thought, but rather that thought and language were inseparably and mutually interactive. Similarly, the fascination the Humanists felt for classical form was much more than an aesthetic delight in the beautiful word. In spite of the repeated warnings of some Christian humanists against the dangers of pagan literature, the neo-paganism of the Italian Renaissance which Burckhardt has emphasized to the point of exaggeration, was clear proof that the boundaries between form and content exist only in the abstract maps of remote theory. The nationalistic and religious impulse of the vernacular languages added a new dimension to the problem. Behind such an impulse there was no doubt a pre-romantic association between the "spirit" of each nation and its own language, an act of rebellion against the medieval conception of the Empire and the supremacy of the Roman Church. Latin thus progres-

[25] See R. H. Robin, *A Short History of Linguistics* (Indiana, 1967), Chapters 4 (The Middle Ages, pp. 66–93) and 5 (The Renaissance and After, pp. 94–132).
Also Vernon Hall, *A Short History of Literary Criticism* (New York, 1963), Chapter 5 (Dante), 6 (Bocaccio) and 7 (Renaissance Critics).

sively became what Mulcaster called "a symbol of the old bondage." The fact that Latin remained the official University language until well into the eighteenth century, and that thereafter it was instinctively associated with neo-scholasticism and Roman Catholic worship, indicates clearly the proportions of this fundamental change and its impact upon the birth of a modern mentality.

The contest between rhetoric and dialectic in the Renaissance was really a conflict between two divergent conceptions of language itself. The dialectician insisted upon the priority of thought over speech; his ideal was to formulate in symbols the inferential rules of all human reasoning. Consequently the sciences of discourse (grammar and rhetoric, correction and ornamentation) were considered secondary and subordinated to the supreme science of dialectic. Their *paideia* was directed to the "thinker" rather than to the "speaker"; their model was Aristotle rather than Cicero or Quintilian. The Humanists on the other side were convinced that the power of speech was man's distinguishing and most noble feature; that the beauty, order, and lucidity of language were inseparable from clear and straight thinking. Rhetoric was therefore the acme of human education and Quintilian their indisputable master. Valla, the most radical anti-dialectician of early humanism, maintained that philosophical jargon corrupted the freshness and integrity of ordinary language – "people speak better than the philosophers"; and that philosophical reflection always arrives *post festum:* "the orators deal with these problems in the midst of life long before the philosophers chatter about the same problems in their dark corners." Valla preferred Quintilian to Cicero because the latter had occasionally fallen victim to the temptation of dialectic. According to the Humanists, therefore, the pedagogic ideal of the dialecticians was both wrong and inhuman. It was based upon the false premise that man first thinks and then speaks. It left out of consideration the most human side of speech, the art of communicating, the strategy of persuading, the technique of teaching, the intelligent play with emotions and feelings, the natural delight and power of rhythm, order and beauty. The impact of Agricola and Ramus on the educational establishment of western Europe from the middle of the sixteenth century to the Logic of Port Royal a hundred years later, bears witness to the magnitude of the Renaissance confrontation between dialecticians and humanists. Today's gap between the advocates of artificial languages and the champion of ordinary language philosophy or literary existentialism and phenomenology represents, *mutatis mutandis*, a similar situation.

Although much has been written about the cult of form by the Humanists, the predominant feature of their attitude toward language was probably much more pragmatic than aesthetic. The rhetorization of philosophy during the Renaissance was a tribute paid to the power of speech in human intercourse, in the classroom, and in the Courts, in the secret meetings of the diplomats and in public assemblies and debates. Even poetry was considered by Bocaccio, Scaliger, and Harvey as a form of teaching, thus returning to a primitive conception which Plato's intellectualism had attempted to erode. Linguistic behavior became in the Renaissance a powerful reinforcer of new social relationships; the efforts of literary critics to distinguish between aristocratic literary genres (tragedy, epic) and the plebeian ones (comedy, farce); the large number of manuals dealing with refinement and gentility; the cult of an obscure and esoteric idiom in poetry; the attempt to shape the vernacular according to the usage of the upper class ("King's English"), are facts of great interest to contemporary psycho and socio-linguistics.

Another linguistic topic abundantly discussed in the Renaissance was the origin of language itself. The conventionalistic and empirical tradition of Aristotelianism had been powerfully reinforced by the nominalists and terminists. According to Ockham there were two kinds of 'signs': the natural or concept, and the artificial or spoken and written word. The main argument of the conventionalists was obviously the plurality of languages. The undisputed assumption was that man's conceptual reflection of reality was one and the same through time and space, and that the different languages were nothing but totally artificial and conventional signs of this universal repertoire of conceptual pictures of reality. The opposite tendency was to emphasize the natural character of the linguistic symbol. The main argument was to insist upon the onomatopoeic character of primitive languages, a way of reasoning the Stoics had used and frequently abused. There was, of course, an easier way to defend the natural symbolism of speech: to appeal to an original divine revelation and consequent oral tradition. This explanation, which assumed the fact of monogenesis, was the very center of cabalistic philosophy of language, and confirmed Hebrew as the mother of tongues and all human speech. According to the cabalists, words – or at least some proper names – were endowed with a magic power illuminating the essence of the thing or person they referred to. Such power of the word came from God Himself, who, in the same instant, created the essence of a thing (or person), enligtened the human mind to understand it, and gave it a name. According to Cabalism, then, thought and its verbal utterance melt together into one reality. To name is to know; the one who knows the name of something not only knows it, but in some way masters it and possesses it. The magical powers of the cabalists are based upon this knowledge of names and numbers. Cabalism is therefore a type of mystical innatism. The contemporary struggle between descriptive empiricism in linguistics – Bloomenfield and Skinner – and rationalistic explanatory theory – Chomsky, Cassirer – is but a more sophisticated and refined version of the sixteenth century contest between Aristotelian empiricism and Ockhamistic nominalism on one side and Platonic 'anamnesis', Augustinian 'enlightenment' and cabalistic magic on the other.[26]

The rediscovery of cabalistic literature during the Renaissance was intimately associated with another linguistic problem of the age: the exegesis of the Bible. The Protestant emphasis upon the self-explanatory character of the revealed word and the cabalistic faith in the primitive, unadulterated Hebrew text provoked in those years an extraordinary and entirely new philological effort only matched in intensity by the historical criticism of nineteenth century German exegetes. This sixteenth century 'philology' – of which Erasmus of Rotterdam is by far the most representative figure – had to cope with several hermeneutic and literary problems still very controversial today. One of the most characteristic was the theory of translation, a problem which arose from the heated theological controversy over the reliability of Saint Jerome's translation of the Bible (the Vulgate edition). Problems such as the semantic incomensurability of two language-vocabularies; the dependence of meaning on cultural patterns, systems of values, and grammatical structure; the discussion of different 'levels' and 'units' of meaning, were much debated in those days, although in scholastic jargon and within a theological framework which has ceased to be of paramount importance. As far as literary criticism is concerned, the trappings were equally theological, but the issues themselves were no less modern and exciting. Protestant exegesis tended toward a formalistic analysis of the text itself as a self-enclosed entity directly available

[26] On Renaissance cabalism see Joseph Leon Blau, *The Christian Interpretation of the Cabala* (New York, 1944). Blau was complemented and criticized by François Secret in his article "L'interpretazione della Kabbala nel Rinascimento," *Convivium*, XXIV (1956), pp. 541–552. Secret deals also with Spanish Cabalism in "Les débuts du Kabbalisme Chrétien en Espagne et son Histoire à la Renaissance," *Sefarad*, XVII (1957), pp. 36–48. Other specialists in cabalism are M. G. Scholem, F. Baer, A. Franck, A. Jellineck, and W. W. Westcott. Spanish cabalism has been especially investigated by M. Asín y Palacios, A. Bension, Carreras y Artau, and Cantera Burgos.

to the individual reader. Thus philological propaedeutics was exclusively directed toward a determination of the text in its total integrity. Catholic exegetes on the other hand insisted on the 'intention' of the writer as one of the essential moments in the formation of the written word and, therefore, demanded an oral tradition as authoritative 'interpretation' of the text. It goes without saying that Catholic exegetes were much more inclined to admit allegorical and hidden senses in the Scripture as long as they were 'confirmed' by a respectable tradition and the authority of the Church.

The history of modern hermeneutics is only a prolongation of this sixteenth century contest between Protestant and Catholic conceptions of the written word. The latter have progressively admitted that the exact ("scientific") determination of the text is a problem of critical philology anterior to any interpretation. The Protestants on the other hand have come to recognize that the Biblical text in itself is not the divine Word but rather what is important is its interpretation by a human writer (Barth); it is not the object of Faith but Faith itself in its own self-presentation that is critical (Bultmann). The Catholic distinction between the literal and the spiritual sense shares with the Protestant distinction between God's word and the human word the conviction that Biblical literary expression is more than just the conscious work of an individual human writer conditioned by time and space. Jung's collective unconscious is a godless but still mythical echo of the Christian faith in a divine inspiration. In both cases words mean more than their exclusively literal import because the author of the written work is larger than and transcends the actual scrivener of the book.[27]

Renaissance attitudes toward language did not always corroborate the strong faith of biblical scholars; on the contrary some of them were inspired by the emerging voices of skepticism, relativism, and anti-metaphysical positivism which have since directed the erratic courses of modern philosophy. There is no doubt that Erasmus' subordination of speculation to "grammar" was one of the first indicators of modern skepticism. The syncretism of Pico della Mirandola – widely imitated in every corner of Europe – was based upon the assumption that even the most divergent philosophical opinions such as those of Plato and Aristotle were only *verbal* and superficial differences covering up a common, universal system of thought. Pico's equation of apparently

[27] For a history of hermeneutics see J. M. Robinson and J. B. Cobb *New Frontiers in Theology* (New York, 1965), pp. 1–77.

different philosophical terms was really a lesson in practical relativism. Nicholas of Cusa on the other hand proclaimed loudly and clearly the limitations of language. According to him man was endowed with a twofold power: discursive reason (*ratio*) and intelligence (*intellectus*). Reason was governed by the principle of contradiction and the incompatibility of opposites; its object was the finite and the contingent. The intellect, however, dealt with the Infinite where opposites coincide in a Supreme Unity. For him language was not the tool of the intellect, but only the instrument of discursive reason. The intellect uses language not to make statements but to make suggestions through mathematical symbols and "the milk of comparisons." Nicholas' rejection of a rational natural theology, the admission of an 'unspeakable' noetic power, and his emphasis on the suggestive power of metaphor, were highly explosive novelties which had an extraordinary impact upon his contemporaries and were systematized and transmitted to posterity by the first martyr of modern rationalism, Giordano Bruno.

That Spain played a highly significant role in the linguistic undertakings of the Renaissance, has been already suggested in other parts of this book. We do not need to remind the reader that most of those Parisian logicians who provoked the fierce criticism of humanists and rhetoricians were Spanish professors at Paris (Gaspar Lax, Fernando Enzinas, Jerónimo Pardo, Juan Celaya, the brothers Coronel, Juan Dolz). Less known is the fact that such a brand of logicians *ad modum Parisiense* was not extinguished in Spain throughout the Renaissance, and that the Universities of Salamanca and Alcalá were enlivened by the controversies centered around the teachings of Fray Alfonso de Córdoba, Diego and Juan Naveros, and Alfonso de Prado. The nominalist writings of Pedro Ciruelo and Sancho Carranza de Miranda bear witness to the Iberian delight in a gallant fight for moribund causes and ideas.[28]

The best informed and the most devastating criticism of terminist logicians was written, however, by another Spaniard, Juan Luis Vives, who in his book *Adversus Pseudo-Dialecticos* rebelled against his own teachers and dealt a serious blow to the reputation of the Parisian University, the medieval center of Christian learning. (*See above*, pp. 24–33).

I frequently tell my Parisian friends that although we should congratulate ourselves about the times in which we live, it is certainly a pity that precisely in Paris, from whence all the light of true erudition should emanate, some

[28] On Ciruelo and Sancho Carranza, see Marcial Solana, *Historia de la Filosofía Española* (Madrid, 1941), 3 vols., III, pp. 36–38.

men should stubbornly attach themselves to this ugly monstrosity, the most vain and stupid of all sophistry . . .

And I do not only beg but adjure our Spaniards to put an end to this nonsensical and ludicrous absurdity, and to dedicate their beautiful talents to the study of beautiful things.[29]

Vives' example was widely imitated in Spain, and the controversies surrounding the Aristotelian *Organon*, the relationship between dialectics and rhetoric, and the problem of method produced an enormous literature. Here we should emphasize that most of these authors contributed also a great deal to the progress of grammar. Vives was once again the leader of this movement. His *Exercitatio Linguae Latinae* (1538) was not a theoretical treatise of grammar, but rather a series of dialogues to be used in the classroom as a practical compendium of vocabulary, idioms, and models of sentence structure. In spite of the strong competition provided by a similar book of Erasmus and other authors, Vives' *Dialogues* were the most widely used in central and northern Europe, and were published fifty times in the second half of the sixteenth century. In his pedagogical works Vives attempted a concise summary of grammatical theory (*De ratione studii puerilis*, 1523) and formulated the fundamental principles of grammar. Vives' encyclopedic book *De disciplinis* (1531) dealt extensively with the same subject. He opposed the popular view (Valla's thesis) that the only permissible Latin expressions were those to be found in classical works on the ground that grammatical rules derived from accepted usage had the power to generate new but acceptable combinations:

Some masters think that anything that they do not remember having read should be immediately rejected because, deprived as we now are of Latin and Greek-speaking people, the norm of language ought to be learned from the authors of books . . . Some go even further and reject not only words which they have not read, but also combinations of words and sentences; according to which opinion it would be impossible to say things like 'Petrum diligo,' or 'Rem mihi gratam vos tres feceritis', sentences you will never find in any Latin author. I feel, however, that one can create new combinations of words on the analogy of those used by old authorities.[30]

The task of grammar, therefore, was to combine inductive generali-

[29] "Id enim fere agimus, ut gratulemur nostro saeculo maxime queri illi solent Parisiis, unde lux totius eruditionis manare deberet, mordicus homines quosdam foedam amplecti barbariem, et cum ea monstra quaedam disciplinarum, velut sophismata, quibus nihil neque vanius est, neque stultius . . . Nostros tamen Hispanos no tam moneo, et hortor, quam per quicquam est sacrorum obtestor obsecroque, ut finem jam faciant ineptiendi, ac delirandi, et pulcherrima ingenia studio dedant rerum pulcherrimarum."

(*In Pseudo Dialecticos*, *Vivis Opera Omnia*, III, pp. 37 and 66.)

[30] *Ibid.*, VI, pp. 79–80.

zations from accepted models with the study of the models themselves. Grammar, thus understood, was a mixture of explanatory and descriptive theory and not merely an introductory discipline but a serious component of high education directed toward a "comprehensive understanding of language itself," without which mankind would relapse into the obscurantism of the Middle Ages.

Vives' recommendation was not ignored in Spain; Hebrew, Greek, Latin, and Castilian grammars were published in considerable numbers throughout the sixteenth century. The best known and by far the most significant was Francisco Sánchez el Brocense's (not to be mistaken with the sceptic author of *Quod nihil scitur*) massive book *Minerva, seu de causis linguae latinae* (1587), the product of twenty years of hard work. Sánchez's methodological principles followed exactly Vives' conception of grammar. The very title of the book (*de causis*) suggests the Aristotelian inspiration and the philosophical ambition of the author and also his connection with the medieval tradition of speculative grammar. Menéndez y Pelayo calls Sánchez "the father of grammar and of the philosophy of language," a paternity which, unlike some, has been widely claimed by many other writers. One can certainly say without exaggeration that Sánchez, J. C. Scaliger, and W. Lily, wrote the most interesting Latin grammars of the Renaissance, and that their names deserve an honorific mention in the history of linguistics.

The Latin, Greek, and Spanish grammars of Simón Abril too deserve here a special mention because of two important innovations: first, they were written in the vernacular; second, they were based upon a bilingual juxtaposition of texts, a method which unfortunately is still widely used by those who want to acquire quickly a deceptive and illusory mastery of foreign languages. Another interesting book of those days was the dialogues written by the Humanist Pérez de Oliva. Anxious to prove the equal dignity of Latin and Castilian, Pérez de Oliva wrote a bizarre mixture of Latin and Castilian words which could easily be understood without any mastery of Latin vocabulary.

The popularity of Valla's philological and rhetorical ideas through the works of Herrera and Nebrija; the amazing impact of Erasmian piety and Biblical scholarship; the eclecticism of Fox Morcillo; the rescue of classical texts through commentaries and translations of Epictetus (Sánchez, El Brocense), Aristotle (Sepúlveda, Felipe Ruiz, Villalpando), Virgil and Cicero (Govea), Plato (Simón Abril, Pedro de Rhua), Hippocrates and Galen (Vallés); the reform of scholastic Latin through Vitoria and Melchor Cano; these and other significant linguistic achievements of the Spanish Renaissance, prove beyond the shadow of a doubt the full participation of Spain in the mainstream of Renaissance ideas and concerns.

Other more typically Spanish features of the same literary enterprise deserve fuller attention here. It goes without saying that Spanish missionaries and explorers played a decisive part in reporting the linguistic characteristics of the American Indians. The struggle of the vernacular had also a distinctive Spanish flavor in that it was intimately associated with the problems of regional separatism and the birth of a truly national consciousness. It can be said that in the first half of the sixteenth century Castilian became for the first time "the Spanish language." The symbol for such an event was the linguistic behavior of Ferdinand of Aragón whose speech became progressively Castilian under the influence of his wife Isabella, born and educated in Avila, the very heart of *Castilla la Vieja*. Although dialect variants (aragonesisms, valencianisms, etc.) remained in the spoken language and even in some written (printed!) texts, Castilian became easily and universally the literary language. The *Cancionero General* of poetry published in Valencia in 1511 was written mostly in Castilian by poets from Aragón, Cataluña, and Valencia. Even the Catalán poets in the Court of Alfonso V of Aragón wrote in Castilian. The greatest Portuguese writers of that age, Gil Vicente and Camoens, wrote both in Portuguese and in Castilian. In fact, the literary production in Castilian was in many cases the work of authors from other peninsular regions: Huarte was from Navarra, Boscán from Barcelona, Herrera from Sevilla.

The indisputable champion of the vernacular during the reign of the Catholic Kings was Antonio de Nebrija, whose *Arte de la lengua Castellana* – published in the year 1492 – was the first grammar of the vernacular ever published in Europe. Nebrija's central idea was that Castilian had reached its full maturity to became the language of an emerging Empire and in no respect was it inferior to Latin. Nebrija himself, however, had been born in Sevilla and his own writing was tainted with frequent Andalucisms which standard Spanish has failed to incorporate, such as *espital* for *hospital*, *escrebir* for *escribir*. Italian influence (Boscán, Garcilaso de la Vega) and Renaissance ideals of *courtier* elegance were strongly felt in Spain during the first years of Charles V's reign. The Castilian *buen gusto* (good taste) – which led Castiglione to call the Spaniards *maestri della corteiannia* – prevailed finally over the affectation of early Renaissance poetry (Juan de Mena). Nevertheless the Castilian language of the sixteenth century maintained almost without exception a delight in words, the slow rhythm and the full-blown verbosity of Guevara's prose.

The next step in the shaping process of Castilian as a national language was taken by Juan Valdés. His *Diálogo de la Lengua* (1535), written in Italy under the influence of Bembo, was a eulogy of Spanish as Spain's 'natural' tongue, a typical case of the Renaissance devotion to the "naturally given." Valdés corrected – not always with great success – Nebrija's Andalusian leanings and established Toledan usage as the supreme norm of standard Spanish. More importantly, Valdés fought every manner of affectation and made the spoken language the norm of the written word: "escribo como hablo" (I write the same way I speak). Valdés' criteria did not prevail in phonetics and the simplified orthography of the *Diálogo* – *sinificar* for *significar*, *acetar* for *aceptar* – which prevailed for almost two centuries, finally lost ground to the present spelling.

The triumph of Castilian as a national language was illustrated by the Emperor himself. At the age of eighteen Charles V did not know a word of Castilian; at age twenty four his speech was a bizarre mixture of French and Spanish; at thirty six, however, he had the audacity to address Pope Paul III in Spanish, "such a noble language –" he said "that deserves to be known by every Christian."

During the reign of Philip II the norm of popular usage dispelled any attempt to perpetuate as a national language the refined speech of the Court and the upper classes. Strangely enough this victory of popularism was achieved mainly by the writings of mystics and preachers, Fray Luis de Granada – the undisputed master –, Saint Teresa of Jesús, Saint John of the Cross. This was precisely the moment Fray Luis de León – the editor of Saint Teresa's works – entered the national scene. The fact that the Renaissance in Spain overcame the evident aristocratic snobbishness of its European, especially Italian, counterpart, precisely through the instrumentality of religious language during the reign of Philip II is, in my opinion, a fact of central importance to an understanding of the cultural history of Spain.

The conflict between a minoritarian and a majoritarian conception of art has nowhere been sharper than in Spain. Although the conflict has never been resolved, most authorities are inclined to see in the popularism of the *romancero*, *libros de caballería*, Cervantes, Teresa, Lope de Vega, Zorrilla, and García Lorca, a more representative side of the Spanish artistic temper than the aristocratic taste of Garcilaso, Góngora, Rubén Darío, and Gabriel Miró. Some critics see in this religious, popular, democratic, folkloric bent of mind the root of everything that is worthwhile in Spanish culture. Others, like Ortega y Gasset in his intriguing book *España Invertebrada*, see in the lack of an enlightened elitism the main symptom of all Spanish diseases and malheurs.[31]

Probably the most important contribution of Spain to the linguistic enterprises of the European Renaissance took place in the field of Hebraic and Biblical studies. The study of Arabic, on the other hand, fell during this time to its lowest level, despite the fact that in 1501 the first Arabic-Spanish dictionary was printed in Spain. Around 1520 only five students were registered in the department of Arabic studies at Salamanca. The shift from the medieval trilingual ideal – Castilian, Hebrew, Arabic – to the new trilingual education of Alcalá – Latin, Greek, and Hebrew – was a linguistic change of great significance. The study of classical Latin and Greek was of course a universal European movement, to which Spain, as we have noted above (*See* p. 186) contributed in a respectable manner. The disappearance of Arabic and the new interest in Hebrew had a distinctive local significance in Spain. The *Moriscos* who remained in Spain after the fall of Granada into the hands of the Catholic Kings failed to assert themselves in the new Spanish society. This was due partly to the fact they were uneducated farmers and small merchants and partly to the attacks of the humanists against any form of Averroism. Also, the constant threat of Islam to the eastern Mediterranean made their intellectual and political respectability highly fragile and vulnerable. With the Jews the situation was entirely different. The relevance of Hebrew to the study of the Bible provided to the well-educated Jewish converts in Spain an extraordinary opportunity to cultivate their ancestral language precisely in defense of their newly acquired Faith, and served as proof of their loyalty to Christianity in those dangerous years of persecution. Due to these circumstances the number and the quality of Spanish Hebraists had no parallel in Europe. (*See below*, p. 199) The fact that most of these scholars were of Jewish ancestry (*cristianos nuevos*) was not ignored by the Spanish Inquisition, and the accusation of *hebraizante* was branded with unbelievable ease against most of those men. The most famous process of this kind was the one initiated by Léon de Castro – probably a Jewish convert himself – against the Patriarch of the Spanish exegetes Arias Montano in Salamanca during the year 1559. The controversy between Castro, a Dominican monk, and Mon-

[31] See Menéndez Pidal, *España y su Historia* (Madrid, 1957), vol. 2, "El lenguaje del siglo XVI," pp. 129–179.

tano, became a landmark in the history of hermeneutics at Salamanca and was finally settled by the cautious book of a Jesuit Father, Mariana, who exonerated Montano from the vicious attacks of Castro. Also involved in this process were the two greatest exegetes of Salamanca, Grajal and Cantalapiedra, considered by many scholars to be the founders of modern biblical exegesis. The central issue at stake in all these processes was precisely the value of the original Hebrew text and of the rabbinical exegesis of the Middle Ages when compared with the Vulgate translation of Saint Jerome (sanctioned by the Council of Trent as the official, dogmatically reliable version of the Holy Scripture). The *hebraizantes* emphasized of course the importance of the former, while the conservative theologians – like León de Castro – admitted only the latter. The bitterness of the persecution was such that Arias Montano, in a moment of despair, described Spain as *gens incultum et barbara semper natio* ("A brutal race and nation of barbarians"). The suspicion against the *hebraizantes* was heightened by the new vigor of Renaissance cabalism. It has become a cliché in Renaissance history to describe Pico della Mirandola as the first cabalist of the age. More critical historians, however, have pointed to the uninterrupted tradition of a Christian Spanish cabalism, a tradition which includes the names of Alfonso de la Torre, the first author ever to use the term *cabala* half a century before Pico. Others have studied in depth the Spanish sources of Agrippa and Ricci and focussed their attention upon the significant number of Christian cabalists during the Spanish Renaissance: Valesius, Miguel de Medina, Jerónimo Osorio, Pedro Galatino, Bartolomé de Valverde, and Juan de Cartagena. These authors were not by any standard thinkers or philosophers of the first magnitude. Their names are known only to a few specialists, but their vision of the world and of language with a heavy emphasis on the mysterious, the symbolic, and the magical was no doubt one of the most compelling symptoms of a revolutionary age in search of new categories and new myths.

C. FRAY LUIS' PHILOSOPHY OF LANGUAGE

To speak of Fray Luis' "Philosophy of Language" might seem to the reader an unforgivable anachronism. It is our contention, however, that Fray Luis' attitudes toward language manifest the most explicit and complex philosophy of language to be found in any Spanish Renaissance writer. We intend, furthermore, to show that Fray Luis' linguistic philosophy was the central source of his intellectual inspiration and the distinguishing trait of his genius. To this purpose we shall make a fundamental distinction between the philosophical insights into the nature of language revealed by Fray Luis' various intellectual enterprises and his explicit declarations on the subject.

Fray Luis represents first of all an eclectic and compromising position in the sixteenth century conflict between grammar and speculation, rhetoric and dialectics, Erasmian philology and scholastic metaphysics, positive and rational theology. The sincerity of this compromise was not always duly recognized. During the first trial of the Inquisition Fray Luis was repeatedly accused of showing a dangerous contempt for scholastic theology:

> It is not clear whether this witness is saying that he heard me teaching these conclusions, or whether he says that he heard from others that I was so doing. In any case it is a big lie ... It is well known that I have taught scholastic theology for fourteen years with as much success and acceptance as any of my colleagues, and that if there is something I know well it is precisely that. Nay, it is well known that I have always taught that scholastic theology is the first requirement to a complete understanding of the Scripture ...[32]

Although most of his life was consumed in the arduous work of teaching theology, posterity sees him almost exclusively as a master of Castilian prose and an inspired poet. Bataillon has even attempted to associate his name with that of Erasmus, and Guy tried very hard to explain his thought without any reference to the scholastic tradition.[33] Fray Luis' massive Latin works nullify any project to leave out of consideration the scholastic origins of his thinking. On the other hand it is true that if Fray Luis' scholastic teaching reveals to us the most conservative aspect of his personality, his linguistic concerns betray

[32] "... no se puede entender si depone como testigo que me oyó á mí afirmar las dichas conclusiones, ó como testigo que no me las oyó á mí, sino que oyó de otros que me las cargaban. Y como quiera que sea ello, es gran mentira ... Y notorio es que yo leo escolástica catorce años há en aquella universidad con tanta acepción y nombre como cualquiera de mis concurrentes, y que si alguna cosa sé medianamente es aquello solo ... Demás desto, toda la escuela es testigo que el San Lúcas del año de 71 dije públicamente en la cátedra, en la primera lición de aquel año, respondiendo á una cédula, porque vino á propósito, dije que para el entero entendimiento de la Escritura era menester sabello todo, y principalmente tres cosas: la teología escolástica, lo que escribieron los santos, las lenguas griega y hebrea; ..." (*Biblioteca de Autores Españoles*, v. 37, part II, p. LVI.)

[33] Alan Guy has censured Gutierrez' book *Fray Luis de León y la filosofía española del siglo XVI* as totally lacking in perspective. Gutierrez attempts to present a picture of Spanish Renaissance thought and to underline Fray Luis' contribution to it. By so doing the book fails to give an account of Fray Luis' intellectual personality and gives instead an inventory of opinions against a very impressionistic and fragmentary view of Spanish Renaissance thought.

him as the "novelty seeker" (*amigo de novedades*) the Inquisition persecuted.

Fray Luis was a lover of words, a typical man of the Renaissance. His mastery of Latin, Greek, and Hebrew exemplified the trilingual ideal of the Renaissance man. In the history of the Spanish language Fray Luis played a decisive role by creating a perfect synthesis of the *llaneza* (simplicity) of Saint Teresa with the refinement of Guevara and Fray Luis de Granada. He was probably the first to raise Castilian to the dignity and perfection of a classical language by introducing "order and harmony" (*número y orden*) into the spoken word, an achievement Lope de Vega celebrated in his play *El Laurel de Apolo:* "*Tú, el honor de la lengua castellana, que deseaste introducir escrita*" (You are the pride of the Castilian language, the language you introduced as a written one). Fray Luis' prose was artistic but not artificial; naturally fluent but patiently and carefully put together, as he himself confessed on several occasions:

> Some of my critics say that I do not write in the vernacular because I do not write loosely and without order, because I use my words with rhythm and regularity, because I choose them carefully and give them their proper position. They think that to write in the vernacular is to write as vulgar people speak, not knowing that right speech requires good judgment to select from the words that everyone uses the most proper ones, the ones with the right sound, the right number of letters, pondering them, measuring them, putting them together, in such a way that they do not only say what they are supposed to, but they say it with harmony and gentleness.[34]

Fray Luis' poetry, which Dámaso Alonso has carefully analyzed in his masterful essays, displayed a perfect combination of highly personal inspiration and a most elaborate technique. This artistry of the poet begins to shed some light upon Fray Luis' conception of Language. For him all human language was essentially poetic, and creative. The connection between the significant and the signified through the mediation of the verbal sign was not a pragmatic, indifferent, and neutral device, but rather a true creation, a *poiesis*. To him poetry was only "tense and heightened language", a second creation. Language

[34] "Y de estos son los que dicen que no hablo en romance, porque no hablo desatadamente y sin orden, y porque pongo en las palabras concierto y las escojo y les doy su lugar; porque piensan que hablar romance es hablar como se habla en el vulgo, y no conocen que el bien hablar no es común, sino negocio de particular juicio, así en lo que se dice como en la manera como se dice. Y negocio que de las palabras que todos hablan elige las que convienen, y mira el sonido de ellas, y aún cuenta a veces las letras, y las pesa, y las mide, y las compone, para que no solamente digan con claridad lo que se pretende decir, sino también con armonía y dulzura." (*Obras Completas Castellanas*, p. 674.)

remains always the result of contrivance. The poet raises language to a second level of significance by the creative constitution of the poetical sign.

We have already mentioned Fray Luis' decisive role in extending the use of the vernacular through the theological domain (*La Perfecta Casada*, *De Los Nombres de Cristo*). We have not yet mentioned, however, that Fray Luis presented battle precisely in the most dangerous field: the vernacular translation of the Bible. His first book in prose (1561) was a Spanish translation of *The Song of Songs*. This choice involved many personal risks and revealed both the daring and the lack of experience of the young Augustinian. Twenty years later – after his encounter with the Holy Tribunal – Fray Luis might have been much more careful. The Council of Trent had just forbidden the publication of vernacular translations of the Bible. *The Song of Songs* was one of the most controversial books of the Scripture, because of its strong erotic symbolism, the doubts about its spiritual meaning, and the primitive naturalism of its language. To make things worse Fray Luis dedicated this translation to Isabel Osorio, a nun at the Monastery of El Espíritu Santo in Salamanca. Arias Montano approved the project with some reservations. It is true that the commentary was never published by Fray Luis himself, but the manuscript leaked to the public and soon hundreds of copies were circulated not only among the students of the University but throughout Spain and even in the American colonies. This book became the central piece of evidence against Fray Luis in his first trial before the Inquisition. After five years of imprisonment Fray Luis was ordered by his superiors to translate the book into Latin. In spite of this terrible experience Fray Luis remained for the rest of his life a champion of the vernacular. The most beautiful apology of Spanish written in the sixteenth century can be found in the dedication of the third part of *De Los Nombres de Cristo* to Portocarrero (a member of the Holy Tribunal!), a dedication written six years before Fray Luis' death:

> Our subject (the names of Christ in the Scripture – my parentheses) could not be treated with propriety if we used low forms of Latin. Words are not dignified because they are Latin, but because they are used with dignity, whether they are French or Spanish. Those who think that Castilian is good only to speak of low subjects just because we call our tongue 'vulgar', are badly mistaken. Plato did not write vulgar books in vulgar style just because he used his own 'vulgar' language nor, Cicero spoke less highly because he used the language which was vulgar in his time. More importantly, Saints Basil, Cyril, Gregory, and John Chrysostomus wrote about the most divine

mysteries of our Faith in the language they received with the maternal milk, the language used by street vendors in the market place.[35]

Fray Luis' edition of Santa Teresa's books and the short apology of 1588 were also events of great linguistic significance in the reign of Philip II. The Spanish commentary to *The Song of Songs* introduces us to the Biblical and Hebraic soul of Fray Luis. The principal cause of Inquisitorial persecution was precisely Fray Luis' constant endeavor to build his personal piety directly upon the literal text of the Holy Scripture. Fray Luis' bitter complaint about the neglect of the Bible by Christians, including the hierarchy of the Church, has been interpreted by Bataillon as an echo of Erasmianism. On this point the illustrious French historian seems to corroborate the Spanish Inquisitors. And both were equally unfair to Fray Luis. What made Erasmus suspect to Catholic orthodoxy was not his positive emphasis upon an inner devotion derived from the Bible, but rather his negative attitude toward the institutional and sacramental aspects of the Church, his bitting sarcasm and his disrespect for authority. None of these negative characteristics are to be found in the words of Fray Luis:

> God inspired the writing of Scripture so that it would be a solace to us amid the trials of life, a clear, unfailing light amid darkness and error, and a salutary remedy for the wounds which sin has inflicted upon our souls. Therefore, He intended Scripture to be available for the use of all men. To this end, He saw to it that it was written in the plainest language, the ordinary speech of those to whom revealed truth was directed.
>
> When, in later days, the knowledge of Jesus Christ was given to the Gentiles, Sacred Scripture was translated into many tongues so that all men could profit by it. Hence, in the early days of the Church, and for many years thereafter, it was considered a grave omission if the faithful did not spend a good part of their time in the study of the Bible . . .
>
> Yet, although the reading of Scripture is good and useful in itself, it has now become the occasion of much harm, as the condition of our age and recent sad experiences teach us. Hence, those who rule the Church were compelled by circumstances to place definite and precise restrictions on the

[35] "Y esto mismo, de que tratamos, no se escribiera como debía por solo escribirse en latín, si se escribiera vilmente; que las palabras no son graves por ser latinas, sino por ser dichas como a la gravedad le conviene, o sean españolas o sean francesas. Que si, porque a nuestra lengua la llamamos vulgar, se imaginan que no podemos escribir en ella sino vulgar y bajamente, es grandisimo error; que Platón escribió no vulgarmente ni cosas vulgares en su lengue vulgar; y no menores ni menos levantadamente las escribió Cicerón en la langua que era vulgar en su tiempo; y por decir lo que es más vecino a mi hecho, los santos Basilio y Crisóstomo y Gregorio Nacianceno y Cirilo, con toda la antigüedad de los griegos, en su lengua materna griega, que, cuando ellos vivían, la mamaban con la leche los niños y la hablaban en la plaza las vendedoras, escribieron los misterios más divinos de nuestra fé, y no dudaron de poner en su lengua lo que sabían que no había de ser entendido por muchos de los que entendían la lengua." (*Ibid.*, p. 673.)

use of the vernacular so that the Bible would be removed from the hands of the uninstructed who would misuse it.

So far as I can see, this unfortunate situation springs from two causes: ignorance and pride, and perhaps more from pride than from ignorrance . . .[36]

What provoked the anger of the Inquisitors was this Biblical emphasis in combination with the despised Jewish ancestry of the author. Four centuries after those events we can today judge much better the significance of the Catholic exegesis in the Counter-Reformation. The Hebraists of Salamanca – Grajal, Cantalapiedra, Arias Montano, and Fray Luis de León, although victimized by the Inquisition, did more to strengthen the Catholic Church than the subtle distinctions of scholastic theologians and the dogmatic definitions of the Council of Trent.

Fray Luis de León's biblical training was completed in Alcalá under the leadership of one of the most brilliant exegetes of that time, Cipriano de la Huerga. In Alcalá he became acquainted with Arias Montano, a professor of the Trilingue College at that time. In Salamanca Fray Luis had Grajal and Cantalapiedra among his colleagues and friends. Fray Luis' main intent in translating *The Song of Songs* – to reproduce the *literal* text of the Bible in the vernacular – points to a main achievement of sixteenth century hermeneutics. The nature of inspiration and the unerring character of the Bible – fashionable topic of today's exegesis – were not at the center of sixteenth century disputes, but rather a twofold problem: the critical fixation of the text and the hermeneutic rules governing the relations between the literal and the non-literal senses of the Scripture were of paramount impor-

[36] "Notoria cosa es que las Escrituras que llamamos Sagradas las inspiró Dios a los Profetas, que las escribieron para que nos fuesen en los trabajos de esta vida consuelo, y en las tinieblas y errores de ella clara y fiel luz, y para que en las llagas que hacen en nuestras almas la pasión y el pecado, allí, como en oficina general, tuviésemos para cada una propio y saludable remedio . . .

Pero, como decía, esto, que de suyo es tan bueno y que fué tan útil en aquel tiempo, la condición triste de nuestros siglos y la experiencia de nuestra grande desventura nos enseñan que nos es ocasión ahora de muchos daños. Y así, los que gobiernan la Iglesia, con maduro consejo y como forzados de la misma necesidad, han puesto una cierta y debida tasa en este negocio, ordenando que los libros de la Sagrada Escritura no anden en lenguas vulgares, de manera que los ignorantes los puedan leer; y como a gente animal y tosca, que, o no conocen estas riquezas o, si las conocen, no usan bien de ellas, se las han quitado al vulgo de entre las manos.

Y si alguno se maravilla, como a la verdad es cosa que hace maravillar, que en gentes que profesan una misma religión haya podido acontecer que lo que antes les aprovechaba les dañe ahora, y mayormente en cosas tan sustanciales, y si desea penetrar al origen de este mal, conociendo sus fuentes, digo que, a lo que yo alcanzo, las causas de esto son dos: ignorancia y soberbia, y más soberbia que ignorancia; en los cuales males ha venido a dar poco el pueblo cristiano, decayendo de su primera virtud." (*Ibid.*, pp. 379, 380, 381.)

tance. The Protestants in general maintained the primacy of the original Hebrew text and attacked the authority of the Vulgate. Some Salamanca theologians – most of the *cristianos viejos* (old Christians) like Melchor Cano, Bartolomé Medina, and the fiery León de Castro – opposed the Hebrew text on the basis that Jewish interpreters had corrupted it on purpose in order to confuse Christian exegetes. Grajal, Cantalapiedra, and Fray Luis León maintained a middle position. They recognized, against Protestant interpreters, that the Hebrew text had been altered by Jewish exegesis, but they held that it was still possible to find the unadulterated text, and rejected the opinion that the rabbinic tradition had purposefully corrupted it. As for the Vulgate Fray Luis taught the following: a) that the Vulgate was Saint Jerome's translation, an opinion he maintained against Erasmus, Budé, and even his colleague Cantalapiedra; b) that the Greek and Hebrew texts were in some passages more clear than their Vulgate rendition; c) that the Vulgate translation had not been inspired by God; and finally d) that the authority of the Vulgate according to the Council of Trent meant only that it was free from dogmatic errors. Those were, in substance, the points that Fray Luis himself made in his own defence against the accusations of the Inquisition:

> As to the first charge let it be said that the defendant has never held that the Bible contains errors: on the contrary he has always taught that the Bible is all true. The defendant has only taught that the Latin translator had no prophetic gift nor was literally inspired by the Holy Ghost; that some passages could have been translated more clearly, more accurately, and more elegantly; that wherever the original Hebrew allows different interpretations, the Latin interpreter gave us the true and Catholic one, although without excluding others he chose to leave out.[37]

Led by these principles – which Catholic Theology has long since accepted without any controversy – Fray Luis' biblical work was directed toward a translation of the Bible from the original Hebrew into the vernacular. His translations both in prose (*The Song of Songs*, *Book of Job*) and in verse (*Psalms*, *Book of Job*, *The Song of Songs*) were

[37] "Al primero capitulo dijo que lo quél ha dicho es lo que está en sus escriptos que presentó en Salamanca, en los cuales este nunca ha dicho que tiene falsedades; antes expresamente dice que no hay en ella falsedad ninguna ni que pueda engendrar error, sino que toda ella es verdadera, y que solamente dijo que el intérprete no fué profeta ni tradujo cada palabra por instinto del Espíritu Santo; y que así, hay algunas palabras que se pudieran traducir más clara y más significante y más comodamente; y que en los lugares ádonde el original hebreo hace muchos sentidos, el sentido que tradujo el intérprete latino es verdadero y católico; pero no de manera que el otro sentido o sentidos que dejó se hayan de desechar, ..." (*Biblioteca de Autores Españoles*, v. 37, part II, pp. XXXI–XXXII.)

masterpieces in their genre, but more importantly for our purposes they included several paragraphs where the author discussed his own theory of translation. In his introduction to the commentary on *The Song of Songs* Fray Luis declared his intention to deal exclusively with the literal meaning of the text, *la corteza de la letra*. Several difficulties had to be overcome. First of all, the sacred text dealt with love, and the words of the writer did not seem to keep pace with the apparently unrelated and erratic zig-zag of the passion they attempted to signify. Secondly, Hebrew was a language of limited vocabulary in which words have a variety of meanings. Thirdly, the customs, the style, and the value system (*el estilo y juicio de las cosas*) of the Jewish people was very different from his. In spite of these dangers and difficulties Fray Luis attempted to translate word by word in such a way that the translation would correspond to the original text not only in vocabulary and sentence structure, but even more importantly in the harmony and feeling of the whole (*el concierto y aire*). To achieve this Fray Luis tried – not always successfully – to use in the translation exactly the same number of words as in the original, and to use those words of Castilian which have the same quality and variety of significations (*la misma cualidad y condición y variedad de significaciones*) as the Hebrew words of the original text. Whenever the translation necessitated new words in order to reproduce the sentence structure and the full meaning of the original, Fray Luis promised to have those words in brackets – a promise he did not always keep. Here is the entire passage in an English translation of my own which probably does not satisfy the high standards defined by Fray Luis:

> This book is difficult, first because it deals with strong passions and emotions, love especially, where reasons run mixed and unrelated... The second source of obscurity is the very nature of Hebrew in which the book was first written, a language of limited vocabulary and concise idioms rich in a variety of meanings. Furthermore, the style and the values of those people were totally different from ours. Some of the comparisons which the Bride and the Bridegroom use to mutually praise their beauty seem to us odd and exotic. Such, for instance, are the metaphors of a neck as a tower, teeth as a flock of sheep.
>
> In this translation I shall first of all attempt to translate each word of the original; secondly to declare in a few words not each word of the original text but only the more obscure passages ... Regarding my first task I have tried to make a translation which corresponds to the original not only in words and the structure of the sentence, but even in their flavor and style by imitating their metaphors and idioms in our own language, which, by the way, resembles Hebrew in many respects. The translator ought to be faith-

ful and exact, and when possible, should count the words in order to have as many in the translation, neither more nor less, of the same quality and condition, with the same variety of meanings as the original. He should further avoid to narrow down the original experience to his own individual interpretation and opinion, so that the reader of the translation may be capable of grasping the entire variety of meaning, which the original could suggest, and is free to choose his own. It is true that in our translation we were not always able to follow the original thus closely. The style and conditions of our language forced me occasionally to add a few little words, without which the very meaning of the whole would remain concealed; but these are few words and will be bracketed in our text.[38]

In this short introduction Fray Luis deals with all the problems of a theory of translation: the incommensurability of vocabularies, the impact of social conditions on meaning, the importance of structure, the relationship between syntax and meaning, the relation between meaning and context, the connotative theory of meaning, the complex character of the literal sign, etc. Biblical translations in the sixteenth

[38] "Hace dificultoso su entendimiento, primeramente, lo que suele poner dificultad en todos los escritos adonde se explican algunas grandes pasiones o afectos, mayormente de amor, que, al parecer, van las razones cortadas y desconcertadas; ...

Lo segundo que pone oscuridad es ser la lengua hebrea en que se escribió, de su propriedad y condición, lengua de pocas palabras y de cortas razones, y ésas llenas de diversidad de sentidos; y juntamente con esto por ser el estilo y juicio de las cosas en aquel tiempo y en aquella gente tan diferente de lo que se platica ahora; de donde nace parecernos nuevas, y extrañas, y fuera de todo buen primor las comparaciones de que usa este Libro, cuando el Esposo o la Esposa quieren más loar la belleza del otro, como cuando compara el cuello a una torre, y los dientes a un rebaño de ovejas, y así a otras semejantes ...

Lo que yo hago en esto son dos cosas: la una es volver en nuestra lengua palabra por palabra el texto de este Libro; en la segunda, declaro con brevedad no cada palabra por sí, sino los pasos donde se ofrece alguna oscuridad en la letra, ... Acerca de lo primero procuré conformarme cuanto pude con el original hebreo, cotejando juntamente todas las traducciones griegas y latinas que de él hay, que son muchas, y pretendí que respondiese esta interpretación con el original, no sólo en las sentencias y palabras sino aun en el concierto y aire de ellas, imitando sus figuras y maneras de hablar cuanto es posible a nuestra lengua, que, a la verdad, responde con la hebrea en muchas cosas. De donde podrá ser que algunos no se contenten tanto, y les parezca que en algunas partes la razón queda corta y dicha muy a la vizcaína y muy a lo viejo, y que no hace corra el hilo del decir, pudiéndolo hacer muy fácilmente con mudar algunas palabras y añadir otras; lo cual yo no hice por lo que he dicho, y porque entiendo ser diferente el oficio del que traslada, mayormente Escrituras de tanto peso, del que las explica y declara. El que traslada ha de ser fiel y cabal y, si fuere posible, contar las palabras para dar otras tantas, y no más ni menos, de la misma cualidad y condicición y variedad de significaciones que las originales tienen, sin limitarlas a su propio sentido y parecer, para que los que leyeren la traducción puedan entender toda la variedad de sentidos a que da ocasión el original, si se leyese, y queden libres para escoger de ellos el que mejor les pareciere. El extenderse diciendo, y el declarer copiosamente la razón que se entiende, y el guardar la sentencia que más agrada, jugar con las palabras añadiendo y quitando a nuestra voluntad, eso quédese para el que declara, cuyo propio oficio es; y nosotros usamos de él después de puesto cada un capítulo en la declaración que se sigue. Bien es verdad que, trasladando el texto, no pudimos tan puntualmente ir con el original; y la cualidad de la sentencia y propriedad de nuestra lengua nos forzó a que añadiésemos algunas palabrillas, que sin ellas quedara oscurísimo el sentido; pero éstas son pocas, y las que son van encerradas entre dos rayas de esta manera ( )." (*Obras Completas Castellanas*, pp. 28–30.)

century are a fascinating chapter in the history of linguistics because through them modern man approached, in a theological context later to be easily disposed of, the most complex problems of semantics, lexicography, structure, social and comparative linguistics, and syntactic theory.

Biblical exegesis on the other hand forms also an integral part in the history of literary criticism. The sixteenth century marked not only the beginning of modern textual criticism but also a decisive reformulation of hermeneutical theory previously scattered through the writings of the Fathers of the Church and the voluminous writings of medieval theologians. Such theory was reduced to a system of principles by Pagnini (*Isagogue*, 1528), by Sixtus of Siena (*Bibliotheca Sancta*, 1566), by Martín de Cantalapiedra (*Hypotypus*, 1565), and, finally, by Salmerón (*Prolegomena Biblica*, 1592). The recent discovery of Fray Luis' hermeneutical treatise *De sensibus Sacrae Scripturae* – published for the first time in 1956 – has clearly shown that Fray Luis was not only one of the greatest Spanish exegetes of his time, together with Ribera, Arias, Montano, Maldonado and others, but also one of the co-founders of Counter-Reformation hermeneutics.

Fray Luis starts his treatise with a fundamental distinction between the literal and the spiritual – or "mystical", or "allegoric" – sense of the Bible, a distinction which is in accord with Patristic, Rabbinic, and scholastic authorities.

> The Holy Scripture contains a literal sense, which the Bible itself calls also a historical or grammatical sense. In its accepted interpretation it signifies whatever is common both to the Scripture and to any other writing. It also contains a mystical or spiritual sense, so called because it is more difficult to understand than the literal sense and is contained therein; it is therefore concealed, covered, hidden.[39]

The literal sense is the primary source of dogmatic proof. In opposition to an opinion which today is widely held by Catholic exegetes Fray Luis accepted the multiplicity of literal senses. In addition to Saint Augustine's authority Fray Luis adduced the following argument. The literal sense of the Scripture depends upon the intention of the writer. God intends all the interpretations of the text which He foresees to be made by readers familiar with the workings of the language.

[39] "Continet sacra Scriptura sensum litteralem, quem etiam sacra Littera historicum sive grammaticum appellat. Et primo sensu accepta significat quod commune est ipsi cum ceteris scripturis. Et rursus continet sensum mysticum sive spiritualem; quia quantum et difficilior est intellectu et aliqua ratione in litterali sensu continebatur, idcirco dicitur mysticus, id est, absconditus, latens, occultatus ..." (*La Ciudad de Dios*, Vol. 170, 1957, p. 297.)

Therefore all such legitimate interpretations, are, in fact, the literal sense of the Scripture as intended by its Divine Author.

Saint Augustine held that the Scripture contains a multiplicity of literal senses and gave the following beautiful proof for it. Nature and philosophy teach that words are signs for concepts. The concepts of God are immense and infinite. Therefore the Saint thought that it would be most proper to believe that the Scripture in which the words and the voice of God are recorded contains under a single letter a plurality of meanings.[40]

Fray Luis' opinion has not fared well with Catholic interpreters. The multiplicity of possible literal senses seems to dull the sharp dogmatic edge of the Bible and overestimates the subjective interpretation of the reader at the expense of the unequivocal, defined interpretation of ecclesiastical authority. Furthermore, Fray Luis' doctrine was based on a narrow definition of literal sense, a danger which contemporary theologians have carefully avoided.

As for the spiritual sense Fray Luis defended a middle position between the "figurists," according to whom every event of the Old Testament was a figure of the New Testament; and the so-called "antifigurists," who believed that only those events of the Old Testament presented as symbols of the future by the New Testament have such pre-figurative value. His position on the subject was, however, obscured by a fluctuant terminology. It is interesting to observe that while the Spanish commentary to *The Song of Songs* was an attempt to fix the literal sense of the text, the Latin version of the same dealt almost exclusively with the spiritual sense. One has the definite impression that the project of building an inner form of piety and devotion on the basis of an immediate enjoyment of the Scripture – clearly the intent of the popular Spanish commentary – was much closer to Fray Luis' heart than the dogmatic interpretation of the Old Testament as the figure of the Church – the aim of the Latin commentary which Fray Luis was ordered to write by his superiors and by the Inquisitors.[41]

[40] "Si quis vero quaerat quae ratio moverit divum Augustinum ad asserendos plures hos sensus sub una littera, illa certe pulcherrima est. Nam primo, cum voces, philosophia ipsa et natura teste, sint signa conceptuum, et conceptus Dei sit inmensus atque infinitus, vidit summus ille vir non esse inconveniens, sed potius convenientissimum quod sacra Scriptura, in qua verba Dei et voces continentur, sub una littera comprehendat plures sensus.

Secunda ratio quae sumitur ex divo Augustino est, quia ille est sensus litteralis quem Scripturae auctor illis verbis intendit significare. Sed Spiritus Dei praevidit quemcumque sensum occursurum lectori sub illa littera, imo vero et ipse fecit ut occurreret, quia est vera lux omnium mentium; ergo sequitur quod omnis ille sensus est litteralis.

Tertia ratio est, quia nihil est magis dignum sapientia Dei et ubertate eloquii divini, quam ut eisdem verbis in plures veniamus sensus eorum verborum ..." (*Ibid.*, p. 304.)

[41] See P. Mariano Revilla's comprehensive article "Fray Luis de León y los estudios bíblicos en el siglo XVI," *Religión y Cultura*, II (1928), pp. 482–528. Also, José López de Toro,

Fray Luis' insistence on the multiplicity of the literal sense and his devotion to it – as evidenced by his numerous translations and by most of his commentaries – springs forth from a philosophical conception of language according to which all languages are "full of secrets and mysteries." In the first chapter of *De Los Nombres de Cristo* Fray Luis proposed a theory of names which contains his most explicit thoughts on the subject. Before we make some observations on this magnificent document we want to present it to the reader in its unabridged translation.

A name is a word which is substituted for that to which it refers and takes the place of that which it represents. A name is the very thing which is designated, not in its real and true existence, but in that existence which our mouth and understanding give it. In order to understand this, we should realize that beings which possess an intellect are one in themselves but capable of becoming all that they know. In this way they resemble God, who contains all things within Himself, and the more they grow in knowledge, the more they approach Him and become like Him. Thus, each of us may become a perfect world, or microcosm, in the sense that all things may be in us and we in all things.

This is a perfection of the rational creature, and since each person naturally desires his own perfection and nature does not fail to provide for our basic desires, it has provided for this with admirable dexterity. Material things as such cannot dwell in one another; therefore, in addition to its physical being, nature has given each material thing a more spiritual being by which it can dwell in the minds of rational creatures. Nature has likewise ordained that these things should proceed from the intellect by means of the spoken word. This can be illustrated if we stand before several mirrors. The image of one and the same face is reflected at the same time in each of the many mirrors.

Therefore, whatever we know with our minds and name with our tongues exists in our intellects. And if our ideas and words are true, those things exist in our minds as they are in themselves. They are the same by reason of a certain likeness, although they are different in their mode of existence. In themselves they are beings of body and quantity, but in the mind of the knower they become like the mind: spiritual and immaterial. To put it briefly, in themselves they are true, but as they exist in the mind and in words they are representations of truth. They are images or symbols which are substitutes for the things themselves. In themselves they are what they are, but in our mind and mouth they are names. Hence, a name is an image

"Fray Luis de León y Benito Arias Montano," *Archivo Augustiniano*, 50 (1956), pp. 6–28; Sandalio Diego, "Fray Luis de León y Francisco de Ribera en el comentario de Abdías," *Estudios Eclesiásticos*, VIII (1929), pp. 5–22. Father Olegario García de la Fuente has introduced and edited Fray Luis' treatise on the interpretation of the Scripture in his article "Un tratado inédito y desconocido de Fray Luis de León sobre los sentidos de la Escritura," *La Ciudad de Dios*, 170 (1957), pp. 258–334.

or representation of the thing spoken about; it is the thing disguised in another way or a substitution for the thing known.[42]

This beautiful document has clearly some limitations. First of all there is no doubt that, except for a few lines on interjections and prepositions, Fray Luis deals almost exclusively with 'names.' But even this particular limitation is not without significance. Scholastic logicians had always distinguished between primary words, (nouns and verbs) and secondary words (adjectives, adverbs, conjunctions, prepositions). The role of the latter is not to signify anything by themselves but only in conjunction with a primary word. They are not 'predicates' but 'co-predicates' or 'syncategorematic' terms. In a slightly oversimplified manner we could say that the study of syncategorematic terms became the task of logicians interested in the bearing of such terms on the truth or falsity of propositions, while the primary terms were the special domain of the more Aristotelian minded grammarians attempting to investigate the relationships between the basic ingredients of reality (substance, change) and the essential terms of a proposition (noun or subject, verb or predicate). Fray Luis' approach to language was clearly more in line with the speculative grammarians than in the direction of the dialecticians.

What Fray Luis was really seeking was a general explanatory theory of language rather than a formalization of logical inference. His theory of names, incomplete as it is, was an interesting document of his age.

[42] "– El *nombre*, si habemos de decirlo en pocas palabras, es una palabra breve, que se sustituye por aquello de quien se dice y se toma por ello mismo. O *nombre* es aquello mismo que se nombra, no en el ser real y verdadero que ello tiene, sino en el ser que le da nuestra boca y entendimiento.

Porque se ha de entender que la perfección de todas las cosas, y señaladamente de aquellas que son capaces de entendimiento y razón, consiste en que cada una de ellas tenga en sí a todas las otras y en que, siendo una, sea todas cuanto le fuere posible; porque en esto se avecina a Dios, que en sí lo contiene todo. Y cuanto más en esto creciere, tanto se allegará más a El, haciendosele semejante. La cual semejanza es, si conviene decirlo así, el pío general de todas las cosas, y el fin y como el blanco adonde envían sus deseos todas las criaturas.

Consiste, pues, la perfección de las cosas en que cada uno de nosotros sea un mundo perfecto, para que por esta manera, estando todos en mí y yo en todos los otros, y teniendo yo su ser de todos ellos, y todos y cada uno de ellos teniendo el ser mío, se abrace y eslabone toda esta máquina del Universo, y se reduzca a unidad la muchedumbre de sus diferencias; y quedando no mezcladas, se mezclen; y permaneciendo muchas, no lo sean; y para que, extendiéndose y como desplegándose delante los ojos la variedad y diversidad, venza y reine y ponga su silla la unidad sobre todo ...

Pues siendo nuestra perfección aquesta que digo, y deseando cada uno naturalmente su perfección, y no siendo escasa la naturaleza en proveer a nuestros necesarios deseos, proveyó en esto como en todo lo demás con admirable artificio. Y fué que, porque no era posible que las cosas, así como son, materiales y toscas, estuviesen todas unas en otras, les dió a cada una de ellas, demás del ser real que tienen en sí, otro ser del todo semejante a este mismo; pero más delicado que él y que nace en cierta manera de él, con el cual estuviesen y viviesen cada una de ellas en los entendimientos de sus vecinos, y cada una en todas, y todas en cada una ..." (*Obras Completas Castellanas*, pp. 392–393.)

Fray Luis begins with a definition of name: "Name is . . . a short word (*palabra breve*) which substitutes for its reference (*que se sustituye por aquello de quien se dice*). The wording of such a definition is clearly borrowed from terminists dialectics, but the ensuing explanation excludes unequivocally any nominalist interpretation. There is nothing more distant from Ockham's '*flatus vocis*' than Fray Luis' theory of language. According to him a name is the very thing named not in its real entity but in the kind of being which "our mouth and our intelligence" gives to it. The perfection of a created being consists in possessing as much of the reality of everything in itself as possible, thus attempting to imitate God who contains everything in the indestructible Unity of His Infinite Being. The perfection of man consists in being a world of his own, in reducing to the unity of his consciousness the enormous variety of the Universe. To make this possible God gave every creature a two-fold existence: one, rough and material (*material y tosca*) in real existence; another "more delicate" (*más delicada*) in their intelligible entity. The latter is entirely similar to the former (*del todo semejante*) and is "born out" from it (*nace en cierta manera de él*). Through this device the whole cosmos resides in each human intelligence, "all in each and each in all" (*cada una en todas y todas en cada una*) without any limitation of time and space. The total reality of the universe, past, present, and future is thus reflected in the multitude of individual minds, as the image of a single face would be reflected in a large number of mirrors. Words are to these mental images what concepts are to reality. They are also "born from" the intellect and are entirely similar to it.

Such is basically the metaphysical world-view of Fray Luis' theory of language. The Neo-Platonic emphasis upon contemplation as the unifying principle is entirely obvious. In the unity of the apperception the differences of things known become mixed but differentiated, multiple and one, at the same time (*quedando no mezcladas se mezclan, y permaneciendo muchas, no lo sean*). As for the immediate source of Fray Luis' Neo-Platonic undercurrents there is some variety of opinion among scholars. Menéndez y Pelayo, for example, underlines the impact of Alexandrian Neo-Platonism upon sixteenth century aestheticians and thinkers; Rousselot selects the Pseudo-Dionysius as Fray Luis' best known source of inspiration; Guy, on the other hand, has emphasized the influence of the Spanish Jewish philosophers Avicebron and Maimonides.[43] Surprisingly enough nobody has carefully examined

[43] See Miguel de la Pinta Llorente, O.S.A., *Estudios y polémicas sobre Fray Luis de León* (Madrid, 1956).

the possible impact of Nicholas of Cusa and Marsilio Ficino whose writings abound in similar ideas. It is relevant to our purpose, however, to analyze the consequences of this clearly Neo-Platonic inspiration upon Fray Luis' theory of language.

According to Fray Luis the three orders of reality, intelligibility, and verbal expression are reduced to unity by the creative act of God. God's exemplary ideas shape the essential nature of created things, their conceptual intelligibility by man's reason, and the verbal sign in man's mouth. Things, their mental conceptualizations, and their verbal expressions (names), are only three different aspects or dimensions of one and the same reality. To think and to speak, therefore, are truly secondary creations perfectly matched with the original one through a divine pre-established harmony of the real, the intelligible, and the word. Of these three orders the supreme one is contemplation. By becoming objects of consciousness things are "raised" (*ascienden*) from their rough materiality (*tosco y grosero*) to their more "delicate" and spiritual existence in the human mind where the disturbing multiplicity of time and space surrenders to the immateriality of pure ideality and unity. Unlike many contemporary epistemologists the tension between consciousness and its object is resolved by Fray Luis in favor of the former. Man's consciousness is not lost "outside" in the awareness of its objects; on the contrary the objects of consciousness are absorbed and purified into God-like light of man's spiritual mind.

Fray Luis' position would seem to be based on an original divine revelation of language and thus dangerously close to what in the nineteenth century was going to be called 'traditionalism' (Bondi, Gioberti, Lamennais), an unorthodox theory condemned by the Vatican Council as a threat to the supernatural character of Revelation. Fray Luis' exegesis of the first chapters of *Genesis* and his insistence upon the primacy of Hebrew over all other languages (*la madre de todas las lenguas*) could be interpreted in that direction. However, the dominant trend of his thought does not point to an initial act of God communicating language to man – and through language the knowledge of everything as the traditionalists would later claim – but rather to the divine plan of guaranteeing a perfect correspondence between words and things. Fray Luis' definition of names, "short cyphers where God enclosed whatever man can understand" (*cifras breves en que Dios encerró todo lo que se puede entender*) should then be understood as a short statement of the inseparable and mutual interdependence of thought and language within the context of God's creative Wisdom and Planning.

His most original contribution to a theory of language consists precisely in his description of the natural connection between the signifying word and the signified concept. In his book *De los Nombres de Cristo* Fray Luis limits his explanation to proper names, and even more explicitly (although not exclusively) to the Hebrew names of Christ in the Holy Scripture.The very title of the chapter, "Of Names in general", the theoretical tone of its content, and some of Fray Luis' examples are enough to indicate a comprehensive theory of language. Fray Luis, as explained above, insists that names are 'born' from the objects they name. Less metaphorically he explains that names are related to their objects by a) their original signification, b) their sound, and c) their configuration.

When the name of a thing is derived from some other word or name, the word from which it is derived must signify something characteristic of the thing to which the word applies. If this be so, as soon as the word is spoken, it evokes in him who hears it the image of that particular property or characteristic. For example, those who bear the rod of justice are called judges, a name which takes its origin from their proper office, which is to judge. Hence, when one hears the word *judge,* he understands what the person so signified is or ought to be.

The second element essential to perfect conformity between a name and the thing signified is the sound of the word. This means that whenever it is possible, the name of anything should by its very sound connote the quality or characteristic which it designates. If it is the name of a creature that has a distinctive sound of its own, then the name of that thing should as far as possible imitate that sound.

The third element of conformity between a name and the thing signified is the form of the word itself, that is, the number and arrangement of the letters of the word. There are numerous examples of these last two elements in the original language of Scripture. With respect to the sound, scarcely any of the words in Scripture which signify something that speaks or has its own characteristic sound fail to imitate the same sound or some other sound very similar to it.[44]

44 "... Pero, como decía, esta semejanza y conformidad se atiende en tres cosas: en la figura, en el sonido, y señaladamente en el origen de su derivación y significación. Y digamos de cada una, comenzando por esta postrera.

Atiéndese, pues, esta semejanza en el origen y significación de aquello de donde nace; que es decir que cuando el nombre que se pone a alguna cosa se deduce y deriva de alguna otra palabra y nombre, aquello de donde se deduce ha de tener significación de alguna cosa que se avecine a algo de aquello que es proprio al nombrado; para que el nombre, saliendo de allí, luego que sonare, ponga en el sentido del que le oyere la imagen de aquella particular propriedad; esto es, para que el nombre contenga en su significación algo de lo mismo que la cosa nombrada contiene en su esencia. Como, por razón de ejemplo se ve en nuestra lengua en el nombre con que se llaman en ella los que tienen la vara de justicia en alguna ciudad, que los llamamos *corregidores*, que es nombre que nace y se toma de lo que es *corregir*, porque el corregir lo malo es su oficio de ellos, o parte de su oficio muy propia. Y así, quien lo oye, en oyéndolo, entiende lo que hay o haber debe en el que tiene este nombre. Y también a los

Etymology, onomatopoetics, and word structure play an important part in his linguistic theory. Derivative names are made from words which closely signify the object they name. Thus a *corregidor* (corrector) names the one whose duty it is to 'correct' the behavior of others; *casamentero* (the one who 'mentions' wedding to a third party) names the one whose task it is to announce to others a proposal of marriage. The Biblical names chosen and assigned by God Himself (Abraham, Sarah, Jacob, Joseph, Peter) always signify the office and authority of those thus named. Hebrew, more than any other language, approximates this ideal of linguistic signification. In what manner this order of signification applies to names in general remains unexplained in Fray Luis' theory.

The second connection between the significant and the signified is the sound of the linguistic symbol. Names – Fray Luis explains – should sound like the things they name. *De los Nombres de Cristo* does not provide more information on this subject. It would then be out of place to see in such a statement a full theory of the onomatopoeic origin of language. What seems important is the emphasis on the mimetic character of the same. The verbal expression is 'born from' or 'generated' by the concept it signifies in the same way that the concept is born and generated by the object it refers to. The combination of sounds of a given name, and even as Fray Luis points out somewhere else, (*Cantica*, Chapter 4) the tone of voice and the gesture of the speaker, are essential co-significants in any spoken language. The study of Fray Luis' poetry reveals that sound meant much more than strict onomatopoeia; it meant an

que entrevienen en los casamientos los llamamos en castellano *casamenteros*, que viene de lo que es hacer mención o mentar, porque son los que hacen mención del casar, entreviniendo en ello y hablando de ello y tratándolo. Lo cual en la Sagrada Escritura se guarda siempre en todos aquellos nombres que, o Dios puso a alguno, o por su inspiración se pusieron a otros. Y esto en tanta manera, que no solamente ajusta Dios los nombres que pone con lo propio que las cosas nombradas tienen en sí; mas también todas las veces que dió a alguno y le añadió alguna cualidad señalada, demás de las que de suyo tenía, le ha puesto también algún nuevo nombre que se conformase con ella, como se ve en el nombre que de nuevo puso a Abrahám; y en el de Sara, su mujer, se ve también; y en el de Jacob, su nieto, a quien llamó Israel; y en el de Josué, el capitán que puso a los judíos en la posesión de su tierra; y así en otros muchos.

"... Y sea la segunda lo que toca al sonido; esto es, que sea el nombre que se pone de tal cualidad que, cuando se pronunciare, suene como suele sonar aquello que significa, o cuando habla, si es cosa que habla, o en algún otro accidente que le acontezca. Y la tercera es la figura, que es la que tienen las letras con que los nombres se escriben, así en el número como en la disposición de sí mismas, y la que cuando las pronunciamos suelen poner en nosotros. Y de estas dos maneras postreras, en la lengua original de los Libros divinos y en esos mismos Libros hay infinitos ejemplos; porque del sonido, casi no hay palabra de las que significan alguna cosa que, o se haga con voz, o que envíe son alguno de sí, que, pronunciada bien, no nos ponga en los oídos o el mismo sonido o algún otro muy semejante de él." (*Obras Completas Castellanas*, pp. 395–396–398.)

indirect and derivative form of onomatopoeic association plus the unexplored and mysterious power of sound combinations (combinations of vowels and consonants, verse rhythm, rhyme) to awaken deep-rooted synaesthetic experiences. Fray Luis' *Oda a Salinas* unveils the Pythagorean sense for the intimate connection between the order of the universe and the phonetic harmonious proportion and *concierto* of music, poetry, and language.

Oh! suene de contino,
Salinas, vuestro son en mis oídos,
por quien al bien divino
despiertan los sentidos,
quedando a lo demás amortecidos.[45]

The third and final element mentioned by Fray Luis applies not to the spoken but to the written word. The configuration of names is to the written language what sound is to oral expression: both are creative mimicry. In dealing with the 'secrets and mysteries' of word configuration Fray Luis occasionally paid an excessive tribute to the cabalistic fad of his age. In spite of his repeated assertion that cabalistic analysis of words, although permissible (*yo no condeno*) was a trivial and irrelevant (*cosas demasiado menudas*) means of explaining the name of Jesus, and especially the name of God or the tetragrammaton, Fray Luis indulged with obvious relish in such extravagant considerations.

Dabar is Christ's name according to His divine nature, not only because it applies to Him rather than to the Father or the Holy Ghost, but because this one name signifies everything that is said of Him by all other names. This is true no matter how we regard this name, either taken as a whole or considered by letters and syllables. The letter D has the function of an article, and an article is used to specify something in particular in order to avoid confusion or to give it added emphasis. All these are functions of Christ as the Word of God, for He is the cause, the measure, and the harmony of all things. He directs all things, restores them if they are impaired, and elevates them to their greatest good.

The letter B, as St. Jerome teaches, means an edifice, and this also applies to Christ, because He is the original edifice or plan of all things which God has made. Whence He is also called Tabernacle, as St. Gregory of Nyssa states: 'The only-begotten Son of God is a Tabernacle, for He contains all things in Himself and He has made a tabernacle of us.' All things were in Him from all eternity, and when they were made He brought them into existence. He is a Tabernacle because we abide in Him; we are tabernacles, because He dwells in us.

The letter R, according to St. Jerome, means the head or beginning, and Christ is properly called Beginning, as we read in St. John's Gospel, for in

[45] (*Ibid.*, pp. 1458–1459.)

Him all things had their origin. He is their Exemplar and He confers on them their existence and substance. He is the Beginning also because He holds the place of pre-eminence. He is the Head of all that is good and the Source who communicates to others whatever good they possess. 'He is the Head, . . . the Beginning, the Firstborn from the dead, that in all things He may hold the primacy.' In the order of being He is the Beginning from whom all other things come into existence; in the order of goodness He is the Head which governs and refashions them. He is the first to resurrect the body and is the power that resurrects others in glory. He is the King of kings, the supreme High Priest, the Good Shepherd, the Prince of the angels, and the omnipotent Lord of all.

The letter R, says St. Jerome, also means spirit, a word which applies to all three Persons of the Trinity and is properly appropriated to the Holy Ghost to indicate the manner of His procession. Nevertheless, it also applies to Christ for a particular reason. First, the Word is the Bridegroom of the soul; but the soul is spiritual and hence it is necessary that He also be such so that He may become the soul of the soul and the spirit of the spirit. Secondly, in His union with the individual soul He carefully observes the laws and conditions of the spirit, which comes and goes without your knowing how or whence, as St. Bernard beautifully illustrates in his sermons.

Thus, each letter of the name Dabar signifies some attribute of Christ, and if we join the letters into syllables, they are even more significant, for *Bar* signifies Son, and *Da-Bar* means 'This is the Son.'[46]

[46] "... Y así, en el primer nombre que decimos *Palabra*, el original *es Dabar*, y en el segundo nombre *Jesús*, el original es *Lehosuah*; pero los traslados son estos mismos nombres, en la manera como en otras lenguas se pronuncian y escriben. Y porque sea más cierta la doctrina, diremos de los originales *nombres*.

De los cuales, en el primero, *Dabar*, digo que es nombre de Cristo, según la naturaleza divina, no solamente porque es así de Cristo que no conviene ni al Padre ni al Espíritu Santo, sino también porque todo lo que por otros nombres se dice de él lo significa sólo éste. Porque *Dabar* no dice una cosa sola, sino una muchedumbre de cosas; y dícelas como quiera y por doquiera que le miremos, o junto a todo él o a sus partes cada una por sí, a sus sílabas y a sus letras. Que lo primero, la primera letra que es D, tiene fuerza de artículo, como *El* en nuestro español; y el oficio del artículo es reducir a ser lo común y como demostrar y señalar lo confuso, y ser guía del nombre y darle su cualidad y su linaje, y levantarle de quilates y añadirle excelencia; que todas ellas son obras de Cristo, según que es la *Palabra* de Dios. Porque El puso ser a las cosas todas, y nos las sacó a luz y a los ojos, y les dió su razón y su linaje; porque El en sí es la razón y la proporción y la compostura y la consonancia de todas; y las guía El mismo, y las repara, si se empeoran, y las levanta y las sube siempre y por sus pasos a grandísimos bienes.

Y la segunda letra, que es B, como San Jerónimo enseña, tiene significación de edificio, que es también propiedad de Cristo, así por ser el edificio original y como la traza de todas las cosas, las que Dios tiene edificadas y las que puede edificar, que son infinitas, como porque fué el obrero de ellas. Por donde también es llamado *Tabernáculo* en la Sagrada Escritura, como Gregorio Niseno dice: *Tabernáculo es el Hijo de Dios unigénito, porque contiene en sí todas las cosas, el cual también fabrica tabernáculo de nosotros.* Porque, como decíamos, todas las cosas moraron en El eternamente antes que fuesen, y cuando fueron El las sacó a luz, y las compuso para morar El en ellas. Por manera que, así como El es casa, así ordenó que también fuese casa lo que nacía de El. Y que de un tabernáculo naciese otro tabernáculo, y de un edificio otro, y que lo fuese el uno para el otro y a veces. Es el Tabernáculo, porque nosotros vivimos en él; nosotros lo somos, porque El mora en nosotros. *y la rueda está en medio la rueda, y los animales en las ruedas, y las ruedas en los animales*, como Ezequiel escribía. Y están en Cristo ambas las ruedas, porque en El está la divinidad del Verbo y la Humanidad de su carne, que

Fray Luis' cabalistic speculations were not only the tribute of a genius to trendy patterns of thought, but also an eloquent expression of the intriguing complexity of his soul. As a man of the Renaissance Fray Luis was fascinated by the study of language and the power of beautiful form; as a Christian he believed in the pre-established harmony of the sign and the signified object; as a Spanish Jew he shared the rich medieval heritage of Talmudic wisdom and speculation; as a philosopher he was deeply concerned with finding a satisfactory theory of meaning. The words of Fray Luis de León on the nature of language are far from being a technical essay on semantics but are explicit enough to justify the title of this chapter.

contiene en sí la universidad de todas las criaturas ayuntadas y hechas una en la forma que otras veces he dicho.

La tercera letra de *Dabar* es la R, que, conforme al mismo Doctor San Jerónimo, tiene significación de *cabeza o principio*, y Cristo es principio por propiedad . . ." (*Ibid.*, pp. 760, 761.)

CHAPTER FOUR

JUAN HUARTE'S NATURALISTIC PHILOSOPHY OF MAN

Those historians of ideas, who see the Renaissance as a radical departure from medieval Christianity and as the first outbreak of modern secular values, are often inclined to question the very existence of a Renaissance of thought in Spain – the home of scholastics, theologians, mystics, counterreformers, and Inquisitors. Most accounts of Spanish sixteenth century thought are indeed restricted to scholastic philosophers and mystic writers, the two groups which fit in better with a stereotyped version of the Counter-reformation. This way of writing history blatantly ignores the complexity of human events. The Renaissance was obviously more entangled in tradition than has been recognized, and Spain paid more tribute to novelty than most people are willing to concede. The first point does not merit much discussion, having been widely proved by eminent scholars. The second claim is still a matter of dispute.

To characterize sixteenth century Spain as a land of theologians and mystics is simply a gross caricature which leaves aside our great classicists (Fox Morcillo, Juan de Sepúlveda and Pérez de Oliva, among others), our sceptics and heretics (Miguel Servet, Francisco Sánchez, Juan de Valdés and Pedro de Valencia), and, finally, an extraordinary group of physicians, educational reformers, and humanists who shared the same crudely naturalistic approach to the study of man (Gómez Pereyra, Sabuco de Nantes, Fernando Vallés and Juan Huarte de San Juan). This chapter is concerned with Huarte, not only because he was the central figure of that group, but because he reveals most clearly the vulnerability of the Spaniard to the enticements of Renaissance naturalism.

A. MEDICINE AND RENAISSANCE NATURALISM

Even the least orthodox trends of European Renaissance thought found abundant echo among Spanish thinkers; and this newly discovered freedom of thought was intimately related to the revival of classical medicine in Spain.

Among the cross-currents and streams of ideas which make up the complexity of the Renaissance one can detect a pervasive and strong naturalism. By 'naturalism' I mean a polymorphous complex of attitudes, values, concerns, and theories which stresses the basic similarity and interrelatedness of man and the universe; which sees the cosmos as a self-contained system of forces to be manipulated by man; which frees the mind from authority and institutional bondage; which emphasizes the worldliness of the human condition and ignores for all practical purposes any reference to man's eternal destiny; and which delights in the beauty of the outward universe and the excellence of the human body. In this wide interpretation of the word even the pious educational reformers of Northern Humanism can be called 'naturalists'. The fundamental assumption of men like Vives, Thomas More, and even Erasmus, was that the improvement of man's earthly life depended more upon the proper refinement of his natural talents through an intelligent educational process than upon the orthodoxy of his religious beliefs, or membership in the right religious denomination. Their faith in education was Pelagian in ancestry, a mixture of dogmatic indifference and ethical naturalism. Furthermore, the admiration for classical form, which either followed or caused the rediscovery of ancient literature, art, and philosophy, ended in most cases in an irrepresible fascination for pagan civilization itself.

In this explosion of naturalism Medicine played a decisive role. In rediscovering nature man rediscovered first of all his own body. The body appeared to the men of the Renaissance not as the temple of the Holy Ghost, but as an integral part of the system of nature, subject to its laws, both beautiful and vulnerable. The desire to live, and to live a long and healthy life, inspired all the efforts of Renaissance physicians. Disease appeared to them not as a consequence of sin which prayer could cure, but rather as a lack of harmony which nature itself had to correct. Inspired by these views Renaissance medicine made extraordinary conquests. The superstitious respect for the body, which for centuries had made the dissection of corpses impossible, gave place to a new scientific curiosity which allowed an extraordinary renaissance of anatomical studies. The frontispiece of Vesalius' *De humani Corporis fabrica*, which represents a dissected corpse in the very center of the temple of Aesculapius, surrounded by an excited crowd of students and teachers, is a compelling symbol of Renaissance science. Leonardo da Vinci dissected ten human bodies for the study of the veins alone. The practical results of anatomical research were of capital importance. Leonardo da Vinci was the first to give an accurate representation of the uterus; Berengario da Carpi made the first careful examination of the tympanum and of the pineal gland; Vesalius corrected Galen's mistakes about the anatomy of the liver, the maxillae, the veins, and the heart; Fallopio discovered the tubes which bear his name, and gave an accurate account of the ocular muscles and cerebral nerves; Coiter investigated the exudates of the brain and the spinal cord. The printing press made possible a wider usage of textbooks and perfected the art of engraving anatomical plates which are still worth studying.

The progress of anatomy encouraged similar advances in physiology. By far the most interesting of those was the discovery of the circulation of the blood, a discovery initiated by the Spanish physician Miguel Servet (1511–1553), and by the Italians Colombo de Cremona (1510–?) and Andrea Cesalpino (1519–1603), before its definite and clear description by Harvey in the generation to follow (1578– 1657). Pathology, too, became highly specialized in the Renaissance, and yielded amazing results. Plague, leprosy, and collective mental disorders such as Saint Vitus' dance, practically disappeared. New diseases, however, challenged the progress of Renaissance medicine: smallpox, measles, chickenpox, influenza, sweating sickness (*sudor anglicus*), and especially syphilis, were the object of intensive research. Gerolamo Fracastoro (1478–1553) made an outstanding study of all forms of contagion; Guillaume de Baillou was the first to describe whooping cough and rubiola. Surgery, which was considered a particular talent of certain barbers in the Middle Ages became an important branch of Medicine in the Renaissance. Paré put an end to the application of cautery and boiling oil to wounds, and began using simple bandages for the control of bleeding. Obstetrics, ophtalmology, and pharmacology also made spectacular advances.[1]

The contributions of Spanish physicians to the Renaissance of medicine in the sixteenth century were truly outstanding. In the Middle Ages Spain – together with Sicily – had become the depository of

[1] Renaissance medicine has been the object of intensive study. Besides the general histories of medicine, such as Arturo Castiglioni's *A History of Medicine* (New York, 1958), we should mention the following: C. Singer, *The Discovery of the Circulation of the Blood* (London, 1922); G. Vorberg, *Ueber den Ursprung der Syphilis* (Stuttgart, 1924); F. R. Packard, *Life and Times of Ambrose Paré* (2nd ed., New York, 1926); C. A. E. Wickersheimer, *La Médecine et les médecins en France à l'époque de la Renaissance* (2 vols, Paris, 1936); A. Castiglioni, *The Renaissance of Medicine in Italy* (Baltimore, 1934).

Arabian medicine, in which the thought of Hippocrates and Galen had become fused with Syrian, Jewish and Oriental traditions. Some of the most prestigious Arabian physicians were Spanish Arabs from Córdoba, such as the encyclopedic writer Abulcassis (who died circa 1013) and the renowned scholars Ben Shaprut, Ibn Golgol, Ibn-Al-Wafid, and Al-Bakri. In the twelfth century Spain produced three great Arabian physicians: Avempace, Avenzoar, and last but not least, Averroes. Ibn Al-Baitar, from Málaga, was perhaps the greatest botanist of the Middle Ages. Among the Jewish doctors the great Maimonides should be mentioned first of all; although a philosopher and Talmudist, he was also the author of very popular books on the art of sexual intercourse, rabies, and poisons. Peter of Spain, Raymond Lull, and especially Arnaldo de Vilanova, all of them masters of Medicine at the University of Montpellier, were famous Christian medieval physicians.

The revival of medicine in the sixteenth century was preceded by an impressive improvement in Spanish schools of Medicine. Toward the end of the fifteenth century and in the three first decades of the sixteenth Huesca, Zaragoza, Sevilla, Barcelona, Alcalá de Henares, Valencia, Toledo, and Mallorca founded new Universities with hospitals and schools of Medicine. The study of Greek medicine was carried on with great enthusiasm at the University of Alcalá de Henares. In Valencia there were eight chairs exclusively dedicated to the study of Hippocrates' and Galen's works. The hospital attached to the Monastery of Guadalupe became a powerful center of medical research. The hospital of San Cosme y Damian, in Zaragoza, had received royal authorization in 1488 to dissect corpses; since that time the study of anatomy had made spectacular progress. The presence of Vesalius in Spain as personal physician to Charles V greatly promoted the study of human anatomy. Among the first-rank anatomists of the sixteenth century we should at least mention Juan Valverde de Amusco, whose *Historia de la composición del cuerpo humano*, published in Spanish (1556), in Italian (1560), and in Latin (1589), became one of the most widely read anatomical books of the Renaissance. Other anatomists included Andrés Laguna, known as "the Spanish Galen;" Luis Vasseo, author of very popular anatomic drawings; and Pedro Ximeno, specialist in auricular anatomy. Of special importance was the Spanish contribution to the study of contagious diseases: Luis Mercado (1541–1606) and Francisco Vallés (1524–1592) excelled in the diagnosis of "tabardillo"; Francisco López de Villalobos was the author of a much respected book on the treatment of syphilis; Francisco Diaz is to be remembered as the author of one of the finest works on the urinary tract, and some historians of medicine call him the founder of modern urology. The treatise of Lobera de Avila, *Libro del regimiente de la salud y de las enfermedades de los niños* (Valladolid, 1551) was one of the first books on pediatrics ever written in the vernacular. The study of botany and pharmacology received a new impulse through the discoveries and reports of Spanish chroniclers in America, such as Gonzalo Fernández de Oviedo, Nicolás Monarde, Father José de Acosta, and many others.[2]

These achievements of Renaissance medicine are important to the history of ideas not only because they reveal the naturalistic temper of the age, but because they point to the enormous vitality of the medical schools from which modern science was about to emerge. Historical circumstances, religious prejudices, and currents of ideas had helped to convert late medieval schools of medicine into centers of secularized research, and in some instances at least into headquarters of anticlerical attitudes. The study of medicine, with its emphasis upon the body, was frequently considered incompatible with an ecclesiastical vocation. In 1131, the Council of Rheims forbade the study of Medicine to clerical students. In Paris the Faculty of Medicine was the first to be open to married laymen in 1422. Thus a gap was created between the clerical faculties of Arts and Theology on one side, and the lay Faculty of Medicine. For that reason medicine never flourished in Paris, the center of Catholic medieval Theology and orthodoxy, but took refuge instead in Montpellier and Toulouse. In Italy the separation of Theology and Medicine was even more pronounced. At Padua there was only a Faculty of Medicine besides that of Arts; at Pisa and Bologna Theology was practically reserved to members of the mendicant orders. The result was that at those institutions Aristotelian philosophy was studied in preparation for medicine rather than for Theology, and thus it escaped the close surveillance of dogmatic orthodoxy. As Randall has abundantly proved, this "Aristotelianism

[2] The best known histories of Spanish medicine are Anastasio Chinchilla, *Anales históricos de la Medicina. Historia de la medicina española* (Valladolid, 1841).

A. Hernández Morejón, *Historia bibliográfica de la medicina española*, 6 vols. (Madrid, 1842).

F. García del Real, *Historia de la medicina en Espana* (Madrid, 1921).

F. Garzón Maceda, *La medicina en Córdoba* (Buenos Aires, 1916).

See also Marcelino Menéndez y Pelayo, *La Ciencia Española*, Edición Nacional de las Obras Completas (Madrid, 1953), v. 59, pp. 403–438 ("Esplendor y decadencia de la cultura científica española"), and v. 60, pp. 276–295 ("Ciencias médicas").

without the benefit of clergy" was destined to be the cradle of modern science.[3]

Two other concrete historical circumstances helped further in this direction. The first was the fact that Latin Averroism, with its rationalistic and naturalistic temper, found a favorable refuge in the Northern Italian Universities after its expulsion from Paris in the thirteenth century. The second was the rediscovery of the genuine Greek text of Aristotle in the early Renaissance, and the allegiance of Italian humanists, philosophers and physicians to the commentaries on Aristotle by Alexander of Aphrodisias. Pomponazzi's philosophy, with its naturalistic ethics and relentless criticism of the traditional arguments in defense of the immortality of the soul, was the outstanding example of this secular rationalism. The naturalistic interpretation of Aristotle made fashionable by the medical schools was reinforced by the renewed study of Hippocratic and Galenic medicine in their original Greek. Thus an entirely new set of world-views and theoretical models began to influence the career of philosophical speculation. The two most distinguished expressions of Renaissance philosophy – the philosophy of nature and the search for a scientific method – were substantially indebted to the medical schools. Cusanus, Cardano, and Patrizi were all, at one time or another, students at Padua; Paracelsus was an anti-Arabian physician; Gerolamo Fracastoro, a teacher of medicine at Padua; Telesio, "the Father of the Moderns" in Bacon's words, was an eager student of Galen.

Spain was no exception to these trends of thought. The medical profession, traditionally linked with liberal freethinking and lukewarm religiosity in Latin countries, produced an extraordinary phalanx of bold thinkers and philosophers in the sixteenth century – men like Miguel Servet, Gómez Pereyra, Francisco Vallés, León Hebreo, Francisco Sánchez, and Juan Huarte de San Juan. The fact that most of these men were of Jewish ancestry, and that their rationalistic leanings were often incompatible with their religious beliefs, seems of decisive importance in understanding the undercurrents of Spanish thought in that century. If, as Menéndez y Pelayo claims, the Inquisition was relatively mild in its control of scientific output, the explanation does not lie in the enlighted magnanimity of the Holy Tribunal, but partly in the ritualistic protestations of orthodoxy which were

[3] See J. H. Randall, *The Career of Philosophy* (New York, 1962), Part II, "The Intellectual Revolution: The Reconstruction of the Intellectual Traditions," pp. 171, 363. Also, "The School of Padua and the Emergence of Modern Science", *Journal of the History of Ideas*, I (1940), pp. 177–206.

expected (and almost always obtained!) from these men, and partly in the incapacity of the Inquisitors to draw all the conclusions from the premises and principles they were supposed to anathematize.[4]

The philosophical speculations of the Spanish physicians were based upon the firm persuasion that all failures of past medicine were derived from "ignoring and misrepresenting the true nature of man; a mistake which itself was born from wrong philosophical principles" (Sabuco de Nantes). The renewal of medicine was impossible without a new philosophy of man. This new philosophy had to stress, first, the mutual dependence of body and soul; and, second, the mutual dependence of man and the universe. The first of these trends was clearly derived from the naturalistic Aristotelianism of the Alexandrists; the latter was reinforced by a fresh appreciation of Hippocratic medicine.

The rediscovery of the Hellenic Aristotle was not by any means a task reserved for Italian humanists. Spanish classicists also made a considerable effort to recover the unadulterated text and thought of the Philosopher. The leader of the Spanish Aristotelians was Juan Ginés de Sepúlveda (1490–1577), a student under Pomponazzi at Bologna, whose name is more intimately associated with his dramatic confrontations with Bartolomé de las Casas regarding the 'natural slavery' of the American Indians (*See above*, p. 100) Sepúlveda translated into Latin several Aristotelian treatises (*Parva Naturalia*, *De coelo*, *De Republica*, *Ethics*), and was the first Renaissance scholar to translate into Latin the fashionable Greek commentaries of Alexander of Aphrodisias (1527). The three best known Spanish commentators on Aristotle, Gaspar Cardillo de Villalpando, Juan Bautista Monllor and Pedro Martínez, displayed a complete mastery of Greek, a thorough knowledge of Alexander of Aphrodisias' thought, and great familiarity with the scholarship of their own age (Scaliger, Budé, Pomponazzi and others). All of them rejected Pomponazzi's thought on the immortality of the soul and attempted very hard (but with little success) to vindicate Alexander from any materialistic interpretation of Aristotle. In sharp contrast with their conservative Peripatetism, other Spanish commentators on Aristotle proved themselves more vulnerable to the naturalistic trend of the day. Characteristically enough, this group was made up almost entirely of physicians. The Aristotelian commentaries of Vallés, the Court physician of Phillip II, betray the same independence of thought and crude scepticism of his main book *De Sacra Philosophia* (1537), a work which was generously expurgated

[4] *La Ciencia Española*, v. 59, pp. 12–13.

by the Inquisition. The physicians Andrés Laguna, Antonio Luis, Francisco de Escobar and Luis de Lemos translated the most important books of Aristotle on physics, botany, and zoology into Latin and Castilian. This immediate contact with the original sources of Aristotelian thought resulted in a large number of treatises which emphasized the mutual dependence of the somatic and the psychic. This emphasis further led to some far-reaching conclusions on the difference between man and the beasts, on the influence of the body upon moral behavior, on the distinction between sense and intellect, and finally, on the spiritual and immortal character of the soul.

Lobera de Avila stresses the psychic character of somatic diseases in his *Libro del regimiento de la salud.* The *Ars Medendi* by Vega, a professor of Medicine at Alcalá de Henares, recommends bodily hygiene as a condition of virtue. Alonso López de Corella, another Alcalá professor described the brain as "the organ of wit" (*el órgano del ingenio*) and the complexion of the body as "the root of good and bad behavior" (*raíz de las buenas y malas costumbres*). According to Vallés, the difference between man and the beasts was not rationality, which both enjoy albeit in different degrees, but only in man's capacity for wisdom: *animal sapientiae capax.*

By far the most revealing expressions of this vortex of new ideas about man in Spanish sixteenth century thought (besides Huarte's *Examen de Ingenios*) were Gómez Pereyra's *Antoniana Margarita* (1555) and Sabuco de Nantes' *La Nueva Filosofía de la Naturaleza del Hombre* (1587). Gómez Pereyra was a bold and independent thinker, the champion of the anti-Galenists of his time, but also a recognized authority in the treatment of leprosy, elephantiasis, and contagious diseases. A century before Descartes, Pereyra maintained that the brutes were automata deprived of sensation. If the brutes were capable of sensing, Pereyra argued, they would also be capable of reasoning, and thus the difference between man and animal would be obliterated. To Pereyra the difference between sensitive and intellectual knowledge was not a qualitative but a quantitative one. With the same boldness Pereyra denied the existence of *species impressa*, common sense, prime matter, and substantial forms; he favored the corpuscular theory of Democritus (made fashionable again by another physician, the Italian Fracastoro) and considered memory an organic power localized in the occipital lobe of the brain.[5]

[5] On Gómez Pereyra see Solana, *Historia de la Filosofía Española*, vol. I, pp. 208–271. M. Menéndez y Pelayo, "*La Antoniana Margarita* de Gómez Pereyra," *La Ciencia Española*, Obras Completas, vol. 59, pp. 277–357. While Menéndez y Pelayo exaggerates the influence of Pereyra upon Descartes, as is to be expected, Benito Feijóo, *Teatro Crítico Universal* (Madrid,

La Nueva Filosofía del Hombre was printed under the name of Doña Oliva Sabuco, the daughter of the author Sabuco de Nantes, whose life still remains shrouded in mystery. Sabuco proceeds on the assumption that traditional medicine had been a terrible failure: "Only two or three people out of thousands live through their natural life-span and reach a natural death." This failure developed entirely from a philosophical misconception of man that ignored the overwhelming impact of the emotions of the soul upon the health of the body. Chapters I to XXI of the book describe the somatic ill-effects of depression, (*enojo y pesar*), anger, sadness, fear, love, excessive joy, distrust, hatred, shamefulness, anxiety, excessive compassion, sensuality, boredom, jealousy, and spirit of revenge. These emotions disturb the balance of bodily humours because they squeeze the humidity and humor of the brain, "where the divine soul is located" (*donde está el alma divina*), a humor which is supposed to permeate the entire organism. Chapters XXV to XXX and LVII–LXI discuss the emotions of the soul which promote the well-being of the body: hope, moderation, love, friendschip, gratefulness, magnanimity, prudence, wisdom, and happiness. The rest of the book, to be discussed below, emphasizes the other aspect of this naturalistic conception of man, the dependence namely of the human composite upon cosmic conditions and causes.[6]

The second source of novel ideas in the Renaissance philosophy of nature was the return to the original Hippocratic tradition. In Spain this movement was led mostly by physicians of Jewish origin who revolted against the medieval dominance of Arabian medicine. An interesting aspect of this revolt was the disagreement of Renaissance physicians about the significance of Galen with respect to Hippocrates. Galenists and anti-Galenists passionately disputed whether the Roman physician was an authentic and loyal disciple of the Asclepiad. An important sequel of such discussion was the increasing attention given to the problem of scientific methodology, an issue Galen raised with much more sophistication and explicitness than the Greek founder of western medicine. The translations, commentaries, apologies, and refutations of Hippocrates and Galen form a very extensive chapter in the history of Spanish Renaissance thought. Physicians who mastered both Greek

1777), vol. III, p. 191, clarifies the different points of departure of both thinkers. Eloy Bullon Fernández has made two special studies of Pereyra: *Los precursores españoles de Bacon y Descartes* (Salamanca, 1905), and *El alma de los brutos ante los filósofos españoles* (Madrid, 1897).

[6] On Sabuco de Nantes see Solana, *Historia de la Filosofía española*, vol. I, pp. 273–289. Sabuco's book is reproduced in *Biblioteca de Autores Españoles*, vol. LXV, pp. 325–376. See also Alain Guy, *Les Philosophes Espagnols d'hier et d'aujourd'hui* (Toulouse, 1956), pp. 78–83.

and Latin – a typical Renaissance miracle of talent and education – imposed upon themselves the immense task of recovering the original text and thought of classical medicine. In his *Historia bibliográfica de la medicina española* Antonio Hernández Morejón lists twenty-seven treatises on Hippocratic medicine written and published in Spain during the sixteenth century. Two of the professors of Juan Huarte de San Juan in Alcalá de Henares, Fernando de Mena and Cristobal de la Vega, published extensive commentaries and translations of Hippocrates' works. Francisco Vallés alone wrote four commentaries on Hippocrates (*In Aphorismos, In Prognosticum, De ratione victus, De morbis popularibus*) and five on Galen (*De locis, De urinis, De temperamentis, Ars medicinalis, De differentia febrium*).

The rediscovery of the authentic Hippocratic tradition led, as suggested before, to an increased awareness of man's subjection and dependence upon cosmic events. Sixteenth century medicine in Spain repeatedly emphasized the relevance of weather, the seasons, geographical location, food, air, water, and even astrological combinations upon man's bodily and spiritual health. The outstanding expression of this trend was, once again, Sabuco de Nantes *Nueva Filosofía de la Naturaleza del hombre*. Less romantic and mystic than Paracelsus, but perhaps more crude, Sabuco wrote extensively on the influence of the macrocosmos upon the microcosmos of man (Chapter LXII). Among the cosmic events discussed by Sabuco we should mention geography (Chapter XXXIV), the cycle of the moon (Chapters XXXV and LV), external noises (Chapter XXXVIII), food and drink (Chapter XLII), weather (Chapters XLVIII and XLIX), and the sun (Chapter L). Sabuco's two favorite symbols of man, a tree up-side down (with the brain as the roots, Chapter LXVI) and a moon going through the phases of increase (youth) and decrease (old age, Chapter LXIII) eloquently reveal the naturalism of his vision of man. A large number of medical treatises on geopathology, climatology, dietetics, hygiene, genetics, alchemy, and pharmacology, which were inspired by the same spirit, belong with Sabuco's original book.

The obsession of the anatomists to localize different 'faculties' of the soul in their corresponding bodily organ (especially the brain or the heart) was another expression of the same naturalism.

The contribution of Spanish physicians and philosophers to the scientific methodology of the Renaissance was obviously much more modest than that of their Italian counterparts, but still more significant than it is generally recognized. Although their ideas on method were not followed up in the seventeenth century, – as were those of Italian men of science, resulting in spectacular break-throughs – they contributed in a powerful manner to make possible the scientific attitude and frame of mind which made those achievements possible. Men like Vives, Gómez Pereyra, Vallés, Sabuco de Nantes, Servet, and Francisco Sánchez were eloquent champions of the two basic principles of the modern scientific outlook: freedom from authority (even Aristotle's) and reliance upon observation. The active participation of two Spanish scholars in the controversy about Ramus also proves the free exchange of ideas between Spain and the European community of that time. One of the most forceful refutations of Ramus was written by Antonio de Govea in his popular book *Pro Aristotele responsio* (1543); and Pedro Juan Núñez (1522–1602), a former student of Ramus in Paris, also turned against his master in his *Avisos para estudiar las artes en particular.*

B. JUAN HUARTE'S EXAMEN DE INGENIOS

The best known, the most original, and the boldest expression of Spanish Renaissance naturalism was Juan Huarte de San Juan's book *El Examen de Ingenios.*[7]

Juan Huarte de San Juan (also known as Juan de San Juan, Huarte de San Juan, San Juan de Ugarte, Juan de Duarte) was born in 1529, in a small village in the province of Navarra which has belonged to France since 1660. Américo Castro has suggested that the Huartes were Jewish conversos, without presenting any convincing evidence.[8] However, the second half of Chapter XV of the *Examen* seems to confirm Castro's views. In a most personal and persuasive manner Huarte tries to prove that by nature the Jews had a high degree of intelligence and a very special aptitude for the study of theoretical medicine. Huarte's reflections upon the meaning of *hidalguía* (Chapter XVI) also fit in perfectly with the worldviews and attitudes of a Spanish Jewish convert in the social context of that century. Huarte emphasizes the im-

[7] Besides some specific studies of Huarte's thought, which will be cited in the body of this essay, the best and most authoritative work on Huarte is Mauricio de Iriarte's *El Doctor Huarte de San Juan y su EXAMEN DE INGENIOS. Contribución a la Historia de la Psicología Diferencial*, 3rd ed., (Madrid 1948). See also, Gregorio Marañón, "Notas Sobre Huarte" *Obras Completas*, (Madrid, 1967), vol. 3, pp. 265–282. Miguel Artigas, *Notas para la bibliografía del EXAMEN DE INGENIOS* (San Sebastián, 1928); J. M. Guardia, *Essai sur l'ouvrage de J. Huarte: Examen des aptitudes pour les sciences* (Paris, 1855); Foster Watson, "The Examination of Wits," *The Gentleman's Magazine*, March 1905, pp. 238–55; Anton Klein, "Juan Huarte und die Psychognosis der Renaissance, "Doct. diss. (Bonn, 1913); José Zalba, "El doctor Huarte y su *EXAMEN DE INGENIOS*," *Euzkadi*, September 1913.

[8] *The Structure of Spanish History* (Princeton, 1954), p. 575.

portance of good deeds and "second birth" as the solid foundations of social respectability. The Huartes left Navarra when Juan was still a child and established themselves in Baeza, a prosperous Castilian town where Juan studied Latin and Philosophy. Philosophy as taught at the University of Baeza – an institution just approved by Pope Paul III in 1538 – was very similar to that taught at Paris. Peter of Spain, the Aristotelian *Organon*, and an all-too-quick introduction to physics, ethics and metaphysics, occupied most of the three academic years. In a rather immodest page of the *Examen* Huarte describes himself as an "eagle" in Philosophy:

> Three of us entered school the same year to study Latin; one of us learned it easily, the other two were never able to put an elegant sentence together. But of all of us passing on to dialectic one of the two who had not been able to learn grammar became a royal eagle in that art, while the other two did not open their mouths the entire year. Then all three of us coming to hear Astrology it is worth noting that the one who could learn neither Latin nor Dialectic knew more in a few days than our master had taught us, and the other two never could learn it.[9]

In 1553 Huarte began to study Medicine at Alcalá of Henares, the Spanish University founded by Cardinal Cisneros. Around 1550 Alcalá had eight or ten chairs of Medicine. Although some of the teachers (Mena, Vega and Laguna), were well-known Galenists, the writings of Hippocrates constituted the bulk of textbooks and lectures. The study of anatomy and the practice of corpse dissection was approved in 1550. Alcalá de Henares, perhaps more than any other sixteenth century Spanish institution, led the struggle to guarantee the high professional standards of medical practice. At Alcalá the future physician had to pass a theoretical test (*probanza de assistencia*), a practical test (*tentativa*), and three years of intensive examinations which ended in a public, all-day discussion with physicians, philosophers, and the Dean of the University (*Alfonsina*). Juan Huarte received his License in Medicine in December 1559, and two weeks later the Doctoral biretta. In 1571 Huarte was practising Medicine in Baeza, had married, and was a father of three children. The *Examen de Ingenios* was first published in

[9] "Porque entramos tres compañeros á estudiar juntos latin, y el uno lo aprendió con gran facilidad, y los demas jamas pudieron componer una oracion elegante. Pero pasados todos tres á dialéctica, el uno de los que no pudieron aprender gramática salió en las artes un águila caudal, y los otros dos no hablaron palabra en todo el curso. Y venido todos tres á oir astrología, fué causa digna de considerar que el que no pudo aprender latin ni dialéctica, en pocos dias supo más que el propio maestro que nos enseñaba, y á los demas jamás nos pudo entar." (*Examen de Ingenios*, ed. Biblioteca de Autores Espanoles, (Madrid, 1953), vol. 65, p. 415 B.)

Baeza in February 1575. Thirteen years later, after a quiet and uneventful life, Juan Huarte died in Baeza (1588).

Huarte wrote only the one book, (the *Examen de Ingenios*), to which he owes his entire reputation. After a slow start the success of the book was extraordinary. At the time of Huarte's death the book had been edited ten times, and had been translated twice into French and three times into Italian. In 1583 the book was included in the Spanish *Index* of Cardinal Quiroga, but outside of Spain, especially in the Low Countries (Leyden, 1591, and 1652; Anvers, 1593 and 1603; Brussels, 1702; Amsterdan, 1662) it was repeatedly reprinted. Huarte himself corrected the book to appease the Inquisition and the new version was published after his death in 1594. This new version was reprinted four times in the seventeenth century (Medina, 1603; Barcelona, 1607; Alcalá, 1640; Madrid, 1660). In the nineteenth century the two versions were combined into one text by Dr. Ildefonso Martínez. This combination of the original texts was the one chosen by the *Biblioteca de Autores Españoles*, and because it is easily available, rather than because of its accuracy, it is also the edition used in this chapter on which the English translations are based. The *Examen* was translated into French by Gabriel Chappius in 1580 and was reprinted twelve times in the seventeenth century. A new translation, by Union d'Alibray was made in 1650 and reprinted in 1655, 1661 and 1668. The third French translation, by Savinien d'Alquien, was published in Amsterdam in 1672. In 1582 Camilo Camilli translated the *Examen* into Italian, a version which was reprinted in 1586 and 1590. In 1600 Salustio Gratii made a new Italian translation which was published again in 1603 and 1604. Richard Carew translated the Italian version by Camilli into English in 1594, and this English edition was published again in 1596, 1604, 1616, and finally in 1969. M. Bellamy made a direct translation from the original Spanish into English in 1698. Finally the *Examen* was translated into German by Lessing in 1752, and into Dutch by Johan Huydekooper in 1659.

A statistical study of the sources of the *Examen* has been made by Father Iriarte. The book contains, among others, one hundred and twenty-seven references to Aristotle, one hundred and two to the Holy Scriptures, forty-two to Cicero, one hundred and fifty to Galen, ninety-eight to Hippocrates, sixty-three to Plato, and less than five references each to Saint Augustin, Plutarch, Homer, and Saint Thomas. Huarte seems to have carefully avoided any references to contemporary writers, although Cajetan, Nebrija, and Tostado are all mentioned once. It appears that Huarte used the Latin translation of Hippocrates made by Cornario (Basel, 1538), the Latin translation of Plato by Marsilio Ficino, the Latin translation of Aristotle by Nicolao Gaza, and the Latin translation of Galen by Andernaco (Basel, 1536). The Hippocratic work most frequently quoted by Huarte, *De aere, aquis et locis*, emphasizes the dependence of man's bodily and mental health upon cosmic causes. Perhaps that is why the *Timaeus* was Huarte's favorite Platonic dialogue. Among the Aristotelian works Huarte found strong inspiration in *De anima, De partibus animalium, and De memoria.* Still, the Aristotelian book most generously quoted by Huarte (sixty quotations) was the *Problemata*, a compilation of Hippocratic and Theophrastus' writings attributed to Aristotle and printed in a single volume by Nicolao Gaza, with the commentaries of Alexander of Aphrodisias. Galen, "the foundation of all my work," as Huarte confesses, was by far the strongest inspiration of the *Examen de Ingenios*. The theory of temperaments made up of the four elements and the four qualities, the centrality of the brain, and the influence of the temper of the brain upon intellectual and moral perfection, were all guidelines taken from Galen's works. Nevertheless, Huarte maintained his strong independence of thought even from Galen's influence, and as we shall presently see, he did not hesitate to disagree with the opinion of the Roman physician on repeated occasions. The *Examen* does not suggest any serious knowledge of medieval tradition, neither in medicine nor in philosophy. The rich content of the *Examen de Ingenios* will now be summarized, together with a generous measure of direct translations from the original Spanish text. Huarte's book is divided into eighteen chapters which have been organized into four different sections for our purpose: A) The Somatic Base of Wit (I–IX); B) The Pedagogical Application (X–XVI); C) Eugenics and Dietetics (XVII and XVIII); D) The Moral Concern (passim).

1. The Somatic Base of Wit

Huarte's point of departure is a proven fact of experience: The enormous variety of human 'ingenios.' The Spanish word 'ingenio' has been translated into English as 'wit' or 'genius,' into French as 'esprit,' into Italian as 'ingegni,' into German as 'Faehigkeiten.' Huarte added one entire chapter (I) to the first version of the *Examen* to "declare what sort of thing 'ingenio' is, and to show how many variations of it one can find among men." In this chapter Huarte indulges in some fashionable etymological analysis of the word, which he relates to the Latin verb 'generare.' 'Ingenio' to Huarte is the human power to generate the arts and sciences. 'Diferencia de ingenio' is then the difference in natural aptitude to learn a given art or a given science. The *Examen de Ingenios*, however, does not always abide by this well-defined intellectualistic interpretation of the word, but adds to it a vague connotation of personality types, of personal development, moral habits, motivation and emotional states. Most of the book, nevertheless, focuses upon individual differences in learning skills, the central theme of Huarte's ideas. It is in this sense that the English word 'wit' has been used, in spite of his unrelated connotations.

In the second chapter of the *Examen* Huarte describes four different types of men. The first is made up of people who are "mentally castrated," "without energies or natural heat to generate any concept of wisdom." These people are totally helpless: no human art can help them in any way. The second group consists of those who have a very moist brain. They can hardly conceive the first principles of any science and need great effort to draw some conclusions. They lack the power to retain their 'concepts,' and these die as soon as they are born. The third type is characterized by an extremely uneven and heterogenous brain, "very thick and firm in one part, extremely thin and irregular in another" (*por unas partes es sutil, por otras grueso y destemplado*). These types are rich in ideas, but utterly disorganized and confused; they are prolific, but their creatures tend to be misformed and monster-like. To the fourth type belong those rare people who conceive easily and in orderly fashion, but without knowing the ultimate reasons, "the *propter quid* of what they know and understand." These observations – which obviously include theoretical explanations not immediately given by experience – are complemented in another section of the *Examen* by a multitude of penetrating remarks about the impact of age, sex, and geographical location upon the skills of the individual. Huarte's observations on age constitute a modest but insightful sketch of developmental psychology. The main concern of the author was to recommend an order of studies adapted to the different stages of the child's development.

He who wants to learn Latin or any other language ought to begin in his childhood, for if he waits until the body is hardened and acquires all the perfection it can achieve, he will never learn it. In his second age, namely the adolescence years, he should study the art of reasoning (for at that time the understanding begins to manifest its strength) which art has the same relation to Logic as shackles have to the feet of untrained mules: after using them for a while they learn to walk with a certain grace. Thus, our understanding, shackled with the rules and precepts of dialectic afterwards acquires a graceful method of reasoning and arguing. Then comes youth, the time to learn all the sciences which belong to the understanding . . .

Intelligence shares development, growth, and decline with other animals and plants. It begins in adolescence, develops during the time of youth, remains stationery in middle age, and declines in old age. Let it be known to those who inquire at what age man's understanding enjoys the most power, that it is from the age of thirty-three to fifty, more or less. This is the period in which we should give most credit to those authors who held different opinions during their lifetime. He that wants to write books, let him do it about this age, neither before nor after, if he does not want to retract himself and change his opinions. Man's age, however, does not always have the same limits; in some childhood ends at the age of twelve, in others at fourteen, in others at fifteen or even eighteen. These people have long lives: their youth lasts almost until they are forty years old, maturity until they are sixty, plus another twenty years of old age, so that their lives amount to eighty years, which is the limit of the most powerful ones. Those whose youth ends at twelve are very short-lived; they begin to reason at an early age, their beards sprout early, their wit lasts for a short time, they begin to decline at the age of thirty, and die when they are fortyeight years old.[10]

These changes in the natural aptitude of the individual at different stages of his development are easily explained by the changes in his body:

[10] "El que ha de aprender latin ó cualquiera otra lengua, lo ha de hacer en la niñez, porque si aguarda á que el cuerpo se endurezca y tome la perfeccion que ha de tener, jamas saldrá con ella. En la segunda edad, que es la adolescencia, se han de trabajar en el arte de raciocinar, porque ya se comienza á descubrir el entendimiento, el cual tiene con la dialectica la misma proporcion que las trabas que echamos en los piés y manos de una mula cerril, que andando algunos dias con ellas, toma despues cierta gracia en el andar. Asi nuestro entendimiento trabado con las reglas y preceptos de la dialéctica, toma despues en las ciencias y disputas un modo de discurrir y raciocinar muy gracioso. Venida la juventud se pueden apprender todas las demas ciencias que pertenecen al entendimiento, porque ya está bien descubierto.

El entendimiento tiene su principio, aumento, estado y declinacion, como el hombre y los demas animales y plantas; él comienza en la adolescencia, tiene un aumento en la juventud, el estado en la edad de consistencia, y comienza á declinar en la vejez. Por tanto él quiere saber cuándo su entendimiento tiene todas las fuerzas que puede alcanzar; sepa que es desde treinte y tres años hasta cincuenta, poco más ó ménos; en el cual tiempo se han de creer los graves autores, si en el discurso de su vida tuvieron contrarias sentencias. Y el que quiere escribir libros lo ha de hacer en esta edad, y no ántes ni despues, si no se quiere retractar ni mudar la sentencia; pero las edades de los hombres no en todos tienen la misma cuenta y razon; porque á unos se les acaba la puericia á los doce años, á los diez y seis y a otros a los diez y ocho. Estos tienen las edades muy largas, porque llegó su juventud á poco ménos de cuarenta años, la consistencia á setenta, y tienen de vejez otros veinte años, con los cuales se hacen ochenta de vida, que es el término de los muy potentados. Los primeros, á quien se acaba la puericia á doce años ,son de muy corta vida, comienzan luégo á raciocinar y nacerles la barba, y dúrales muy poco el ingenio, y á treinta y cinco años comienzan á caducar, y á cuarenta y ocho se les acaba la vida." (*Ibid.*, 416 a-b; 417 a-b.)

Childhood is hot and wet; adolescence is lukewarm; youth is hot and dry; adulthood, has moderate heat, but is excessively dry; old age is cold and dry.[11]

Sex is also a source of intellectual and moral differentiation. Huarte's remarks on the wit of females are not very complimentary to women:

> Those parents who want to enjoy wise children, with an aptitude for learning, must endeavor to produce males; because females cannot achieve a profound intelligence, on account of the cold and moist qualities of their sex. Some of them might talk with an appearence of knowledge in light and easy matters, in ordinary and well-memorized terms. Once they begin to learn they get no farther than some knowledge of Latin, and this only because it involves memory. It is not women themselves who are to be blamed for their dullness, but the cold and moist qualities which formed them without any wit.
>
> If we consider the flesh of women and children, we will find that it is more tender than that of men, yet in spite of that, men, as a rule, have more intelligence than women. And the reason is that the humors which make the flesh tender, phlegm and blood, are both moist and wet; Galen said of these humors that they make people simple and dull. Where the humors which harden the flesh, the choler and melancholy, make man prudent and wise.[12]

With remarkable ease Huarte adhered to Aristotle's theory of sex differentiation, according to which the female fetus is only a male fetus whose development has been prematurely arrested by the lack of enough heat. Women, therefore, are nothing but imperfect men, or to put it in a more blunt manner, raw and inmature men.

Although it appears otherwise, man only differs from woman in having his genitalia outside his body. If we study the anatomy of a woman, we shall find that she has within her two testicles, two seminal

[11] "La puericia, caliente y húmeda; la adolescencia, templada; la juventud, caliente y seca; la consistencia, templada en calor y frialdad, y destemplada por sequedad; la vejez, fria y seca." (*Ibid.*, 420 b.)

[12] "Los padres que quisieren gozar de hijos sabios y que tengan habilidad para letras, han de procurar que nazcan varones, porque las hembras, por razon de la frialdad ó humedad de su sexo, no pueden alcanzar ingenio profundo; sólo vemos que hablan con alguna apariencia de habilidad en materias livianas y fáciles, con términos comunes y muy estudiados, pero metidas en letras no pueden aprender más que un poco latin, y esto por ser obra de la memoria. De la cual rudeza no tienen ellas la culpa, sino que la frialdad y humedad, que las hizo hembras, estas mismas calidades hemos probado atras que contradicen al ingenio y habilidad."

"Y si no, consideremos las carnes de las mujeres y de los niños ,y hallarémos que exceden en blandura á la de los hombres, y con todo eso, los hombres en comun tienen mejor ingenio que las mujeres, Y es la razon natural que los humores que hacen las carnes blandas son flem y sangre, por ser ambos húmedos, como ya lo dejamos notado; y de éstos ha dicho Galeno que hacen los hombres simples y bobos, y por lo contrario, los humores que endurecen las carnes son cólera y melancolia; y de éstos nace la prudencia, sabiduria que tienen los hombres." (*Ibid.*, 497 a; 441 b.)

vessels, and a uterus shaped exactly as the penis. And this is so true that if, when nature has produced a perfect man, it wants to convert him into a woman, nothing needs to be done but to place his reproductive organs inside. And if nature has created a woman and would like to transform her into a man, all it has to do is to place her uterus and testicles outside of her body.[13]

Using these views as a basis Huarte did not hesitate to draw the conclusion that the intelligence of women remains in inverse proportion to their feminity. The more beautiful, delicate, and fertile they are, the less capable they are of learning any part or science.

The third source for wit variations repeatedly stressed by Huarte was geographical location; the variety among men, both in their bodily make-up and in the condition of their wit and soul, springs from their inhabiting countries of different temperature, and being accustomed to different kinds of food and drink." Chapter XV of the *Examen*, "Wherein it is proved that the theory of Medicine belongs partly to memory and partly to understanding; its practice belongs to imagination," offers a colorful panorama of comparative psychology:

> Good natural philosophy and experience have abundantly proved that barren and arid soils, not those producing a rich harvest, engender men of sharp wit. And, on the contrary, rich and fertile soils bring forth men possessing powerful muscles, who are courageous, and of great bodily strength but poor in intelligence.
>
> It is difficult to find men of powerful imagination in Spain. As we have proved above, men of this region lack memory and imagination, but have a good understanding. The imagination of those who live toward the North is not suitable for medicine, too slow and unreliable; it is good, though, to make clocks, pictures, pins, and other knickknacks which are not of much service to man. There is a great deal of this (vivid) imagination in Egypt; and thus historians never cease mentioning what great enchanters the gypsies (sic!) are, how talented for imagining things, and for finding remedies to their problems.
>
> Greece is the most temperate region in the world. The heat of the air does not exceed the coldness, nor does moisture outbalance dryness. This temperature makes man very wise and gifted in all the sciences, as one can see from the great number of illustrious men who came from Greece: Socrates, Plato, Aristotle, Hippocrates, Galen, Theophrastus, Demosthenes, Homer,

13 "El hombre, aunque nos parece de la compostura que vemos, no difiere de la mujer, segun dice Galeno, más que en tener los miembros genitales fuera del cuerpo. Porque si hacemos anatomía de una doncella, hallarémos que tiene dentro de sí dos testículos, dos vasos seminarios y el útero con la misma compostura que el miembro viril, sin faltarle ninguna delineacion. Y de tal manera es esto verdad, que si acabando naturaleza de fabricar un hombre perfecto, lo quisiese convertir en mujer, no tenía otro trabajo más que tornarle adentro los instrumentos de la generacion. Y si hecha mujer, quisiese volverla en varon, con arrojarle el útero y los testículos fuera, no habia más que hacer." (*Ibid.*, P. 492 a.)

Thales Milesius, Diogenes Cynicus, Solon, and other infinitely wise men mentioned here and there, whose deeds we find full of wisdom ... Thus, we see, that of those philosophers, many who were born and educated outside Greece none of them arrive at the perfection of Plato or Aristotle; those who are physicians, do not compare with Hippocrates and Galen; the orators, are far from Demosthenes; and the poets, very inferior to Homer. In all the other sciences the Greeks have always been first, without any question. At least Aristotle's theory is truly verified by the Greeks; because they are indeed the most beautiful men of the world, endowed with the highest degree of intelligence. Unfortunately, they have been oppressed by force, held in bondage and crudely treated by the Turks, who banished all learning and caused the University of Athens (?) to move to Paris, where it continues to this day. Thus, for the lack of proper care, many men of talent, comparable to those we have just mentioned, are completely lost. Although there are great schools to this day no outstanding scholar has yet been produced.[14]

This is the chapter where Huarte proves at length that the climate, the food [the manna], and the pure waters of the desert combined to make the Jews the most talented physicians of mankind. The chapter ends with these ironical, and touching remarks:

Like the negroes in Spain (i.e., the Moors) who transmit their skin color to their children through their seed, – without being in Ethiopia (*Sic*) – the

[14] "Y esto es cosa muy averiguada, así en buena filosofia natural como en experiencia, que las regiones estériles y flacas, no paniegas y abundosas en fructificar, crian hombres de ingenio muy agudo; por lo contrario, las tierras gruesas y fértiles engendran hombres membrudos, animosos y de muchas fuerzas corporales, pero muy torpes de ingenio.

Esta diferencia de imaginativa es mala de hallar en España, porque los moradores de esta region hemos probado atras que carecen de memoria y de imaginativa, y tienen buen entendimiento. Tambien la imaginativa de los que habitan debajo del Septentrion no vale nada para la medicina, porque es muy tarda y remisa; sólo es buena para hacer relojes, pinturas, alfileres, y otras brujerías impertinentes al servicio del hombre. Solo Egipto es la region que engendra en sus moradores esta diferencia de imaginativa, y así los historiadores nunca acaban de contar cuán hechiceros son los gitanos y cuán prestos en atinar las cosas y hallar los remedios para sus necesidades.

Grecia es la region más templada que hay en el mundo, donde el calor del aire no excede á la frialdad, ni la humedad á la sequedad. La cual templanza hace á los hombres prudentísimos y hábiles para todas las ciencias, como parece considerando el gran número de varones ilustres que de ella han salido: Sócrates, Platon, Aristóteles, Hípocrates, Galeno, Theophrasto, Demóstenes, Homero, Táles, Milesio, Díogenes, Cinico, Solon y otros infinitos sabios de quien las historias hacen mencion, cuyas obras hallarémos llenas de todas las ciencias.

Y así vemos que cuantos nacen y estudian fuera de Grecia, si son filósofos, ninguno llega á Platon y Aristóteles; si médicos, a Hipócrates y Galeno, si oradores á Demóstenes, si poetas ó Homero, y así en las demas ciencias y artes, siempre los griegos han tenido la primacía, sin ninguna contradiccion. A lo ménos el problema de Aristóteles se verifica bien en los griegos, porque realmente son los más hermosos hombres del mundo, y de más alto ingenio, sino que han sido desgraciados, oprimidos con armas, sujetos y maltratados por la venida del turco; éste hizo desterrar las letras y pasar la universidad de Aténas a Paris de Francia, donde ahora está, Y así, por no cultivarlos se pierden ahora tan delicados ingenios como los que arriba contamos. En las demas regiones fuera de Grecia, aunque hay escuela y ejercicio de letras, ningum hombre ha salido en ellas muy eminente." (*Ibid.*, 469 b; 468 a; 484 a-b.)

people of Israel, who also come from there, pass on their sharpness of wit, without remaining in Egypt or eating manna; for to be ignorant or wise is as much a man's accidental quality as it is to be white or black. True, they are not as sharp and intelligent now as they were a thousand years ago, for from the time they stopped eating manna and began eating other food, inhabited different countries, and drank water not as pure as that of the desert, they have been losing part of their wit. It is also due to their mingling with those who descended from the Gentiles and lacked this excellence of wit. One thing, though, cannot be denied: and that is that they, the Jews, have not lost their wit altogether.[15]

Having described the empirical fact of the diversity of wit in man, Huarte proceeds to argue that such diversity is inborn and not acquired; that it can only be fully explained by a 'natural,' hereditary, innate trait of the individual himself. The first proof is the authority "of all ancient philosophers, who found from experience, that where nature does not dispose a man to knowledge, it is superfluous to toil in the rules of art." The second proof is this fact of experience itself:

At least if I were a teacher, before admitting any student into my school, I would test him in many different ways until I discovered the quality of his wit. If I found him naturally talented for the discipline I taught, I would willingly receive him, for it is a source of great joy to a teacher to teach those who are capable of learning; otherwise I would advise him to take up the discipline for which he showed a greater talent. But if I saw that he had no disposition toward any sort of learning, I would tell him in the most friendly way: My brother, you have no talent to follow the path you have chosen. I advise you to find another way of life, one which does not require as much ability as learning does.

Experience confirms this every day: we see a large number of students who register in this or that course – be the teacher very good or very bad. At the end some students acquire great erudition, others some learning, and still others after wasting their time and money end up in frustration without learning anything.

All this is based on the assumption that man has a natural talent. Otherwise 'He that goes a beast to Rome, returns a beast again.' It does not help the dull student to go to Salamanca, where there is no chair of understanding, nor wisdom, nor a man to teach it.[16]

[15] "Y de la manera que los negros comunican en España el color á sus descendientes por la simiente sin estar en Etiópia, así el pueblo de Israel, viniendo tambien á ella, puede comunicar a sus descendientes la agudeza de ingenio, sin estar en Egipto ni comer del maná, porque ser necio ó sabio tan bien es accidente del hombre como ser blanco ó negro. Ello es verdad que no son ahora tan agudos y solertes como mil años atras, porque desde que dejaron de comer del maná lo han venido perdiendo sus descendientes poco á poco hasta ahora, por usar de contrarios manjares, y estar en region diferente de Egipto, y no beber aguas tan delicadas como en el desierto, y por haberse mezclado con los que descienden de la gentilidad, los cuales carecen de esta diferencia de ingenio; pero lo que no se les puede negar es, que áun no lo han acabado de perder." (*Ibid.*, 472 b.–473a.)

[16] "Yo á lo ménos, si fuera maestro, ántes que recibiera en mi escuela algun discipulo

Huarte argues further that this inborn trait which causes the difference in wit cannot be found in the soul but in the body. At this point the author blindly embarks upon a highly metaphysical speculation commonly held by the great Spanish scholastics of those days, Dominicans as well as Jesuits.[17] The soul, as the *actus corporis*, is only the formal cause of man's specific and substantial perfection, not of man's individual differences. The souls of all mankind, males and females, children and mature men, men from different regions and age, are all of identical perfection. The source of individual differentiation can, therefore, only be traced back to the other substantial component of man, the body.

All the rational souls are of identical perfection, the soul of a learned, as well as the soul of an ignorant. We cannot say that the soul makes a man witty; otherwise all men would have the same degree of wit and knowledge. . . . In confirmation thereof let us consider the different stages in man's development. As an infant, man is but a dumb animal who makes use only of his irascible and concupiscible instincts; when adolescence sets in, man reveals an admirable wit which lasts for a while but not for very long; in his old age, this wit declines steadily and finally disappears. This variety of wit cannot proceed from the soul which is the same throughout, with no alteration whatsoever in its power and substance, but from the temper and diverse disposition of the body in each age, according to which childhood, adolescence, and senility are marked by different actions.[18]

habia de hacer con él muchas pruebas y experiencias para descubrirle el ingenio, y si se halláre de buen natural para la ciencia que yo profesaba, recibiérale de buena gana, porque es gran contento para el que enseña instruir á un hombre de buena habilidad; y si no, aconsejarle que estudiase la ciencia que á su ingenio más le convenia; pero entendido que para género de letras tenía disposicion ni capacidad, dijérale con amor y blandas palabras: hermano mio, vos no teneis remedio de ser hombre por el camino que habeis excogido, y que busqueis otra manera de vivir que no requiera tanta habilidad como las letras.

Viene la experiencia con esto tan clara, que vemos entrar en un curso de cualquier ciencia gran número de discípulos (siendo el maestro ó muy bueno ó muy ruin), y en fin de la jornada, unos salen de grande erudicion, otros de mediana, otros no han hecho más en todo el curso de perder el tiempo, gasta su hacienda y quebrarse la cabeza sin provecho ninguno.

Todo esto se entiende impuesto que el hombre tenga buen ingenio y habilidad, porque si no, quien bestia va á Roma, bestia torna; poco aprovecha que el rudo vaya á estudiar á Salamanca, donde no hay cátedra de entendimiento ni de prudencia ni hombre que la enseñe." (*Ibid.*, 415a.–b.; 416b.)

17 See, Domingo de Soto, *Liber predicamentorum* (Salamanca, 1553), Chapter V, quest. 2; also *Commentarii Collegii Coimbricensis Societatis Jesu in tres libros De Animae Aristotelis Stagiritae* (Coimbra, 1589), Book II, Chapter 1, Queast. 5.

18 "Todas las ánimas racionales sean de igual perfeccion, así la del sabio como la del necio, no se puede afirmar qué naturaleza, en esta significacion, es la que hace al hombre hábil; porque si esto fuese verdad, todos los hombres tendrian igual ingenio y saber ...

"Y pruébase claramente, considerando las edades de un hombre sapientísimo, el cual en la puericia no es mas que un bruto animal, ni usa de otras potencias más que de la irascible y concupiscible; pero venida la adolescensia comienza a descubrir un ingenio admirable, y vemos que le dura hasta cierto tiempo y no más, porque viniendo la vejez, cada dia va perdiendo el ingenio, hasta que viene a caducar. Esta variedad de ingenios, cierto es que nace del ánima racional, porque en todas las edades es la misma sin haber recibido en sus fuerzas

According to Huarte, then, the soul which is of the same perfection in all men, does not grow, does not decay. It remains unaffected through time, it lacks history. Every individual differentiation in mental ability, emotional balance, motivation, and patterns of individual behavior, is, strictly speaking, physiological in character. Speculative psychology is, therefore, barren in any pedagogical, social, ethical, and therapeutic applicability. Applied psychology is based upon psychophysiology. The *Examen de Ingenios* thus signals an important step both in the pragmatic and in the reductionistic trends of modern psychology.

Having reached the conclusion that some inborn trait of the body explains all the individual differences in wit, Huarte sets out to determine in concrete ways where this trait is to be found. In fact, the author was convinced that such a task was his own personal vocation, and that all previous philosophers and physicians had remained inexcusably vague on this most important point.

It is common opinion among ancient philosophers that Nature gives the ability to learn, art makes it easy by means of its rules and precepts, use and experience of particular things makes man powerful in action: *Natura facit habilem, ars facilem, ususque potentem.* Yet none of these philosophers has ever shown specifically what sort of thing 'nature' is, nor what its origin is. They just affirmed that whoever did not have such a 'nature' would not be helped by art, experience, teachers, books or hard work'[19]

In spite of this sweeping criticism, Huarte's own theory, in its general features at least, is only a modified and enriched version of traditional but still fashionable patterns of thought. The two key theories assumed by Huarte were, first the theory of temperament; second, the consideration of the brain as the organ of the mind.

The theory of temperament was a biological application of Empedocles' cosmology, promoted by the cosmic emphasis of Hippocrates' teaching, widely accepted by Alexandrian physicians, and definitively formulated by Galen. The four elements (air, water, earth, and fire) combine with the four qualities (cold, hot, dry, wet) to make up the sublunar universe. The human organism includes four humors which

y sustancia ninguna alteracion, sino que en cada edad tiene el hombre vario temperamento y contraria disposicion, por razon de la cual hace el ánima unas obras en la puericia, y otras en la juventud, y otras en la vejez," (*Ibid.*, 419b.–420a.)

[19] "Sentencia es muy comun y usada de los filósofos antiguos, diciendo: naturaleza es la que hace al hombre hábil para aprender, y el arte con sus preceptos y reglas le facilita, y el uso y experiencia que tiene de las cosas particulares le hacen poderoso para obrar. Pero ninguno ha dicho en particular qué cosa sea esta naturaleza, ni en qué género de causas se ha de poner. Sólo afirmaron que faltando ella en el que aprende, vana cosa es el arte, la experiencia, los maestros, los libros y el trabajo." (*Ibid.*, 417b.–418a.)

correspond to the four cosmic qualities: blood (collected in the heart) is hot, phlegm (collected in the brain) is cold, yellow bile (collected in the liver) is dry, black bile (collected in the spleen and the stomach) is wet. Man is healthy when all these four humors are in equilibrium; an irregularity in their mixture produces disease. Furthermore, the constitutional dominant character of one of these four humors in the individual explains the four different 'temperaments' or levels of emotional reactivity: blood prevails in the sanguine, phlegm in the phlegmatic, yellow bile in the choleric, and black bile in the melancholic. Galen was also the first to write a book on the relation between 'temperament' and moral character.

Huarte's thought on 'temperament' is presented in rather disorderly fashion from Chapter V to IX. Chapter V, (missing in the first version of the *Examen de Ingenios*), deals with the relationship between temperament and moral behavior, a subject we shall discuss later (*see below*, under letter D). Chapter VI discusses which of the dominant qualities of the brain affects the temperament. Chapter VII is a baffling digression on innatism. Chapter VIII, by far the most important, describes temperament as the combination, in different degrees of the three qualities (hot, dry, and wet) in the brain; it also discusses the impact of temperament upon the three hegemonic faculties, memory, imagination, and understanding. Chapter IX answers some objections.

Before we proceed to summarize Huarte's thought on temperament we need to return to the second key theory assumed in the entire discussion: the centrality of the brain as the organ of man's cognitive faculties (Chapter VI). Huarte here relies upon the fundamental Aristotelian principle that each human power or 'faculty' must be endowed with its corresponding instrumental organ.

> Man's body has so many different parts and powers, each one applied to a different end, that it is incumbent upon us to show, which member was ordained by nature to be the main instrument of man's wisdom and prudence. It is clear that we do not reason with our feet, nor walk on our head, nor see with our noses, nor listen with our eyes, but that every one of these parts has its own use and disposition for the work which it is supposed to accomplish.
>
> As long as the rational soul dwells in the body it cannot perform different operations if it did not possess the proper instrument for each one. This is obvious in the animal soul, whose various external senses function according to their differing structure. The eyes have one, the ears another, and so do taste, smelling, and touch. If it were not so we would have but one kind of action and operation, and all the operations would be seeing, or tasting, or

touching. Because the instrument determines and modifies the faculty for one action and for no more.[20]

Huarte summarizes the traditional controversies about the instrumentality of man's rational powers in the following manner:

> Before Hippocrates and Plato were born it was generally assumed by natural philosophers that the heart was the principal organ where the rational faculties were located, and the instrument of the soul to achieve prudence, wisdom, diligence, memory, and understanding . . . When these two wise philosophers came into the world they gave evidence that such opinion was false, and proved by many arguments that the brain is the principal seat of the rational soul. Everyone accepted this opinion, except Aristotle. Being eager to contradict Plato whenever possible, he revived the former opinion and made it plausible by means of persuasive arguments. Today, however, there is no way of questioning which of these two is the true opinion. No philosopher now doubts that the brain is the instrument ordained by nature to see that man grows wise and prudent . . .[21]

That the brain was the central organ of the rational soul was, then accepted by Huarte as a fashionable and commonplace theory which did not deserve further discussion. He believed that for the brain to function efficiently it had to have the correct structure (shape, size, four 'ventricles'), the proper connection and contact between its different parts; the right 'temper', and the right texture (*de partes sutiles y muy delicadas*). Although the brain was the main organ of the rational soul, this did not mean that the soul did not also use other parts of the

[20] "Tiene el cuerpo humano tanta variedad de partes y potencias, aplicadas cada una para su fin, qué no será fuera de próposito ántes cosa necesaria, saber, primero, que miembro ordenó naturaleza por instrumento principal para que el hombre fuese sabio y prudente; porque cierto es que no raciocinamos con el pié, ni andamos con la cabeza, ni vemos con las narices, ni oimos con los ojos, sino que cada una de estas partes tiene su uso y particular compostura para la obra que ha de hacer.

Estando el ánima racional en el cuerpo, es imposible poder hacer obras contrarias y diferentes, si para cada una no tiene su instrumento particular. Vese esto claramente en la facultad animal, la cual hace várias obras en los sentidos exteriores, por tener cada uno su particular compostura. Una tiene los ojos, otra los oidos, otra el gusto, otra el olfato y otra el tacto. Y si no fuera así, no hubiera más que un género de obras, ó todo fuera ver, ó gustar, ó palpar porque el instrumento determina y modifica la potencia para una acción y no mas." (*Ibid.*, 425b; 433b.)

[21] "Antes que naciese Hipócrates y Platon, estaba muy recibido entre los filósofos naturales que el corazon era la parte principal donde residia la facultad racional y el instrumento con que nuestra alma hacia las obras de prudencia, solercia, memoria y entendimiento. Pero venidos al mundo estos dos grandes filósofos, dieron á entender que era falsa aquella opinion, y probaron con muchas razones y experiencias que el cerebro era el asiento principal del alma racional; y así lo recibieron todos, sino fué Aristóteles, el cual, con ánimo de contradecir en todo á Platon, tornó á refrescar la primera opinion, y con argumentos tópicos hacerla probable.

Cuál sea la más verdadera sentencia ya no es tiempo de ponerlo en cuestion; porque ningun filósofo duda en esta era que el cerebro es el instrumento que naturaleza ordenó para que el hombre fuese sabio y prudente." (*Ibid.*, 426a.)

body to exercise its rational powers. Toward the end of Chapter VI Huarte mentions the 'vital spirits' and the arterial blood (*espíritus vitales y sangre arterial*). The vital spirits are concentrated in the heart, but they 'run' (*andan vagando*) through the entire body following the directions of the imagination. As important links between the brain and the rest of the body, their 'temper' is obviously of direct relevance to the individual, especially in connection with action and choice. The 'temper' of the paternal and maternal seed is also extremely important since it decides the 'temper' of the child's brain. Furthermore, Huarte claims a close connection between the maternal uterus and the paternal testicles through their corresponding brain.

To specify that the brain is the organ of the rational soul was not enough for Huarte. Abandoning the Aristotelian tradition which attributed five powers to the soul, Huarte remained constantly loyal to his tripartite model (three qualities, three dominant characters of wit, three kinds of science,) by assigning three hegemonic powers to the rational soul: memory, imagination and understanding. The problem was to localize the three different organs possessing these three different powers in the brain.

If it is true that every operation requires its own instrument there must necessarily be an organ for the understanding, another for memory, and another for the imagination within the brain. For if the brain were organized in an entirely uniform manner it would consist only of memory, or understanding, or imagination. But we see that there are different operations, since there must be a variety of instruments. However, if we open the skull and show the anatomy of the brain, we shall find that all of it is organized uniformly, that it consists of one kind of substance, without any variety of heterogeneous parts; we shall find only four small ventricles which, when closely observed, display the same composition and shape, without having anything in between to separate them.[22]

Huarte rejects Galen's theories of localization and then gives his own opinion:

The truth of the matter is that the fourth ventricle has the task of absorbing and altering the vital spirits, for the purpose we have mentioned before.

[22] "Pero si es verdad que cada obra requiere particular instrumento, necesariamente allá dentro en el cerebro ha de haber organo para el entendimiento, y órgano para la imaginativa, y otro diferente para la memoria; porque si todo el cerebro estuviera organizado de una misma manera, todo fuera memoria, o todo entendimiento, ó todo imaginacion, y vemos que hay obras muy diferentes; luego forzosamente ha de haber variedad de instrumentos. Pero abierta la cabeza y hecha anatomía del cerebro, todo está, todo está compuesto de un mismo modo de sustancia homogénea y similar, sin variedad de partes hetereogénas; sólo aparecen cuatro senos pequeños, los cuales (bien mirados) todos tienen una misma composicion y figura, sin haber cosa por medio en que puedan diferir." (*Ibid.*, 434a.)

This is why nature separated it from the rest and made it into as separate a brain as possible, so that its functions would not hinder the operations of the rest. Nature made the three front ventricles for no other purpose than to reason and to philosophize. This is revealed by the fact that after intensive study and contemplation the frontal part of the head is the one which hurts.[23]

By this ingenious device Huarte manages once again to preserve his own structural trichotomy. The difficulty, however, remains: "Now the problem is to find out in which of these ventricles the understanding is placed, in which one the memory, and in which one the imagination." To make things worse these frontal ventricles of the brain are so close together that it is hard to distinguish one from another. Huarte 'solves' the problem in the following manner:

Considering that understanding cannot work without memory being present... and that memory cannot function without the assistance of imagination (as we declared above), we shall quickly understand that all three faculties are placed together in each ventricle, so that understanding is not alone in one, memory in another, and imagination in the third...[24]

We are, finally, ready to understand Huarte's notion of 'temperament.' Assuming, as he does, that the typology of wit is determined by the dominant character of one of the three hegemonic faculties (memory, imagination, understanding); and assuming further that these three faculties reside in the same frontal ventricles of the brain, the only possible source of differentiation left is the different combination of qualities in that part of the brain. Rather capriciously Huarte discards cold: "all the physicians," he says, "leave it out as totally useless regarding the operations of the soul" (once again the ternary paradigm prevails); and thus reaches the conclusion that the strength of memory, imagination and understanding depends entirely upon the degree of heat, humidity and dryness of the frontal ventricles of the

[23] "La verdad que parece en este punto es, que el ventriculo cuarto tiene por oficio cocer y alterar los espíritus vitales, y convertir los animales para el fin que tenemos dicho. Y por esto lo apartó naturaleza en tanta distancia de los otros tres y le hizo cerebro aparte y dividido, y tan remoto como aparece, porque con su obra no estorbase la contemplacion de los demas. Los tres ventriculos delanteros, y no dudo sino que los hizo naturaleza para discurrir y filosofar. Lo cual se prueba claramente, porque en los grandes estudios y contemplaciones siempre duele aquella parte de la cabeza que responde á estas tres concavidades." (*Ibid.*, 434a.–b.)

[24] "Considerando que el entendimiento no puede obrar sin que la memoria esté presente, representándole las figuras y fantasmas, conforme aquello (Arist., 13, *De anima*) 'oportet intelligentem fantasmata speculare'; ni la memoria sin que asista con ella la imaginativa (de la manera que atras lo dejamos declarado), entendéremos fácilmente que todas tres potencias están juntas en cada ventrículo, y no está solo el entendimiento en el uno, ni sola la memoria en el otro, ni la imaginativa en el tercero," (*Ibid.*, 434b.)

brain. The only issue to be solved is to find a one to one correspondence between the three constituents of wit and the three qualities of the brain. With remarkable facility Huarte resolves the puzzle by relating memory to humidity, imagination to heat, and understanding to dryness.

> The office of memory is to preserve the images (*fantasmas*) to the end that the understanding may contemplate them . . . And this being its operation it is obvious that it depends on humidity, because this quality makes the brain tender and pliable, and the image is stamped upon it by way of pressing. To prove this we have an evident example in early childhood, at which age man enjoys a very strong memory, and the brain is most humid . . .
>
> Imagination is born from heat, which is the third quality, for there is no other reasonable power in the brain, nor any other quality to which it might be assigned. Besides, the disciplines which belong to the imagination are those uttered by the sick in the heat of high fever, and not those which belong to understanding and memory.
>
> Finally, everyone agrees that dryness makes man very wise, although they do not specify which of the rational powers it helps . . .[25]

The classification of wit and its determination by the three qualities is further reinforced by declaring these types to be mutually incompatible. Since dryness and humidity are opposite qualities, the temper which causes a strong memory is physically incompatible with the temper which produces a keen intelligence. For the same reason a powerful imagination excludes a strong memory, since the heat which causes the former excludes the humidity of the latter. On the other hand experience shows that a man of great imagination is rarely a man of sharp intelligence, although in this particular case the reason is unknown, since the heat of the imagination and the dryness of intelligence are not – at least in a certain range of intensity-incompatible qualities. Huarte also notices that an overly intensive quality tends not to refine the corresponding rational power, but rather to disrupt it entirely.

Although Huarte was obviously pleased by the neatness of his conclusions and the prospect of promising applications and relationships

[25] "Y el oficio de la memoria es guardar estos fantasmas para cuando el entendimiento los quisiera contemplar. Y siendo este su uso, claramente se entiende que depende de la humedad, porque ésta hace el cerebro blando, y la figura se imprime por via de compresion; en la cual edad aprende el hombre más de memoria que en todas las demas, y el cerebro le tiene humedisimo . . .

De calor (que es la tercera calidad) nace la imaginativa; porque ya ni hay otra potencia racional en el cerebro, ni otra calidad que darle; allende que las ciencias que pertenecen á la imaginativa son las que dicen los delirantes en la enfermedad, y no de las que pertenecen al entendimiento y memoria.

"Finalmente, todos convienen que la sequedad hace al hombre my sabio; pero no declaran á cual de las potencias racionales ayuda más." (*Ibid.*, 436a.–b.; 437a.; 435b.)

between his types and other considerations such as sex, age and geography, he was also painfully aware of the vulnerable artificiality of some of his premises and principles. Chapter IX of the *Examen de Ingenios*, which begins with a touching confession of ignorance, is an attempt to solve some of the large number of questions suggested by the preceding chapters. Is human intelligence an organic power? Is memory the same as reminiscence, as Aristotle claimed? What is the realtionship between the temperament of the brain and other parts of the body? How can humidity explain the retentive power of memory? What is the correspondence, if any, between the basic three types of rational wit and the four (emotional) temperaments described by Galen? Why is it that theoretical and practical reason are seldom combined in one individual?

Some of these questions obviously deal with matters of little relevance; others, however, touch upon serious philosophical and theological matters. The first part of the *Examen*, which we have just summarized, contains philosophical positions open to severe criticism from an orthodox and traditional point of view. These include, first the criticism of authority; second, a new conception of the natural sciences; and, third, a naturalistic philosophy of man.

Huarte's ideas on the role of authority in philosophical speculation and scientific research, and his faith in the constant possibility of progressive discoveries, are a faithful echo of Vives' general principle: "Truth is accessible to everybody and has not been appropriated by a few. A great portion of it is left for future generations." Those who insist on denying that sixteenth century Spain made a radical break with medieval allegiance to authority and tradition, should carefully consider the following words of Juan Huarte de San Juan:

> If your wit is of a common and vulgar nature, I am sure you are convinced that the sciences, in all their perfection, were discovered long ago by ancient writers. Your reason for this is very simple: as they found nothing else to say, there cannot be anything new to say. If that is the way you think, stop right here and do not read another page of this book: for you will suffer when you realize what a miserable wit you have been alloted.
>
> The philosopher of nature who thinks that a proposition is true just because Aristotle made it, without justifying it further, lacks any kind of understanding. Truth is not found in the mouth of the speaker, but in the subject matter itself, which loudly proclaims its nature and the purpose for which it was ordained. Those who listen to nature learn much about it; others need a teacher to be told what the animals and the plants proclaim themselves.[26]

[26] "Si tu ingenio es de los comunes y vulgares, bien sé que estás persuadido que el número

In the particular case of Medicine, Huarte writes "experience is stronger than reason, and reason stronger than authority." The scientific and rationalistic thrust of the age reappears, even more emphatically, in Huarte's consideration of the very nature of scientific research. Huarte begins with a short story:

Once upon a time there was a philosopher who liked to discuss matters with a Grammarian. One day an inquisitive Gardener came to them, and asked why the soil did not bring forth the vegetables he had sown in it, although he took such care of it, digging, turning, dunging and watering it; whereas the grass bred by the soil itself grew with such abundance. The Grammarian answered that it was due to Divine Providence, which had ordained everything toward a good arrangement of the world; the natural Philosopher laughed at this, seeing that the Grammarian referred everything back to God because he ignored the discourse on natural causes, and the manner in which they produced their effects. The Grammarian, seeing the other laugh, asked him whether he was making fun of him, or why he was laughing. The Philosopher answered that he was not laughing at him, but at the teacher who had taught him so poorly; for the solution of those things which resulted from Divine Providence being supernatural operations, had to be dealt with by the metaphysicians (or 'theologians' as we call them today); but the question put by the gardener belonged to the domain of the Philosopher of nature, for there are manifest and well-ordered causes for these effects.[27]

de las ciencias y su perfeccion há muchos dias que por los antiguos está ya cumplido, movido con una vana razon, que pues ellos no hallaron más que decir, argumento es que no hay otra novedad en las cosas; y si por ventura tienes tal opinion, no pases de aquí ni leas más adelante, porque te dará pena ver probado cuán miserable diferencia de ingenio te cupo.

El filósofo natural que piensa ser una proposicion verdadera, porque la dijo Aristóteles, sin buscar otra razon, no tiene ingenio, porque la verdad no está en la boca del que afirma, sino en la cosa de que se trata, la cual está dando voces y grita enseñando al hombre el sér que naturaleza le dió, y el fin para que fue ordenda.

El que tuviere docilidad en el entendimiento y buen oido para percibir lo que naturaleza dice y enseña con sus obras, aprenderá mucho en la contemplacion de las cosas naturales, y no tendrá necesidad de perceptos que le avise y le haga considerar lo que los brutos, animales y plantas están voceando." (*Ibid.*, 404a.; 410 a–b.)

[27] "Estando un filósofo natural razonando con un gramático, ille ó á ellos un hortelano curioso, y les preguntó qué podia ser la causa que haciendo él tantos regalos á la tierra, en cavarla, ararla, estercolarla y regarla, con todo eso, nunca llevaba de buena gana la hortaliza que en ella sembraba; y las yerbas, que ella producia de suyo, las hacia crecer con tanta facilidad. Respondió el gramático que aquel efecto nacia de la divina Providencia, y que así estaba ordenado para la buena gobernacion del mundo; de la cual respuesta se rió el filósofo natural, viendo que se acogia á Dios por no saber el discurso de las causas naturales, ni de qué manera producian sus efectos.

El gramático, viéndole reir, le preguntó si se burlaba de el ó de qué se reia. El filosófo le dijo que no se reia de él, sino del maestro que le habia enseñado tan mal; porque las cosas que nacen de la Providencia divina, como son obras sobrenaturales, pertenece su conocimiento y solucion á los metafísicos, que ahora llamamos teólogos; pero la cuestion del hortelano es natural, y pertenece á la jurisdiccion de los filósofos naturales, porque hay causas ordenadas y manifestas, de donde tal efecto pueda nacer." (*Ibid.*, 418a.)

The task of the philosopher of nature, is thus to investigate the causal relationships among the secondary (*causas segundas*) or intermediary (*causas intermedias*) causes. Any appeal to the first cause or Divine Providence, or any appeal to vague and mystical causes such as 'Nature,' 'instinct' and their like is unscientific and misleading. Man leans toward this superstition, sometimes glorified as 'modesty,' for the following reasons:

I have often asked myself why vulgar people are so inclined to impute all things to God, rather than nature, and to abhor natural causes...

First, because men are for the most part impatient and anxious to get whatever they covet. Knowing, that God is omnipotent and performs whatever he wants in one second; and knowing also that natural means take time, they become impatient and expect God to give them health as miraculously as he did to the paralytic ...

The second reason is that men are arrogant and conceited; many of them desire in their hearts that God bestow some particular favor upon them...

Thirdly, men are naturally lazy, and the natural causes are such that they require work and labor in order to obtain their effects...

The last reason is that many vulgar people are religious and they like to see God magnified and honored, an effect which is better achieved by miracles than by natural causes; they ignore that God performs wonderful and supernatural works only to prove to those who do not know that He is Omnipotent, to prove the truth of His doctrine. But when it is unnecessary, He does not do so.[28]

Impatience, arrogance, laziness and false religiosity are opposed to the relentless, long and modest inquiry by the true philosopher of nature. God created an ordered Universe: it is the task of science to discover

[28] "Pero yo muchas veces me he puesto á considerar la razon y causa de donde pueda nacer que la gente vulgar sea tan amiga de atribuir todas las cosas á Dios, y quitarlas á la naturaleza y aborrecer los medios naturales. Y no se si he podido atinar, á lo ménos bien se deja entender, qué por no saber el vulgo que efectos se han de atribuir immediatamente á Dios, y cuáles a naturaleza, los hace hablar de aquella manera, fuera de que los hombres, por la mayor parte, son impacientes y amigos de que se cumpla presto lo que ellos desean; y como los medios naturales son tan espaciosos y obran por discurso del tiempo, no tienen paciencia para aguardarlos. Y como saben que Dios es omnipotente y que en un momento hace todo lo que quiere, y de ello tienen muchos ejemplos, querrian que él les diese salud como al paralítico ...

"La segunda causa es que los hombres somos arrogantes y de vana estimacion; muchos de los cuales desean allá adentro de su pecho que Dios los haga á ellos alguna merced particular.

"La tercera razon es ser los hombres amigos de holgar y estar dispuestas las causas naturales, por tal órden y concierto, que para alcanzar sus efectos es menester trabajar ...

La última causa es ser mucha la gente vulgar religiosa y amiga de que Dios sea honrado y engrandecido, lo cual se consigue mucho más con los milagros que con los efectos naturales; pero el bulgo de los hombres no sabe que obras sobrenaturales y prodigiosas las hace Dios para mostrar á los que no lo saben que es omnipotente, y que usa de ellas por argumento para comprobar su doctrina, y que faltando *esta* necesidad nunca jamas las hace." (*Ibid.*, 418b.–419a.)

the sequence of cause and effect in the realm of creation in order to be able to master nature for the sake of man. The emphasis is not on formal but on efficient causes, not on contemplative theorizing but on pragmatic guidelines of action. Such a task is never complete nor is it freely undertaken without hard toil and effort.

Huarte's views on the nature and mutual dependence of the soul and body were by far the most controversial matters of the book. A review of the Inquisitorial objections to the *Examen* sheds much light on the subject. Some of those objections were no doubt ridiculous and personal. Alonso Pretel, a professor of Patristic Theology at the University of Baeza, violently objected to Huarte's claim that those who were gifted to teach Positive Theology were men of powerful memory but weak intelligence. A more serious criticism was directed against the use of the expression *potencia orgánica* to describe the understanding. Huarte's emphasis on the dependence of the understanding upon such material circumstances as the heat, dryness and humidity of the frontal ventricles of the brain, was seen by the Inquisition as an indirect denial of the spiritual character of the human soul. This impression was reinforced by other sections of the *Examen* where Huarte did not hesitate to grant animals some kind of understanding, prudence, and even moral virtue (Chapter VI); or where he seemed to exaggerate the positive and negative influence of bodily temperament upon moral behavior and free choice (Chapter V); or finally, the last pages of the book where he gave the natural reasons for the excellence of Christ's brain. (Chapter XVIII). To forestall this anticipated criticism Huarte wrote an entire chapter (VII) on the problem of the immortality of the soul. The result, however, was to make things worse, and the controversial chapter was left out in the second version of 1594. This chapter, which is obviously a digression and does not fit in at all with the general plan of the book, was a blunt confession of fideism regarding the truth of the soul's immortality.

> Obviously the infallible certainty we have about the immortality of the soul is not based on human reasons, nor are there any arguments to support proof that it is corruptible: there are always possible objections to them. It is only our Faith that makes us certain and sure that our soul lasts for ever.[29]

Human reason cannot prove that the soul is immortal. Huarte is so firmly entrenched in this position that he does not even bother to refute

29 "Y así es cierto que la certidumbre infalible de ser nuestra ánima inmortal no se toma de las razones humanas, ni ménos hay argumentos que prueban es corruptible; porque á los unos y á los otros se puede responder con facilidad: sola nuestra fe divina nos hace ciertos y firmes, que dura para siempre jamas." (*Ibid.*, 443b.)

the traditional arguments based on the immateriality of some of the operations of the rational soul. On the other hand, human reason can destroy the arguments proving that the soul is in fact corruptible and mortal. The very title of the chapter accurately describes its content; "Where it is shown that, although the rational soul is in need of the temper of the four [*sic*] qualities to reside in the body and to be able to reason and discourse, it does not follow that it is mortal or corruptible." To infer the corruptibility of the soul from its dependence upon brain is to repeat Galen's erorr, who always held the truth of the soul's immortality in doubt for such "minor reasons."

> Galen had no reason to entangle himself in such flimsy reasoning; all work performed by the mediation of an instrument can be defective without it being the fault of the main agent, according to natural philosophy. The painter who paints well with a brush which suits his artistry, is not to blame when he paints poor shapes with a poor brush; and it is not a good argument to say that the writer had an imperfection in his hand, when through default of a well-made pen he was forced to write with a stick.[30]

To say that the human soul is poor in intelligence because the brain is too wet does not denote an imperfection of the soul itself, only an imperfection of the instrument it uses to reason and discourse. This dependence in no way proves that the nature of the main agent is the same as the nature of the instrument it is forced to use in the course of this earthly life. It is not necessary to follow Huarte, step by step, in his refutation of Galen. The intent of the chapter is very clear. The reliance of the soul upon the material condition of the brain does not necessarily involve the material condition of the soul itself, but it is enough to weaken and to cast doubt on the traditional arguments in favor of the immortality of the soul. Thus the only refuge left is Christian Faith in Divine revelation.

2. *The Pedagogical Application*

The *Examen de Ingenios* is an eloquent expression of Renaissance faith in social improvement through education. The aim of the book is clearly formulated in its dedication to Philip II:

[30] "Pero no tuvo razon Galeno de embarazarse con tan livianos argumentos, porque las obras que se hacen mediante algun instrumento, no se colige bien en filosofía natural haber falta en el agente principal, por no salir acertadas. El pintor que dibuja bien teniendo el pincel cuando conviene á su arte, no tiene culpa cuando en el malo hace les figuras vorradas y de mala delineacion; ni es buen argumento pensar que el escribano tenía alguna lesion en la mano cuando por falta de pluma bien cortada le fué forzado escribir con un palo." (*Ibid.*, 443b.–444a.)

To the end that the work of our productive men reach the perfection which the welfare of the republic demands, I think, Royal Catholic Majesty, that a law should be promulgated that no carpenter be allowed to do the job of a farmer, nor a tailor that of architect, nor a lawyer that of physician, nor a physician that of lawyer, but that each one exercise only that art for which he has a natural talent... Now, to the end that he may not make a mistake in choosing that profession which best fits his own nature, there should be some deputies in the commonwealth, some men of great prudence and knowledge, able to discover the wit of every child and to force him to study a specific science aggreeable to him, rather than leaving him a free choice ...[31]

The introduction to the *Examen*, drawing on the authority of Plato, spells out in detail what Huarte calls "three true conclusions" (*tres conclusiones muy verdaderas*) which in fact are the undisputed assumptions of his general theory:

The first is that of many varieties of wit to be found among men, only one is eminent in every individual ...
The second is that only one science corresponds to each type; so much so that unless you choose the right one, you will be mediocre in the others, even if you work day and night.
The third is, that after discovering which discipline is best adapted to your personal wit, there is still another problem, namely, to know whether your talent is better suited to the theory or to the practice of it, because these two kinds of wit are so different from each other that where there is one, the other is missing.[32]

The second half of the book, which begins with Chapter XI, tries to show the correspondence between individual gifts and specific sciences.

[31] "Para que las obras de los artífices tuviesen la perfecion que convenia al uso de la república, me pareció, Católica Real Majested, que se habia de establecer una ley. Que el carpintero no hiciese obra tocante al oficio del labrador, ni el tejedor del arquitecto, ni el jurisperito curase, ni el médico abogase, sino que cada uno ejercitase sólo aquel arte para el que tenía talento natural, y dejase los demas.

"Y porque no errase en elegir la que á su natural estaba mejor, habia de haber diputados en la república, hombres de gran prudencia y saber, que en la tierna edad descubriesen á cada uno su ingenio, haciéndole estudiar por fuerza la ciencia que le convenia y no dejarlo á su eleccion." (*Ibid.*, 403a.)

[32] "La primera es, que de muchas diferencias de ingenio que hay en la especie humana, sola una te puede, con eminencia, caber, si no es que naturaleza, como muy poderosa, al tiempo que te formó, echó todo el resto de sus fuerzas en juntar solas dos ó tres, ó por más no poder, te dejó estulto y privado de todas.

La segunda, que á cada diferencia de ingenio le corresponde, en eminencia, sola una ciencia no más; de tal condicion, que si no aciertas á elegir la que corresponde á tu habilidad natural, tendrás de las otras gran remision aunque trabajes dias y noches. La tercera, que despues de haber entendido cuál es la ciencia que á tu ingenio más le corresponde, te queda otra dificultad mayor por averiguar, y es: si tu habilidad es más acomodada á la práctica que á la teórica, porque estas dos partes (en cualquier género de letras que sea) son tan opuestas entre sí y piden tan diferentes ingenios, que la una á la otra se remiten como si fuesen verdaderos contrarios." (*Ibid.*, 404 a.–b.)

Throughout this part of the book the word 'wit' (*ingenio*) is used almost exclusively to signify "learning ability." At the beginning of the chapter Huarte proclaims, with great self-assurance and no small amount of dogmatism, the division of the sciences according to the dominant role in them by one of the three hegemonic faculties:

The arts and sciences which are developed by memory are Latin, Grammar, or any other language, theory of Law, Positive Theology, Cosmography, and Arithmetic. Those which belong to the Understanding are Scholastic Theology, Theoretical Medicine, Logic, Natural and Moral Philosophy, and the Practice of Law. All the arts and sciences which require shape, proportion, harmony and interrelated parts, such as Poetry, Eloquence, Music, the Art of Preaching, the Practice of Medicine, Mathematics, Astrology, Government, Art of Warfare, Painting, Drawing, Writing, Reading, and the art of being pleasant, witty and practical, are derived from a good imagination. The talent of the handyman, all the devices and engines which artificers make, the art of dictating different matters to four different writers in good order and sense – a special skill which vulgar people admire very much – also belong to the imagination.[33]

Huarte admits that it would be endless (*Sería nunca acabar*) to prove each one of those assignments. By way of example he attempts to prove that learning languages is mostly a matter of memory, that scholastic theology 'belongs' to the domain of the understanding, and that poetry lies in the realm of the imagination. The first of these examples gives Huarte a chance to discuss a fashionable topic: the nature of language and the merits of the vernacular:

In the catalogue of sciences which we ascribed to memory we placed Latin and the other languages spoken in the world. Nobody will deny this: because languages were invented by man to communicate, and to explain their concepts to each other. There is no other hidden mystery in the existence of language but that men, as Aristotle said, just decided to agree upon framing words and giving each one its own signification. From this there grew such a great number of words and manners of speech, far beyond any rule of reason, that if man had no memory, no other faculty would help him to learn a language. How little understanding and imagination help in this

[33] "Las artes y ciencias que se alcanzan con la memoria son las siguientes: gramática, latin y cualquier otra lengua; la teórica de la jurisprudencia, teología positiva, cosmografía y aritmética. Las que pertenecen al entendimiento son: teología escolástica, teórica de la medicina, la dialéctica, la filosofía natural y moral, la práctica de la jurispericia que llaman abogacía. De la buena imaginativa nacen todas las artes y ciencias que consisten en figura, correspondencia, armonía y proporcion: éstas son poesía, elocuencia, música, saber predicar, la práctica de la medicina, matematicas, astrología, gobernar una república, el arte militar, pintar, trazar, escribir, leer, ser un hombre gracioso, apodador, pulido, agudo in agibilibus, y todos los ingenios y maquinamientos que fingen los artifices, y tambien una gracia de la cual se admira el vulgo, que es dictar á cuatro escribientes junto materias diversas, y salir todas muy bien ordenadas." (*Ibid.*, 447a.)

matter can be proved by the fact that a child, who lacks those two faculties more than at any other age, learns languages more readily than do mature men, although they are endowed with better understanding. Experience confirms this: how often do we see a Basque who comes to live in Castile at the age of thirty or forty [Probably Huarte's own father and mother. – Translator's note] and never learns the Castilian language; but if he had come as a boy [Himself? – Translator's note] after two or three years you would think that he had been born in Toledo . . .

Since languages are nothing but a contrivance of man, it stands to reason that sciences can be taught in any language, and that it is possible to say the same thing in all languages. Hence none of the great authors of the past had to look for a foreign language to express their concepts; the Greeks wrote in Greek, and the Romans in Latin, and Moors in Arabic, and I do so in Spanish (*en mi Español*), which is the language I know best.[34]

Chapters XII to XVII deal specifically with the following disciplines: Rhetoric (XII), Theology (XIII), Law (XIV), Medicine (XV), Art (?), War (XVI), and Government (XVII). The main purpose of these lengthy and poorly organized chapters was to establish the triadic relation, dominant quality-wit-discipline, which sustains Huarte's theory. The amazingly neat results of Huarte's inquiry can be appreciated in the following chart:

Prevalent quality of the brain	Prevalent mental power	Most fitting discipline and profession
Humidity	Memory	Languages Theory of Law Positive Theology Geography Arithmetic

[34] "En el catálogo de ciencias que dijimos pertenecer á la memoria pusimos la lengua latina y las demas que hablan todas las naciones del mundo; lo cual ningun hombre sabio puede negar, porque las lenguas fué una invencion que los hombres buscaron para poder entre sí comunicarse, y explicar los unos á los otros sus conceptos, sin haber en ello más misterio ni principios naturales de haberse juntado los primeros inventores, y á buen pláceme, como diijo Aristóteles (lib. 1 De interpret.), fingir los vocablos y dar á cada uno su signifiacion. Resultó de alli tanto número de ellos, y tantas maneras de hablar, tan sin cuenta ni razon, que si no otra potencia, ésta es imposible poderse comprender. Cuán impertinente sea la imaginativa y el entendimento para aprender lenguas y maneras de hablar pruébalo claramente la niñez, que con ser la edad en la cual el hombre está más falto de estas dos potencias con todo eso, dice Aristóteles (30 sect. probl. 3) que los niños aprenden mejor cualquiera lengua que los hombres mayores, aunque son más racionales. Y sin que lo diga nadie nos lo muestra la experiencia; pues vemos que si á Castilla viene á vivir un vizcaino de treinta á cuarenta años, jamas aprende el romance, y si es muchacho, en dos ó tres años parece nacido en Toledo. De ser las lenguas un plácito y antojo de los hombres y no más, se infiere claramente que en todas se pueden enseñar las ciencias, y en cualquiera se dice y declara lo que á la otra quiso sentir. Y así ninguno de los graves autores fué á buscar lengua extranjera para dar á entender sus conceptos; ántes los griegos escribieron el griego, los romanos en latin, los hebreos en hebreo, y los moros en arábigo, y así hago yo en mi español, por saber mejor esta lengua que otra ninguna." (*Ibid.*, 447a.–b.)

Heat	Imagination	Poetry, Eloquency, Music Practice of Medicine Politics
Dryness	Intelligence	Theology Theory of Medicine Philosophy Practice of Law

Huarte was aware of the artificiality of this clear-cut trichotomy as is shown by his insecure manner in refuting the possible objections of the reader. Having decided that the theorist of the Law is a "memory-type" and the practitioner of the Law an "understanding-type," Huarte writes:

> There is a possible objection to this doctrine, apparently a serious one. If the understanding has to submit a particular case to the Law, and defines it by making the proper distinctions, limitations, generalizations, and inferences, and if understanding is the faculty which has to respond to the arguments of the other party, how is all this possible unless memory first presents all the specifications of the Law to the understanding? This argument certainly proves that the perfect lawyer ought to have a powerful intelligence and an excellent memory, a conclusion I am willing to accept. But, what I really meant was, that since it is impossible to find great intelligence with great memory, it is better for the lawyer to be of sharp intelligence and poor memory than vice versa, because there are many remedies for a poor memory, such as books, files, notes, and other human devices; if intelligence is lacking, nothing can be done about it.[35]

One of the most startling conclusions of this theory was the emphasis on the alleged incompatibility between different gifts, abilities, and professions. Since eloquence is a combination of memory and imagination (humidity and heat), it excludes a high degree of intelligence (dryness). Biblical and Patristic theologians constantly need the leadership of scholastic theology "if they do not want to wake up and find themselves facing the Inquisition" (*si no quieren amanecer en la Inquisición*). The reason, according to Huarte, is very simple:

[35] "Pero una dificultad se ofrece en esta doctrina, y al parecer no es liviana, porque si el entendimiento es el que asienta el caso en la propia ley que lo determina, distinguiendo, limitando, ampliando, infiriendo y respondiendo á los argumentos de la parte contraria, como es possible hacer esto el entendimiento, si la memoria no le pone delante todo el derecho? Este argumento prueba que es necesario que para que él abogado tenga perfeccion se junten en el grande entendimiento y mucha memoria, lo cual yo confieso; pero lo que quiero decir es que ya que no se hallar grande entendimiento con mucha memoria (por la repugnancia que hay), que es mejor que el abogado tenga mucho entendimiento y poca memoria, que mucha memoria y poco entendimiento, porque para la falta de memoria hay muchos remedios, como son, los libros, las tablas, abecedarios y otras invenciones que han hallado los hombres; pero si falta el entendimiento, con ninguna cosa se puede remediar." (*Ibid.*, 462a.)

Those who are endowed with a combination of memory and imagination, courageously embark on the interpretation of the Holy Scripture, convinced that, because they master Latin, Greek, and Hebrew, they have everything needed to find the spirit of the text (*el espíritu verdadero de la letra*), but in reality they are lost. Firstly, because the words and manners of speech of the Scriptures have more meanings than those Cicero knew in Latin. Secondly, because such people lack the understanding to verify whether a Catholic or a depraved meaning is intended; understanding is the faculty which can select the truest and most Catholic statement from among the two or three most likely meanings of the text.[36]

The incompatibility between the theoretical and practical mastery of any art applies to all disciplines without exception. The legal expert does not make a prudent judge or a persuasive barrister. The former memorizes the letter of the Law but subjects his understanding to that of the law-giver; the latter excels in understanding the Law in order to subsume the concrete, singular case under the universal provision of the Law. A professor of medicine has to be a man of great memory and sharp intellligence – a most rare combination – but the practitioner of medicine has to be generously endowed with imagination, "just one degree less than that of the poets," to find the chain of causes and effect. Courage excludes prudence, intelligence excludes excellence in style, theoretical understanding makes practical skill impossible. "These are hard facts," Huarte comments, "but what is even harder is that there is no appeal to these limitations nor any pretense that we have been unfairly treated." There is only one profession which requires the perfect balance of all qualities and talents, that of being a King.

We still have to show to the different wit to which the art of being a King belongs – a King as the commonwealth expects a King to be – and to list the signs by which we might recognize the man who has such art and ability . . . Of the nine temperaments which mankind possesses, only one makes man as prudent as possible, wherein the first qualities are so balanced that heat does not exceed cold, nor is there more moisture than dryness, but are found in such proportion and harmony as if in reality they were not contrary to each other. *Hence* a perfect instrument results, so well adapted to the operations of the rational soul, that man has a perfect memory of things past, a great ima-

[36] "Los que alcanzan esta junta de imaginativa y memoria entran con grande ánimo á interpretar la divina Escritura, pareciéndoles que por saber mucho hebreo, mucho griego y latin, tienen el camino andado para sacar el espiritu verdadero de la letra, y realmente van perdidos. Lo uno, porque los vocablos del texto divino y sus maneras de hablar tienen otras muchas significaciones, fuera de las que supo Ciceron en latin. Lo otro, que á los tales les falta el entendimiento, que es la potencia que averigua si un espiritu es católico ó depravado; ésta es la que puede elegir con la gracia sobrenatural, de dos ó tres sentidos que salen de una letra, el que es más verdadero y católico." (*Ibid.*, 453 a.)

gination to foresee the future, and a sharp intelligence to distinguish, infer, argue, judge and to make the proper choices.[37]

Such an extraordinary combination, frequently formed in Greece, was extremely rare in Spain. In fact, Huarte confesses that he knew of only one case, his Royal Majesty Philip II, to whom he had dedicated his book!

For these principles to be applicable in practice, parents and educators were to know the "signs" (*señales*) which point to the different talents of the child. Some of the chapters under discussion end with a short inventory of the signs characteristic of a given *ingenio*. For instance, these are the signs for telling a future lawyer:

> The signs by which we know that the one who is going to study Law has a natural talent for it, have already been mentioned. But in order to refresh our memory and to prove it in more detail, let it be known that the child who learns the alphabet quickly is endowed with good memory . . . Also the ability to write fast and clearly reveals a good imagination. Therefore, the boy who uses his hand well within a few days and writes straight with neat letters of even size, gives evidence of poor intelligence, because that work is performed by the imagination, and these two powers, as noted before, are mutually incompatible.[38]

The military genius is known by many different signs, according to Huarte: he is pleasant, careless about his dress and external appearance, bald, sparing in words, of honest speech, lucky in his enterprises and long-lived. The man who has a natural gift to be a ruler ought to have golden hair, "between red and white," to be of good countenance, virtuous, long-lived, prudent, the father of many children, moderate in eating and drinking, self controlled, healthy and kind.

[37] "Solo conviene mostrar á qué diferencia de ingenio pertenece el arte de ser rey, y tal cual la república lo ha menester, y traer las señales con que se ha de conocer el hombre que tuviere tal ingenio y habilidad. De nueve temperamentos que hay en la especie humana, solo uno dice Galeno que hace al hombre prudentisimo en todo lo que naturalmente puede alcanzar, en el cual las primeras calidades están en tal peso y medida, que el calor no excede á la frialdad, ni la humedad á la sequedad, ántes se hallan en tanta igualdad y conformes, como si realmente no fueran contrarias ni tuviran oposicion natural. De lo cual resulta un instrumento tan acomodado á las obras de ánima racional, que viene el hombre á tener perfecta memoria para las cosas pasadas, y grande imaginativa para ver lo que está por venir, y grande entendimiento para distinguir, inferir, raciocinar, juzgar y elegir." (*Ibid.*, 484a.)

[38] "Con qué señales se podrá conocer si el que quiere estudiar leyes tiene la diferencia de entendimiento que esta facultad ha menester, ya lo hemos dicho atras en alguna manera, pero para refrescar la memoria y probarlo más por extenso, es de saber que el muchacho que puesto á leer conociere presto las letras y dijere con facilidad cada letra cómo se llama (salteada en el A B C), que es indicio de tener mucha memoria. Tambien el escribir con facilidad y hacer buenos rasgos y letras dijimos que descubria la imaginativa, y así el muchacho que en pocos dias asentáre la mano é hiciere los renglones derechos y letra pareja y con buena forma y figura, ya es mal indicio para el entendimiento, porque esta obra se hace con la imaginativa, y estas dos potencias tienen la contrariedad que hemos dicho y notado." (*Ibid.*, 464b.-465a.)

It is the duty of educators and State officials to pay due attention to these signs and thus to orient the student in the choice of his profession. This bold emphasis upon professional orientation supervised and enforced by the State gives Huarte's thought a sharp socialistic overtone, most unusual in the second half of the sixteenth century.[39]

This is the central thought of Chapters XII to XVII. This part of the book, however, is rich in interesting digressions. Besides the long-winded examples from classical and Biblical sources which Huarte – according to the fashion of the day – recites with evident gusto, the author takes his time to discuss the social role of the orator, theologian, lawyer, physician, soldier and ruler. The advantages and limitations of rhetorical education, the relation of scholastic and positive theology, the reformation of the law, the nature of Jurisprudence, the preparation for Medicine, the relation of theory and practice both in Law and Medicine, the ethical character of the military profession, the nature of war and the qualifications of the political ruler, were among the important subjects in the history of sixteenth century ideas discussed by Huarte with daring, novelty and insight. Together with these reflections these chapters also abound in less closely related discussions such as the benefits of learning chess, the ability of the Jews to study theoretical medicine, and the nature of original sin.[40]

By far the most interesting detour occurs in Chapter XIV, where Huarte reveals his empiricist and even skeptical leanings:

> We must admit that although understanding is the highest and most powerful faculty of man, there is none which errs as easily. That is what Aristotle meant when he said that the senses always are truthful, but that in most cases the understanding reasons badly. This is further confirmed by experience, for if it were not so, why should there be such diversity of opinions among philosophers of serious reputation, physicians, theologians and jurists, and so many disputes, so many opinions, although there is never more than one truth? We can see why the senses believe with such great certainty in their objects while the understanding is so easily fooled, when we consider that the objects of the senses and the species by which they are known have a

[39] See above, notes 31 and 16.
For Huarte's ideas on professional orientation, see C. A. Figuerido, *La orientación profesional y el médico navarro Juan de Huarte* (Bilbao, no date); J. M. Guardia, *Essai sur l'ouvrage de J. Huarte: Examen des aptitudes pour les sciences* (Paris, 1855); Gregorio Marañón, "Notas sobre Huarte," *Obras Completas* (Madrid, 1967), vol. 3, pp. 265–283; Antonio Simonena y Zabalegui, *Un precursor de la orientación profesional: El Doctor Juan Huarte* (San Sebastián, 1927); Ricardo Roya Vilanova, *La orientación profesional o El Examen de Ingenios en las vocaciones médicas* (Zaragoza, 1926).

[40] The latter had been discussed by C. M. Hutchings in his article "The '*EXAMEN DE INGENIOS*' and the Doctrine of Original Sin," *Hispania* (Stanford), XIX, (1936), pp. 273–82.

firm, real and stable being before they are actually known. The truth to be contemplated by the understanding, however, if it is not framed and shaped by the understanding itself, has no formal being of its own; it is entirely shapeless, its elements are scattered as in a building reduced to a mass of stones – earth, timber and tiles, with which it is possbile to construct as many errors as man can conceive with his imagination. . . . The senses are free, because the eyes do not provide the color, nor taste the different flavors, nor touch the palpable qualities; but all these are formed by nature before any of them can become acquainted with its object.

Because men forget about the bad and sad condition of their understanding, they dare to express their opinions with bold confidence, without knowing what kind of wit they possess and whether or not it corresponds to truth.

This variety of tastes and appetites is also found in the concepts of the understanding. If we bring a hundred men of learning together and ask them a particular question, each one will deliver a different judgement and reason in a different manner. One and the same argument will seem a fallacy to one, a probable argument to another, apodictic demonstration to a third. And this applies not only to different types of understanding, but experience shows that it applies also to one kind of understanding on different occasions: the same proof will convince a man at one, but not at another time. Thus men change their opinions every day. Some men improve their intelligence with the passing of time, recognizing the mistaken reasoning which moved them before; others, on the contrary, lose the good temper of their brains and in time come to hate Truth and love Error . . .[41]

[41] "Es de saber que aunque el entendimiento es la potencia más noble del hombre y de mayor dignidad, pero ninguna hay que con tanta facilidad se engañe acerca de la verdad como él. Esto comenzó Aristóteles (lib. De anima, cap. III) á probar, diciendo que el sentido siempre es verdadero, pero el entendimiento por la mayor parte raciocina mal. Lo cual se ve claramente por experiencia, porque si no fuese así, ¿habia de haber entre los graves filósofos, médicos, teólogos y legistas, tantas disensiones, tan várias sentencias, tantos juicios y pareceres sobre cada cosa, no siendo más de una la verdad? De dónde les nazca á los sentidos tener tanta certidumbre de sus objetos, y el entendimiento ser tan fácil de engañar con el suyo, bien se deja entender, considerando que los objetos de los cinco sentidos y las especies con que se conocen tienen sér real, firme y estable por naturaleza ántes que los conozcan. Pero la verdad, que el entendimiento ha de contemplar si él mismo no lo hace y no la compone ningun sér formal tiene de suyo, toda está desbaratada y suelta en sus materiales, como casa covertida en piedras, tierra, madera y teja, de los cuales se podran hacer tantos errores cuantos hombres llegasen á edificar con la imaginativa. De estos errores y opiniones están reservados los cinco sentidos, porque ni los ojos hacen el color, ni el gusto los sabores ni el tacto las calidades tangibles; todo está hecho y compuesto por naturaleza ántes que cada uno conozca su objecto. Por no estar advertidos los hombres en esta triste condicion del entendimiento se atreven á dar confiadamente su parecer, sin saber con certidumbre cuál es la manera de su ingenio, y si se compone bien ó mal la verdad. Toda esta variedad de gustos y apetitos extraños se halla en las composturas que el entendimiento hace; porque si juntamos cien hombres de letras, y les proponemos alguna cuestion, cada uno hace juicio particular y razona de diferente manera: un mismo argumento á uno parece razon sofistica, á otro probable, y á otro le concluye como si fuese demostracion. Y no sólo tiene verdad en diversos entendimientos, pero áun vemos por experiencia que una misma razon concluye á un mismo entendimiento en un tiempo, y en otro no. Yasi vemos cada dia mudar los hombres el parecer, unos cobrando con el tiempo más delicado entendimiento, conocen la falta de razon que ántes los movia, otros perdiendo el buen temperamento del cerebro, aborrecen la verdad y aprueban la mentira." (*Examen de Ingenios*, ed. cit., 462b.–463b.)

Huarte's faith in education shares the naturalistic assumption of Northern Humanism, that the improvement of man's individual and social life depended more upon the proper refinement of his natural powers through education, than upon the orthodoxy of his religious beliefs. The influence of Vives upon Huarte in this connection is undeniable. All the naturalistic ingredients of Huarte's pedagogy were formulated by Vives forty years before publication of the *Examen:* the criticism of authority, the importance of observation and uselessness of excessive speculation; the pragmatic character of knowledge and interaction between the passional and cognitive faculties of man; the psychological foundations of pedagogy and the educational responsibility of secular powers; the impact of the environment upon the individual and the importance of hygiene; the diversity of individual talents and the need for professional orientation. On the other hand, Huarte's insistence upon the limitations of man's natural talents to one given discipline, and consequently to one specific role in the organic structure of society, pointed toward an emphasis on specialization totally opposed to the more Italian Renaissance ideal of the well-rounded individual.

3. Eugenics and Dietetics

The last and by far the longest of the *Examen's* chapters (XVIII) carries the amazing title "In what manner parents may beget wise children possessing wit for learning." In this part of the book all the naturalistic premises of Huarte's thought inevitably lead to the most startling conclusions. If the learning ability of the child is correlated to the dominant quality of his brain, and if such quality is itself an hereditary trait received from the paternal and maternal seed, it ought to be possible to predetermine and control the wit of the off-spring through proper mating and breeding. Such is the conclusion of Huarte's thought. Thus, the last part of the book is supposed to be a practical manual on the proper mating of prospective parents, on sexual orientation, and on the proper breeding of children. This section is an incredible mixture of vision and gullibility, of primitive physiological theories and futuristic insights, of ridiculous examples and utopian expectations. The reader ought to beware of scorning the doctrine of this chapter too easily on account of its obsolete idiom and models; he should rather be encouraged to translate Huarte's thought into the contemporary paradigm of genes and chromosomes. Only thus will he be able to appreciate the daring, originality, and incredible foresight of Huarte's thought.

The chapter is divided into five sections, some of them as long as the preceding chapters of the book. It opens with the following reflection:

It is worth noting that although nature is prudent and wise, full of power and insight; and although man is her most carefully planned creation, for every wise and prudent man she provides, an infinite number of men are born without any wit. Having asked myself about the reasons for this, I discovered for myself that parents approach the sexual act in ignorance of the art and order established by nature and of the conditions which ought to be observed if children are to be born prudent and wise.[42]

To beget wise children, then, is an *art* which needs to be learned. Man has neglected this art because "in the moment of copulation, out of a feeling of modesty, he forgets to practice the diligence necessary for the child to partake in the wisdom of his father." This feeling of natural modesty results from the union of the soul with a body "similar to that of the beasts." Out of modesty man can inflict serious damage to himself on different occasions:

We find men so modest that although they have a terribly strong desire to urinate, they cannot do it if somebody is looking at them, whereas left alone, they urinate right away . . . And the same happens to the seed with relation to the seminal vessels, as happens to the urine with relation to the bladder. For in the same way that urine irritates the bladder, the seed damages the vessels. And Aristotle's opinion that man and woman do not endanger their health by retaining the seed is contrary to the judgement of all physicians, especially of Galen, who teaches that many women who were widowed in their youth lost their senses, motion, the proper method of breathing, and finally their lives. And Aristotle himself tells of many diseases men suffer for being chaste.[43]

[42] "Cosa es digna de grande admiracion, que siendo naturaleza, tal cual todos sabemos, prudente, mañosa, de grande artificio, saber y poder; y el hombre una obra quien ella tanto se esmera; y para uno que hace sabio y prudente, cria infinitos faltos de ingenio. Del cual efecto buscando la razon y causas naturales, he hallado por mi cuenta que los padres no se llegan al acto de la generacion con el órden y concierto que naturaleza estableció, ni saben las condiciones que se han de guardar para que sus hijos salgan prudentes y sabios. Porque por la misma razon que en cualquiera region templada ó destemplada naciere un hombre muy ingenioso, saldrán otros cien mil, guardando siempre aquel mismo órden de causas, si esto pudiésemos remediar con arte, habriamos hecho á la república el mayor beneficio que se le podria hacer." (*Ibid.*, 490b.)

[43] "La misma proporción dice Galeno que tiene la simiente con los vasos seminarios que la orina con la vejiga. Porque de la manera que la mucha orina irrita la vejiga para que la echen de allí, así la mucha simiente molesta los vasos seminarios. Y pensar Aristóteles que el hombre y la mujer no vienen á enfermar y morir por retencion de simiente es contra la opinion de todos los médicos, mayormente de Galeno, el cual dice y afirma que muchas

Before going into this subject matter, Huarte promises the reader to respect a certain measure of propriety and to deal with the problems of sexuality in a delicate, but frank manner:

Taking into account this natural modesty of the ear, I have endeavored to avoid crude and rough terms and to use only delicate and indirect manners of speech. Wherever I failed in this purpose, I apologize to the reader. For one of the things most important to the republic is to perfect the art by which men produce children, so that these may be born virtuous, gentle and healthy, and be able to enjoy a long life.[44]

Huarte first of all tackles the problem of sterility. "The first task is to show the qualities and temper which man and woman ought to possess in order to procreate." Here Huarte presents his theory of sex differentiation. The distinction between male and female is a difference in development, such that both sexes possess a primitive stage of common sexuality. The source of this distinction is the difference in the amount of heat. Heat of a certain temperature expands the genitalia out of the body in the case of the male, while a lower degree of heat keeps the sex organs inside the female body. Sex changes and intermediate forms of sex are not only possible and frequent, but also the physiological explanation of homosexuality, bisexuality, hermaphroditism, and androgynic personalities. Huarte derives the conditions of fertility for man and woman from this very theory. A fertile woman is the one who obviously possesses the two qualities – humidity and coldness – which determine her feminity:

In order to be fertile, Aristotle says, women have to be cold and moist; otherwise they could not have the menstrual flow, nor the milk to retain the fetus in their wombs for nine months and for feeding the child for two years after its birth.

All philosophers and physicians maintain that the belly of a woman has the same relation to man's seed as the earth has to wheat or other grain. If the earth is not cold and moist the farmer does not dare to sow therein. The most fertile soils are those which are more cold and moist, as in the northern regions of England, Flanders and Germany, whose abudance of fruit aston-

mujeres, quedando mozas y viudas, vinieron á perder el sentido y movimiento, el pulso y la respiracion, y tras ello la vida.

Y el mismo Aristóteles cuenta muchas enfermedades que padecen los hombres continentes por la misma razon." (*Ibid.*, 491a.–b.)

44 "Tomando, pues, en cuenta esta honestidad natural del oido, procuré salvar los términos duros y ásperos de esta materia, y rodear por algunas maneras blandas de hablar; y donde no se pudiere excusar, habráme de perdonar el honesto lector; porque reducir á arte perfecta la manera que se ha de tener para que los hombres salgan de ingenio muy delicado, es una de las cosas que la república más ha menester. Allende que por la misma razon nacerán virtuosos, gentiles hombres, sanos y de muy larga vida." (*Ibid.*)

ishes those ignorant of the reason for it. And in countries like these no married woman was ever unable to have a child, [Here an early English translator wrote on the margin of the page: 'you are much mistaken'.] nor do they know what sterility means; they are all prolific because of the coldness and humidity.[45]

That Huarte was not in the least concerned about the obvious exaggeration of his claim that English, Flemish and German women were never sterile, is a clear indication of his compulsion to use artificial and grand generalizations adapted to the preconceived schemes of his mind.

The conditions for male fertility are not as clear-cut and limited as are those for females. Men can be hot and dry (the most 'masculine' combination), but also hot and wet. The combinations cold-wet (women) and dry (or wet)- hot (men) admit of three different degrees which are characterized by certain 'signs' (*señales*) as the following chart shows:

DEGREES OF COLD-WETNESS	SIGNS for women						
	WIT	BEHAVIOR	VOICE	WEIGHT	SKIN	HAIR	BEAUTY
1	sharp	rough	deep	light	dark	much	ugly
2	standard	normal	mezzo	moderate	fair	blonde not much	very pretty
3	poor	pleasant	high	heavy	very fair	blonde scarce	beautiful
DEGREES OF DRY-HEAT	SIGNS for men						
1	good			weak,			
1	good memory	delicate	high	weak, light	fair	blonde	handsome
2	good understanding	easy going	mezzo	moderate	normal	normal	normal

[45] *Ibid.*, 492 b. "La mujer para ser fecunda dice Aristóteles que ha de ser fria y húmeda, porque si no fuese, era impossible venirle la regla ni tener leche para sustentar nueve meses la criatura en el vientre, y dos años despues de nacida toda se la gastára y consumiera.

La misma proporcion dicen todos los filósofos y médico que tiene el útero con la simiente viril, que tiene la tierra con el trigo ó cualquiera otra semilla, y vemos que si la tierra no está fria y húmeda, los labradores no osan sembrar ni se traba la simiente. Y entre las tierras, aquellas son más fecundas y abundosas en fructificar que tienen más frialdad y humedad, como parece por experiencia, considerando los lugares de Norte, Inglaterra, Flándes y Alemania, cuya abundancia en todo lo frutos espanta á los que no saben la razon y causa; y en tales tierras como éstas, ninguna mujer casándose, jamas dejó de parir, ni saben allá qué cosa es ser esteril; todas son fecundas y prolificas, por la mucha frialdad y humedad." (*Ibid.*, 491b.)

3	good imagination	proud, witty, a "lover"	deep	muscular	dark	much (beard)	ugly

Based upon these theoretical principles and practical signs of recognition Huarte finds it surprisingly easy to decide "which type of woman ought to marry a certain type of man, so that they may have children" (Article II). Fertility results from the proper balance of heat and coldness, humidity and dryness, and therefore results in the proper mating of men and women. Women are not completely sterile and in most cases at least, sterile only in relation to a given type of man. "There are men who are unable to procreate with certain women, but with others they are fertile and beget children." Experience proves, Huarte claims, "that couples separate upon pretence of impotency; thus he takes another wife, and she takes another husband, and both have children." The ideal combinations for fertility are:

Woman first degree cold and wet with man first degree hot and dry or with man second degree hot and wet (but danger of early miscarriage).
Woman third degree cold and wet with man third degree hot and dry.
Woman second degree cold and wet with man second degree hot and dry or with man second degree hot and wet.

Combinations which would certainly produce sterility would be a woman in the first degree of coldness and wetness – a woman of sharp intelligence, deep voice, light weight, much body hair, rough and ugly – with a man in the third degree of heat and dryness – a man of vivid imagination, witty, muscular, bearded, ugly, strong, and of dark complexion.

Having 'solved' the problem of sterility Huarte proceeds to show the 'art' of having boys instead of girls (Article III). Such 'art' is extremely important, firstly, because "girls, on account of the cold and moisture of their sex, cannot be endowed with a sharp intelligence;" and, secondly, because the order of nature has been altered to the point that "today six or seven females are born for every male." The order of nature "at the beginning of the world and for many years thereafter" was that two children were always conceived at one time, one male and one female." The purpose of this natural disposition was, "that there should be a wife for every man so that mankind could increase more speedily." This entirely fantastic assumption was complemented by an equally misinformed physiological theory about the difference between the right and the left testicles:

In addition to this nature did another admirable thing: she gave a great deal of heat and dryness to the right kidney and right testicle, and much humidity and coldness to the left kidney and left testicle. Thus the seed which is formed in the right testicle comes out hot and dry, while the seed formed in the left testicle is cold and humid.[46]

Guided by this theory, Huarte felt able to guarantee the birth of a male child to those parents who followed his instructions closely. The first rule was for parents to eat hot and dry food, such as honey and white wine; but to avoid humid and cold food such as lettuce or brown bread [*sic*]. Second rule: to digest the food thoroughly.

The second instruction is to eat this food in moderate quantities, so that the stomach may digest it easily; because, although the food be hot and dry by nature, it turns cold and humid if the natural heat of the body fails to cook it . . . For this reason most rich and important people are burdened with more daughters than the humble and poor, for they eat and drink what their stomachs cannot digest . . .[47]

The third instruction is to "engage in more than just moderate physical exercise, to consume the excessive moisture of the body and to warm and dry it." This again is the reason why poor people, who eat little and work hard and have to walk a great deal, usually have strong, healthy boys, instead of the effeminate weaklings so frequently born to aristocratic parents. The fourth rule is to delay sexual intercourse until the seed is "well formed and mature." The intensity of sexual desire, increased by self-control and moderation, reveals the readiness of the seed to create a male. The fifth rule is to have intercourse six or seven days before the oncoming menstruation, because the male seed needs more food to support itself. That the fetus is male may be recognized by the beauty of the pregnant mother.

Hippocrates said that a woman pregnant with a male fetus looks beautiful and fair. The reason is that the intense heat of the boy consumes all the impurities which usually spoil the face of the mother, leaving it like a wet piece of cloth . . . The contrary happens when a woman conceives a girl. Because

46 "Con esto hizo naturaleza otra cosa digna de gran consideracion, y es, que al riñon derecho y al testículo derecho les dió mucho calor y sequedad, y al riñon izquierdo y al testiculo izquierdo mucha frialdad y humedad; por donde la simiente que se labra en el testículo derecho sale caliente y seca, y la del testículo izquierdo fria y húmeda." (*Ibid.*, 497b.)

47 "La segunda diligencia que dijimos, era comer estos manjares en tan moderada cantidad que el estomago los pudiese vencer; porque aunque los alimentos sean calientes y secos de su propia naturaleza, se hacen frios y húmedos si el calor natural no los puede cocer.Por donde, aunque los padres coman miel y beban vino blanco, harán la simiente fria de estos manjares, y de ella se engendrará hembra y no varon. Por esta razon la mayor parte de la gentle noble y rica padece este trabajo de tener muchas más hijas que los hombres necesitados; porque comen y beben lo que su estómago no puede gastar," (*Ibid.*, 498a.)

of the excessive coldness and humidity they eat very little and manifest a great deal of impurity. Thus the mother of a girl looks dry, and has thousands of perverse little whims, and needs twice the time to purify herself after the birth.[48]

The last rule to follow is to ensure that the seeds of both husband and wife enter into the right side of the womb, "for males are engendered in that place, which is next to the liver and therefore very hot." Huarte suggests this can easily be accomplished if, after copulation, the woman rests on her right side with her head down and her heels up. Having observed these rules, Huarte assures the reader," it is impossible for a female to be conceived."

The final part of this amazing sketch of eugenics instructs the parents on ways of conceiving boys who are witty and wise. This, unfortunately, is by far the longest, most contorted and incredible section of the entire chapter. Article IV begins with a wordy and obscure refutation of Aristotelian cosmology and Galen's theory of cosmic heat. The purpose of this digression is to show that the amount of heat communicated to the seed is not a cosmic event which defies human art and control, but rather a combination of actions skillfully controlled by man. Thus Huarte emphasizes the importance of food and drink to produce the right balance of qualities in the paternal seed and in the maternal menstrual blood, "the two ingredients which are required for the creation of a child." The rest of the chapter, and practically the rest of the book, provides a manual of dietetics whose details are of scarce interest, but which is symbolic of significance in expressing the concern of the Renaissance man with hygiene. Huarte recommends white bread, salt, partridges, and muscatel wine to sharpen the intelligence; trouts, salmon, lampreys and eels to strengthen the memory; pigeons, goats, garlic, onions, pepper and vinegar to develop the imagination. The problem in dietetics stems from the incompatibility of qualities. The concupiscible faculty thrives on heat, but wisdom requires dry cold. The threptic powers which are opposed to the cognitive faculties of the soul rely on hot humidity.

Article IV ends with a strange theory of sexual reproduction. Huarte

[48] "Y así dice Hipócrates que la mujer que ha concebido varon está de buen color y hermosa, y es que el niño, con su mucho calor, le come todos aquellos excrementos que suelen afear el rostro y llenarlo de paño.

Al reves acontece siendo el preñado de hembra, que por la mucha frialdad y humedad de su sexo, comen muy poco y hacen mucho excrementos. Y así la mujer que ha concebido hembra está seca y pañosa, y se le antojan mil suciedades, y en el parto ha de gastar doblados dias en mundificarse que si pariera varon." (*Ibid.*, 499b.)

accepts the Hippocratic teaching that when a male and a female seed (he uses the same word, 'seed,' for both the sperm and the ovum) fertilize each other, the more powerful of the two becomes the formative agent (*agente y formador*) and feeds on the other. "Nature provided that in the procreation of a creature two seeds should concur; once they are mingled together, the stronger should do the forming, and the other serve as nourishment." This theory explains how it is possible for women to become pregnant with the seed of dogs, bears, monkeys and even of fish [*sic*], "as many authentic stories confirm." But, mostly, it helps to clarify and explain the reason for some statistical data of great social significance.

Having said all this, finally we are now in a position to solve the main problem by saying that the children of intelligent men are almost always formed from their mother's seed, because the paternal seed (for reasons given above) is not good enough to procreate and only helps to nourish the maternal seed. Now the man who is formed from a woman's seed cannot be witty, because of the cold humidity of her sex. Hence it is certain that if a boy is born witty and sharp he was formed from his father's seed . . .

What is the reason that bastard children usually look like their fathers, and of a hundred legitimate children at least ninety look like and behave like their mothers? Secondly, why is it that bastards are usually kind, courageous and intelligent? Finally, why is it that if a bad woman becomes pregnant she cannot induce a miscarriage even if she takes much poison and bleeds herself, while the honest wife who has become pregnant by her husband can suffer a miscarriage very easily? . . .

The man who seeks a woman other than his own wife is filled with that fertile, well formed, and mature seed from which the fetus will necessarily be formed . . . The contrary happens in the case of legitimate children. Since married men always have their wives sleeping by their side, they never wait until the seed is mature and prolific; rather they ejaculate the seed with great violence and movement upon any small excitement, whereas in the case of women, (passive as they are during the carnal act), the seminal vessels [sic] never yield any seed unless it is well formed and mature . . . Therefore the father who wants a child formed from his own seed ought to withdraw from his wife for a few days, and wait until his seed has matured, and then it is certain that his seed will prevail, and the maternal seed will serve as nourishment . . .

The answer to the last question is that the fetus of bad women is almost always formed by the male's seed, which being small and strong fastens itself to the uterus with strong roots . . .[49]

[49] "De todo lo dicho, aunque nos hemos algo tardado, podrémos ya sacar respuesta para el problema principal, y es, que los hijos de los hombres sabios casi siempre se hacen de la simiente de sus madres, porque la de los padres, por las razones que hemos dicho, es infecunda para engendrar, y no sirve en la generacion más que de alimento. Y el hombre que se hace de simiente de mujer no puede ser ingenioso ni tener habilidad, por la mucha frialdad

The title of the last article (V) reads: "What efforts are to be made to preserve the wit of children after their birth." Huarte recommends special foods, hard work, moderate sleep, firm bedding, exposure to all kinds of weather, walking, discipline, games in moderation, and baths. The chapter ends with some thoughts on the perfection of Christ's brain, a part of the book the Inquisition found extremely uncouth. As in the case of professional orientation, Huarte did not hesitate to recommend the intervention of public authorities in directing the mating of prospective parents, and in the supervision of domestic hygiene.

To deal with the first point; we have already alleged on the authority of Plato, that in a well ordered commonwealth there ought to be some official supervisors of marriages (*casamenteros*), capable of knowing the attributes of the people to be married, so that they could assign to each man the woman who best fits his temper, and to each woman a man who corresponds to her qualities.[50]

4. The Moral Concern

Although the main thrust of the *Examen de Ingenios* is obviously the socio-

y humedad de este sexo (3). Por donde es cierto que en saliendo el hijo discreto y avisado, es indicio infalible de haberse hecho de la simiente de su padre.

Algunas dudas se ofrecen á los que tratan de entender muy de raiz esta materia; la respuesta de las cuales es muy facil en la doctrina pasada. La primera es, ¿de dónde nace que los hijos bastardos parecen ordinariamente á sus padres, y de cien legítimos los noventa sacan la figura y costumbres de las madres? La segunda, ¿por qué los hijos bastardos salen ordinariamente gentiles hombres, animosos y muy avisados? La tercera, ¿qué es la causa que si una mala mujer se empreña, aunque tome bebidas ponzoñosas para mover, y se sangre muchas veces, jamas echa la criatura; y si la mujer casada está preñada de su marido, con livianas causas viene á mover?

Luego el hombre que va á buscar ia mujer que no es suya, ya va lleno de aquella simiente fecunda, cocida y bien sazonada; de la cual forzosamente se ha de hacer la generazion; porque en paridad, siempre la simiente del varon es de mayor eficacia, y si el hijo se hace de la simiente del padre, forzosamente le ha de parecer.

Al reves acontece en los hijos legítimos, que por tener los hombres casados la mujer siempre al lado, nunca aguardan á madurar la simiente ni que se haga prolífica: ántes con la contínua irritacion la echan de si, haciendo gran violencia y comocion; y como las mujeres están quietas en el acto carnal, nunca sus vasos seminarios dan la simiente sino cuando está cocida y bien sazonada y hay mucha en cantidad. Por donde las mujeres casadas hacen siempre la generacion, y la simiente de sus maridos sirve de alimento.

Por donde el padre que quisiere que su hijo se haga de su propia simiente, se ha de ausentar algunos dias de su mujer, y aguardar que se cueza y madure, y entónces cierto que él hará la generacion, y la simiente de su mujer servirá de alimento.

A la tercera duda se responde que el preñado de las malas mujeres casi sienpre se hace de la simiente del varon; como es enjuta y muy prolífica, trábase en el útero con fuertes raíces." (*Ibid.*, 515b.–516b.)

[50] "Venidos, pues, al primer punto, ya hemos dicho de Platon que en la república bien ordenada habia de haber casamenteros, que con arte supiesen conocer las calidades de las personas que se habian de casar, y dar á cada hombre la mujer que le corresponde en proporcion, y á cada mujer su hombre determinado." (*Ibid.*, 492a.)

pedagogical one, the book also betrays a constant concern with the triadic relation, 'temper of the brain-character-moral behavior.' In the second edition of the book Huarte added an entire chapter (V) "wherein it is discussed how much the temperament makes man prudent and moral." The chapter begins with a refutation of Galens's extreme naturalism. According to the Roman physician 'all the habits and powers of the rational soul parallel the temper of the body," to such an extent that the main task of the physician was truly "to weaken the vices of man and to introduce the opposite virtues."

Such an opinion is false and contrary to the common belief of moral philosophers who maintain that virtues are spiritual habits, inherent in the rational soul. The nature of the accident corresponds to the nature of the substance where it inheres. Furthermore, since the soul moves and the body is moved, the virtues reside in the agent, not in the patient. If virtues and vices were habits dependent on temperament, man would cease to be a free agent and would become a 'natural' agent, according to the good or bad appetites derived from his temperament. Besides, man's actions would not be subject to reward or punishment . . . Hence it should be understood that prudence and wisdom and all other virtues reside in the soul, and do not depend on the composition and temper of the body, as Hippocrates and Galen believed. It is, however, worth noting, that these two skilled physicians, together with Aristotle and Plato, held a wrong opinion on this matter.[51]

After this solemn proclamation of orthodox conservatism – which was not enough to appease the Spanish Inquisition – Huarte proceeded to present his own thought on the matter. In spite of his pretended moderation, Huarte occasionally seemed to relapse into the same kind of crude naturalism he began by condemning, proving beyond any doubt the dominant trait of his thought. In this particular case, as in many other sections of the *Examen*, one senses deeply troubled waters under the apparently calm surface.

Huarte's ideas on the relationship between bodily temperament and moral behavior are based upon certain philosophical and theological

[51] "Pero esta opinion es falsa y contraria al comun consentimiento de los filósofos morales, los cuales afirman que las virtudes son hábitos espirituales, sujetados en el alma racional; porque, cual es el accidente, tal ha de ser el sujeto donde cae; mayormente que como el alma sea el agente y movedor, y el cuerpo el que ha de ser movido más á propósito caen las virtudes en el que hace que en el padece, y si las virtudes y vicios fuesen hábitos que dependieran del temperamento, sequirse habia que el hombre obraria como agente natural, y no libre necesitado, con el apetito bueno ó malo que le señalase el temperamento, y de esta manera las buenas obras no merecerian ser premiadas ni las malas castigadas, Por donde se entiende que la prudencia y sabiduriá y las demas virtudes humanas están en el alma, y que no dependen de la compostura y temperamento del cuerpo, como pensaron Hipócrates y Galeno. Pero con todo eso, hace mucha fuerza que estos dos graves médicos, y con ellos Aristóteles y Platon, hayan dicho esta sentencia, y que no digan la verdad." (*Ibid.*, 421a.–b.)

assumptions. Philosophically speaking, one needs to point to the central position of the imagination in Huarte's theory of freedom. For him the imagination is the focal point where man's cognitive powers, volitions, emotions and physiological reactions become mutually interrelated in the process of human action. The imagination is free to choose its content by simply paying attention to it. The imagined object sends the vital spirits to the organs of the irascible faculty (the heart) and to the organs of the concupiscible faculty (the liver and testicles). The imaginations's influence upon the organs of irascibility and concupiscence through the mediation of the vital spirits is such that it can change the temper of those organs, thus facilitating or rendering more difficult the final decision of the will. However, Huarte emphasizes, saying that the imagination is free to choose its contents does not imply that it is not dependent on the previous temper of the organs and on the temper of the brain itself.

Theologically speaking, Huarte's thought was closely influenced by his own conception of original sin and the effects of Redemption on man's nature. One of the most interesting digressions of Chapter XVII (*See above* p. 240) is a short theological reflection on the nature of Adam. Huarte was convinced that man's nature is not conducive to virtue: the proper temper of brain, heart, liver, and testicles produces a combination which makes man, in most cases, inclined to vice.

Galen is mistaken on this point. For it is impossible to create a man perfect in all his powers, no matter how temperate his body might be. It is quite impossible to avoid the irascible and concupiscible faculties from being superior to reason, and from inciting man to sin. Therefore, however moderate a man may be, it is not right to let him follow his natural inclination without the restraints and corrections of reason.

. . . Hence it follows that a man who is well equipped and organized will have excessive heat in his heart, for otherwise the irascible faculty will be too weak; and if the liver is not very hot he will not be able to digest his food nor produce enough blood for his own nourishment; and if the testicles did not have more heat than coldness, man would be impotent since these organs are as strong as we have said, it necessarily follows that the brain will be disturbed by so much heat, one of the qualities which most hinders the use of reason; and what is even worse is that the will, although free, becomes inclined to surrender to the base appetites. Thus it is clearly shown that nature cannot make a man who will be perfect in all his powers and inclined to virtue.[52]

[52] "Pero en esto no tiene razon Galeno; porque es imposible componerse un hombre, que sea en todas sus potencias perfecto, como es el cuerpo templado; y que la irascible concupiscible no salga superior á la razon y la irrite á pecar. Y así no conviene dejar á ningun hombre (por templado que sea) que siempre siga la inclinacion natural, sin irle á la mano y

The theological confirmation of Huarte's theory was that although Adam was the most perfect man created (with the exception of Christ), "yet if God had not infused him with a supernatural ability to control his baser instincts, it would have been impossible (according to the principles of his own nature) for him not to be disposed to sin."

Considering the way in which the first man was created, it is easy to prove that it is against man's nature to be virtuous . . . Because the irascible and concupiscible faculties were so powerful on account of the great heat, and the rational faculties too weak and feeble to resist them, God provided Adam with a supernatural quality, which theologians call Original Justice by which the baser appetites were restrained, the rational element remained superior, and man tended to be virtuous. But when our first parents sinned, they lost this quality, and the irascible and concupiscible powers retained their natural strength and remained superior to reason . . . Hence it follows in good natural philosophy that whenever man wants to perform a virtuous act the contrary to the instincts of his flesh, it is impossible for him to carry it without the help of grace.[53]

Huarte's thought contains unorthodox views about man's nature and his dependence on grace to perform moral acts. That man needs supernatural help to undertake a virtuous act is not and never was Catholic doctrine; it is rather a Jansenist theory with a strong Lutheran flavor. In strict orthodox theology – from the point of view of the Spanish Inquisitors – man certainly needs God's help to conform to the Natural Law, but such help is not supernatural. Grace, in the strictly supernatural sense, is needed only to carry out acts of supernatural merit. Huarte never made this distinction perfectly clear, although in Chapter

corregirle con la razon. De aquí se infiere claramente que si el hombre está bien compuesto y organizado, ha de tener por fuerza calor excesivo en el corazon, sopena que la facultad irascible quedára muy remisa; y si el higado no es caliente en exceso, no podrá cocer los alimentos ni hacer sangre para la nutricion; y si los testículos no fuesen más calientes que frios, quedaba el hombre impotente y sin fuerza para engendrar. Por donde, siendo estos miembros tan fuertes como decimos, necesariamente se ha de alterar el cerebro con el calor, que es una de las calidades que mas perturba la razon, y lo que peor es, que la voluntad, siendo libre, se irrita é inclina á condescender con los apetitos de la porcion inferior. A esta cuenta parece que la naturaleza no puede hacer un hombre que sea perfecto en todas sus potencias, y sacarlo inclinado á virtud." (*Ibid.*, 485b.–486a.)

[53] "Cuán repugnante es á la naturaleza del hombre salir inclinado á virtud, pruébase claramente considerando la compostura del primer hombre. Siendo, pues, la facultad irascible y concupiscible tan poderosa por el mucho calor, y racional tan flaca y remisa para resistir, proveyó Dios de una calidad sobrenatural, que llaman los teólogos justicia original, con la cual se reprimen los ímpetus de la porcion inferior, y la parte racional quedó superior, y el inclinado á virtud. Pero en pecando, nuestros primeros padres perdieron esta calidad, y quedó la irascible y concupiscible en su naturaleza y superior á la razon. De esta doctrina se infiere en buena filosofía natural que si el hombre ha de hacer algun acto de virtud en contadiccion de la carne, es imposible poderlo obrar sin auxilio exterior de gracia." (*Ibid.* 486a.–487a.)

V he explicitly declared that his discussion had nothing to do with supernatural virtues.

Keeping these philosophical and theological views in mind, it is not hard to understand the position of our author on the relationship of temperament and moral behavior. As a rule (*ordinariamente*) men have moral habits which correspond to their temperaments. The reason being that to act against one's temperament requires a 'perfect virtue' and a painful effort. God Himself, in granting supernatural gifts to men, ordinarily takes the natural disposition of the individual into consideration. Fasting when the stomach has an insatiable appetite is indeed more difficult than after a good meal. To remain chaste is harder when the testicles are burning with passion than in cold, old, age. Coldness is the quality which helps virtue more because it weakens both the irascible and concupiscible powers of man. Thus sexuality is best controlled by fasting, corporal penance, and moderate sleep. The imagination of hell helps to cool off the natural heat of the body. Praying helps because it raises the heat of the brain, but makes the rest of the body cold and weak. The varying moral dispositions of man in his different stages of development confirm the close relationship of temperament and moral character. Childhood, which is hot and wet, makes man tender, shy, charitable, humble and chaste. Adolescence (14–25) is mild and temperate, most inclined to virtue and prudence. Youth (25–35), which is hot and dry, makes man most vulnerable to temptation. Maturity (35–45) again suggests moderate temper: the age of moral conversion. Old age, cold and dry, is the time of prudence and temperance. Similar considerations apply to sex and geographical location.

Huarte's moral concern permeates the entire *Examen de Ingenios*. In addition to chapter V, the book abounds in reflections on the impact of bodily temperament upon the mores of the individual. Thus, for instance, in discussing the dominant character of imagination in preachers, Huarte sounds a warning about the moral dangers of that profession.

> Those who have a strong imagination possess a very hot temperament and three principal vices spring from this quality in man: pride, gluttony and sensuality . . . Hence, such people try to interpret the Scriptures in ways which flatter their natural inclinations. They preach to the ignorant flock that priests are allowed to marry, that there is no need for Lent and fasting, and that people are not obliged to confess their sins to the priest in the Sa-

crament of Penance. With such tricks, misinterpreting the Scriptures, they glorify their own vices and force people to respect them as saints ...[54]

These are the leading ideas contained in Huarte's *Examen de Ingenios*. The book is also rich in numerous observations of unequal accuracy and interest which betray both the weakness and the virtues of Huarte's thought. Among the former we again have to mention Huarte's uncritical assumption of popular beliefs, his leaning toward sweeping generalizations, and the excusable reliance upon old-fashioned scientific models. The greatest virtues of the book are the independence, and relentless curiosity of the author.

As has been noted the *Examen de Ingenios* quickly became a European sensation in spite of its obvious defects and limitations. There is no doubt that Huarte's unique work drew much attention in the 17th century world of ideas. Father Iriarte has traced the book's influence on the thought and the literature of Spain.[55] Iriarte has also suggested the impact of Huarte upon such first-rate European thinkers as Bodin, Charron, Descartes, Sorel, Montesquieu, Rousseau, Bacon, Thomasius, Lessing (who translated the *Examen* into German), and Gall. Whether or not these relationships can be fully justified in each case, there is no doubt that Huarte's *Examen de Ingenios* was and remains an important document in the history of ideas.

[54] "Los que tienen fuerte imaginativa, ya hemos dicho atras que son de temperamento muy caliente, y de esta ealidad nacen tres principales vicios al hombre: soberbia, gula y lujuria; Y así trabajan de interpretar la Escritura divina de manera que venga bien con su inclinacion natural, dando á entender á los que poco saben, que los sacerdotes se pueden casar, y que no es menester que haya cuaresma ni ayunos, ni manifestar al confesor los delitos que contra Dios cometemos. Y usando de esta maña (con Escritura mal traida) hace parecer virtudes á sus malas obras y vicios, y que las gentes los tengan por santos." (*Ibid.*, 458a.)

[55] Iriarte, *El Doctor Huarte*, Chapter VII, pp. 275–333. The influence of Huarte upon Cervantes has been the object of much attention. See e.g., Rafael Salillas, *Un gran inspirador de Cervantes, El doctor Juan Huarte y su EXAMEN DE INGENIOS* (Madrid, 1905); A. Cuevas, *EL QUIJOTE y el EXAMEN DE INGENIOS* (Habana, 1917).

BIBLIOGRAPHY

Abad y Cavía, Fidel. *El dominico español Fr. Francisco de Vitoria y los principios modernos sobre el derecho de la guerra.* Madrid, 1905.

Albertini, Quiricus, *L'oeuvre de Fr. de Vitoria et la doctrine canonique du droit de la guerre.* Paris, 1903.

Alcocer Martínez, Mariano. *Historia de la Universidad de Valladolid.* Valladolid, 1928.

Allen, P. S. and H. M., eds., *Opus Epistolarum Des. Erasmi Roterodami.* Oxford, 1906–1965.

Allevi, Luigi, "Francisco de Vitoria e il renascimento della scolastica nel secolo XVI," *Rivista de Filosofia Neoscolastica,* XIX (1927), pp. 401–441.

Alonso, Dámaso. *Poesía Española.* 4th ed., Madrid, 1962.

Alonso Getino, Luis G. See *Getino.*

Arconada, Mariano. *Vida Pública de Fray Luis de León.* El Escorial, 1928.

Arigita y Lasa, Mariano. *El Doctor Navarro Martin de Azpilcueta y sus obras.* Pamplona, 1895.

Arjona, M. M. "Crítica de las Obras poéticas de Fray Luis de León," *La Ciudad de Dios.* XV, (1888), pp. 459–468.

Arriaga, G. de. *Historia del Colegio de San Gregorio de Valladolid.* Valladolid, 1928.

Artigas, Miguel. *Notas para la bibliografía del EXAMEN DE INGENIOS.* San Sebastián, 1928.

Azorín, Martínez, Ruiz, José. *Los dos Luises y otros ensayos.* Madrid, 1961.

Barcia Trelles, Camilo. *Francisco de Vitoria. Fundador del Derecho Internacional Moderno,* third part, "El derecho y la guerra," pp. 131–218. Valladolid, 1923.

Barthelémy, Joseph. *Francisco de Vitoria.* Paris, 1904.

Bataillon, Marcel. *Charles Quint et Son Temps,* "Charles-Quint, Las Casas, et Vitoria." Colloques Internationaux du Centre National de la Recherche Scientifique. Paris, 1949.

—. *Erasmo y España,* trans. Antonio Alatorre. México, 1950.

Bate, John Pawley. *Relectio De Indis,* ed. Ernest Nys. Washington, 1917.

Battaglia, F. *Cursos de Filosofía del Derecho,* trans. F. Elias de Tejada and P. Lucas Verdú. Madrid, 1951.

Baumel, Jean. *Le droit international public, la découverte de l'Amérique et les théories de Francisco de Vitoria.* Montpellier, 1931.

Bell, Andrey F. G. *Luis de León. A Study of the Spanish Renaissance.* Oxford, 1925.
—. "The Chronology of Fray Luis' Lyrics," *MLR*, XXI, (1926), pp. 168–177.
Beltrán de Heredia, Vicente. *El Maestro Francisco de Vitoria. Su naturaleza Vitoriana.* Vergara, 1932.
—. *La Patria del Maestro Francisco de Vitoria a la luz de la crítica histórica.* Vitoria, 1930.
—. *Los Manuscritos del Maestro Francisco de Vitoria.* Madrid, 1928.
—. "Accidentada y efímera aparición del nominalismo en Salamanca," *La Ciencia Tomista.* LXII (1942), pp. 77–78.
—. „En que año nació Francisco de Vitoria? Un documento revolucionario," *Anuario de la Asociación Francisco de Vitoria.* VI (1943–1945), pp. 1–29.
—. "Final de la discusión acerca de la patria del Maestro Vitoria: La prueba documental que faltaba," *La Ciencia Tomista.* April-June 1953, pp. 276–289.
—. "Ideas del Maestro Francisco de Vitoria anteriores a las Relecciones *De Indis* acerca de la colonización de América, Según documentos inéditos," *La Ciencia Tomista*, 122, March-April (1930), pp. 145–165.
—, Ed. *Francisco de Vitoria, O. P., Comentarios a la Secunda secundae de Santo Tomás.* Salamanca, 1932–1935.
—, Ed. *Summa Sacramentorum Ecclesiae ex doctrina Francisci a Vitoria.* Salamanca, 1566.
Bertini, G. M. *Influencia de algunos renacentistas italianos en el pensamiento de Vitoria.* Salamanca, 1934.
Beuve-Mery, H. *La théorie des pouvoirs publics d'après François de Vitoria et ses rapports avec le Droit contemporain.* Paris, 1928.
Biederlack, Joseph. "Das Verhaeltnis von Kirche und Staat bei Franz von Vitoria, O. P.," *Zeitschrift für Katholische Theologie.* Innsbruck, LI, (1927), pp. 548–555.
Blanco García, Francisco. *Fray Luis de León. Estudio biográfico.* Madrid, 1904.
—. "Acta de reposición de Fray Luis de León en una cátedra," *Revista de Archivos*, 1900.
—. "Segundo Proceso contra Fray Luis de León," *La Ciudad de Dios*, LXI (1896).
Blau, Joseph Leon. *The Christian Interpretation of the Cabala.* New York, 1944.
Bochenski, L. M. *A History of Formal Logic*, trans. Ivo Thomas. Indiana, 1961.
Boehner, Philotheus. Collected Articles on Ockham, ed. by Eligius M. Buytaert. ("Franciscan Institute Publications, Philosophy Series" No. 12).
—. *Medieval Logic. An Outline of its Development from 1250 to 1400.* Manchester, 1966.
Brandi, John. *The Emperor Charles V; the Growth and Destiny of a Man and of the World-Empire*, Eng. trans. C. V. Wedgwood. London, 1960.
Brown Scott, James. *The Spanish Origin of International Law, Francisco de Vitoria and his Law of Nations.* Oxford, 1934.
Bullón Fernández, Eloy. *El alma de los brutos ante los filósofos españoles.* Madrid, 1897.

—. *The Spanish Origin of International Law, Francisco de Vitoria and his Law of Nations*. Oxford, 1934.
Camón Aznar, José. *El Renacimiento y Fray Luis de León*. Cuenca, 1928.
Carrión, A. "Los maestros Vitoria, Bañez, y Ledesma hablan sobre la conquista y evangelización de las Indias," *La Ciencia Tomista*, Salamanca, XLII (1930), pp. 34–57.
Castan Tobenas, J. "El Derecho y sus rasgos en el pensamiento español," *Revista general de Legislación y Jurisprudencia*, XCVII (1949), pp. 646–707.
Castiglioni, Arturo. *A History of Medicine*. New York, 1958.
—. *The Renaissance of Medicine in Italy*. Baltimore, 1934.
Castro, Américo. *The Structure of Spanish History*. Princeton, 1954.
Catry, J. "La liberté du commerce international d'après Vitoria, Suarez et les scolastiques," *Revue générale de droit international public*. 1933, pp. 193 ff.
Cayuela, A. M. "Las grandes perspectivas cristianas en Fray Luis de León," *Razón y Fé*, LXXXVIII (1928).
Chacón, Pedro. *Historia de la Universidad de Salamanca*. Salamanca, 1569; ed. Antonio Valladares de Sotomayor, *Semanario Erudito*, VIII (1789), pp. 3–67.
Chenu, M. B. *L'Humanisme et la Réforme au Collège Saint-Jacques de Paris*, Archives d'histoire Dominicaine, Paris, 1946.
Chinchilla, Anastasio. *Anales históricos de la Medicina. Historia de la medicina española*. Valladolid, 1841.
Cobb, J. B. See *J. M. Robinson*.
Conning, Herman. *Opera Omnia*. Brunswich, 1730.
Coster, Adolphe. "Luis de León," *Revue Hispanique*, LIII (1921) pp. 1–468.
Cuevas, A. *EL QUIJOTE y el EXAMEN DE INGENIOS*. Habana, 1917.
Delos, J. T. "La doctrine de Monroe, la politique Américaine et les principes du droit public de Vitoria," *La Vie Intellectuelle*, I(1 928), pp. 461–475.
—. *La Société internationale et les principes du droit public*, Paris, 1929.
Dempf, Alois. *Christliche Staatsphilosophie in Spanien*. Salzburg, 1937.
Díaz de la Lastra. *El Burgalés Francisco de Vitoria*. Burgos, no date.
Diaz Güemes. See Díaz de la Lastra.
Diego, Gerardo. *Actualidad poética de Fray Luis de León*. Montevideo, 1930.
Diego, Sandelio. "Fray Luis de León y Francisco de Ribera en el Comentario de Abdias," *Estudios Eclesiásticos*. VIII (1929), pp. 5–22.
Diferman, B. "Estudio específico del Derecho Natural y Derecho Positivo según los clásicos agustinos españoles del siglo XVI," *La Ciudad de Dios*, CLXIX (1956), pp. 253–285.
—. "La orden agustiniana y los estudios jurídicos en la época clásica española," *Anuario de Historia del Derecho Espanol*, XXV (1955), pp. 775–790.
Dominguez Carretero, P. E. "La escuela teológica Agustiniana de Salamanca," *La Ciudad de Dios*, CLXIX (1956), pp. 638–685.
Dominguez, Ursino. "Fray Luis de León. Su doctrina acerca de la predestinación y reprobación," *La Ciudad de Dios*, CLIV (1942), pp. 65–84.
—. "Fray Luis de León. Su doctrina Mariológica," *Ibidem*, CLIV (1942), pp. 413–437.
Echard, J. et Quetif, J. *Scriptores Ordinis Praedicatorum Recensiti*. Paris, 1719–1721.

Ehrle, Franz. "Die Vaticanischen Handschriften der Salmantizenser Theologen des 16. Jh.," *Der Katholik*, Mainz, II (1884), pp. 495 ff.
Esperabé Arteaga, Enrique. *Historia de la Universidad de Salamanca.* 2 vols., Salamanca, 1914–1917.
Feijoó, Benito. *Teatro Crítico Universal.* Madrid, 1777.
Fernández Montana, L. *Los Covarrubias.* Madrid, 1935.
Fernández Quintana, Guillermo. "Las bases filosóficas de la teología de Fray Luis de León," *Revista de la Universidad de Madrid*, XIII (1963), pp. 346–367.
Figuerido, C. A. *La orientación profesional y el médico navarro Juan de Huarte.* Bilbao, no date.
Fitzmaurice-Kelly, James. *Fray Luis de León. A biographical fragment.* Oxford, 1921.
Golgado, Avelino. "Los tratados *De Legibus* y *De iustitia et iure* en los autores españoles del siglo XVI y primera mitad del XVII," *La Ciudad de Dios*, CLXXII (1959), pp. 225–302.
Galán, Eustaquio. "La teoría del poder público según Francisco de Vitoria," *Revista general de Legislación y Jurisprudencia.* Madrid, July–August, (1944).
García de Castro, Rafael. *Fray Luis de León, teólogo y escriturario.* Granada, 1928.
García de la Fuente, Olegario. "Un tratado inédito y desconocido de Fray Luis de León sobre los sentidos de la Escritura," *La Ciudad de Dios*, CLXX (1957), pp. 258–334.
García del Real, F. *Historia de la medicina en España.* Madrid, 1921.
García, Félix. See *Luis de León, Obras Completas.*
García, Ricardo. See *Villoslada, Ricardo G.*
Garzón Maceda, F. *La medicina en Córdoba.* Buenos Aires, 1916.
Getino, L. G. Alonso. *El Maestro Francisco de Vitoria y el Renacimiento filosófico-teológico del siglo XVI.* Madrid, 1914.
—. *El Proceso de Fray Luis de León.* Salamanca, 1906.
—. *La autonomía universitaria y la vida de Fray Luis de León.* Salamanca, 1904.
—. *Relecciones Teológicas del Maestro Vitoria.* 3 vols. Madrid, 1933–1935.
—. "Vitoria y Vives. Sus relaciones personales y doctrinales," *Anuario de la Asociación Francisco de Vitoria*, II (1931), pp. 277–309.
Giorgi, A. de. *Delle vita a delle opere di Alberico Gentili.* Parma, 1876.
Godet, Marcel. *La congrégation de Montaigu.* Paris, 1912.
González, Anselmo. "Guillermo de Ockham, *De Praedestinatione:* Introducción de Anselmo Gonzalez," *Ideas y Valores*, VI (1963–64), pp. 303–360.
González Palencia, Angel. *Fray Luis de León en la poesía castellana.* Madrid, 1942.
Grabmann, Martin. *Die Geschichte der Theologie.* Freiburg, 1933.
Guardia, J. M. *Essai sur l'ouvrage de J. Huarte: Examen des aptitudes pour les sciences.* Paris, 1855.
Gutiérrez, Constancio. *Españoles en Trento.* Valladolid, 1951.
Gutiérrez, P. David. "Del origen y caracter de la escuela teológica hispano-agustiniana en los siglos XVI y XVII," *La Ciudad de Dios*, CLIII, n. 2 (1941), pp. 227–255.
—. "La doctrina del Cuerpo Místico de Cristo en Fray Luis de León," *Revista Española de Teologia*, II, (1942), pp. 727–753.

Gutiérrez, Marcelino. *Fray Luis de León y la Filosofía Española del Siglo XVI.* Madrid, 1885.
Guy, Alain. *Les Philosophes Espagnols d'hier et d'aujourd'hui.* Toulouse, 1956.
Hall, Vernon. *A Short History of Literary Criticism.* New York, 1963.
Hamilton, Bernice. *Political Thought in XVI Century Spain.* Oxford, 1963.
Hernández Morejón, A. *Historia bibliográfica de la medicina española.* Madrid, 1842.
Hinojosa y Navarro. "Los precursores españoles de Grocio," *Anuario de Historia del Derecho Español,* Madrid VI (1910), pp. 220–236.
Hornedo, Rafael María. "Algunos datos sobre el petrarquismo de Fray Luis de León," *Razón y Fé,* LXXXV (1928), pp. 336–353.
Huarte, Juan. See *San Juan, Juan Huarte de.*
Humbert, A. *Les Origines de la Théologie Moderne.* (Vol. I) Paris, 1911.
Hutchings, C. M. "The '*EXAMEN DE INGENIOS*' and the Doctrine of Original Sin," *Hispania,* XIX (1936), pp. 273–82.
Iriarte, José, S. J. "Fray Francisco de Vitoria, del linaje de los Arcaya de Vitoria-Alava," *Hispania,* XXXVI (1952), p. 43.
Iriarte, Mauricio de. *El Doctor Huarte de San Juan y su EXAMEN DE INGENIOS. Contribución a la Historia de la Psicología Diferencial.* Madrid, 1948.
Jesús, Crisógono de. "El misticismo de Fray Luis de León," *Revista de Espiritualidad,* I (1942), pp. 30–52.
Kaltenborn, Karl. *Lehrbuch der Rechtsphilosophie.* Leipzig, 1848.
Klein, Anton. "Juan Huarte und die Psychognosis der Renaissance," Doctoral Dissertation. Bonn, 1913.
Kohler, Joseph. "Die Spanischen Naturrechtslehrer des 16. und 17. Jahrhunderts," *Archiv fuer Rechts- und Sozialphilosophie.* XXI, (1927), pp. 235–263.
—. „Die Spanischen Naturrechtslehrer des 16. und 17. Jahrhunderts," *Archiv fuer Rechts- und Wirtschaftsphilosophie.* X (1916), pp. 236 ff.
Kosters, J. "Les fondateurs du Droit des Gens," *Bibliotheca Visseriana.* Vol. 4, The Hague (1925).
Kottman, Karl. *Law and Apocalypse: The Moral Thought of Fray Luis de León. (1527–1591).* Vol. 44 of the International Archives of the History of Ideas. The Hague, 1972.
Labrousse, Roger. *Essai sur la philosophie politique de l'ancienne Espagne.* Paris, 1938.
Larequi, J. "El Derecho Internacional en España durante los siglos XVI y XVII," *Razón y Fé.* LXXXI (1927), pp. 222–232.
—. "Del *Ius Gentium* al Derecho Internacional," *Razón y Fé.* LXXXIII (1928), pp. 21–37.
Larramendi de Olarrea, María Luisa. *Miscelánea de noticias romanas acerca del D. Martin de Azpilcueta.* Madrid, 1943.
León, Luis de. *Cantar de los Cantares,* ed. Jorge Guillen. Madrid, 1936.
—. *Correspondencia. Documentos Inéditos para la Historia de España,* vol. XLI, Madrid, 1862.
—. *De Legibus,* ed. Luciano V. Pereña. Madrid, 1963.
—. *Informes Inéditos,* ed. Eustasio Esteban. *La Ciudad de Dios,* vol. XXVI.
—. *La Perfecta Casada,* ed. José Sanchez Rogerio. Madrid, 1912.

—. *Obras Completas Castellanas*, ed. Felix García O.I.A. 2 vols., Madrid, 1957.
—. *Obras latinas de Fray Luis de León*, ed. Blanco García. *La Ciudad de Dios.* CLIV (1942), pp. 413–437.
—. *Poesías de Fray Luis de León*, ed. A. C. Vega. Madrid, 1953.
—. *The Names of Christ*, trans. Edward J. Schuster. Binghamton, 1955.
—. "Escritos Latinos de Fray Luis de León," ed. Marcelino Gutiérrez. *La Ciudad de Dios*, XXII (1891).
—. "Segundo proceso contra Fray Luis de León," ed. Francisco Blanco García. *La Ciudad de Dios*, XLI (1896).
Leturia, Pedro. "Maior y Vitoria ante la Conquista de América," *Estudios Eclesiásticos*, XI (1932), pp. 44–83.
Lisarraga, Salvador. "Un texto de Francisco de Vitoria sobre la potestad política," *Revista de Estudios Políticos*, Madrid, April (1941).
López de Toro, José. "Fray Luis de León y Benito Arias Montano," *Archivo Agustiniano*, L (1956), pp. 6–28.
Losada, Angel. "Luis Vives en la actualidad internacional," *Revista de Filosofía*, VII (1952), pp. 151–155.
Lukasiewicz, Jan. "Zur Geschichte der Aussagenlogik," *Erkenntnis*, V (1935), p. 127.
Maravall, Juan Antonio. *Carlos V y el pensamiento político del Renacimiento.* Madrid, 1960.
Marañón, Gregorio. *Tres ensayos sobre la vida sexual.* Madrid, 1927.
—. "Notas Sobre Huarte," *Obras Completas*, III, pp. 265–282, Madrid, 1962.
Martínez Ruiz, José. See *Azorin.*
Mellizo, Felipe. "Fray Luis de León en Menéndez y Pelayo," *La Ciudad de Dios*, CLXX (1957), pp. 464–471.
Menéndez Reigada, I. G. "El sistema ético-jurídico de Vitoria sobre el Derecho de Gentes," *La Ciencia Tomista*, XXXIX (1929), pp. 307–330.
Menéndez y Pelayo, Marcelino. *Boletín de la Real Academia de Historia.* Madrid, 1892.
—. *Discurso leído en la Universidad Central.* Madrid, 1889.
—. *Ensayos de crítica filosófica.* Madrid, 1918.
—. *Historia de las Ideas Estéticas en España.* Madrid, 1940.
—. *La medicina en Córdoba.* Buenos Aires, 1916.
—. *Mística Española.* Madrid, 1956.
—. "La *Antoniana Margarita* de Gómez Pereyra," *La Ciencia Española.* Obras Completas, vol. 59.
Mesnard, Pierre. *L'essor de la philosophie politique au XVIe siècle.* Paris, 1936.
Millás Vallicrosa, J. M. "Probable influencia de la poesía sagrada hebraico-española en la poesía de Fray Luis de León," *Sefarad*, XV (1956), pp. 261–285.
Montolín, Manuel. *El alma de España y sus reflejos en la literatura del siglo de Oro.* Barcelona, no date.
Moody, Ernest E. *Truth and Consequence in Medieval Logic.* Amsterdam, 1953.
—. "William of Ockham," *The Encyclopedia of Philosophy*, ed. Edwards, P., Vol. VIII, pp. 306–317.
Muñoz Iglesias, Salvador. *Fray Luis de León, teólogo.* Madrid, 1950.
Naszalyi, Emilio. *El Estado según Francisco de Vitoria.* Madrid, 1948.

Nys, Ernest. *Le Droit de la Guerre et les Précurseurs de Grotius.* Bruxelles, 1882.
—. *Les Origines du Droit International.* Bruxelles, 1894.
Packard, F. R. *Life and Times of Ambrose Paré.* New York, 1926.
Palacio, José Maria de. See *Pinta y Llorente.*
Parry, J. H. *The Spanish Theory of Empire in the Sixteenth Century.* Cambridge, 1940.
Pereña Vicente, Luciano. *Diario YA*, 24 April (1953), Madrid.
—. *La Universidad de Salamanca, forja del pensamiento español en el siglo XVI.* Salamanca, 1954.
—. "El concepto del Derecho de Gentes en Francisco de Vitoria," *Revista Española de Derecho Internacional*, V (1952), pp. 603–628.
—. "El descubrimiento de América en las obras de Fray Luis de León," *Revista Española de Derecho Internacional*, VII (1955), pp. 587–604.
—. See Luis de León, *De Legibus.* Madrid, 1963.
Pinta y Llorente, Miguel de la. *Estudios y polémicas sobre Fray Luis de León.* Madrid, 1956.
—., (and José M. de Palacio). *Procesos Inquisitoriales contra la familia judía de Juan Luis Vives.* Madrid, 1964.
—. "En torno al proceso de Fray Luis de León," *Archivo Agustiniano*, XLIV (1950), pp. 53–66.
Pradelle, A. de la. *Maîtres et doctrines du droit des gens.* Paris, 1939.
Prantl, Karl v. *Geschichte der Logik im Abendlande.* Graz, 1955.
Puig Peña, F. „La influencia de Francisco de Vitoria en la obra de Hugo Grocio," *Revista de Ciencias jurídicas y sociales*, XVI (1933), pp. 543–606; XVII (1934), pp. 12–113; 213–314.
Quetif, J. See *Echard.*
Randall, J. H. *The Career of Philosophy.* New York, 1962.
—. "The School of Padua and the Emergence of Modern Science," *Journal of the History of Ideas*, I (1940), pp. 177–206.
Rashdall, H. *The Universities of Europe in the Middle Ages*, 3 vols., Oxford, 1936.
Rassow, G. *Die Kaiser-idee des Karls V dargestellt an der Politik der Jahre 1528–1540.* Berlin, 1932.
Recasens Siches, D. L. *Las teorías políticas de Francisco de Vitoria.* Vol. II, Madrid, 1931.
Regout, R. *La doctrine de la guerre juste de S. Augustin à nos jours, d'après les théologiens et les canonistes catholiques.* Paris, 1935.
Renaudet, Augustin. *Préréforme et Humanisme à Paris pendant les premières guerres d'Italie (1494–1517).* Paris, 1953.
Revilla, P. Mariano. "Fray Luis de León y los estudios bíblicos en el siglo XVI," *Religión y Cultura*, II (1928), pp. 482–528.
Ríos, P. F. Marcus del. "La doctrina mística de Fray Luis de León," *Religión y Cultura*, II (1928), pp. 531–543.
Robin, R. H. *A Short History of Linguistics*, Indiana, 1967.
Robinson, J. M. and J. B. Cobb. *New Frontiers in Theology.* New York, 1965.
Rodríguez, Conrado. "Fray Luis de León, Horaciano o Virgiliano?" *La Ciudad de Dios*, vol. CXLIII.
Rollin, Alberic. *Le Droit Moderne de la Guerre.* Bruxelles, 1920.

Rousselot, Pierre. *Les Mystiques espagnols*. Paris, 1867.

Roya Vilanova, Ricardo. *La orientación profesional o El Examen de Ingenios en las vocaciones médicas*. Zaragoza, 1926.

St. Joseph, Bruno de. "Où naquit François de Vitoria?", *Revue Néo-Scolastique de philosophie*, XXXIV (1932), pp. 247–249.

Salvioli, J. *Il concetto de guerra justa negli scrittori anteriori a Grocio*. Naples, 1915.

Salillas, Rafael. *Un gran inspirador de Cervantes, El doctor Juan Huarte y su EXAMEN DE INGENIOS*. Madrid, 1905.

San Juan, Juan Huarte de. *El Examen de Ingenios*, Biblioteca de Autores Españoles, vol. 65, Madrid, 1953.

—. *The Trial of Wits*, trans. Richard Carew, 5th edition. London, 1969.

Santiago Vela, Gregorio. "La Universidad de Salamanca y Fray Luis de León," *Archivo Hispano Agustiniano*. V (1916).

—. "Oposiciones de Fray Luis de León a la cátedra de Biblia," *Ibidem*, VI (1916).

Schuster, Edward J. See Luis de León, *The Names of Christ*.

Shapiro, Herman. *Motion, Time and Place According to William Ockham*. ("Franciscan Institute Publications, Philosophy Series" No. 13). New York, 1957.

Secret, François. "L'Interpretazione della Kabbala nel Rinascimento," *Convivium*, XXIV (1956), pp. 541–552.

Serrano, Luciano. *Los conversos D. Pablo de Santa María y D. Alfonso de Cartagena*. Madrid, 1942.

Simonena y Zabalegui, Antonio. *Un precursor de la orientación profesional: El doctor Juan Huarte*. San Sebastián, 1927.

Singer, C. *The Discovery of the Circulation of the Blood*. London, 1922.

Solana, Marcial. *Historia de la Filosofía Española. Epoca del Renacimiento*. Madrid, 1941.

Soto, Domingo de. *Commentarii Collegii Coimbricensis Societatis Jesu in tres libros De Animae Aristotelis Stagiritae*. Coimbra, 1589.

—. *Liber predicamentorum*. Salamanca, 1553.

Stegmueller, Friedrich. *Francisco de la Vitoria y doctrina de la Gracia en la Escuela Salmantina*. Barcelona, 1934.

—. "Die Spanischen Handschriften der Salmantizenser Theologen," *Theological Revue*, XXX (1931), pp. 361–365.

—. "Zur Literaturgeschichte der Salmanticenser Schule," *Theological Revue*, XXIX (1930), pp. 55–59.

Tejada, Elías de. See *Battaglia*.

Tischleder, Peter. *Die naturrechtlichen Grundlagen der Staats-, Kirchen-, und Kolonialpolitik nach der Lehre des Fr. de Vitoria*. Köln, 1932.

Torrubiano Ripoll, Jaime. *Relecciones teológicas del Maestro Vitoria*. Madrid, 1917.

Tour, Imbart de la. *Les Origines de la Réforme*. 4 vols., Paris, 1905–1935.

Urbano, L. "La Sociedad de las Naciones y los principios tomistas del Maestro Fray Francisco de Vitoria," *La Ciencia Tomista*, XXIX (1929), pp. 37-59, 348–369.

Valbuena Prat, A. *Historia de la literatura española*. Barcelona, 1960.

Valdés, Juan de. Index, edited by Rea. Academia Española, *Tres índices expurgatorios de la Inquisición española en el siglo XVI*. Madrid, 1952.

Valladares, Antonio. See *Pedro Chacón*.

Vanderpol, Alfred. *La Doctrine Scolastique du droit de la Guerre*. Paris, 1918.

—. *Le Droit de la Guerre d'après les Théologiens et les Canonistes du Moyen Age*. Paris, 1911.

Vega, A. C. See *Luis de León, Poesias*.

Verdú, Lucas. See *Battaglia*.

Villoslada, Ricardo G. *La Universidad de Paris durante los estudios de Francisco de Vitoria O.P.* (1507–1522). Rome, 1938.

—. "Erasmo y Vitoria," *Razón y Fé*, (1935), pp. 19–38, 340–350.

Vitoria, Francisco de. *Comentarios a la Secunda Secundae de Santo Tomás*, ed. Beltrán de Heredia. 2 vols., Salamanca, 1932.

—. *De Indis et de iure belli relectiones*. ed. Ernest Nys. The Classics of International Law, Washington, 1917.

—. *De Indis recenter inventis et de iure belli*. Ed. Walter Schaetzel, Tuebingen, 1952.

—. *De Iustitia*, ed. Beltrán de Heredia. 3 vols., Madrid, 1934–35.

—. *Los manuscritos del Maestro Fray Francisco de Vitoria*, ed. Beltrán de Heredia. Madrid, 1928.

—. *Relecciones teológicas*, trans. Jaime Torrubiano. 3 vols., Madrid, 1917.

—. *Relecciones teológicas del Maestro Fray Francisco de Vitoria*, ed. Vicente Beltrán de Heredia. 5 vols., Salamanca, 1932–1935.

—. *Relecciones Teológicas del Maestro Fray Francisco de Vitoria*, ed. L. G. A. Getino. 3 vols., Madrid, 1933–1935.

Vives, Juan Luis. *Vives Opera Omnia*, ed. Gregorio Majans. Valencia, 1790.

Vorberg, G. *Ueber den Ursprung der Syphilis*. Stuttgart, 1924.

Vossler, Karl. *Luis de León*. Munich, 1943.

Wallace, William. "The Enigma of Domingo de Soto," *Isis*, LIX (1968), pp. 84–401.

Watson, Foster, "The Examination of Wits," *The Gentleman's Magazine*, March (1905), pp. 238–255.

Wedgewood, C. V. See *Brandi*.

Welzel, Hans. *Derecho Natural y Justicia Material*, trans. Felipe González Vicen. Madrid, 1957, pp. 131–141.

Wheaton, Henri. *Histoire du progrès du droit des gens*. Leipzig, 1841.

Wichersheimer, C. A. E. *La Médecine et les médecins en France à l'époque de la Renaissance*. 2 vols., Paris, 1936.

Wright, Herbert F. *Francisco de Vitoria 'De iure belli' relectio*. Washington, 1916.

—. *Vitoria and the State*. Washington, 1932.

Zalba, José. "El doctor Huarte y su *EXAMEN DE INGENIOS*," *Euzkadi*, September (1913).

INDEX